TITANIC CAPTAIN

THE LIFE OF EDWARD JOHN SMITH

TITANIC CAPTAIN

THE LIFE OF EDWARD JOHN SMITH

G.J. COOPER

All images from the author's collection unless otherwise stated.

First published 2011

The History Press
The Mill, Brimscombe Port
Stroud, Gloucestershire, GL5 2QG
www.thehistorypress.co.uk

British Library Cataloguing in Publication Data.
A catalogue record for this book is available from the British Library.

ISBN 978 0 7524 6072 7

Typesetting and origination by The History Press
Printed in the EU for The History Press.

CONTENTS

To my parents William and Barbara Cooper
and in memory of my uncle Peter Tomkinson,
the first historian in the family.

ACKNOWLEDGEMENTS

I t would have been difficult if not impossible to have written this book without the interest and assistance of a number of institutions and individuals. The author would therefore like to start by thanking the staff of the following establishments: the Maritime History Archive at the Memorial University of Newfoundland, Canada; the National Archives, Kew, London; the Merseyside Maritime Museum, Liverpool; the National Maritime Museum, Greenwich; the New Brunswick Museum, St John, New Brunswick, Canada; Paris Smith LLP, formerly Paris, Smith and Randall, solicitors, Southampton; the University of Keele Library; Hanley Central Library and Archives; Liverpool Library; Lichfield Library.

The list of private individuals I wish to thank begins with Ernie and Pauline Luck who have pretty much been my co-conspirators in this work. Ernie introduced me to Captain Smith's family link with the Mason and Spode pottery dynasties, then went out of his way to trace the exact address of the house that Smith was born in and the credit remains with him for that. Both Ernie and Pauline also proofread a number of my chapters and prevented a few of my barbarisms getting into print. Via Ernie I would also like to thank a number of other people whose information contributed to this biography: the late Marjorie Burrett; Lyane Kendall; and Barbara Faruggio. I would also like to thank the members of the Mason's Pottery Collectors Club for allowing me to give a talk on Captain Smith and for the many kind comments I received afterwards.

Another person who has my sincerest thanks is Norma Williamson, a descendant of Captain Smith's uncle George. Her research into her family history came as a pleasant revelation saving me a great deal of legwork and filling in a few otherwise embarrassingly large blanks in the Smith family tree.

Other individuals I wish to thank are: my friend and work colleague Paula Brown, who proofread several of my chapters and brought a number of points to my attention; Martin Biddle who helped me out of a number of geneaological holes; Steve and Gill Jones who provided me with the location of the grave of Smith's mother and were good enough to send me some photos; Susan M. Wickham who put me onto Kate Douglas-Wiggin's memoirs; and in a very useful info swap, novellist Ann Victoria Roberts and her husband Captain Peter Roberts, master of the heritage steamship *Shieldhall*, pointed out a number of researcher's and landsman's errors in my work that I had not noticed. G.W. Robinson, Geoffrey Dunster RD, RNR, and Lt. Commander Raymond J. Davies RD, RNR, contributed useful information to my earlier research and deserve to be thanked here still. So too does Jeff Kent, who many moons ago published my first book on Captain Smith. Two other individuals I would like to thank (though they may both have long since forgotten about me) are Biddie Garvin, who in 1987 during a college trip to Stratford to see a production of *The Taming of the Shrew*, gave me the idea for my first book on Smith and started me on this path; and Mike Disch, an American actor who in 2003 contacted me out of the blue for any insights I might have into Smith and rekindled interest in what for me had by that time become a rather dusty subject.

One major difference between this work and my original research, is that the online community has provided me with a wealth of research and opinions to draw upon, most notably on Philip Hind's excellent *Encyclopedia Titanica* website. Though I have by no means corresponded with all of the individuals listed here, to paraphrase Lightoller somewhat, their online comments, knowledge and good common sense in the face of much *Titanic*-related silliness has given me much guidance and food for thought and it would be churlish not to acknowledge the fact. I should note, though, that any opinions expressed in this work, are mine and mine alone. I would, therefore, like to thank, in no particular order: Inger Shiel, Mark Chirnside, Michael H. Standart, Erik Wood, Dave Gittens, David G. Brown, Bob Godfrey, Brian J. Ticehurst, Bill Wormstedt, Tad Fitch, George Behe, Addison Hart, Scott Blair, Samuel Halpern, Senan Molony, and Randy Bryan Bigham. Dustin Kaczmarczyk of the German Titanic Society contacted me privately pointing out a number of problems with my original text that needed addressing and has my thanks for that. Mark Baber, along with his many contributions to the *Titanica* site, also very kindly provided me with the fruits of his research showing that Captain Smith had been unfairly blamed for the grounding of the SS *Coptic* in 1889. Another community member, Parks Stephenson was good enough to contact me with information on the installation of Marconi wirelesses on White Star vessels, for which he too has my thanks. I have no doubt there are others, but it is difficult to recall everyone and should I have obviously missed anyone out they have my apologies.

Last, but by no means least, I would like to thank my family and friends who, without badgering me too much over the years, have continued to be interested in the progress of my research.

I

MADE IN THE POTTERIES

Hanley in North Staffordshire, where Edward John Smith, the future captain of the *Titanic*, was born in 1850 was one of six towns that by the time of his birth were known collectively as the Potteries. Only two centuries before, the district had not existed. Hanley and its near neighbours, Tunstall, Burslem, Stoke, Fenton and Longton, had still been a group of small moorland farming settlements, but the heavy upland soil and higher than average rainfall made for poor farming and circumstances had obliged the inhabitants to indulge in supplementary crafts to make ends meet. The local abundance of clay and coal had made pottery-making the natural choice in this respect and over time the locals had earned a reputation for the production of a wide range of domestic wares and pottery storage jars that were sold at the larger county markets. With the advent of the Industrial Revolution during the eighteenth century, these village crafts rapidly blossomed into full-blown industries and the small settlements had grown as people flooded into the area looking for work. So successful had the subsequent rise of the area been, that by the middle of the eighteenth century the six towns of the Potteries supplied the bulk of the pottery used in Britain and by the beginning of the nineteenth century the area was well on the way to dominating the world's ceramic market.

Success, though, had come at a heavy price. As photographs of the Potteries in the nineteenth century reveal, 100 years of industry had produced a grim urban landscape and visitors to the area met with an interesting, if rather apocalyptic scene. When a German traveller, Johann Georg Kohl, first saw the district in about 1843, he was put in mind of an embattled line of fortifications. On approaching the Potteries from Newcastle-under-Lyme, the first thing he noticed was the thick cloud of smoke that spread out over the region. This poured from hundreds of factory chimneys and bottle ovens – the distinctively shaped pottery kilns of the region – of which dozens were often gathered close together looking, Kohl noted, 'like colossal bomb-mortars' in the distance. The conical slag heaps of the local collieries, the high roofs of the drying-houses and warehouses and the thick walls that enclosed the factories, along with the piles of clay, coal, flint, bones, cinders and other matters lying scattered about, served only to strengthen the illusion. Nor did the Potteries diminish in interest as he passed its borders. In the sooty cobbled streets between the great factories, or pot banks as they are known locally, he spotted the small terraced houses of the workers, the shopkeepers, the painters, the engravers, the colourmen, and others, while here and there the intervals were filled up by churches and chapels, or by the grander houses of those who had grown rich as a result of the pottery industry.[1]

Sprawled across the south-western slope of a gently rising hill, Hanley lay roughly in the centre of the Potteries conurbation. With a population of just over 25,000 people in 1851, it was the largest of the six towns. Like its neighbours, its inhabitants were largely employed in the pottery industry or down the local pits. The bulk of the town's pot banks, though, were situated away from the town centre and Hanley had developed into the commercial heart of the region. Perhaps because of this, even today Hanley town centre – now the city centre of Stoke-on-Trent – still largely retains its eighteenth-century street plan, relatively unaltered by later developments; its winding streets, scattered squares and 'banks' forming an 'archipelago of island sites', as the *Victoria History* has described the seemingly random knot of buildings at its core. The majority of the old village buildings had been demolished before E.J. Smith was born and had been replaced with much more imposing structures. A small, stone-built covered meat market – now the Tontines – was built in 1831, while a new town hall complete with columns and a classical pediment was erected in Fountain Square in 1845. Until the late 1840s, Market Square had been dominated by a large coaching inn, the old Swan Inn, but this too had been demolished and replaced with a new market hall which opened in 1849. This market was the grandest structure of all, with an impressive stone façade three storeys high with balustrades and a row of ornamental stone vases set above a row of tall shop windows. These shops were probably the first of Hanley's more ambitious shop fronts, 'far above the standard of everything else in the Pottery district', and they quickly became the focal point of the town.[2]

Houses were being built too, hundreds of them. A sudden influx of newcomers into the town in the late 1840s and 1850s – not only pottery workers, but also new workers for Lord Granville's collieries – had caused serious overcrowding in the available housing in the lower part of town and in Shelton. This had created further problems with serious outbreaks of disease that caused much death and misery. In response, new housing sprang up in previously underpopulated areas, such as Northwood, Far Green and Birches Head. Another major development, and one more pertinent to our story, occurred to the east of the main town, where what became the Wellington estate started to expand from Well Street where Captain Smith was born, down over the other side of the hill across previously untouched farmers' fields.

Well Street

Just as the older buildings were giving way to grander structures, so too were the colloquial street names of yesteryear being exchanged for more glorious titles. As the name of the new Wellington estate implied, many of its streets would be named after famous men or events associated with the Napoleonic Wars – Wellington Road, Nelson Place, Picton Street, Waterloo Street and Eagle Street. The names of the older streets, though, situated on the edge of the old village were more parochial in style and Well Street was one of these. It predated the new estate and was so named because it was the site of, or was situated near to, two old wells. One of these, the Woodwall well, had been the main source of water for the entire town in the eighteenth and early nineteenth centuries. By the 1840s, it was accessed via a street pump from which the local housewives drew water for their household needs and a water cart run by a 'higgler' filled up. This higgler then drove his cart around the town selling his water for ½d a bucketful. Today it seems primitive, but at the time it was a valuable and useful trade, for in the early years of the nineteenth century piped water was still a rarity and often of an inferior quality to this natural spring water. Because of this, the Woodwall well and other natural springs were still regularly used as late as the 1840s and even though the supply of water had grown limited due to the flow being diverted on many of its underground streams, there are indications that it may still have been used by people in the neighbouring streets as late as the 1850s. Even today these ancient springs still flow, though the waters of the Woodwall well now run through a conduit that empties into the nearby Caldon Canal.

Well Street also still exists, but like the wells it was named for it is not what it once was. In the not so distant past the street was much longer and like nearby Charles Street, reached up to Bucknall New Road. In the 1960s, the upper part of the street was demolished and the space given over to the construction of a series of maisonettes and blocks of flats. What remained also survived the construction of the modern bypass known as the Potteries Way, the building of which, in the 1980s, removed several old streets from the map. Modern houses have replaced the old Victorian houses down one side of what remains of Well Street. Down the other side there still exists a row of old Victorian terraced houses that run down the bank from number 51, to the Rising Sun pub at the junction with Waterloo Street. In these we may fancy that we catch a glimpse of what Well Street once looked like, but only in late Victorian times, for it seems that most of these houses did not exist until after 1891 and although a Rising Sun pub had been on the site for years, the present building did not appear until 1886.

To see Well Street how it was prior to this, we need an old map and a little imagination. The map is extant. Produced in 1865, the large-scale map of the Potteries, surveyed by Captain E.R. James RE, clearly shows the layout of the upper part of the Wellington housing estate that year. It was probably a typical street of the locality and the period, with a simple dirt track, or a cambered cobbled road with blue brick pavements. The upper part of Well Street was given over to the terraced houses that Kohl had noted on his peregrination, the monotony of which was broken by the occasional shops that were simply houses converted by their owners. Most of the terraced houses in Hanley were built back-to-back with small yards to each, containing ash pits and privies. The houses were built of brick with tiled roofs and most had only four rooms. The ground floor was paved with bricks or quarries, there was a front parlour and behind it a living room with a cooking range and possibly a boiler for washing clothes in, while the upper storey had two bedrooms.

Of course, the conditions inside each home varied with the wealth, social background and disposition of the occupants. One visitor to the area noted some workers' houses, the windows of which were decked with flowers in pots that would put London parlours to shame.[3] These pots were often placed on mahogany chests of drawers which were themselves clear indications of some small wealth. On the other hand, an article in the *Morning Chronicle* spoke of grimy parlours containing wretched sofas, all rickety boards and dirty calico that served as beds for some members of the family. An official report into the state of large towns in the region noted that though small and gloomy, the houses locally were not deficient in ventilation, but the inhabitants being for the most part engaged in warm manufactries were mortally afraid of cold air and the illnesses it might engender and blocked most of the vents and gaps.[4]

The lower half of Well Street, though, would have come as a pleasant surprise to anyone expecting a continuation of these typical working-class dwellings. Clearly marked on James' map, three quarters of the way down the now steeply inclined bank and set back from the road, was a large property of quality fronted by an ornamental garden. This was 'The Cottage', a large house owned by George Fourdrinier, a local paper manufacturer who had made his fortune producing paper transfers for the pottery industry. The quality of his establishment can be gauged from the details in the sales advertisement for the property carried in the first copy of the *Staffordshire Sentinel* of 7 January 1854, following Mr Fourdrinier's retirement to Rugeley just prior to his death. There were dining rooms, a drawing room, a breakfast room, four bedrooms, a kitchen and school rooms. Included in the household goods up for sale over the four days 16 to 19 January 1854 were: a mahogany bagatelle board, a pair of globes, a solar lamp, a magnificent fourteen-day Parisian timepiece, an eight-light chandelier, a six and a half-octave pianoforte by Collard and Collard, a collection of oil paintings by eminent masters, 100 volumes of books and electroplated tea and coffee sets. The list moved on to more mundane items, but also listed a six-year-old carriage horse (16½ hands) and a 'useful bay horse'. These could be harnessed into either the 'Capital, well-built four wheel Dog Cart' or the 'handsome Barouche, with turn over back seat, in good condition.'[5]

For the people of Well Street, the main benefit provided by The Cottage would have been the large ornamental garden in front of it, its numerous trees and bushes adding a splash of colour to the soot-stained bricks and cobbles of the neighbouring houses. These gardens stood on land now occupied by the remaining terraced houses of Well Street. The garden is clearly depicted on James' 1865 map, showing that The Cottage was still occupied years later and proving that many if not all the houses there today are later additions.

The presence of such a high-class house also alters somewhat the perception of Well Street as the largely working-class street that it later became. We are instead looking at an area in transition, if The Cottage predated most of the surrounding terraces. After all, prior to the start of construction of the Wellington estate, Well Street was on the rural edge of the village, the perfect place for a rich manufacturer to make his home. The construction of the Wellington estate began in the 1830s and the church of St Luke's, which on James' map can be seen just to the east of The Cottage, was not built until 1853–54. Fields to the west of Well Street, where Gilman Street now stands, plus others further to the east, support this idea. Also many of the back yards to those houses down the western side of Well Street even appear to have had trees in them. So, though not perhaps a rural idyll, Well Street was on the other hand not a blighted urban slum. Nature still had its place. It seems to have been a good spot to settle and raise a family.

The Smith Family

One couple that did just that were Captain Smith's grandparents, Edward and Elizabeth Smith, who arrived in Hanley in the early years of the nineteenth century. For the next sixty or perhaps seventy years, three generations of their family lived there, raising their children and, in the case of E.J. Smith's branch of the family, rising in social status. Edward Smith first appears in Well Street as an apparently humble working-class tenant, but when the last of the family finally quit the street and the Potteries in the late 1870s, they were lease holders on at least two properties.

A little is known about the life of Edward Smith senior. He was the son of Edward Smith and Jane Blakemore who had married in Bradley, near Stafford, on 27 December 1760. They seem to have had a number of children, their son Edward being born on 16 April 1775 and baptised at St Mary's Church, Stafford, on 21 May that year. Twenty-three years later on 10 September 1798, at Ranton parish church, the younger Edward married twenty-year-old Elizabeth 'Betty' Tams, the daughter of John and Catherine Tams from the village of Salt. The couple may have settled locally at first, but by the early 1800s, drawn perhaps by the promise of better wages and greater opportunities, they had moved north to the Potteries where they settled in Well Street. Here, Edward started working as a potter.

In 1807, the first appearance of the name Edward Smith can be found amongst hundreds of other mundane entries in the 1807–08 Hanley Rate Book. There are no street names or house numbers given in this large red tome and the most that can be gleaned from the book is that one Edward Smith occupied property No.4375, owned by a certain William Tambs; the rate on the house was 2s 4d. As there are no remaining rate books for the years 1808–62, it is impossible to trace this particular Edward Smith any further. However, in 1818 an early trade directory of the Staffordshire Potteries was published, which proved to be more informative. In the section covering Hanley, we find the following entry: 'Smith, Edward, potter, 8 Well Street, Old Hall Street.' The presence five doors away of Samuel Sneyd, grocer at number 3 Well Street, indicates that this was indeed Captain Smith's grandfather. Mr Sneyd and Edward Smith's family were in the same houses relative to one another, at the time of the 1841 census.[6]

Between 1807 and 1822, at least seven children were born in Hanley whose parents were named Edward and Elizabeth Smith. The eldest of these, Edward, was baptised on 10 May 1807, while Mary Ann (or Mary Anne) is listed as being baptised twice, on either 10 or 28 May 1809. One Thomas Smith was baptised on 30 October 1814, Jane on 11 September 1816, William on 1 June 1818, and Phyllis was baptised on 16 September 1821. All of these children had been christened at St John's, the town's Anglican church, but the last child, George, was baptised at the Charles Street Wesleyan Chapel. His details are more complete; he was born on 28 October 1822 and baptised on 1 December 1822.[7] Although the double entry for Mary Ann Smith raises some questions, the chances are very good that this is a full list of Edward and Elizabeth Smith's children. There is supporting evidence that Edward and George, the eldest and the youngest, were related, as they were both still living with their mother in 1841 when the census was taken. We also know that Jane Smith was their sister, as Edward would be a witness at her wedding and her daughter was lodging with his family in 1861.

From the information contained in the 1851 and 1861 census returns, it seems that Edward Smith junior, the father of Edward John Smith, was actually born in 1805, two years before the St John's baptism. That he received some education in his youth can be seen from the fact that he was able to write his name in a strong and practised hand when he later married. What form this education took is unknown, but from 1805 to 1817, when the building was demolished, a Sunday school for local boys operated in Hanley's old market hall, a small, ugly brick building supported on iron pillars, which stood at the top of the present-day Market Square. His schooling, though, would have been a very perfunctory affair, lasting at best only a few years, for by his early teens, Edward, like hundreds of other youngsters across the district, was apprenticed as a potter.

To most people the term 'potter' conjures up an image of a man sitting at a potter's wheel throwing finished wares. In Stoke-on-Trent, however, 'potter' is very much a generic term covering a dozen or more occupations on a pot bank. What evidence there is, namely a single reference on his death certificate, indicates that Edward had actually worked as a pottery presser, pressing clay into plaster moulds to form the shape of the pot. Though not as skilled a job as throwing, pressing nevertheless requires speed, dexterity and plenty of hard experience in order for its practitioner to make a living. Pressers produced the more complex, often ornamental pottery shapes such as square or oval-bodied wares that could not be produced on a wheel. Hollowware statuary was also largely press-moulded, the best known pieces being the cheap flatbacks, fairings and Staffordshire dogs that ornamented many a Victorian mantelpiece.

On 23 May 1838, the family suffered a loss when the head of the family, Edward Smith senior, died at the age of sixty-five. According to his death certificate he still lived in Well Street and the cause of his death was given as asthma, brought on perhaps by his years spent working in warm, dusty pot banks. He may have been ill for some time, as according to the death certificate he had prior to his death been reduced to working as a labourer. Two days later, his nephew George Redfern, who lived only a few doors away in Well Street, went to notify the registrar of his uncle's demise. Edward Smith was buried at St John's churchyard, Hanley, on 27 May 1838.

The death of Edward Smith senior could not have come at a worse time for his daughter Jane, who was planning to marry. Less than two months later, on 16 July 1838, Jane married potter Thomas Privet at Wolstanton parish church. Both bride and groom were at that time living in Tunstall. The witnesses to the marriage were her brother Edward Smith and a woman named Priscilla, whose surname is difficult to make out on the certificate. The reason for the marriage in haste only a matter of weeks after her father's funeral seems to have been that Jane Smith was pregnant, her daughter Ellen being born just a couple of months later.

The 1841 census was the first survey of the British population to list individuals and households. This from a researcher's point of view is a positive boon, compared to the simple head counts provided by the three previous censuses, but it was by no means perfect. The 1841 census listed street names, but not house numbers; individuals were named and their employment given, but their marital status, relationships to the head of the household and birthplace were not recorded, while the age of most people over the age of ten years was 'rounded down' to the nearest five years. Thus a man of thirty-seven would be 'thirty-five' in the census return, or a woman of fifty-three, would be 'fifty', though the rule was not always enforced rigorously. The enumerator who covered Well Street often stated a person's true age, or rounded them down to the nearest decade.

On the night of Sunday, 6 June 1841, three people were listed as living at one particular house in Well Street, Hanley. The eldest of these was sixty-three-year-old Elizabeth Smith, whose profession was listed as 'Ind' – presumably shorthand for independent. The second individual was Edward Smith, whose age was given as thirty, though he was actually nearer thirty-five or thirty-six years old. Under profession, the census return has the words 'J. Potter', which probably stands for 'Journeyman Potter', in other words a skilled workman, but not yet a master potter; he was later described as such on his wife's death certificate. The last person in the household was eighteen-year-old George Smith, who worked as a gilder, applying gold decoration to pottery.

The next household contained the large Simpson family and apparently three guests or lodgers, a widowed transferer, thirty-five-year-old Catherine Hancock, and her two children, ten-year-old Joseph and six-year-old Thirza. If the entry is correct then there were thirteen people living, or at least staying, in the house, a rather unlikely scenario given such a small building. Instead, Catherine and her children probably lived in the neighbouring house and the enumerator merely failed to indicate this. Still, there were connections between the Smiths, Simpsons and Hancocks. One of these is of considerable importance to our story, for by 1841, Edward Smith and Catherine Hancock were lovers and marriage was in the air.

Mother and Child

The mother of Captain Smith had been born Catherine Marsh, the daughter of potter Ralph Marsh, in Penkhull in about 180 . She appears to have received little or no education as a girl and on both of her subsequent marriage certificates Catherine signed with her mark. Indeed, the first time she appears in any documentation is on the occasion of her first marriage. This took place, after banns, at Wolstanton Church on 13 June 1831, when she married potter John Hancock. Although John and Catherine were married at the parish church, the available evidence, namely the baptisms of their children, indicates that they were in fact Methodists. They had probably not changed their religious beliefs in the interim, the simple fact was that Methodists had to get married in the parish church. In 1753, Lord Hardwicke's Marriage Act had defined a legal marriage as one which took place in the Church of England, after banns and according to the rubric, old style common-law marriages being effectively outlawed. Only Quakers and Jews were exempt from this law, so between 1754 and 1837 all nonconformist marriages took place in Anglican churches. There seems to have been very little opposition to this, Methodists after all believed in many of the same religious tenets as Anglicans. Catherine seems to have been traditionally minded and even after 1837 she still preferred to get married in an Anglican church rather than one of the new-fangled registry offices.

Her first marriage was a short but fruitful one. John and Catherine's first child, Joseph, was born on 26 June 1832; the second child, John, came along on 6 February 1834 and was baptised at the Wesleyan Methodist Chapel, Burslem, on 2 March 1834. John, though, only lived for eighteen months and his burial took place at Tunstall Christ Church on 30 August 1835. Then, on 1 January 1836, Catherine had a daughter, or possibly twin girls. Certainly local baptismal records show two girls named Thirra and Thirza, daughters of John and Catherine Hancock, as being born that day. On 7 January 1836, one Thirra, daughter of John and Catherine Hancock, was baptised at Wolstanton parish church. Thirza, however, was baptised at the Tunstall Primitive Methodist Chapel on 17 January. Thirra never appears after this, but Thirza certainly prospered, living to a grand old age and having children of her own. Thirra could have been her twin and perhaps died in infancy, though no burial entry has yet been found. The most likely explanation, though difficult to prove, is that they were the same person, namely Thirza Hancock. Perhaps she was a sickly child and her parents feared for her life, which would certainly explain the hurried Anglican baptism – any port in a storm – but she rallied and ten days later was rebaptised in her parent's Methodist faith, her name being changed or corrected in the process.

There were no more children born to the couple, for in either 1838, or 1839, John Hancock died. The exact date of his death is not known for sure, as there were at least five separate John Hancocks who died locally at this time.

Up until this point, Catherine and her family had lived in the Penkhull-Wolstanton-Tunstall area, so what exactly prompted her move to Hanley in or around 1840? The Simpson family may have been the link. William and Hannah Simpson had eight children and the names of the three youngest were Joseph (seven years old), Catherine (five years) and Thirza (six months). It could be coincidence that these children had exactly the same Christian names as the Hancocks, or it could be an indication that the Simpsons were friends or relatives of Catherine's, who had taken her and her children in, or put her into the neighbouring property that was up for rent in Well Street.

Certainly the Simpsons knew the Smiths, as Hannah Simpson was present a mere six days after this census was taken when, on 12 June 1841, Elizabeth Smith died at home. Two days after that, it was Mrs Simpson who went to the town hall to inform the local registrar of the death. The death certificate gives Elizabeth's cause of death as 'dropsey'(sic), otherwise known as edema, a condition caused by the abnormal accumulation of fluid in the body tissues or cavities, which causes painful swelling in the affected parts. Dropsy, it is now known, is a symptom of an underlying condition rather than a direct cause of death, the latter being most often caused by congestive heart failure brought on as a result of the condition.

Elizabeth Smith was buried at St John's Church, Hanley, on 15 June. Many graves were exhumed in the twentieth century when the graveyard was reduced in size. Details of the memorial inscriptions of those graves that were removed were recorded, but there is no mention of Elizabeth Smith's or her husband's being amongst these, so they may still be there, though much of the site surrounding the sadly neglected church is today off-limits to the public.

The hasty burial was followed just under two months later by a happier event, namely the marriage of Edward Smith and Catherine Hancock. This took place at St Marks Church, Shelton, on 2 August 1841. According to the marriage notice carried in the *North Staffordshire Mercury*, Edward and Catherine were married at the 'same time and place' as another couple, Thomas Meigh and Isabella Lightfoot, both of Hanley.[8] The surnames of the witnesses at Edward and Catherine's marriage are difficult to make out, but they appear to read William and Julia Laynton. The information on the marriage certificate clears up one curious notion that has grown up concerning Captain Smith's father. The dearth of information on Edward Smith prior to this event has led to speculation that he had contracted an earlier marriage and had children some time in his twenties, but on the certificate we read that Edward was a bachelor and there is no reason to believe otherwise. For a marriage to again occur so swiftly after a family tragedy seems rather unusual, but perhaps the match had been planned for some time. Whatever the case may have been, Catherine and her children Joseph and Thirza now set up home with her new husband.

For nine years afterwards we hear little of the Smiths or the Hancocks, a fairly sure sign that they settled down and lived their lives quietly. It was not until the end of the decade that they come into sight once again and when they do, it becomes clear with hindsight that subtle changes in their fortunes had taken place. These changes would eventually see the Smiths and Hancocks of this story leaving the Potteries for good and would propel the as yet unborn E.J. Smith to his long career at sea and eventually into the limelight.

The most notable differences were in the careers some of them had now begun to follow. Catherine Smith had given up working as a transferer on a pot bank and had begun working as a grocer, either on her own, or on some other premises, while her daughter Thirza found employment as a milliner and dressmaker. This may have been a family trade for the Hancocks, as in 1818 another Thirza Hancock is listed as a milliner and dressmaker in Hanley. The biggest break, though, and the most significant in the development of this story, came in late 1849 or early 1850, when Catherine's eldest son, Joseph, left the Potteries entirely, travelled to Liverpool and entered the merchant navy. Why he did so is unknown, but it is clear from one account that Joseph, as either an example, or an active advocate, was later the chief cause of his half-brother choosing to go to sea himself.

That little half-brother, who would first emulate, but then surpass Joseph, now enters his own story. In 1849, Catherine Smith found that she was again pregnant and on 27 January 1850 she gave birth to a baby boy. He would be her last child and the only one born of the union of Edward and Catherine. They named their new son Edward John Smith, the first name doubtless after his father and the middle name came either from Catherine's late husband, or in memory of the son she had lost fifteen years before.

The number of the actual house where the future captain of the *Titanic* was born has long been something of a bone of contention, as there is no house number given in the birth certificate, which merely states that he was born in Well Street. It has formerly been stated that Edward John Smith was born at 51 Well Street. The oft-quoted number 51 comes from the 1851 census where it appears alongside the street name beside the Smith family entry.[9] However, the number here is not that of a particular house, but rather the schedule number, in other words the fifty-first building visited by one particular enumerator that day, not necessarily 51 Well Street. The matter of the house number was further confused over the following decades as the houses were renumbered on at least two occasions, probably as Well Street and the surrounding estate expanded. That this was indeed the case rather than the family simply moving house, is borne out by the fact that the Smiths and many of their neighbours occupied the same houses relative to one another over this period. Thus, by 1861, the Smiths' home had become number 17 Well Street and by 1871, the last occasion that Edward John Smith was included on a census in his native town, his old family home had become 30 Well Street. The clue to the real number of the house where he was born can be found in the 1851 edition of *Slater's Classified Directory for Birmingham, Worcester and the Potteries*. Though Edward's address had no number, two grocers on either side were numbered. Totting up the numbers in between, it seems that in 1850 the Smiths actually lived at number 86 Well Street. As further confirmation, when Edward's brother George Smith got married a couple of years later he gave his address as 86 Well Street where he was still living with his brother and his new family.[10]

At the time of Edward John Smith's birth, the property comprised a 'house, shop and yard'. This was probably just an ordinary house, the front parlour of which was converted into a store – a fairly common practice even in the late twentieth century. Certainly the Smiths' store easily converted back into a family home when Catherine Smith left the area in the late 1870s. In the 1851 edition of *White's Gazetteer and Directory of Staffordshire*, Edward Smith of Well Street is listed as a 'Shopkeeper', though, as noted elsewhere, it was probably Catherine who actually kept the shop. Though both Edward and Catherine were at times described as grocers, they are not here listed under that heading. The same distinction was made in the 1852–53 edition of *Slater's Classified Directory*. The Smiths appear to have run something akin to a general store selling (according to *White's Directory*) flour, cheese and other household goods as well as groceries.

Schooldays

Though no baptism record has yet been found, young Ted Smith, as he was known in his youth, was probably a Methodist. He certainly attended the Methodist British School in the nearby village of Etruria. This seems to have occupied the old Sunday school building at the rear of the New Connection Wesleyan Chapel which still stands in Lord Street, Etruria, not far from the Wedgwood pottery factory around which the village was originally built. The school later reverted to being a Sunday school, while the regular day pupils were absorbed into the Etruria Board School that opened in 1881 and was finally demolished in 2005. The old British School building itself is long gone and no pictures of it seem to exist. The closest we get is in a photograph of Etruria taken in 1865, in which the side walls of the chapel can be discerned, the Etruria British School, though, is out of the picture. As if to echo this lack of an image, surprisingly little textual information survives about the school, the *Victoria History* for Staffordshire barely notes it and E.J.D. Warrillow's *History of Etruria* tells us only a little more. There is scant information about its origins, though it became very closely tied to the Etruria Unsectarian School. This had been an infants school founded in 1847 by Francis Wedgwood, the grandson of the famous Josiah Wedgwood, which later effectively became the British School's infants department. This suggests that Francis also endowed the British School, but as a junior school to take the children who had attended the Unsectarian School.

The British School was founded in 1851; the earliest reference to it in the local directories was in 1852–53, but it appears to have had a good reputation from the start and embraced the Methodist doctrines that the Smiths obviously wanted their child to inherit. Like all schools of its ilk, the Etruria British School was a private institution. Parents had to pay for their children's education as free compulsory state education did not start until 1890. As there are no figures for the school Smith attended, we can only make comparisons. For instance in 1843, children at the nearby Shelton British School paid 2d a week, while in 1862, the Etruria Unsectarian School that took over from the Etruria British School, charged 3s a month. The sums demanded seem paltry today, but even these small amounts were often more than the average family could afford in such a poor area. In 1843, the Shelton School had 180 boys and 108 girls on its books, but as the teachers admitted only 100 of the former and eighty of the latter attended regularly. The rest were absent in the main because their parents could not afford the fees every week, or even a decent set of clothes to send them in. It was also revealed that many boys were taken out of school early to start work, while girls were required to look after the home while their mothers went out to work. Joseph Lundy, the master at the Shelton School, felt that this was a great pity, as those pupils who stayed on for any length of time did well in their studies.

The Etruria British School was a monitorial school, so called because the responsibility for a great deal of the teaching was delegated down a chain of pupil monitors from one class teacher. The schools of this type were usually subdivided by religious faith; the Anglican community was largely catered for by the National Schools, while the Nonconformists sent their children to the British Schools. These employed the Bell or Lancaster systems of tuition respectively. Both were systems (arrived at separately) whereby a very limited number of teachers could hand the lessons over to the monitors, who would see that the large classes each got the same amount of tuition per pupil. Both systems demanded heavy regimentation of the schoolchildren, and inevitably analogies have been drawn with the factory system then in operation. Despite the overtones, though, this was not a middle-class ploy designed to produce workers ready for the factories, it was simply the best method for the situation; only in this way, as Joseph Lancaster noted, could 500 children be taught from one book instead of 500. In fact, at its simplest the monitorial system was a variation on the theme of learning by rote that had been employed for centuries. Such a method of learning could have remarkable results – Shakespeare, for instance, learnt his lessons by rote. But, as critics of the monitorial system noted on more than one occasion, less able pupils were left behind as the lessons steamrollered on and the benefits to all were lost if the teaching was poor, while real problems would result if the monitors under the teacher's tutelage did not fully understand what he or she had been taught.

The schools' governing bodies supplied each local branch and school with a simple set of 'readers'. These were printed sheets bearing excerpts from books that could be held up in front of a class for the pupils to copy. At first in both National and British Schools, these readers were drawn almost exclusively from the Scriptures, but by the 1850s, both societies had come to realise that the Bible, though a useful and familiar text for children to begin with, had its limitations in the increasingly complex society that was nineteenth-century Britain, where secular knowledge counted for much more than familiarity with the Scriptures. As a direct result of this realisation, a set of secular readers had been introduced in the mid-1840s. Instead of the old religious tracts written by divines, these were written by people who espoused the 'new religion' of political economy that had come with the rise of industry. These new readers extolled the habits that children were expected to cultivate in this new order such as diligence, forethought, frugality and temperance and explained the perils of neglecting them, allied to dire warnings of the dangers to the working man of rocking the economic boat. The laws of political economy were also invoked to argue against trade unionism and the futility of government intervention in wage disputes. Basically, it embodied all of the principles that the middle class wanted the working class to believe in.

Not that the children were aware of this, and the pill was sweetened by presenting it in many varied and often very familiar forms. For the youngest, there were fairy stories and fables, the traditional moral endings of which were given a new slant to fit the new belief system. As the children grew older, the new secular readers provided a much wider range of textual material that would give them a much better grasp of the wider world. One suggested curriculum for schools using the new readers was drawn up by a training college inspector in 1848, '...biography (of good men); natural history; the preservation of health; cottage economy; horticulture; mechanism; agriculture; geography; history; grammar; natural and experimental philosophy; money matters; political economy; popular astronomy.' [11]

In most monitorial schools, the school day was regulated with almost military efficiency. Discipline was strict and disruptive pupils were punished quickly. There were, however, no beatings in a British School. Being a Quaker, Joseph Lancaster had opposed the use of the cane under his system and he instead advocated punishments that would shame, exhaust or terrify the malefactors. These could range from something as simple as having the pupil wear a dunce's cap, to thoroughly Byzantine punishments, like fastening a heavy log around the children's necks and making them walk around the school until they dropped, tying them up in sacks, or hoisting them up to the ceiling in a basket until the end of the lesson.

Though ousted from its paramount position in the curriculum, piety was still rigorously enforced, as too was deference to their elders, children being drilled to 'know their place' and 'respect their betters'. In National Schools, the attitude towards such indoctrination was that it taught the children to put up with their lot in life now, and to happily accept the existing status quo when they became adults;

the attitude in British Schools, though, was different and to twenty-first-century eyes surprisingly modern. Though the emphasis was still there to respect God and their elders, the education they received was instead extolled as a benefit by which they could better their lot in life. This was a subtle difference, but a telling one nevertheless, and indeed in later times many of the old boys of the Etruria British School did exceptionally well in their chosen careers, Ted Smith being one of them.

The Patriotic Schoolmaster

Good teachers helped to push the message home and the Etruria British School seems to have been able to attract better than most. The trade directories of the time tell us the names of the head teachers at the school. The first of these, mentioned in the 1852–53 edition of *Slater's Classified Directory*, was Jane Vickers. In a separate entry in the same book, one John Vickers is noted as being a schoolmaster at Etruria, though at which school it does not say. The Vickers' tenure, though, would be brief and the school soon had a new head teacher who would have a profound effect on the pupils he taught.

We all remember our favourite teachers, the people who influenced us and helped to shape us for adult life, and the boys of the Etruria British School were no different. By the mid-1850s, the school had as its headmaster Alfred Smith, a native of Derbyshire, who was a much loved and respected teacher by the standards of the time. Spencer Till, a school friend of Ted Smith's, later recalled their 'much respected master', while another old school fellow, Joseph (Joe) Turner, called him 'dear old Alfred Smith'. Only a few years after Ted left his school, Alfred Smith was appointed as the first secretary to the Hanley School Board, whilst he also spent time giving private tuition to future local luminaries such as Cecil Wedgwood, a scion of the famous potting family who in 1910 became the first mayor of the newly federated Stoke-on-Trent. A measure of the esteem in which he was held can be gained by seeing how in later life many of the old boys, including Ted Smith, would attend a reunion in their old teacher's honour.

Alfred Smith died at the age of seventy-eight in 1911, but in the 1850s he was still a vital young man in his twenties and, it seems, a fiery patriot. According to Joe Turner, the boys under his charge were taught to love 'God, Queen and Country' and he often regaled them with tales of brave British deeds. This would make a deep impression on many a lad. Joe Turner, who would himself later go to sea, wrote, 'I have often thought that there are few schools in our country that produced the number of soldiers and sailors that the Etruria British School did, and this was in a great measure owing to the patriotic fervour of our schoolmaster.'[12]

Ted Smith for one certainly took Alfred Smith's teachings to heart and he was instilled with a deep love of his country and its achievements that never left him. In the aftermath of the *Titanic* disaster, though his name was essentially wrapped in the flag by the popular press, those who knew him personally vouched for the fact that Smith was indeed very proud to be British. The publisher J.E. Hodder Williams wrote:

> He was very British, almost insular for a man who had travelled so widely. His last command as the waters rose to the bridge, 'Be British,' was what we expected and wanted him to say. He belonged to the race of the old British sea dogs. He believed with all his heart and soul in the British Empire. He had added that to his creed.[13]

We even know of one of the tales that may have fired Smith's patriotism and inspired him in his hour of need, for Joe Turner recalled with some irony in later life how he had listened with fascination to Alfred Smith's rendering of the wreck of the *Birkenhead*.

The HMS *Birkenhead* had been a troopship ferrying soldiers drawn from several regiments, plus their wives and children, to Algoa Bay, Cape Colony to take part in the 8th Kaffir War. Its journey from Britain had passed without incident, but early on the morning of 26 February 1852, as it neared its final destination, haste and a strong prevailing current resulted in the ship being driven too close to the coast where it impaled itself on a rock off Danger Point on the outskirts of Cape Town. As the ship began to break apart the crew discovered that there were not enough serviceable lifeboats for all on board and so at the request of their officers the soldiers famously formed ranks and stood firm as the ship broke up and went under, thereby allowing the women and children to escape in the remaining boats. Of the 643 people on board only 193 survived the disaster and the soldiers' chivalry gave rise to the 'women and children first' protocol that male passengers and crew were expected to abide by should they be unlucky enough to be caught in a shipwreck.

This astonishing story of self-sacrifice fascinated the Victorian world in many of the same ways that the story of the *Titanic* would the people of the twentieth century, and the conduct of all future evacuations, including the *Titanic*, would be measured against this yardstick. Doubtless Ted Smith heard this tale, if not from his teacher then certainly at some point during his long career at sea, and it seems more than likely that the hard lessons taught by the men of the *Birkenhead* had a bearing on how he tried to manage his own evacuation half a century hence.

A Day at School

If he had started school as an infant, doubtless Ted's mother or father, or perhaps even Thirza, would have taken him to school at first, but as he got older and made friends, Ted began to go to school in the company of other boys. One of these, William Jones, later recalled how half a dozen of them used to travel into school every morning. 'I remember how Vincent Simpson used to call on me first and how we would call for

Johnny Leonard. Then the three of us would knock at Ted Smith's door and having collected the others we would run down Mill-street and Etruria-road to school.'[14]

The route they took still exists, though it has changed a great deal in the interim. Jones'Mill-street and Etruria-road' are now Etruria Road and Lord Street respectively. They form part of a busy thoroughfare linking the Potteries and Newcastle-under-Lyme and serve a number of brash out-of-town superstores and multiplexes. In the middle of the nineteenth century, though, Mill Street was bordered by corn fields and Etruria Road was guarded by a toll gate and passed through a thick copse of mature trees, known simply as the Etruria Grove. Prime dawdling country for your typical schoolboy if ever there was any.

School would start at 9a.m. for all classes. At the Shelton British School there were classes for boys, girls and infants in separate classrooms. The Etruria School was apparently the same, though only boys are ever mentioned in the accounts that have survived. Before the lessons began, the school said the morning prayer, then the senior monitor called out all the lesser monitors and asked for a head count of each class. Considering that Ted Smith was to spend the majority of his adult working life in a job where a hierarchical chain of command governed his existence, such roll calls would remain very familiar.

After the head count, on command the children sat down on bare wooden benches and waited for their orders. The head monitors received the lesson from the teacher or headmaster, then gave out the letters or phrases to be copied and these were written either on a blackboard, or on a card, which was held up before the whole class, who then copied it out on their own small slates. When they were all done, the senior monitor called out, 'Hands down. Show slates,' and the monitors then did the round checking for any mistakes before further orders of 'Lay down slates,' 'Clean slates,' and 'Show slates clean,' were issued. Then a fresh set of words and phrases were set out and it started all over again.

Age largely dictated what they were taught. The younger pupils usually had their mornings given over to writing or reading and spelling lessons, where groups of children would be brought out to read from the board. Alternatively a monitor would come in with a card bearing the alphabet and the class would say each letter out loud as it was called out. The children were also tested on their ability to count to 100 accurately. As the pupils grew older, though, the lessons would have become much more involved and taxing. The new readers encouraged pupils to analyse and dissect the passages or subjects they were studying and they often came with a list of questions or critical notations. The teacher would take the pupils through the passage and question them as to what it meant, or at least be asked to give their own interpretation of its meaning.

At about 10.30, there was a five-minute break before they returned to their lessons. These carried on until about 11a.m., when the class had to study their catechism or religious induction, so important to the Victorian sense of religion: the Creed, the Lord's Prayer, the Ten Commandments and a few psalms, all taught in the same manner as the alphabet. After that was done, the class said grace 'before meat' and at noon went home.

Lessons resumed at about 2p.m. The children said grace 'after meat' and then got back to their routine. For the youngest pupils, the afternoon was spent in the same manner as the morning, but as the scholars got older the afternoons were given over increasingly to arithmetic, tables and accounts. At 4.30, more prayers were said, followed perhaps by evening hymns. Then, finally, the children were allowed to go home.

Of course, it is only possible to speculate how close all this was to the routine Ted knew at school, as the system did vary, but that the school did operate along these lines is perhaps borne out by the fact that Ted numbered among his closest friends boys that quite often were many years his junior, so if he had taken up the duties of a class monitor, he would have had occasion to meet many of them from day to day. For instance, there was Edmund Jones who knew him as a senior boy at the school and considered him to be 'a quiet, respectable, courageous lad who never put himself to the front too much'. Jones also recalled that Ted was always on hand to defend the weaker and younger boys if anyone ever fell to bullying them.[15] Spencer Till, the son of an Etruscan grocer who was to remain lifelong friends with Ted, was seven or eight years his junior.

Joe Turner was two years younger than Ted. He, though, remembered him in a rather different light, as 'a high-spirited lad' as Alfred Smith was want to call such boys, and at first the two of them were at odds with one another:

Ted Smith quarrelled with me many times and used to punch my head, and I returned the obligation. These quarrels became so incessant that our dear old schoolmaster cautioned us before our class that they must be stopped, but if we wanted to cudgel ourselves, we must go out in Hall Fields and cudgel each other to our hearts' content. I am sorry to say that we both took such advice and met after close of school. My second was Herbert Greatbach. Ted Smith's was my brother Edward. After the fight had progressed for some time with sword sticks, I inadvertently struck Ted Smith on the neck, and this so infuriated Smith that he rushed on me, put down my guard, and thrashed me until I howled.[16]

Like most schoolboy quarrels, though, one good fight seems to have cleared the air and in time Ted and Joe grew to be the best of friends.

Out of school, Ted spent a good amount of his spare time out playing with his mates. The gang of lads who ran down to school with him every morning seem to have numbered amongst his close friends. William Jones recalled that he and the others spent many happy hours together before and after school. The reporter who interviewed Mr Jones after the *Titanic* disaster, was shown an old faded photograph of the six boys, 'in which the bright, determined face of the boy who was to be the leading figure in the world's greatest maritime disaster stands out conspicuously.'[17]

These though were not the public school boys of *Tom Brown's Schooldays,* or the perfect children of the woodcut illustrations in Joseph Lancaster's education books, all well dressed and well spoken. Working-class children usually stripped off their better clothes at home and often played barefoot in the street, where they spent most of their time. Also the accent and dialect with which Ted Smith and his friends spoke at this time would have been pretty impenetrable to anyone from outside the area, full of its own idiosyncratic words and pronunciations that still find an echo in the milder modern Potteries dialect. Depictions of Smith as the skipper of the *Titanic* have him speaking in more generalised English or mid-Atlantic accents, which working in such a cosmopolitan international society he may well have adopted, though it is unlikely that he lost his local accent completely. There is a telling comparison that can be used to illustrate the point. A century before Smith was born, his fellow Staffordshireman, Dr Samuel Johnson, author of the first English dictionary, despite having spent years in London amongst its fashionable society, was often pulled up by members of his clique for his broad Staffordshire accent. James Boswell noted how Johnson pronounced 'there' and 'once', as 'theer' and 'woonse'.[18] Though the Potteries accent was a much harsher version of Dictionary Johnson's Lichfield brogue, the former are typical Staffordshire pronunciations and the chances are good that in later life Smith also sometimes lapsed back into the colloquialisms of his youth.

Pirates of the Barbary Coast

A great deal had happened to the Smiths and Hancocks during Ted's childhood and schooldays. These events were personal family affairs that young Ted Smith would have witnessed or heard about at first hand. The first and certainly the most dramatic of these concerned Ted's half-brother Joseph, who had broken from the Potteries completely, gone to Liverpool and had begun to make a career for himself in the merchant navy. He had first gone to sea at the age of seventeen as an apprentice aboard the ship *Acadia* in April 1850, shortly after Ted was born, and between 1853 and 1856, he served as an able seaman aboard two other sailing ships, the *Rimac* and the *Simonds*. He gained his second mate's certificate of competency, No.14721, on 17 April 1856 and a few days later signed on in that capacity aboard the 400-ton Liverpool-registered barque *Hymen*, commanded by Captain James Smith. On 23 April, the ship set off from Liverpool with a crew of fourteen including the owner as a passenger and a cargo of 600 tons of coal bound for Ancona in Italy.[19]

The ship made a trouble-free passage down the French and Iberian coasts and on through the Straits of Gibraltar. On 12 May, though, the wind dropped and for two days the *Hymen* lay becalmed off the coast of Barbary, modern-day Morocco. This was a dangerous place to be at that time as the seas thereabouts were plagued with Riff pirates who preyed on passing merchantmen.

At first there was no immediate danger, the *Hymen* was far out to sea, but by 14 May the current had pushed her to within 15 miles of land and about the same distance west of Cape Tres Forcas. It was now that the vessel was spotted from the shore and at about 11a.m. two carabos, or boats, manned by between seventeen to twenty-five Moorish pirates from the Benibugllafar tribe, all armed with muskets, pistols and swords, set out towards her. These boarded the barque at about 1.30p.m., quickly overpowering Captain Smith, Joseph Hancock and the rest of the crew. The first pirates were soon joined by nine other boats and the raiders began plundering the *Hymen* of every moveable object that they could find, badly damaging the ship in the process. The owner and crew were seized by the pirates and taken ashore as captives. They were then forced to endure a march into the interior almost barefoot and under a blazing sun, with scarcely a drop of water to quench their thirst. For twenty days they were kept prisoner by the pirates, subsisting on a meagre diet of barley bread and water, with no idea of what was going to happen to them, or even if anyone knew that they were missing.

In fact, by this time many people did know about the fate of the *Hymen* and her crew and efforts were well underway to secure the mens' release. Though the two separate accounts of the capture of the *Hymen* given in *The Times* are vague and contradictory as to how the release of Joseph and his fellow prisoners was secured, it seems that a great deal was owed to one Morobito, the chief of the Benisaid tribe. When the wrecked *Hymen* drifted ashore at a beach known as Nufter or Pasani, 9 miles east of Cape Quilate, Morobito seems to have secured the wreck and somehow gained the release of four of the *Hymen's* crew. It was probably as a result of Morobito's intervention that word of the incident reached Colonel Don Manuel Buceta, the govenor of the Spanish fortress of Melilla at Cape Tres Forcas, who immediately went to check on the wreck and investigate the capture of the sailors.

Though Morobito seemed confident that he could soon secure the release of the remaining captives, it was beholden on Govenor Buceta to inform the British authorities of the loss of one of their ships. He therefore sent a report to William Penrose Mark, the British Consul at Malaga, who in turn dispatched a note to the Govenor of Gibraltar suggesting that a British warship be sent post-haste to Melilla, to act in concert with Govenor Buceta.

In the event, our man in Gibraltar sent two warships, HMS *Ariel* and HMS *Retribution*. A force drawn from these was placed under Commander Frederick Maxse of the *Ariel* and then sent on a raid against the pirate camp.[20] This was a complete success and the remaining prisoners, all of whom were now reportedly in a very wretched state, were rescued. Tired, hungry and by now dressed in rags, they were taken aboard the *Ariel*, where they were treated with great kindness by the officers and crew. They were immediately transported to Tangiers and thence on to Gibraltar before being taken back to Britain.

However, the memoirs of J.W. Gambier, who served as a midshipman aboard the *Retribution* tells a different tale. Gambier reported that when his ship arrived at

Melilla, which he described as 'one of the most terrible places on the face of the earth for cruelty and barbarity,'[21] the crew of his ship were feasted by the governor and his pretty wife, then joined in taking pot shots at the Riff tribesmen who were settled outside in almost permanent siege of Melilla. Gambier then notes:

> Next day my ship proceeded to a spot where the English captives were to be handed over. This was done without much ceremony, and, as far as I know, without any ransom. That, probably, was extorted from the Sultan. The rescued men were a scratch lot, hardly worth all the fuss made over them – though possibly they themselves thought otherwise – and when we midshipmen heard that for six or eight months they had been living comfortably in the interior, had been gazelle-hunting, and had had the run of the whole place, we could not see what they had to growl at, and felt sure that we ourselves would willingly have gone into captivity for any number of months under the same conditions.
>
> There were eleven of these mariners: their brig, the Hymen, had been captured by the pirates while lying becalmed off the coast.[22]

Obviously wild rumours were already circulating about the capture of the *Hymen* and though Gambier's views of what he thought of the men are valid from an observer's point of view, the story of their luxurious and prolonged captivity seems just so much fantasy. The stark difference between his account and that given in *The Times* perhaps indicates that Morobito managed to get some other captives handed over before the navy launched its raid on the pirate camp.

The only casualty of the whole sorry affair over the *Hymen* was the ship itself. Despite the efforts of the Spanish to refloat her, the ship broke up and the remains were scavanged by the locals. It was reported that the ship was only half insured and the loss to the owner, who was doubtless still traumatised by the whole ordeal, was doubly heavy; nonetheless a claim was being made via the consul at Tangiers on the Moorish government, who were seen as having failed in their duty, so recently ratified in an international agreement, to quell the pirates operating from their shores. The claim was successful and the Emperor of Morocco eventually paid out £3,278 in lieu of the *Hymen* and her cargo.[23]

Today incidents such as that which overtook the *Hymen* would be reported almost as soon as they happened, but communications in the 1850s were slow and in some ways this was a good thing as it often spared the families the worry of too much waiting; by the time people in Britain received the news from abroad the incidents had often resolved themselves and such was the case here. As already noted, the story made the papers, but the first report was not published in *The Times* until 12 June, two days shy of a month since the *Hymen* had been captured. A second more detailed report culled from the *Gibraltar Chronicle* was printed by *The Times* a week later, by which time the crisis had been resolved and Joseph and his crewmates were on their way home.

Yet it must have been an anxious time for his family when they heard the news, no matter how short a time it was. Joseph was not settled permanently in Liverpool, so he probably returned home to the Potteries when he finally reached Britain. The celebrations at his safe return can be easily imagined, as too can the curiousity of family, friends and neighbours keen to hear what he had gone through.

Despite the harrowing experience and any sufferings he may have endured, Joseph's experience on the *Hymen* does not seem to have dented his love for his chosen career. By 7 July he was back in Liverpool explaining the loss of his second mate's certificate to the authorities. A few days later on 10 July, he received a new certificate and a new number, No.15310, to replace that lost with the *Hymen*. The next day, on the 11th, Joseph signed on as second mate aboard the St John, New Brunswick-registered vessel *David G. Fleming*, an emigrant ship bound for Melbourne, Australia.

The Highs and Lows of Family Life

Joseph was away from home for the best part of a year, landing safely back in Britain on 8 June 1857. Though he was often away, Joseph had nevertheless stayed in regular contact with the Potteries. He had other reasons besides the obvious one of visiting his family, for there was a young woman by the name of Susanna Wrench, who demanded his attention. Susanna, later known to her relatives as 'Anna', was the twenty-year-old daughter of engraver Thomas Wrench and his wife Fanny. The Wrenchs lived nearby in Bethesda Street, Hanley, but how Joseph and Anna first met is unknown, though it was probably a long-standing affair, as Joseph had precious little time at home in the early years of his career. Clearly their affection for each other had allowed the two of them to maintain a relationship despite Joseph's time at sea and by this time they had decided to marry. Thus on 2 July 1857, they were wed at St Peter Ad Vincula Church in Stoke.

Joseph and his new wife spent two months together before he returned to work, signing on at Liverpool on 19 September 1857 as second mate aboard the St John-registered *Sovereign of the Seas* for a quick jaunt over to New Brunswick and back. Joseph then applied for and gained his first mate's certificate of competancy in December, but according to his records he did not return to the sea for two years. He may have taken work locally, tiding himself over until he could settle his family more permanently before returning to his career.

All this while, Joseph and Anna both gave their addresses as Hanley, so they were probably lodging with the bride's parents in Bethesda Street. Certainly that was where she gave birth to their first child just over a year after they were married; this was George John Hancock, born on 24 July 1858. So, at the tender age of eight, Ted Smith had become an uncle, and as will be seen due to the similarity in ages, he later enjoyed a strong bond with his half-nephews and not only with those by this marriage.

On 25 June 1859, Ted's half-sister, Thirza, also got married, to engineman William Harrington, at Wolstanton parish church. William came from Burslem and his father James was a manager, possibly of a pot bank. The description of William as an engineman is rather vague, though he probably worked one of the steam engines on a pottery. These were good positions. The men who ran the steam engines had to keep their machines up and running, as these powered most of the other machines on the factories via a series of ropes and belts. If the steam engine broke down, the factory would grind to a halt as too would its profits. As a result, the enginemen were well paid for their trouble.

For Thirza it would prove to be a good marriage and the Harringtons would prosper as time went on. If their gravestone is to be trusted, though, theirs would be a life regularly tinged with tragedy as beneath their own inscriptions the names of five children are inscribed. The first of their surviving children that we know about was James William Sidney Harrington, who was born in Well Street on 7 October 1861. He too would be close to his uncles Joseph and Edward and served under the latter during his early years in the merchant navy. At the time of the census that year, William and Thirza had a house of their own at 18 Well Street, next to the Smiths' grocer's store. Living with them was sixteen-year-old Louisa Wooley, a cousin of William's. Thirza was working as a dress maker and Louisa was her assistant.

Of course, though the closest, these were not Smith's only relatives, as he had many cousins in the area. Ted's uncle George now had a number of children, the eldest of whom, Elizabeth Smith, born in 1855, would later make her own mark in the Smith family history when she married Mark Spode Mason, the impoverished grandson of Charles James Mason, the patentee of Mason's Ironstone pottery and husband of Sarah Spode, the granddaughter of the famous Josiah Spode. Through this relationship, therefore, Captain Smith's family became distantly related to both the Mason and Spode pottery dynasties. Whether Smith and his cousin Elizabeth actually saw or knew much of each other is hard to say as by 1861 George Smith and his growing family had moved from Hanley and were living a few miles away in May Bank, Wolstanton.[24]

Other cousins though were closer by and at number 17 Well Street, Edward and Catherine Smith had extra mouths to feed. Two-year-old George Hancock had been left with his grandparents and there was also twenty-two-year-old Ellen Privet, the daughter of Edward's younger sister Jane. Ellen was working on a pot bank as a paintress. Ted is there too, but his age on this return is incorrect; the census claims that he was ten, but he was in fact eleven years old and was listed as a 'scholar'.

The young George Hancock may have been left in the care of his grandparents as during this time Susanna may have been at work because Joseph had returned to the sea. From March 1860 to November 1862, he served as mate aboard the *Princess Royal* followed by the *General Williams*. Then in December 1862, having accrued the necessary sea time, Joseph gained his master's certificate. As he never applied for an extra master mariner's certificate, the course of Joseph's career over the next few years is harder to track, but the family's joy and pride at what their son had achieved must have been great. Much seems to have been later made of Ted Smith gaining his master's certificate thirteen years later, so there were probably similar if not greater celebrations when Joseph became the first in the family to have gained this great prize.

Family events at this time were not all happy ones, though. Ted's father, Edward Smith, was becoming increasingly ill as a result of phthisis, a form of pulmonary tuberculosis, and on 7 October 1864 he died at home aged fifty-nine. Three days later Thyrza (as she henceforth spells her name) appeared before the local registrar to report the death and it is from this document that we learn that Ted's father had worked as a pottery presser.

Edward Smith was buried on 11 October 1864, at Hanley's municipal cemetery, actually situated in Shelton. The burial record is at odds with the death certificate, as here Edward Smith is listed as a grocer. The burial service with the family gathered around the grave was carried out by the Revd C.J. Slating. Edward's grave plot was 21204 in consecrated ground, but if there was ever a gravestone, it is now long gone and the burial place of Captain Smith's father lies unmarked.

Etruria Forge

It is impossible to say for certain at what age Ted left school. He certainly received a relatively good education that he was later able to build upon in pursuit of his career, so he probably stayed on into his early teens. As already seen, Edmund Jones remembered him as a senior boy at the British School, while in 1912, William Jones recalled that 'Something like 48 years ago, he [Smith] was a scholar at Etruria'[25], giving us an approximate date of 1864, the same year that his father died. Perhaps after his father's death, the family's circumstances demanded that fourteen-year-old Ted finish school and start work to earn his keep.

When he did though, Ted quickly found work at the Etruria Forge, one of Lord Granville's iron foundries, the chimneys of which can be glimpsed behind the trees of the Etruria Grove on the 1865 photo of Etruria. Ted would have been familiar with the Forge, as it was near to his old school, being situated on the bank of the Trent & Mersey Canal, just to the west of the Wedgwood factory. The manager of the Forge at this time was the grandfather of Edmund Jones who had known Ted at school. Here he was trained up to operate a Nasmyth steam hammer, a monstrous contraption built in the shape of a large inverted letter 'Y'. This was used to shape the largest of wrought-iron components with blows of its mighty hydraulic hammer and the original had been designed to make the paddle shafts of the steamer SS *Great Britain*. The *Great Britain*'s paddles soon gave way to propellors, but the steam hammer survived and its maker, James Nasmyth, claimed in a rather self-aggrandising manner that his machine was so well engineered that, with a skilled operator, the hammer could hold an egg without breaking it. Ted's job fascinated one of his old friends, Joe Turner, who later recalled how one night he stayed away from home to sit with Ted through his night shift in the little box that accommodated the machine's operator.[26]

It seems, though, that Ted was merely biding his time at the Etruria Forge until he was old enough to follow his half-brother Joseph into the merchant navy. In an interview given after the *Titanic* disaster, Ann O'Donnell, a childhood friend of the Smiths who had emigrated to the States, recalled how keen Ted had been on the idea:

> His half-brother was Captain Hancock, who sailed the seven seas from Henley (sic) and the youngster was stirred by the stories told by the elder man and determined to go to sea. There was no denying the lad, and rather than force him to run away from home and sail with strangers, his brother shipped him in his 16th year.[27]

Early in 1867, Ted Smith gave up his job at the Etruria Forge and on 5 February, actually a little over a week after his seventeenth birthday, accompanied by a group of friends, one of whom was Joe Turner, Ted arrived in Liverpool. He had made an appointment to meet his half-brother Joseph, who was by then the captain of an American-built sailing ship the *Senator Weber*, then loading across the Mersey at Birkenhead's West Float Dock. Joe Turner noted in his recollections that he got so excited that he too tried to enlist there '…but was greatly disappointed at Captain Hancock's refusal to take me, as he said I had no outfit or my parents' consent, and he could not take me under such conditions.'[28]

Crestfallen, Joe Turner and the others had to return to the Potteries, though Joe soon found a position on a sailing ship from the port of London and thus realised his own dream. Ted meanwhile was taken to the head offices of Messrs Andrew Gibson & Co. in King Street, Liverpool, where he was officially apprenticed and signed on as 'Boy' aboard the *Senator Weber*.[29]

2

BEFORE THE MAST

They had to take a boat across to Birkenhead and travel some distance inland to the West Float Dock to reach the ship that was to be Ted Smith's home from home for the next couple of years. The *Senator Weber* had started life as the *Wellfleet*, built in Boston, USA, in 1853 and as such she sailed initially for Enoch Train's Boston-Liverpool Line of packets. The ship changed hands in 1854, being transferred to the Regular Line sailing in the Boston-New Orleans packet trade. A few years later, the vessel had a significant role to play in some North American family histories. Numerous American families can today claim descent from two groups of Mormon immigrants who sailed to America aboard the 1,353-ton *Wellfleet* in the summer of 1856. At some point during her *Wellfleet* days a picture of the ship was painted, possibly by the artist Francis Hustwick, showing her in rough seas in full windswept rig, her long, sleek, black hull decorated with a gold band and her upper works gleaming white; a handsome ship, the pride of her owners. But the American Civil War drastically reduced trade and wartime economics dictated that the *Wellfleet* like many other vessels be sold off. Thus, in 1863, she was sold to Hamburg, which as German unification was still a few years off, had its own fleet. There she was renamed *Senator Weber* and flew the flag of Hamburg. In 1866, following Prussia's victory over Austria, Hamburg was incorporated into the North German Confederation and the *Senator Weber* was sold once more, this time to the Liverpool ship owner Andrew Gibson & Co.

By this stage in her life the ship had been stripped down, now weighing in at a more sprightly 1,297 tons, though that still made her a fair-sized vessel for her day. She measured 197.7ft long by 39.4ft wide and 26.1ft deep with a raised quarterdeck of 42 tons. Classified by her rigging as a 'wood ship', she carried three masts, square rigged. Her code letters were NHWB, official number 51475. At this time the *Senator Weber* was one of Andrew Gibson & Co.'s prime trading vessels and so she remained for many years, her portrait being painted once again, this time by the artist Otto Ioop. By 1885, though, the ship had changed hands once again and was owned by Axel Petterson and sailing out of Helsingberg, Sweden, under the command of Captain J.W. Wenck. Following the *Titanic* disaster, Ted's old school pal Joe Turner claimed that in 1903 he had seen the *Senator Weber* working as a coal hulk out of

Port Stanley in the Falkland Islands.[1] He was, however, mistaken, for as numerous newspapers on either side of the Atlantic reported in March 1891, a few days after setting off from Cardiff for Rio de Janeiro, the *Senator Weber* was caught in a heavy gale off the English coast and sank with the loss of fourteen men. This grim fate, though, was still many years distant from that day in early February 1867 when Ted Smith walked up the gangplank and first went to sea.[2]

Ted Smith's first experience of life at sea would be the sort of thing that boyhood dreams are made of, a long journey to an exotic land and back, for the *Senator Weber* was bound for Hong Kong, 'and any ports and places in the Indian, Pacific and Atlantic Oceans and China and Eastern Seas…',[3] as the voyage description on the crew agreement had it. Including Ted himself, the voyage would start with a crew of twenty-six men and boys, all of whom signed on aboard the ship on 5 February even though the ship would not sail for another week. This would give Joseph a full compliment of hands for loading and packing the cargo and ship's provisions.

The crew were a mixed bunch. Most were in their twenties, though there were a few in their thirties, while Manxman Robert Redfern, the carpenter, was the old man of the ship at forty-two. The youngest members of the crew were the other two ship's boys, James Grieve from Roxburgh and Thomas Forster who, like Ted, came from Hanley; both were fifteen. The crew was also mixed nationality-wise. The bulk of the men were British or Irish, but there were men from Germany, Norway, Denmark, Greece, Italy and Ceylon and apart from the three new boys all had been to sea before. The ship would be a crucible, a melting pot for these nationalities and individual temperaments for nearly two years. As will be seen very few stuck the coarse and less than half of those who now signed on aboard the *Senator Weber* came home on her. One by one, the others would quit the ship either by mutual consent, or by deserting. The latter seems to have been something of a curse to the voyage and it is tempting to suppose that Joseph might have been something of a tartar, but in truth, desertion seems to have been rife in the merchant service as sailors tired of the sea or their shipmates or they sought better paid work on other ships. So, it is hard to ascribe any definite reason to the troubles that would beset the *Senator Weber*, it seems merely to have been a case of familiarity breeding contempt.

Ted Smith's first sea journey began on 12 February 1867. It was customary at this time for most of the sailors to join the ship drunk on the sailing day and the crew of the *Senator Weber*, were probably no different, for as Joseph had noted in the crew agreement there was 'no grog allowed'. The prospect of a long, dry journey would have certainly seen the sailors getting their fill prior to sailing in the bars that dotted the waterfront. By the 13th the ship was reported to be on the river outward-bound and by the 14th was at sea.

From references in *Lloyd's List* and contemporary newspapers and the single reference to the Indian Ocean in the voyage description, it seems that the *Senator Weber* then steered a course down past the shoreline of Western Europe then the length of Africa before finally turning east at the Cape of Good Hope. The momentous first leg within easy reach of land would then be followed by a long journey out across the wide blue expanse of the Indian Ocean before they reached their destination. There was as yet no shortcut, the Suez Canal that would halve the journey time would not open until 1869 and as a result the *Senator Weber* would not reach Hong Kong for five or six months.

A Rough School

In one way this was a good thing as it would give Joseph ample time to shake his new ship and crew into some kind of order, especially the ordinary seamen and boys such as his half-brother Ted, undergoing their apprenticeship. This was not designed to turn the novice into a ship's officer. Ted Smith, like his half-brother before him, was being trained as an ordinary seaman. The option was there in years to come to sit his exams for a certificate of competency, but that was for the future. Now, though, as a landsman hoping to become a seaman, Ted had a lot to learn and endure. For though he had doubtless been primed by Joseph, Ted would have had at first only a vague grasp of the realities of the life he had now entered. He had escaped the dust, heat, long hours and hard labour in the pot banks, mines and foundries of the Potteries, but life at sea was no soft option. In later life, Smith himself confirmed to some of his passengers that his early years at sea had been no picnic. The publisher J.E. Hodder Williams recalled how Captain Smith occasionally ribbed some of his more delicate passengers, cossetted as they were in these 'floating hotels' as he called them. Hodder Williams added that Smith 'had served his apprenticeship in a rough school and knew the sea and ships in their uncounted moods.'[4]

That said, there can be little doubt that his relationship with the captain would have put him in the best possible position for getting to 'know the ropes' in his new job. This old nautical term that has fallen into common usage was the mantra that every seaman in the age of sail had to learn. The average sailing ship carried upwards of 200 different ropes and the purposes of each had to be committed to memory and quickly too if a sailor was to do his job properly and not find himself subjected to the ire of the more experienced seamen or the mates. So too did the names and purposes of the numerous masts, spars and sails that powered the ship. Then there were the more technical aspects of seamanship to be mastered such as the more arcane branches of mathematics needed for navigation. The physical practicalities of draught and displacement also needed to be thoroughly understood for the successful navigation of shallower waters, while the careful loading of stores and stowing of cargos was a must if a ship was to sail smoothly; this tricky science, of keeping a vessel balanced on an even keel, provided another sea salt idiom for the English language. These, though, were not aspects of the job that could easily be fitted into the typical working day, so most sailors had to study whenever they could and were probably forced to attend crammer sessions ashore, prior to sitting any exams.

Above all, though, the young sailor had to get to know and understand the great elements around him. The sea was a fickle, changeable mistress, 'the grey widow maker' as knowing sailors called it. It had moods and nuances and there were marked differences between the swell of the deep blue oceans and shallower coastal waters. The sea was only half the equation, the sky dictated life on a ship just as much if not more so, its clouds and winds could make life aboard a square-rigger a tranquil heaven or a living hell.

Not only did ship life improve the brain, but also it promoted brawn. Out in the open air, working at hard and physical jobs, day-in, day-out, seven days a week until the journey ended, unprepossessing boys could grow in a few years into muscular, barrel-chested men. Yet on the downside it might also be said that Smith had adopted a very dangerous life. Besides the ever present menace of being washed overboard, or tumbling from the rigging, the physical extremes of the job also took their toll – muscular strains were the most likely complaints, hernias were also common and there were illnesses ranging from seasickness to more exotic ailments picked up on foreign shores, or those caused by exposure and dampness. It comes as little surprise, therefore, that the merchant navy was not seen as a prudent choice so far as career prospects were concerned. Yet, if the sailor was spared injury or illness and had the wits to get on, there was a wealth of experience to be gained from such a life and there was the added advantage that you got to see the world as few others did. The romance of travel probably gained many recruits for the sea.

When he got aboard ship, Ted would have found his quarters in the cramped forecastle. The fo'c'sle, as it was known, was situated in the pointed bow of the vessel; it was generally spartan in aspect, unheated and with little in the way of ventilation. Men slept upwards of eight to a cabin on bare wooden bunks; their only belongings being the clothes they wore (and usually slept in – changing was made very difficult in such cramped quarters) and a few personal items they may have carried in a sea chest, which could be lashed to the floor by iron rings. The sailor provided his own mattress, oilskins (usually gaiters, a jacket and a hat) and a few oddments such as a knife, fork, spoon, soap and a brush.

The fo'c'sle was the centre of an ordinary sailor's society on a ship, but it was claustrophobic and often unhygienic except when it was washed out by the sea which during rough weather usually found its way into this inner sanctum. All too often the shared quarters were filled with the heavy smells of dirt and worse if illness took a hold. Baths were rare except when the ship was becalmed in tropical waters when the men could take a dip in the sea itself; personal hygiene was more often than not confined to each man taking a cold scrub out of a ship's bucket and many sailors grew beards and wore their hair long as a result. The food aboard such voyages was pretty drab fare, consisting per man per day of a ration of about a pound and a half of dry salt beef or a pound and a quarter of salt pork every other day. These had often been stored for years and as a result had become so hard that rumour had it that bored sailors would whittle model ships out of them. The meat was supplemented by half

a pound of flour on beef days and a third of a pound of peas supplied with the pork.
On top of these each man received a pound of bread, an eighth of an ounce of tea,
half an ounce of coffee and two ounces of sugar every day. There was also a seemingly
endless supply of hardtack, the tough, rock-like ship's biscuits. These could often only
be broken by beating them with a hammer or against the corner of a sea chest. And
no matter how fresh – relatively speaking – they were when taken on board, after only
a few days they would invariably be infested with grub-like weevils. The ship's cook
who usually cooked up the men's rations could indulge in a little experimentation,
producing unleavened bread or 'duff pudding' – bread and fat boiled in a linen bag.
These bare rations, though, could be replaced with more exotic foodstuffs depending
on the ports of call. The official 'Scale of Provisions' for each journey listed foodstuffs
that could be used in lieu of their standard rations. The skippers, in an effort to keep
their crews healthy, on arriving at a port often dipped into their coffers and took on
more perishable supplied such as fruit, vegetables and fresh meat. When these had run
out, or were not available, every twelve days a ration of lime juice was served out to
every crewman to prevent scurvy. Ships on long voyages also carried some livestock,
such as hens or other fowl for their eggs, goats for milk, while the flesh on the animals
could act as an emergency reserve if things got bad.

The able seamen were formed into watches, to one of which Ted would have
been attached. The mate, in this case twenty-nine-year-old Irishman James Teevans,
was in charge of the port watch that looked after the port side and the bowsprit and
trimmed the sails on the foremast, while the starboard watch under the second mate,
twenty-four-year-old Richard Brewer, tended the starboard ropes and the rear of the
ship including the main and mizzenmasts. All of the sailors turned out to set sail and
then worked alternate watches of four hours each, with one watch looking to the
sails and steering, while the off-watch ate or slept. Providing the weather remained
good, this system operated without interruption for the rest of the journey. The
duties whilst on watch could include a stint at the wheel, but the time was usually
spent tending the canvas, making sure that the ropes were taut and untangled and
that they were not sawing each other to bits. Holystoning and swabbing the decks
and greasing the anchor chains were also duties regularly carried out. Generally, such
jobs were not designed to improve the speed of the ship, but to make sure that the
ship was 'ship-shape', in other words, ready for anything.

The most iconic part of a seaman's duty was, however, the setting and furling of
the sails. Setting sail was easy; the canvas was merely let loose from the yards and
after it was dropped, the sail was trimmed to the wind under the supervision of the
mate or master. The position of the sail was then fixed by using the running rigging,
the lengths of rope used to secure the sails to the sides of the ship. These ropes were
apart from the standing rigging and the ladder-like shrouds that were attached to
each mast. When the sails needed to be furled, though, especially in rough weather,
the riggers were ordered aloft. They climbed up the shrouds with their backs to the
wind so that they were pressed against the rigging, until they reached the yardarm.

Quickly, the men shifted their weight from the shroud to the footline beneath the spar and gripping onto the yard, they legged their way along. When everyone was ready, the canvas was slackened off and the corners were winched up to the yard, leaving the sagging belly of the sail to be taken in by hand. Letting go with his hands and supported only by the footline and his stomach resting on the spar, each sailor reached down and grabbed a handful of canvas and hauled it up under his stomach until each man was resting on a cushion of canvas. The sails were not made of a thin, light material, but of a heavy duty weave not far removed in texture from tarpaulin, so the rigours that such a duty entailed, especially if the canvas was wet or if the job had to be done in heavy weather, could be crippling. Then, when the entire mass of sail was drawn up, it was rolled, beaten and finally lashed to the yard.

Working aloft could be a terrifying experience for those new to the job, but the time-served sailors knew their duty and took a sort of pride in the speed and ability of their furling. They also knew that despite being suspended several storeys above the rolling deck or hanging over an angry sea, being aloft for all the perils it engendered did have advantages over being down on the storm-lashed deck, where towering waves could engulf the ship and pick a man off the deck for him never to be seen again.

Though work dominated most of a sailor's time at sea, it was not all hardship and even the lowliest deckhand had his private moments. Sundays were rest days where work was kept to a bare minimum, though it depended very much on the whim of the individual skipper. Some captains were religious-minded and insisted on church service, others, though, left the men to their own devices. Off watch, sailors sometimes amused themselves by carving ornaments or made models from whatever bits and pieces came their way. Today even the most naive of their productions command staggering prices at auction. Music also played a part in their lives, be it the shanties they sang to keep in time as they hauled on the ropes, or the sea songs they composed in moments of reflection. These mingled with popular tunes and jigs and many a sailor was a skilled amateur musician on the fiddle, pipes or Jew's harp. Sport could also be had by fishing, while others attempted to snare the more dim-witted sea birds that visited the ship, anything to break the monotony. They even had a festival of sorts, a tradition still carried on today. For first-timers, 'crossing the line' of the equator was a rite of passage during which one of the more venerable members of the ship's company would dress up as Neptune, Roman god of the sea in all his splendour, trident in hand and goad the crew into ceremonially ducking the first-timers in the ocean, even if it only meant pouring a bucket of sea water over them.

Towards the end of her long haul to the Far East, we do hear something of the *Senator Weber*'s progress. *Lloyd's List* indicates that the ship passed the town of Anjer on the island of Java, on 13 July. Anjer overlooks the Sunda Strait, the narrow strip of sea between the islands of Java and Sumatra. The ship's passage through the Strait would take it past the dormant volcano of Krakatoa, which at that time occupied a lush green island 30 miles offshore in the middle of the Strait. Sixteen years later, however, as is well known, Krakatoa exploded in one of the most cataclysmic eruptions in recorded history, destroying hundreds of nearby coastal settlements and killing thousands of people on both Java and Sumatra, with over 7,000 casualties in Anjer alone.

Having passed through the Sunda Strait, the *Senator Weber* then turned due north through the South China Sea, on the last leg of her long outward journey and the final stage of Ted Smith's first voyage at sea. We do not know whether it had been an arduous or tedious voyage, rough or calm; such details do not seem to exist. For though the log of the *Senator Weber* survives, it tells us nothing of the voyage before early August 1867, when the ship made landfall in distant Hong Kong.

Hong Kong

To a young man fresh from the Potteries, Hong Kong must have seemed an otherworldly place. This far-flung outpost of the Empire had been ceded to Britain at the end of the Opium War in 1841 and by the time the *Senator Weber* sailed into Victoria Harbour in the middle of 1867, Hong Kong was a bustling international port.

This great Asian city was then, as now, an assault on the senses. During the day the harbour was alive with the ships of all nations, Western square riggers from Europe, Australia and the Americas, but also junks and sampans from closer to home. The air almost throbbed with the clamour along the waterfront where stalls, hawkers and shopkeepers, allied by eye-popping coloured silks, banners and paintwork and heady, spiced, unfamiliar smells, vied for the attentions of passers-by. But nineteenth-century Hong Kong was arguably at its best by night when darkness softened the attendant squalour and gave the place a haunting beauty. The mountain upon the base of which the city is built circles around the harbour like a great amphitheatre, and the streets rising up one above the other from the waters edge far up the mountainside were illuminated at that period by thousands of Chinese lanterns that hung over every door and almost every window. These successive tiers of lights were reflected in the shimmering waters below, across which flitted incessantly the lights of the numerous small boats that wove their way in and out of the shipping. For the harbour was home to many Chinese families who lived in bustling amphibious communities on their sampans. These people were more at home in a boat than many a Western sailor and it was no unusual thing to see wiry octogenarians and even toddlers barely able to walk or talk skillfully piloting their boats across the harbour's wide waters.

The *Senator Weber* arrived in Hong Kong during the typhoon season, but there is no indication that nature threw anything too serious at the master and crew during their sojourn in the port. What problems there were mentioned in the ship's log were purely domestic. The proximity of the port and its numerous attractions for young men: the women — the drinking, opium and gaming dens, the brothels, theatres and street shows – seems to have strained relations between Joseph and his crew, who were eager to get ashore, though some it seems were more troublesome than others. The *Senator Weber* seems to have had a knot of ne'er-do-well crew members who could not seem to stay out of trouble and one of these was Edward Smith. This, however, was not Joseph's half-brother; this Edward was a twenty-year-old able-bodied seaman from Scarborough who had formerly encrewed with the ship *Regelia*. It has been suggested that because there were two Edward Smiths aboard, that it was now that young Ted Smith started to be known as 'E.J.' amongst his fellow sailors, an appellation that would stick with him throughout his long career at sea. What is certain is that despite their names, the two young men were poles apart character-wise.

The first indication of trouble came with the first entry in the ship's log, dated 'Monday 6am August 5 1867 … Edward Smith, Seaman refused duty alleging as a reason that he could not agree with the Crew.'[5]

Joseph took this malcontent ashore and had him charged and thrown in prison for three days. The stint in jail, though, seems to have done little to cool Edward Smith's heels and hardly had he returned to the ship on 11 August than he immediately left without leave and did not return for ten days. Smith, though, was not the only member of the *Senator Weber*'s crew eager to get ashore, as earlier that same morning two other sailors, thirty-four-year-old Francis Gallachan and twenty-two-year-old Matthew Mudd, had also absconded. By the next day they were both back on board and suffering their skipper's ire. Joseph had both of them up before a magistrate who promptly fined them four days' pay each.[6]

Others left the ship with much less fuss. On 26 August, the ship's cook, thirty-year-old Henry Goff, was discharged before the local shipping master, 'by mutual consent', a rather bland stock phrase that could perhaps cover a multitude of sins, though Goff's departure does not seem to have been attended by any trouble. This peaceful departure, though, was the exception, as Francis Gallachan was playing up again. Claiming that he had injured himself, he refused to work. Joseph smelt a rat and had him examined by a doctor who did find that Gallachan had a hernia of some years standing, but it was so small to be of no significance and in no way disabled him. The doctor gave him a truss and an otherwise clean bill of health, but all to no avail, the man still refused to work. Two days later Joseph took him ashore to see the local magistrate and at his own request he was examined by another doctor at the civil hospital. The doctor confirmed the previous prognosis that there was nothing substantially wrong with Gallachan and that he could return to work. Gallachan, though, was adamant and told the magistrate that '… he would do no more work aboard the "Senator Weber".' As a result he was sent to jail for a month for refusing duty and fined £5 to pay for the doctor's examination.[7] Precisely one month later on 28 September 1867, Francis Gallachan was discharged before the shipping master.

Joseph was minus one malcontent, but that same day Edward Smith got up to his old tricks and refused duty and backed up his truculence with some insolence. After all the troubles of the past few weeks, Joseph, it seems, had had enough. The man was seized and as Joseph himself wrote, 'I gave him a sound thrashing with a rope's end but he would not return to duty therefore I took him on shore to the Police station.'[8] Two days later on the 30th, Joseph recorded that his half-brother's namesake was committed to jail for six weeks' hard labour and the ship was rid of him at last. The only other entry made during the *Senator Weber*'s stay in Hong Kong recorded how after so many months at sea, Joseph discovered that one of his men, Daniel Materanga, a twenty-six-year-old Italian rated able seaman when he joined the crew in Liverpool, could not steer, had no knowledge of the compass, did not know one rope from another and could do nothing aloft. That he had hidden his inability for so long is remarkable and perhaps points to a lack of perception and distance from the crew on Joseph's part, which may perhaps account for the trouble over the previous two months.

For almost two months we hear nothing more from the skipper and crew of the *Senator Weber*. *Lloyd's List* seems to indicate that there was at least one departure and return to Hong Kong at this time, though there is no corroboration in the ship's documents. Obviously she had offloaded her cargo and now took on more for shipment to her next destination, San Francisco on the eastern coast of the USA. The ship also took on at least one passenger. Henry K. Jones was a sick man and had been in hospital in Hong Kong for some months with pleurisy. He had been advised to leave the colony to recruit his health and the *Senator Weber* took him aboard. That the ship carried at least one passenger implies that others may have travelled to and from Hong Kong aboard her, but if so there is no record of them. That we know so much about Mr Jones is due to the fact that at 12.15p.m. on Monday 23 December 1867, Jones died from his illness. The ship was by this time almost halfway across the Pacific Ocean and, lacking the facilities to store a corpse, the dead man was buried at sea at 4p.m. that same day. The co-ordinates of the burial Lat. 38° 34' North, Long. 175° 22' West, were recorded in the ship's log.[9]

Two days later, on Christmas Day, an inventory of the dead man's belongings was entered in the log. Henry Jones appears to have been a man of means judging by his belongings, which give us an interesting glimpse of what the well dressed and appointed mid-Victorian gentleman abroad wore. These ranged from a pair of wellington boots; four pairs of shoes; five uniform coats; a grey cloth suit; assorted trousers and shirts; a black silk neckerchief; two uniform caps; an alpaca umbrella; shirt collars; cotton socks; gloves; handkerchiefs; vests; cap covers; ties and scarfs; a Bible and Church Service; a gold watch and chain and a gold ring; two bank bills and $18 in silver. His belongings would have then been stored ready to be handed over to the authorities prior to being returned to his family. The log entry is also notable as not only was it signed by Joseph Hancock and his mate James Teevans, but also by 'Edward J. Smith, Boy', as an extra witness. [10]

San Francisco

Nothing else of note occurred during this part of the journey and by mid-January 1868 the *Senator Weber* was sailing up the Golden Gate. The passage to San Francisco today is spanned by the famous Golden Gate suspension bridge, but at this time no such structures existed. San Francisco was nevertheless by this time the capital of America's west coast, with a history dating back to Sir Francis Drake's founding of Nova Albion in the late 1500s. The real catalyst for its growth, though, came twenty years before the arrival of the *Senator Weber* when, in 1848, gold was discovered in California. In the resulting gold rush, San Francisco benefitted from its proximity to the gold fields that brought in thousands of prospectors from around the world. By 1868 the gold was dwindling, but compared to the east coast cities so recently threatened by the American Civil War, San Francisco and its west coast cousins had enjoyed something of a boom and hundreds of ships regularly crowded the bays and waterfront bringing foreign goods and settlers to the city and taking American goods to the world. On the down side poverty, squalour, corruption and crime were growing social problems and there was the ever present danger of earthquakes. A large earthquake had struck the area in 1865 and another would rock San Francisco late in 1868, though long after the *Senator Weber* had departed.

For all that, though, San Francisco and indeed the young United States itself still offered great opportunities to the adventurous as evidenced by the gold rush. Perhaps it was because of this allure that shortly after the *Senator Weber*'s arrival at the city, little by little, the ship's crew all but vanished. Three of the men were legally discharged, but by 21 February, when Joseph appeared before the British consul in San Francisco, a further fourteen of his crew had deserted. What is notable is that those discharged were slightly older, while the deserters were all young men or boys, one of whom was Thomas Foster, the other Hanley lad under his command. Getting a replacement crew for these defaulters, though troublesome, was not a major problem, the local seaman's homes and waterfront bars were full of sailors eager for work or a passage home and the *Senator Weber* soon had enough hands. Again it was a mixed group of nationalities, mainly English, Scots and Irish, but with Swedes, Germans, Belgians and Canadians and most were in their twenties. [11]

The desertions apparently benefitted young Ted Smith, who according to his own service records was first rated as third mate on 8 February 1868. This coincides with the stopover in San Francisco. His promotion may have been the result of nepotism, but Joseph's decision to promote his half-brother, albeit to an unqualified position, was also doubtless prompted by the fact that the crew of the *Senator Weber*, for whatever reason, had suddenly been reduced to just twelve men, including the skipper. Nowhere in the documentation of this voyage is Ted Smith referred to in this new capacity, though he was taken on as such on the next voyage, so it seems he received the promotion to help the official third mate, Henry Tate, who would have been amongst those who had the unenviable task of knocking this new crew into order.

Callao and the Chincha Islands

From San Francisco, the *Senator Weber* sailed south, crossing the equator once more and arriving eventually at Callao, the principal port of Peru and a major destination for trading ships of all nations. Here one man deserted and another was discharged while Joseph appeared before the British Consul with a crewman who was found to suffer from epileptic fits. He kept him on the ship, but the man was downgraded and could not work in the rigging.

Some three decades before the *Senator Weber* arrived at Callao bay, HMS *Beagle* had stopped there for several weeks during her soon to be famous scientific voyage around South America. Aboard her was the young, aspiring naturalist Charles Darwin, making the voyage that would form his ideas on evolution. His journal of the voyage has him discovering wonders around every headland, but Callao was not one of them. The fortress that dominated the town and which had resisted bombardment by the rogue British admiral Lord Cochrane a decade earlier was impressive enough. Darwin, though, did not like the weather, nor the fetid stench that rose from the malarial marshes near to the port. Of Callao and its inhabitants he was equally dismissive:

> Callao is a filthy, ill-built, small seaport. The inhabitants… present every imaginable shade of mixture, between European, Negro and Indian blood. They appear a depraved drunken set of people.[12]

Whatever Darwin's opinions of their appearance and morals, the locals were nevertheless extremely industrious and as an illustration of the port of Callao in the middle of nineteenth century shows, by the time the *Senator Weber* touched there it had become a very busy place indeed. In the distance numerous square-riggers lie at anchor surrounded by smaller vessels, launches and lighters carrying passengers or cargo back and forth. In the middle ground there is the long landing stage with its cranes and warehouses. This later became a rail terminus for goods wagons taking cargos out to the ships. In the foreground can be seen a busy wharf with piles of goods waiting for transport. A few years after the *Senator Weber* touched at Callao, an American visitor, Ephriam George Squier, passed through this wharf and described it in some detail. He noted the large jars filled with 'italia' – a native spirit. Bales of cinchona bark lay beside great heaps of wheat from Chile that was bound for mills along the River Rimac. Blocks of salt and loaves of a crude sugar known as 'chancaca' were wrapped up in plantano leaves and huge bars of hard-won silver from Cerro de Pasco were awaiting shipment to foreign ports. The whole wharf was a hive of activity, not only with sailors and the dock workers, but with harbour-front vendors offering passers-by fish, fresh and salt meat, potatoes, crabs, the juice of bitter oranges, lard, peppers and salt.[13]

Another major export from Callao was guano. This pungent but highly profitable material was the fertiliser of choice for many European and American gardeners and farmers and huge sums were made in its export. Peru boasted a number of small islands from which hundreds of tons of ossified bird dung were collected. The nearby islands of Lobos de Afuera gave some, but the most famous, or infamous by this time, were the Chincha Islands which were the ship's next port of call. Situated some 13 miles off the coast of south-western Peru, these three small islands had just recently sparked a war when, in 1864, covetous of the wealth that the guano islands produced, Spain had occupied the islands sparking the Spanish-Peruvian War of 1864–66. This tragicomic attempt by Spain to recapture some of its imperial glory resulted in a resounding Peruvian victory. By the time the *Senator Weber* arrived there, though, memories of the conflict were fading away.

So too, though, was the supply of guano which had been harvested quite ruthlessly since the 1840s and by 1874 the supply would have quite simply run out. However, in the heyday of the guano trade hundreds of ships crowded into the sounds between these granite-cliffed islands, awaiting their valuable cargo. There were Peruvian settlements on the islands, but the mining was unpleasant work and was largely left to an itinerant population of Chinese workers who then trundled the guano down to the shore in railway trucks there to be loaded aboard ship. It was a labourious process and many ships had to wait sometimes a month or two before it was their turn to load their valuable cargo. While the *Senator Weber* awaited its turn two more men left the vessel, another deserter and a man who was legally discharged.

The last mention of the *Senator Weber* at the Chincha Islands was on 13 August 1868. She must have left the islands shortly after that and made good time around the usually notorious Cape Horn and up through the Atlantic. On 28 October, the ship having docked, Joseph walked into the office of the shipping master at Antwerp in Belgium to deliver the ship's log and crew agreement. The crew were then paid off and went their separate ways. Ted and Joseph returned home to their families in the Potteries for a couple of months. Ann O'Donnell later recalled their homecoming. 'Ted returned home to thrill the youth of the town with his stories of having sailed to America, of his experience in California, where the ship on which he made his first voyage touched, and with his mind firmly made up to spend the rest of his days on the ocean.'[14]

A Trip to Japan

Ted apparently spent Christmas and New Year back home in the Potteries, but by December 1868, Joseph had returned to Antwerp to rejoin the *Senator Weber* and according to *Lloyd's List* then took her to Plymouth. Ted would encrew with him again for the next big journey, but first Joseph had to bring the ship to Cardiff. The ship arrived in early February 1869. There was the usual spate of desertions and official leave takings amongst the crew, but a large number of fresh hands were taken aboard and it was here on 10 February that Ted rejoined the ship, this time as her official third mate.[15]

This journey would again take the *Senator Weber* to the far side of the world, but to an entirely different country, Japan. The land of the rising sun had until just over a decade earlier been the land of mystery, an ancient feudal nation effectively closed to the Western world by its military rulers, the shoguns. In 1854, though, a force of American ships under the command of Commodore Matthew Perry had compelled the Japanese to open up to the rest of the world. The subsequent opening of Japanese ports to western ships and the clash of cultures this set in motion, had resulted in a power struggle between the decrepit shogunate and forces loyal to the forward-looking Japanese emperor, a war that the latter had effectively won in 1868. Now Japan's ports were trading eagerly with the West and it was to the largest of these, Yokohama, in Tokyo Bay, that the *Senator Weber* was now destined.

By this time, the distance to the Indian Ocean and the Far East had been radically shortened by the opening of the Suez Canal in 1869 and Joseph could have taken advantage of this, though there are no indications that he did, quite the contrary. *Lloyd's List* notes the ship's passage through the Sunda Strait in July at around about the same time as she passed there on her previous voyage, but there is no real evidence as to what might have taken place aboard the ship during this long haul to Japan, as after departing Cardiff, the ship's log is again silent until the *Senator Weber* pulled into Yokohama.

Prior to Perry's arrival, Yokohama had been a sleepy little fishing village and was chosen as the principal port for foreigners as it was far enough from Edo, modern-day Tokyo, to prevent unnecessary contact with the foreigners, whom the Japanese authorities regarded as powerful, but uncouth barbarians. Nontheless, the more enterprising locals appreciated the trade and as the foreign merchants flocked to Yokohama, the village was quickly transformed into a hub of commercial activity. The growing town was surrounded by a moat and divided into an inner and outer settlement. The foreigners were located in the inner hub, which developed into the heart of the modern city and it was here that the port was located.

Here, as on the ship's previous journey there followed a litany of desertions, leave-takings and visits from the local constabulary escorting unrepentant sailors, while two new crew members were signed on board. The most notable of these proves the point that despite what their rulers thought, not all Japanese people were introspective and terrified by these foreigners; a thirteen-year-old Japanese lad named Mossa Keechi (sic) enlisted as ship's boy for the duration of the journey back to Antwerp.[16]

The *Senator Weber* left Yokohama in late September 1869 and sailed east. The longer voyage seems to indicate that perhaps the ship did some trading from port to port in the Far East and Americas. Her final destination was the Guanape Isles, another group of guano islands off the coast of Peru, though *Lloyd's List* indicates numerous voyages to and from 'Lima', which seems to indicate that she was operating off the Peruvian coast for a time and the Guanape Isles was probably the last call out of these. The ship arrived there in late March 1870 and as well as taking on a cargo of guano, the ship lost her first mate, Robert Dauthwaite, who left by mutual consent. The second mate William Williams took over Dauthwaite's duties, his promotion being noted in the log. As he had not yet acquired his first certificate of competency, Ted could not be officially promoted to second mate, but as the next in command he probably stepped into Williams's shoes, becoming the ship's unofficial second mate for the rest of the journey.

This ended back at Antwerp on 6 September 1870, where as usual the ship's crew were signed off and went their separate ways. Joseph had been away from home for three months shy of two years and Ted had been away for nineteen months. It was time to go home for a few weeks at least. For the two brothers it would also be a parting of the ways, for this second voyage aboard the *Senator Weber* was the last journey that Ted would take under his half-brother's command. There is no indication as to why this should be, though a few reasons spring to mind. It could be that Ted felt constrained by Joseph's presence; he was afterall the skipper's younger half-brother, which may have been a source of friction amongst the crew. Alternatively, Ted may have wanted to prove himself on his own, a fairly normal attitude for a young man in his late teens or early twenties. Another reason might simply be that Ted wanted more of a social life ashore, a life being denied him during the long months he spent mewed up aboard ship out in the middle of the ocean. He might want to start a family some time and perhaps he feared that his youth was slipping away in very distant latitudes.

Other Ships and Promotion

A little over a month after leaving the *Senator Weber*, Ted made his way to the Briton Ferry docks, just outside Neath in South Wales, where on 18 October, he signed on as an able seaman aboard another Andrew Gibson ship, the 656-ton Halifax, Nova Scotia-registered barque, *Amoy*, commanded by Captain J. McKenzie. As Ann O'Donnell later recalled, it was a point of pride for the famous future captain of the *Titanic* 'that once he was listed on the ship's books as merely an able seaman.'[17] Compared to his previous voyages, though, this would be a short trip. The *Amoy* set sail on 24 October for Norfolk, Virginia. Here the ship took on a cargo of nearly 600 bales of cotton, 200 barrels of rosin plus, '6000 hd and 6200 heading staves'. Quitting Norfolk on 4 February 1871, the ship made good time and just over a month later on 6 March, the *Amoy* pulled into Liverpool docks and Ted along with the rest of the crew was signed off.

According to his own records, eighteen days after this, on 24 March, Ted again signed on as an able seaman, this time aboard the Liverpool-registered ship *Madge Wildfire*, under Captain F. Von Hoffman. She was destined for Canada, but before that both Joseph and Ted returned to the Potteries and were back at home in Well Street lodging with their mother, their sister Thirza and two of her children, James aged nine and Anne aged four, when the census was taken on 2 April 1871. This must have been only a flying visit, for Ted was soon back in Liverpool and by 1 May the *Madge Wildfire* had arrived at St John's, Newfoundland. Her arrival there was noted in the records of the Partridge Island Quarantine Station, since one of the crew had died during the voyage from 'scrofulous ulcers'.[18] Any investigation or quarantine was short-lived, the ship took on a cargo of deals, deal ends, scantlings and battens and by 15 July 1871, Ted and the rest of the crew were back in Liverpool.[19]

During this early part of his career, Ted Smith's life ashore was unsettled and whilst in Liverpool, like many seaman, he lodged at the Sailors' Home. Pictures of this building reveal a tall, gothic Victorian edifice with corner towers and a striking entrance hall. Inside it looked very like a prison with its long open walkways and railings lit by a high glass roof. He probably had friends here, though what kind of social life he led ashore is unknown. The traditional sailor's portside pastimes usually lasted as long as their money did, most of which was spent on drinking, gambling, womanising and 'being young', Ted probably did his share of these. What we do know on this occasion is that he was certainly studying, for when Ted left the *Madge Wildfire* on 15 July 1871, he had clocked up four years, eleven months and twenty-six days at sea. Only four years at sea and a minimum age of seventeen were required of a candidate to take the first step on the ladder of promotion. When he booked into the Sailor's Home this time, Ted began preparing as best he could for the exam for a second mate's certificate of competency.

The rules and regulations governing the examination of masters and mates, had been set down within the pages of the 1854 Merchant Shipping Act. This made it a felony for ships to sail unless the masters and mates held the certificates required under the Act. Prospective candidates for examination had to register a couple of days before the exam and provide testimonials as to their character, sobriety, experience, ability and good conduct. They also needed to show certificates of discharge from the masters of the ships they had sailed on to prove their length of service. Only after these had been provided could the applicant's name be entered for examination. This Ted Smith did on 21 July 1871. The next day he handed over his exam fee of £1 to the Liverpool shipping master and two days after that, on 24 July, he sat the exam.

The candidates had to arrive at the venue early in the morning. There were the usual injunctions still familiar to examinees today – no talking, no copying, specific texts were banned and problems were to be worked out on the papers provided. The exam was a long one, candidates being allowed a full five hours to answer all the questions. These were arranged in three sections dealing with navigation, seamanship and commercial code signals. Some leeway was given to the candidates in that they were allowed to solve the problems by the methods with which they were most familiar, but the margin of error was strictly decreed. For instance on any of the navigation questions a margin of error of one nautical mile from the correct position qualified as correct, anything beyond that was a failure. Furthermore, failure in any one of the three sections meant that the entire exam was failed. The candidate was also failed if he did not complete the exam in the allotted time.

For the navigation section, candidates for a second mate's certificate needed to write in a legible hand and understand the first five rules of arithmetic and the use of logarithms. They had to be able to do a complete day's navigation, including the bearings and distance of the port they were aiming for by Mercator's method. They had to correct the sun's declination for longitude and find their latitude by the meridian altitude of the sun at midday and to work out any other easy questions that might be put to them. They had to understand the use of the sextant, show that they could use it correctly and take the reading from the arc.

In the seamanship section, Ted would have had to give satisfactory answers as regards the rigging and unrigging of ships, the stowing of holds and so on. He had to show an understanding of how to use the log-line, the barometer and the lead-line and be conversant with the rules of the road for both steamers and sailing vessels and familiar with the lights and fog signals carried by them. The section on commercial code signals was an adjunct to this and Ted and his fellow candidates would be examined on their knowledge of 'the Commercial Code Signals for the use of all Nations'. This covered the variety of signal flags flown by merchantmen, the interpretation of such, and perhaps more alien methods of signaling such as the semaphore stations used by the French.

Ted passed the examination and received form Exn.176 from the examiner which entitled him to collect his certificate of competancy from the Superintendent of the Mercantile Marine Office at the port to which he wanted it to be forwarded. This he collected at Liverpool on 12 August that year. With his certificate came his registration number 14102. He then put his newly earned qualifications to the test and on 24 August he signed on as second mate aboard the 1,039-ton Liverpool-registered vessel *Record*, Captain W. Groves, bound for New Orleans.

The second mate learnt his duties under the direction of the first mate and his first and perhaps most significant lesson if he had not learnt it already aboard the *Senator Weber*, was how to control the crew, an important skill as he now had charge of one of the watches. The men generally seemed to regard the second mate as something of an upstart, neither officer or seaman, more a qualified foreman who was expected to maintain his dignity though his priviledges were small. Ted now had the rank to be dignified as 'Mister' Smith, had a cabin of his own at the rear of the ship with the skipper and mate, and his wages were twice as much as an ordinary seaman. These, though, were the sum total of his perks and he was made to work for them. With the officers he was definitely the 'junior' and he still had to go aloft with the men, indeed, all of the sails, masts and rigging were his responsibility. He was also obliged to be on deck most of the time supervising the work of the men during the day and supplying them with the various materials they needed for their work, needles and threads, holystones, buckets and mops, hammers and nails, tar and brushes, all under the charge of the second mate, who had to answer to the captain for any losses.

The *Record* returned from the States with over 1,000 bales of cotton and over 400 bags of oil cake and sundry other goods. Arriving back in Liverpool on 19 January,

Ted was signed off, but in his capacity as second mate he also served aboard two other vessels. The first was the Windsor, New Brunswick-registered ship *Agra*, about which little is known save that he served on her from 28 February to 27 July 1872. The second ship was the Quebec-registered *N. Mosher*, under Captain M. Doyle, making another cotton run to New Orleans. Ted joined the ship on 27 September 1872 and left on 3 March 1873.[20]

With five years at sea, at least one of these as second mate, Ted now had qualifications enough to advance further up the ladder of promotion. On leaving the *N. Mosher*, he put in for the exams that would gain him his first mate's certificate of competency. During that time he had left home for good and when he paid the 10s exam fee on 22 March 1873, he was lodging at 5 Hanover Street, Liverpool. He sat the exams three days later. The exam began with the same questions posed for the second mate's certificate before moving on to more taxing problems put to a prospective first mate. The additional navigational skills required of him were the ability to observe azimuths (the positions of astral bodies) and compute the variation; to compare the ship's chronometers and keep their rates and find their longitude by them after taking an observation of the sun. Ted also had to be able to work out a ship's latitude by the altitude of the sun off the meridian and be able to use and set his sextant by the sun.

The additional seafaring skills demanded of him ran to shifting large spars and sails, sailing a vessel in stormy weather, taking in and making sail, getting heavy weights in and out of the holds, weighing anchors, casting a ship on a lee shore and securing the mast in the event of an accident to the bowsprit. Though much more detailed, Ted once again passed all the tests and he collected his new certificate of competency on 8 April in Bremerhaven in Germany where he was to join his next ship.

Compared to those of the second mate, the duties of the first mate were legion. The job of the captain was the safe sailing and positioning of the ship, but the mate was in charge of the men and it was up to the mate to see that the skipper's orders were carried out swiftly and to the best advantage when he was not around. The mate did not have to work aloft like the other men, he was essentially in charge of the day-to-day running and maintenance of the vessel. On top of the duties also mentioned, he also measured the ship's speed, and took charge of the soundings when the ship came into coastal waters. As a by-now-practiced navigator, the mate carried out many of the duties of the captain, whose job, should anything have happened to him, the mate was expected to take over. Above all, though, he was the mouth of the captain, so when the weather turned sour and the captain decided that the situation warranted it, it was to the mate that he gave the order to call 'All hands', and it was the mate who supervised the setting and the furling of the sails. These, amongst many others, were the duties Smith carried out between July 1873 and May 1875, during three terms aboard another of Andrew Gibson & Co.'s vessels, the 1,095-ton Liverpool-registered sailing ship *Arzilla*, under the command of forty-one-year-old Canadian ship's captain Charles Edward Durkee.

Smith joined the ship at Bremerhaven on 15 April 1873 and the crew list put twenty-three men under his command, though a couple never actually joined. The ship departed Bremerhaven on 20 April, obstensibly bound for South America, but with a jaunt over to Canada en route. As ship's logs go, that of the *Arzilla* for this journey at least is pretty dry reading, the bulk of the entries merely noting the ship's displacement on leaving the various ports it visited. The entries nevertheless plot the ship's course. The *Arzilla* left Quebec on 29 June 1873 and though the log does not note the fact, the crew's particulars and the consular endorsements at the end of the crew list show that the ship arrived at Valparaiso on 13 October and departed on or after 13 November. On 24 November, the ship arrived at Callao and departed three days later. The only notation in the log at this time came on the 26th of that month when a desertion was recorded, though this was by no means the only one as Captain Durkee appears to have been a little lax in keeping records of such events.[21]

The only other note in the log is out of sequence and records the ship's departure from 'Maccabis Island' (sic) on 13 January and nothing more is known of the ship's movements until she arrived in the Victoria Dock of the Port of London on 12 May 1874. Despite the paucity of information on the voyage, as South American jaunts went it had been fairly straightforward, though an attached note indicates that Captain Durkee was queried as to why he had not noted numerous crew discharges in the ship's log. Smith, though, seems to have got along well enough with Captain Durkee and was happy to re-enlist aboard the *Arzilla* on 3 July prior to her setting out on her next voyage four days later.

This time it was a much simpler and shorter journey to the United States and back and after the cautionary note Captain Durkee had received from the marine superintendant regarding the upkeep of his log from the last voyage, this one is more animated, though hardly more exciting.

The ship set out from London on 8 July and eleven days later came the highlight of the trip when two stowaways, James Smith and Charles W. Gresley, were discovered. Unable to put them ashore, Captain Durkee called them aft and signed them onto the ship's books at a shilling a month. It is a question as to whether the men collected any money, for hardly had the *Arzilla* reached Philadelphia on 27 August, than the two of them and another crewman promptly deserted with their effects.[22]

They were not the only departures, though. On 6 September, six crewmen deserted. Extra hands were taken on to replace them, but one final man took unofficial leave of the ship on 26 September, the day the *Arzilla* set off back across the Atlantic to Antwerp, arriving there on about 27 October 1874.

Ted's final voyage as first mate aboard the *Arzilla* began in early 1875, when the ship journeyed to Galveston in Texas, where it took on board over 3,000 bales of cotton and eighty-five barrels of cotton seed oil before setting sail back to Britain on 24 March.[23]

Back in Britain, on 4 May 1875, Ted applied for the exams for the master's ordinary certificate of competency, the great goal that all ambitious seamen strove for. To apply the candidate had to be at least twenty-one years of age and to have been at sea for six years, of which at least one had to have been in the capacity of first or only mate with one year as second mate. He must also have served at least one year in a square-rigged ship.

In addition to the qualifications expected of first mate, candidates for the master's certificate had to be able to find the latitude by a star. He would be asked questions as to the effect of the ship's iron on the compass and as to the method of determining it and examined on the laws of the tides in as much as it allowed him to plot a course and to compare his soundings with those marked on his navigational charts. The candidate would be examined as to his competency to construct jury rudders and rafts and as to how exactly he would preserve his crew in the event of a shipwreck. Other questions taxed his knowledge of lights and fog signals and steering and sailing rules. He would need to show that he possessed sufficient knowledge of what he was required to do by law as to the entry, discharge and the management of his crew and as to penalties and entries to be made in the ship's log and how to prevent the outbreak of scurvy aboard ship. He would then be questioned as to his knowledge of invoices, charter party, Lloyd's agent and as to the nature of bottomry (a form of marine insurance). Last, but not least, he must show that he was acquainted with the leading lights of the channel he had been accustomed to navigate, or which he was to use.

On 19 May 1875, he handed over his £2 exam fee and three days later sat and again passed all three sections of the exams. On 26 May 1875, he picked up his certificate in Liverpool and became a fully fledged master mariner. To commemorate his success, Ted was presented with a loving cup decorated in deep pink, white and gold, showing a Highland scene on one side, while written in gold in the opposite panel were the no doubt welcome words, 'Captain E.J. Smith. 1875.' This cup was later passed to his nephew J.W.S. Harrington after Captain Smith's death. The cup was later briefly on display at the Potteries Museum and Art Gallery in Hanley in 2006.

The Captain of the *Lizzie Fennell*

Smith had now risen to the lofty position through hard work and study, but there was no guarantee that he would get a ship straight away. Many who held master's certificates spent much if not all of their working lives as first or second mates; such over qualification was a common thing amongst sailors. Smith did indeed have to wait for his first ship, though not for too long. Many retrospectives of his career have him commanding his first vessel at the age of twenty-five shortly after he received his master's certificate. Yet when, in 1888, he applied for his extra master mariner's certificate, Smith claimed that it was in May 1876 that he first got his own ship. This agrees with the records of the ship in question, the *Lizzie Fennell*.

Though no images of the *Lizzie Fennell* appear to have survived, the details of her build and size give a fair impression of Captain Smith's first command. Built at Gardiner's Creek, New Brunswick, in 1870, the *Lizzie Fennell* was 174.6ft long, 35.8ft wide and 22ft deep. Her official number was 64485, her code letters were KQVR and she was registered as a 'full-rigged ship'. Weighing in at 1,040 tons, the ship was over 200 tons lighter than the *Senator Weber* in which Ted had first gone to sea, though she was built for the same purpose, namely long-haul, high seas cargo transportation, and on this voyage Ted would be taking her back to Callao, Peru, which he had first visited in his brother's ship eight years earlier.

Ted joined the ship in Antwerp and recruited his crew from that port. Like most merchant crews he had served with they were a mixed group of men of many nations, the bulk of them being Scandinavians, five of whom – presumably a group of friends – came from the same ship. The others were British, French, German, Danish, Italian, Mexican and Estonian. Hearing that the ship was bound for Callao, three Peruvians also turned up unannounced on the morning of departure, eager to take the ship back home, and Captain Smith – as he now was – obliged them. In charge of this polyglot crew, serving as mate on this first voyage, was a twenty-eight-year-old Scot named William Sinclair, who some years later took over as the skipper of the *Lizzie Fennell* when Smith left. Under Sinclair was second mate William Ross from Denmark.

Captain Smith was by no means the youngest man aboard, but there were plenty, like his two mates, who were older than him. According to Smith's nephew, J.W.S. Harrington, who served under his uncle a few years later, at first Smith endured some gentle ribbing from the older hands who apparently looked askance at this stripling at the helm. Smith, he said, '…was twitted for being too young for such a responsible position and won immediate favour by repeating almost precisely the same words as a famous Premier that he would soon grow out of that.'[24]

The voyage began on 13 May 1876 and the ship would be away for ten months. The usual route taken by cargo vessels sailing to Peru was to sail down the western coasts of Europe and northern Africa before making the short hop across the Atlantic at its narrowest point. From there, it was a simple case of following the continent of South America down to Cape Horn. He had been there before, but never in command, and the Horn was a notoriously treacherous spot, with its raging seas and merciless breakers, but there is no indication that the *Lizzie Fennell* suffered any difficulties during her passage.

Once past the Horn, though, the vessel began to suffer some misfortune. On 19 August, during the long haul up the Chilean coast, an Italian crewman died and was buried at sea. Smith reported his death when the ship reached Callao in early September. The other Italian crewman left the ship sick during the three-week stay in port and the three Peruvians were signed off the books, so replacements were hired. On 29 September the ship left Callao and set off to do some trading up the coast. The journey was punctuated on 2 October by another tragedy when three of the five Scandinavians who had joined up together in Antwerp were drowned, possibly during bad weather.[25]

Perhaps because of this tragedy, by 15 November Smith had taken the *Lizzie Fennell* back to Callao where she took on some more men before sailing on to the

Islas Lobos Afuera. These bleak rocks were like the now depleated Chincha Islands, being systematically stripped of their deposits of guano. As with the voyages of the *Senator Weber*, this seems to have been the final destination and cargo for the *Lizzie Fennell*. Once the cargo was loaded they were off and four months later in March 1877 the ship sailed into St Nazaire, France, without it seems having suffered any further misfortunes on the way back.

Smith commanded the *Lizzie Fennell* for three more years and though the journeys undertaken after the long haul to Callao were shorter, they were no less interesting as they took him to a new destination, one he would become very familiar with, namely North America. Two months after the end of the previous voyage, the *Lizzie Fennell* sailed out of St Nazaire bound for the Canadian port of Miramichi, then onto Chatham, both in New Brunswick. She carried a completely different crew and compared to nearly a year away on the previous voyage, this trip there and back took just under four months. Having taken on 132 tons of mixed cargo comprising scantlings, deals and numerous other goods the descriptions of which are obscure, the ship left Chatham on 28 July and she docked at Liverpool on 13 September.[26]

There followed another four-month trip across the Atlantic, this time to Tybee Island off Savannah, Georgia, then onto Galveston, Texas, where the ship arrived on 17 November. With the ship's company on this trip was Ted's nephew, James William Sidney Harrington, at fifteen the ship's boy, probably on his first trip abroad. The ship spent Christmas and New Year in the United States, took on a cargo of 3,000-plus bales of cotton and departed on 20 January 1878, arriving back in Liverpool on 28 February.[27]

The ship managed to squeeze in a couple more trips to the States during 1878. The first of these, beginning on 13 March, was a five-month-long trip to Hampton Roads and Baltimore then back across the Atlantic to Dublin. This journey was punctuated by a rash of desertions and the hiring of replacements in Baltimore and by the death of a crewman, William Prior, who on 30 March was killed when he fell down a hatchway. He was buried at sea some 540 miles west of the Canary Islands. This journey was followed by another five-month jaunt, to Savannah once more, returning to Liverpool in early December.

The next voyage, begun on 10 December 1878, was another across the Atlantic to Galveston, Baltimore, Savannah, Tybee and back, carrying much the same cargos as on the previous two years, principally cotton or cotton-related goods. There were a number of desertions in Savannah in late January, which accounted for the only point of interest on the American side of the voyage. The ship must have then been involved in some coastal trading as the *Lizzie Fennell* and her crew did not return to Europe for over six months. On 11 June 1879, the ship arrived at the Swedish town of Söderhamn in the Gulf of Bothnia off the Baltic Sea. Leaving there a few days later the *Lizzie Fennell* arrived in London on 31 July 1879.

Despite the long stints away at sea, Ted seems to have thoroughly enjoyed the job. He certainly seems to have recalled his time aboard the *Lizzie Fennell* with some fondness in later life, no doubt because she was his first command. Also, sailing in sunnier climes with a relatively small crew and few if any passengers to worry about, plus plenty of time spent in the slightly more decadent and exotic ports of call, his early career must have seemed a lifetime away from his later transatlantic bus service. There is also evidence that during these many trips to the States, Ted made many valued acquaintances, especially in Savannah, Georgia, one of whom he later alluded to in a letter written to his nephew Frank Hancock who had married and settled there in the late nineteenth century. In the letter, after mentioning several other Savannah men, Captain Smith asked his nephew to remember him to one George Walker, who had been very kind to him during his times there with the *Lizzie Fennell*, though Smith suspected that Mr Walker may well have forgotten him after all this time. Whatever the nature of the kindness Walker bestowed on the young captain, it obviously made a deep impression to be recalled nearly thirty years later.[28]

However, as his career thus far had shown, enjoy the life as he may, Ted was ambitious and as he was blessed with the capacity to succeed in his chosen career, he seems to have seen no need to stop where he was. He would have been aware of the advantages of making a career for himself with the bigger shipping companies. The two big rivals at this period were Cunard, whose ships were generally the fastest afloat and the White Star Line who operated the most luxurious vessels. It was the White Star ships that had caught Ted's eye and imagination. Their sleek black and white vessels with their distinctive buff and black funnels were regular visitors to Liverpool's docks and it was the sight of one of their newest, classiest ships that finally lured Ted away from the small sailing ships of Andrew Gibson & Co.

Having left Norfolk, Virginia, on 6 December 1879, with a cargo of 3,622 bales of cotton and 2,037 pine boards, the *Lizzie Fennell* arrived off Liverpool in the first few days of the New Year.[29] The local papers noted that by 3 January she was moored in the Liverpool graving dock, but over the next couple of weeks the ship was shifted first to the Wapping Dock, then to the Herculaneum basin before Smith received further instructions on 31 January to take her to the Wellington Dock further to the west. As he conned his ship down the Mersey, Smith stood chatting with amongst others his nephew James Harrington, noting the other vessels as they passed. Along both shores there was a forest of masts, lines and furled canvas, but here and there the compact lines of one of the new breed of steamers could be seen moored by the docks, or making steam ready for the off. One of those they sailed past, warped into the West Waterloo Dock, was the White Star steamer SS *Britannic*, fresh from her latest transatlantic voyage. The *Britannic* was a beauty by the standards of the time; she weighed 5,004 tons, was 455ft long, her graceful outline dominated by four masts and two large funnels amidships. She was six years old, held records of seven and a half days for both the passages East and West bound to the United States and, since her launch, she and her sister *Germanic* had served as the flagships of the transatlantic run. The luxury of her appointments was still the talk of the shipping world and left passengers and shipping journals highly impressed. Now the glamour of the ship fixed itself on Ted Smith. He pointed her out and according to James Harrington, 'Captain Smith remarked that he would not mind accepting an inferior position in order to hold a berth on such a fine vessel.'[30]

According to another, rather fanciful account, such was the effect on Smith that he resigned as the captain of the *Lizzie Fennell* as soon as the ship had moored. However, he had doubtless seen the *Britannic* or similar ships many times before and it is unlikely that he made such a snap decision; it is more probable that a tour we know he took around the *Britannic* a few days later finally made up his mind for him.

Smith must have been impressed, not only by the look of the ship and its accommodation, but also by the many small comforts it offered for members of the crew. As compared to the Spartan lifestyle of sailors aboard sailing ships, the crew of the *Britannic* could look forward to comfortable beds, freshly laundered bed linen and clothes, medical attention should it be required and perhaps best of all, as Bertram Hayes a future White Star captain and contemporary of Smith noted, there was the prospect of three square meals a day.[31] All these factors probably helped Smith to decide on the course of his future career. Whether Smith had left the employ of Andrew Gibson & Co., before or after this tour of the *Britannic*, is neither here nor there, the fact is that it swung the balance and in March 1880 Edward John Smith joined the White Star Line.

3

WHITE STAR

I t was the red swallow-tailed pennant bearing the five-pointed white star that flew at the mastheads of their ships that gave the White Star Line its popular name. This house flag had originally belonged to a small fleet of sailing ships which, in 1845, had started to carry emigrants, cargo and later gold to and from Australia. At first the company had prospered, but by 1868, changes in circumstance and crippling financial difficulties had forced the original owners to sell off their assets. At this point the White Star name would have vanished from history forever, had not the company goodwill and eponymous pennant been acquired by a young, ambitious Liverpool shipowner named Thomas Henry Ismay.

Ismay was a determined forward-looking entrepreneur who for many years had carried on an extensive shipping business. He had first put in an appearance with the new steam trade as a director of the National Steamship Company where his organisational skills, experience and enterprise paid dividends. Since the early days of steamships he had considered introducing these powerful new vessels to his own trade and with the purchase of the White Star name he decided to pursue the option of adding some steamers to his fleet. He therefore entered into negotiation for an extension in his business and in 1869, in partnership with Mr G. Hamilton Fletcher of Liverpool, a management associate, he formed the Oceanic Steam Navigation Company Ltd. In 1870, Ismay went into partnership with Mr William Imrie, formerly of the firm of Imrie, Tomlinson & Co., the firm with which he had served his apprenticeship. This firm had been the first to open up the steam trade with the West Indies and a partnership with Imrie added to the growing operations of the newly formed firm of Ismay, Imrie & Co., with a considerable influx of new ports and contacts.

The first step taken by the Oceanic Steam Navigation Company Ltd was to enter into a contract with the shipbuilding firm of Harland & Wolff of Belfast regarding the construction of a fleet of steamers for the North Atlantic trade between Liverpool and New York. These were to be of a size and design not yet seen on the Mersey. Harland & Wolff were given carte blanche to make the steamers as efficient and luxurious as possible. The company was, therefore, launched into the North Atlantic trade in direct competition with a number of well-established lines such as Cunard, which had been operating the route since the 1840s. These two companies would in time become great rivals, though Cunard would win out in the end, eventually purchasing White Star in the 1930s.

In the meantime, shares in the new company sold well and in February 1871, White Star's first transatlantic passenger steamer SS *Oceanic* arrived in the Mersey, exciting great curiosity from the public and the rival shipping lines. The ship's long, slender, seemingly fragile design was criticised in some scientific, nautical and commercial quarters, but she soon proved her worth as a relatively fast and dependable workhorse. For her maiden voyage, Thomas Ismay took the trip over to the States, where he had the pleasure of seeing some 50,000 people visit the ship on its open days. His son J. Bruce Ismay would later follow his father's practice of taking passage to the States on the company's new prestige ships, though for him, as will be seen, this was to have tragic consequences.

Following hard on the *Oceanic*'s success, White Star introduced more vessels of a similar design in quick succession. The *Atlantic, Baltic, Republic, Adriatic* and *Celtic* appeared the following year. In 1874 the newly designed *Britannic* and *Germanic* appeared, both nearly 1,000 tons heavier than the older vessels. These had been followed by the much smaller *Gaelic* and *Belgic*. Yet, though it seemed that success had followed success, the history of the White Star Line was shot through with tragedy and two of the worst maritime disasters of the nineteenth century were sharply etched into its history. The loss of RMS *Tayleur* in 1854 had blighted the company's beginnings, the ship sinking on its maiden voyage after striking rocks in foul weather off the Irish coast with the loss of 360 lives. If the company slate seemed to have been wiped clean by Ismay's arrival, the sinking of the SS *Atlantic* in 1873 soon destroyed that image when, on 1 April 1873, that ship also ran onto rocks and sank off the coast of Nova Scotia, with the loss of 535 people. In both of these disasters panic had taken over and in the chaos the women and children passengers had suffered particularly badly. Of the 100 or more women aboard the *Tayleur* only three survived and only one child out of 345 women and children survived the sinking of the *Atlantic*.

Of course, these terrible disasters, both of which compared so poorly to the selfless heroism of the *Birkenhead* disaster, did not get a mention in the company's publications. To read the 1877 *White Star Line Official Guide*, one would think that White Star's history had been one of unmitigated success, for nowhere in this fulsome document is either ship mentioned. This tendency to play down the worst episodes in its history would be repeated after the sinking of the *Titanic*. None of the officers who survived that future disaster would ever gain a White Star command, Smith would be quickly forgotten by the company and the *Titanic* became a dirty word. For White Star, the clean corporate image was everything.

Still, it was perhaps for the best to look to the future, for despite the disasters things were on the upturn. Though business was slow at first in the face of the well-established competition, White Star ships regularly seized the Blue Riband and began to build up a loyal clientele and were quickly earning the reputation for steady travel and luxury accommodation, just some of the factors that seem to have prompted young Captain Smith's decision to join their ranks.

Junior Officer

Like all other applicants, Ted Smith would have first submitted his details to Ismay, Imrie & Co., detailing his service thus far. The firm's partners were obviously satisfied enough to pass his application over to their Marine Superintendent, whose job it was to assess prospective junior officers. This was doubtless an anxious interview. Though Ted's master's certificate had enabled him to rise quickly to the command of a cargo ship in the small firm of Andrew Gibson & Co., the prestigious White Star Line operated a high-class passenger service and there was no guarantee that he would be accepted. He was accepted, of course, but though he had plenty of experience as a seaman, operating steam ships was far different to running a sailing ship, while catering to the rich and famous passengers required a certain polish in an officer that was perhaps at first felt to be lacking in the young sailor and for the first few years with his new employers Ted Smith would find himself serving what amounted to a second apprenticeship as a junior officer aboard a number of White Star vessels.

He did not get his first wish straight away, namely to serve aboard the *Britannic*, instead Ted was employed as fourth and later third officer aboard the SS *Celtic*, a comfortable, but far less glamorous ship than the *Britannic*. Launched in 1872, the *Celtic* weighed 3,867 tons and measured 437ft in length. Primarily an emigrant ship like most of the company's liners, she could carry up to 900 passengers in reasonable style at a top speed of about 14 knots. Before he even took up his position, though, he would need to find an obliging tailor to supply him with a couple of White Star Line uniforms, though there were doubtless several in Liverpool, the line's home port, who could cater to his requirements at such short notice.

For the first few days aboard the *Celtic*, Ted Smith, as the new boy, would have been like a fish out of water: getting lost in the ship's corridors, unsure as to where everything was, or who was who and he was doubtless amazed at the orderly way that everything was organised as compared to the rough-and-tumble way things were done on a sailing ship. At this stage he probably shared a cabin with another junior officer. This may have been the main let down. Having been used to running his own ship and prior to that his own watch, now that he was a junior officer it would have seemed at first that he was again bottom of the heap and had very little to do, but once he got settled into the daily routine, Smith would have found that he had many duties. Also, during his first voyages he would have had plenty of time to become familiar with the power structure in use aboard steamships and liners, a hierarchy far more complicated than that found on the small cargo vessels he had known. Of course the captain was still next to God, but beneath him, power was farmed out to a number of executive officers and heads of departments, but we shall start at the top and work our way down the ladder.

The skipper of the *Celtic* at this time, forty-nine-year-old Captain Benjamin Gleadell, was the kind of master that any prospective steamship captain could have happily modelled himself on. Captain Gleadell had earned a first-rate reputation as a brave and enterprising sailor and it was noted by a magazine reporter in 1886 that the captain was very proud of his pocket watch which had been presented to him by no less a person than Ulysses S. Grant, the former American Civil War general and President of the United States. This had been given in appreciation of Gleadell's bravery for going to the aid of ships in distress, though for which instance is unclear, for Gleadell had had his fair share of drama and had twice gone to the rescue of stricken ships. On the first occasion in 1873, whilst in command of the SS *Atlantic*, he went to the rescue of the brigantine *Scotland*, for which he earned the thanks of the American Congress. Then in 1875 he had gone to the aid of the stricken ship *Oriental*, which foundered in heavy seas, but not before the SS *Baltic* under Gleadell's command had changed course and rescued the luckless crew before their ship sank and then successfully located more crewmen who had previously taken to the lifeboats. He had apparently received numerous other awards and testimonials from individuals and associations for similar deeds of humanity, all of which he likewise treasured. However, Gleadell was not ostentatious about such things and as one reporter noted you had to ask to see them.

Gleadell was a quiet man and regarded by many passengers as being somewhat reserved, venturing nothing more than an occasional 'good morning' as he passed the early risers on the deck. 'I won't say he's a darned disagreeable cuss,' one American traveller commented on the skipper's private manner, 'but he's too dignified to suit me.' In a *Harper's New Monthly Magazine* article there is an engraving of the captain and he does indeed look rather patrician; he has a pleasant enough face, but his balding pate and long sideburns give him the appearance of a parson out of a novel by Trollope. But when he donned his uniform and went up on the bridge this image disappeared and 'he looks every inch a sailor and a fine specimen of physical manhood.'[1]

Benjamin Gleadell, though, was not destined to plough the seas for much longer, dying at sea in 1888, a mere six years after Smith had left the *Celtic*. There was one final connection between the two, however. His body being returned home, Captain Gleadell was buried in St Hilary's churchyard, Wallasey, Birkenhead, the same graveyard that would later hold the remains of Ted's half-brother, Joseph.

Under Captain Gleadell, as on every steamship, there were a number of bridge officers, principally his navigation staff. As the fourth and later third officer on board the *Celtic*, E.J. Smith was one of these odd-bodies officially designated as navigation trainees. In number these could be anything up to eight (on the *Titanic* there were seven officers under the captain). The chief officer was essentially another master, whose duty it was to act in the captain's place in any capacity and was usually, like the captain, an extra master mariner. Next came the first officer, whose job was that of an assistant to the chief, while the second officer was usually in charge of navigating the ship. On modern vessels there is usually a first, a second and a third officer, the third officer normally being a trainee navigator, while undoubtedly aboard the big White Star ships the third to sixth officers were navigation trainees. These men also acted as aides-de-camp to the captain. On an ocean liner the presence of an active number of deck officers also served as useful reference points for the passengers, at the same time providing a good many raw young officers with the chance to hone their social graces.

Other departments on the ships had a similar organisation under their own chiefs. The chief steward was in charge of the stewards and stewardesses who acted as personal room attendants and chambermaids. The head chef organised the galley and cooking arrangements, while the head pantryman was in charge of the stores and both had several assistants. The man with the greatest responsibility after the master was the chief engineer. Like that of the master of the ship, the position of chief engineer was one earned through years of hard work and exemplary service. Under the chief engineer were several assistants, who increased in number with the size of the ship. These engineers, junior and senior, could number over thirty in the biggest ships, such as the *Olympic* and the *Titanic*. All of them were technically proficient marine engineers and they cared for the smooth running, servicing, fuelling and oiling of the engines. All of them were men who had not only served long careers at sea, but had also spent much time in machine shops and drawing rooms, looking over complex design specifications, and as with the progression of the navigation officers, each had had to sit exams to advance up the greasy pole of promotion.

There were other smaller departments, staffed by men of officer's rank, the ship's surgeon and his assistants took care of the health of passengers and crew, while the purser and his assistants took charge of the passengers' valuables and acted as office staff on a busy ship. As accounts show, perhaps because they were outside of the main command structure and they had to rely on them so much, the chief surgeon and chief purser often became good friends and confidants of the captain.

Crossing the Atlantic

The *Celtic* like most of the White Star steamers was making for New York, the great metropolis of the American east coast. Though Smith's journeys thus far had been extensive, there is no indication that he had yet visited this city that he was to become so familiar with over the years. New York had started life in the early 1600s as the Dutch colony of Nieuw Amsterdam, but its name and allegiance had changed in 1664, when it was seized by the British and renamed New York. Under British rule the small settlement on Manhattan Island grew in importance as a trading port. During the American Revolutionary War, New York had served as the principal

British base of operations and several battles were fought out in the near vicinity. Despite the setbacks eventually suffered by the British forces, it remained under British control until the end of military operations in 1783.

New York then became the hub of the young USA, serving briefly as its first capital. It was here that the American Constitution was ratified and where George Washington was inaugurated as the first president of the new republic. Though it soon lost the honour of being the nation's capital, by 1790 it was the largest city in the United States and during the early to mid-nineteenth century had been extensively reorganised and had continued to expand to several of the nearby coasts and islands. In doing so it increased its role as not only a major port, but also the gateway to the Americas, as it was via New York that most of the USA's European immigrants arrived, many of these courtesy of the big shipping companies like the White Star Line. By 1880, New York was a buzzing, vibrant, cosmopolitan city of over 1,200,000 people and though it had yet to gain some of its most famous landmarks such as the Brooklyn Bridge and the Statue of Liberty – these would appear in the next few years – it boasted many impressive buildings and was easily on a par with London, Paris and the other great European cities.

In his capacity as a junior officer, Ted Smith undertook fifteen round trips to New York and back aboard the *Celtic*. These followed a routine that he had grown used to aboard his cargo ships and which with a few differences and with varying degrees of involvement he would follow for the rest of his career. Hardly would their vessel have docked in Liverpool from its previous voyage and the passengers disembarked than the stevedores would come aboard and start offloading the ship's cargo to the porters on the dock, who would transport it to the nearby warehouses. Sometimes, Smith would have been obliged to remain aboard ship during its time in port as part of the ship-keeping crew, though he would also get the chance to go ashore or go home until he was required again.

Before the ship set out, fresh cargos were loaded aboard, as well as supplies of linen, flowers for decoration, food and drink required for a journey of over a week for hundreds of people and, of course, the thousands of tons of coal needed to keep the ship's engines running, which was loaded from barges. The human cargo, first the bulk of the crew including the captain (who never carried out ship-keeping duties in port) followed a few hours later by the passengers, turned up on sailing day. Should tugs or a pilot be required, the shipping company would have arranged for these in advance and these arrived when required to ensure a smooth departure.

Once at sea, Smith stood his four-hour watches like everyone else. There were regular morning duties such as the captain's inspection and provided he was not on watch Smith would have been one of the junior officers trailing along behind Captain Gleadell, taking notes on the state of the vessel as he did his rounds. At noon with the other officers he would have gone on to the bridge to take the midday reading with his sextant. Such duties were part and parcel of life at sea and Smith would have grown used to such routines under sail, but now he also had to divide his time between his sailing duty and service to the passengers, though this always came second. If the weather grew bad, or there were any other dangers to be faced, then his duty was solely to the ship. Such dangers included not only storms, but fog, partially sunken wrecks, other vessels and in the spring months the threat of ice.

If the ship managed to avoid or weather these several dangers, though – and indeed, most journeys were notable for their lack of excitement – shipboard life carried on in the same old manner and a week or so after leaving the shores of Britain, New York and the New World beckoned. On approaching their destination port the same process that attended their departure was gone through albeit in reverse. A harbour pilot would come to meet them to guide them through the intricate approaches and in New York Harbour itself, tugs and a mooring party would have been hired by the company representative. There were few differences for newcomers to the States, the revenue cutter would bring customs men aboard and on landing the steerage passengers went through quarantine, which at New York was initially located at the Battery, though this would later give way to a much larger facility at Ellis Island. Here they would be examined to make sure that they were solvent and healthy, and only then would they be allowed into the country.

Once this was done, the ship was unloaded as at home, the skipper and some of the crew took shore leave and all of the crew had time to rest and catch up on their sleep and any outstanding duties or repairs before the whole round began again.

Something that Smith may have noted during his time on the *Celtic* was that the transatlantic shipping lines attracted a good deal of attention in the New York press, much more than would be lavished on their counterparts today; the transatlantic travelling public, after all, wanted to know what was happening out at sea, such as who operated the best service, which ships were a liability and best avoided and increasingly which captains were the best to sail under. As a result, numerous incidental stories of ocean travel appeared in the New York papers. Often these news articles are the only indication as to what was going on in Smith's life at sea, which was now a much more anonymous existence than it was in the narrow confines of a sailing ship.

Occasionally stories of ocean liners and their officers made the news in Britain too, but most of our information of Smith's time back home is gleaned from more official documents. For instance, the *Celtic* was docked at Birkenhead when the 1881 census was taken on the night of 3 April. The ship had only one occupant that night, the thirty-one-year-old Fourth Officer John Lewthwaite. Third Officer Smith like most of the crew was ashore, in lodgings in Liverpool. A widow, Mrs Georgina Bradshaw of 20 Berkley Street, Toxteth Park, had evidently found her sizeable house too big and expensive for herself, her daughter Laura and their teenage domestic Elizabeth Hart and so hired out a number of rooms. At the time of the 1881 census she had five lodgers: twenty-six-year-old Agnes Williamson from Scotland, Ted Smith, now thirty-one, and three commercial clerks: nineteen-year-old Arthur Speck from York and two of Ted's nephews, nineteen-year-old Frank A. Hancock who would soon emigrate to the States and twenty-two-year-old George J. Hancock.

The 1881 census also brings us up to date with the movements of the rest of Ted's family, most of whom were gravitating closer to Merseyside. Of the rest of Joseph Hancock's family there is no sign, though they were probably somewhere in Liverpool or Birkenhead. Their mother Catherine, now seventy-one, had left the Potteries in about 1879 and set up home at 7 Peel Street, Runcorn, along with her daughter Thyrza and William Harrington and their two children, fourteen-year-old Annie and seven-year-old Edward. Only William Harrington had a profession on the return, being listed as a mechanical engineer, but it seems fairly clear from the Hanley Rate Books of 1879–80, that Catherine had prospered in her last years in Well Street and at her time of leaving owned and leased numbers 4 and 6 Well Street and her own former home at number 30, all of which doubtless provided her with a small independent income.

It would probably have been in late 1881, or early 1882, that Ted heard the bad news that his first command, the *Lizzie Fennell*, was no more, having been lost to a fire at sea. The loss was reported in *The Times* in early October, but if he missed this Ted would most likely have heard the news from one who had been there, namely his nephew James Harrington who had been on board at the time.

After a long voyage back from the Phillipines with a cargo of sugar, the *Lizzie Fennell* had taken on a cargo of West Hartley coal and sailed from the Tyne on 11 June 1881, bound for Valparaiso. On 21 August, off the coast of South America, a spontaneous fire broke out in the hold, probably as a result of the cargo shifting in heavy seas and iron elements in the coal striking a spark. This spread quickly and by the time the fire was detected it was too late. Ted's former first mate William Sinclair, now the ship's captain, sent out a distress call, probably using rockets, but when the flames burst through the deck the crew had no other option but to abandon ship. By this time an American barque, the *Isaac Jackson*, had come to their assistance and the crew of the *Lizzie Fennell* were taken aboard that vessel, from where they now watched their ship consumed by flames. The only good thing that could be said was that nobody had been harmed.

A Board of Trade inquiry was convened at the British Consulate in Valparaiso on 13 October 1881, with the purpose of determining what exactly had happened to the *Lizzie Fennell*, whose captain and mates now sat before them, their certificates of competancy technically on the line. But the story they heard was a familiar one to officials long used to the dangers of putting combustable cargos inside wooden ships. Finding no evidence of any illegal or wrongful act on the part of the crew the court had pleasure in returning the certificates to Sinclair and his mates.[2]

Was there a pang of regret at the loss of the *Lizzie Fennell*? Certainly Smith seems to have looked back with some fondness to his first command, yet the symbolism was not perhaps lost on him. His old boat was now burnt behind him as he started on his new career, which promised great things providing he could successfully work his way up through the ranks.

Pacific Service

Sterling work aboard the *Celtic* earned Smith a promotion and a change of scene
and between March 1882 and March 1884, he served as the second officer aboard the
4,367-ton SS *Coptic*, a relatively new ship built the year before and now under the
command of thirty-seven-year-old Captain William Henry Kidley. Born in Bristol
in 1845, Captain Kidley had a typical seaman's tale to tell of running away to sea at
an early age – eleven years old in his case – before securing a berth as an apprentice.
Having served on numerous vessels around the world, he had joined the White Star
Line in 1870 and had previously served aboard the *Gaelic* before taking command of
the *Coptic*. Nothing is known of his character, but appearance-wise he was a pleasant-
looking individual with a large bushy beard. Apart from the clean-shaven Captain
Gleadell, beards appear to have become de rigueur with White Star's captains; all of
Smith's future skippers would wear them and if Smith himself had not already grown
one he soon did so.

The beginning of Smith's service aboard the *Coptic* coincided with the ship taking
up the Pacific station under charter to the Occidental and Oriental Steamship
Co., to be used on their Pacific mail trade. As second officer, Smith was probably
the navigator for the voyage out which started from Birkenhead's Wallasey Dock on
11 March 1882. Travelling first through the Mediterranean, the ship touched at Malta
before passing through the Suez Canal, the Red Sea, the Indian Ocean and into the
Pacific Ocean. By mid-April, *Lloyd's List* placed the *Coptic* at Singapore, eleven days
later she was reported to have reached Smith's old destination of Hong Kong. By May
she had moved onto another of his old stamping grounds, Yokohama in Japan, before
at last reaching her destination, San Francisco, on 8 June. It was hardly the grand
arrival that the ship could have hoped for, though. At Hong Kong the *Coptic* had
taken 900 Chinese passengers aboard and some of them were unwell and when she
arrived at San Francisco *Coptic* was flying the yellow flag, the signal that there was a
contagion aboard, in this case smallpox.[3]

Judging by the notices in the American newspapers, between July 1882 until she
returned to Britain in early 1884, the *Coptic* made half a dozen round trips from San
Francisco across the Pacific, calling at Shanghai, Hong Kong, Yokohama and Honolulu
and back again, carrying passengers, mails and sometimes news of what was going on in
the Far East. Many of the passengers were Chinese workers either going to the States in
search of work or returning home to their families with their hard-earned cash.

During this time between voyages Smith lodged in San Francisco where he
probably had plenty to see and do. Bertram Hayes, who served aboard the *Coptic*
a few years after Smith, recalled that when between voyages the crew had a very
pleasant time ashore, 'those of us who were off duty would get up picnics to go fishing,
shooting rabbits, and exploring the surrounding country.'[4]

Whilst in San Francisco, Smith made a couple of acquaintances that we know
of. Though the small amount of information that their accounts give us is sadly

lacking in detail, they do indicate that the *Coptic*'s second officer was already a popular individual. Mr G.A. Capen of Sacramento, California, wrote after the *Titanic* disaster:

> I knew Captain Smith very well when he was second officer on the Steamer 'Coptic' on the San Francisco–Hong Kong run. I have watched his steady rise in the Company to which he was a credit; and yet it was no surprise, for he was the ablest man on the 'Coptic's payroll. He once wrote in my album the words 'Nil desperandum'. When I read of his remaining at his post to the last, and maintaining the most perfect order and discipline all through that awful time, he would not have been the E.J. Smith that I knew had he done otherwise.[5]

Another friend at this time was John H. Rinder, himself a future captain of the *Coptic* who later took up US citizenship and went on to captain the Pacific Mail Company steamer *Magnolia*. By 1912, Captain Rinder had given up the sea and was working as a broker in San Francisco. In the 1880s, though, he was a young British junior officer in the Pacific service who got to know Ted Smith fairly well. 'I knew him when he sailed out of San Francisco and he had the reputation of being the inferior of no man that ever trod a ship's bridge.'[6]

In a separate interview Captain Rinder noted that Smith made his home in San Francisco while in port from the Far East, adding, 'After a considerable service in the Pacific, Captain Smith (sic) returned with the Coptic to the Atlantic, when the liner was sent home to be reboilered, and remained on the other coast assuming command at different times of the largest steamships afloat.'[7]

But all good things must come to an end and as Captain Rinder's account indicates, in late 1883, after less than a year and a half in the Pacific service, the *Coptic* returned to Britain. Arriving back in Liverpool in March 1884, the ship being sent to be fitted not with new boilers, but with refrigeration machinery., Smith was signed off her books and returned to the North Atlantic service.

Britannic and *Republic*

This return to the Atlantic service must have been a happy homecoming for Ted, as he was appointed second officer aboard the ship he most admired, the SS *Britannic*, at that time under the command of Captain Hamilton Perry.

Captain Perry was quite a character to serve under. The same *Harper's New Monthly Magazine* article that had described Benjamin Gleadell, took a longer look at Perry perhaps because it found in him something of a conundrum as he did not fall happily into the two categories that most sea captains seemed to occupy, 'either of the jolly, genial type, or of the silent, retiring (I had almost said unsociable) sort.'[8]

Captain Perry was at that time the commodore of the White Star Line. Aged about fifty, he was a tall, stocky, bearded individual. He had been educated at the Royal Naval College in Greenwich, but for whatever reason he had not joined the navy, instead taking employment with the merchant marine. He went to sea in 1853 and joined White Star in about 1871. A year later, already in command of his own ship, Captain Perry had distinguished himself by going to the rescue of the shipwrecked crew of a vessel called the *Allen*. He had found her out at sea in the dead of night, waterlogged and with a shattered rudder, but got the crew off safely for which he was subsequently awarded a medal by the Royal Humane Society and a pair of binoculars were presented to him by the British Government. Four years later in 1876, he earned a bar to the Humane Society medal when he saved the crew of the Norwegian barque *Augusta*. The article commented that Perry had seen many more strange sights and figured in many other daring feats than these during his time at sea, but he had forgotten many of them and it now took something remarkable to surprise this hardened sea dog.

Perry impressed different people differently. 'It depends how you take him,' someone commented on him. He did not suffer fools gladly and if any passengers were rash enough to approach him with some ridiculous question that many were want to tax captains with on transatlantic voyages, they were treated with short shrift and doubtless came away from the interview with the impression that the captain of the *Britannic* was not a very pleasant person. Nor was he to be trifled with if he was about his duties, but if an interviewer caught Perry during quiet periods as he lolled over the rail or strolled idly on the deck and talked to him as they would any other gentleman, then a different picture emerged of a very agreeable man who could talk intelligently on any subject, but never gushed upon any.[9] How Perry was regarded by his officers and crews is never made clear, yet it is noticeable that many comments made about Captain Smith are similar to those made about Perry; one can only assume that something of Perry's no-nonsense nature rubbed off on his juniors.

Smith made fifteen round trips to the United States and back during this first stint on the *Britannic*. Of his life aboard the ship we hear nothing, though the ship and its passengers made the news a couple of times. In June 1884, the American papers reported that the evangelist Ira Sankey and his family were returning home to the States on the ship. Since first arriving in Britain in 1883, Sankey and his partner Dwight Moody had wowed religious British audiences with their new dynamic style of worship and some decidedly catchy hymns, many of which are still sung today. Private business, though, had forced Sankey to return home at this juncture and he boarded the *Britannic* at Liverpool.[10]

Then during the fourth voyage a passenger committed suicide and Smith as one of the senior officers probably witnessed some of the fallout. One Patrick Cronin had joined the *Britannic* as a steerage passenger at Queenstown on 17 July 1884. After the vessel had been out for two or three days Mr Cronin was seen wandering about looking very melancholy and on Thursday 24th whilst on deck he slit his own throat, dying in a few minutes. He was buried at sea the next morning and on Saturday when the *Britannic* arrived in New York, his luggage was sent to the British Consul. Cronin was travelling alone and nothing was known of his family, but his death seriously affected one man. When he took his own life, Cronin was standing near to Edward Hore, the ship's baker, who was severly shocked by what he witnessed and soon afterwards he began to act irrationally. He imagined that his wife in England was being haunted by Cronin's ghost and on the morning of 27 July after baking a batch of bread, Hore seized his coat and hat, jumped on the dock, and ran off. He was pursued by two stewards and was caught after a long chase and taken back to the vessel. The ship's surgeon found that the poor man had been driven insane, and took him to the Jefferson Market Police Court, where Justice Ford committed him for examination.[11]

In July 1885, Smith moved on again, being promoted and appointed as the first officer aboard the SS *Republic*. The *Republic* was a modest-sized ship compared with the monsters Smith was later to command. Like most of the early White Star steamships, she was one of that dying breed of vessels that seemed to present an unhappy amalgam of sail and steam; her single smokestack – a lonely concession to steam power – seemed hidden amid the rigging of her four masts. 470ft long and grossing 3,707 tons, she was nonetheless a neat four-cylinder single-screw passenger liner. She was also the ship destined to be Smith's first White Star command.

The captain of the *Republic*, Peter J. Irving, was scarcely in his forties and despite the impressive beard he sported he was one of the youngest looking of the White Star skippers. Like Captain Gleadell he was a quiet man, but with nothing of Gleadell's apparent stand-offishness and he favourably impressed all who met him. Like many other merchant sailors of his generation, he had learnt the rudiments of his trade aboard the old training vessel *Conway* and had since risen quickly through the ranks of the White Star Line.[12] Like many of his fellow captains he had been involved in a number of rescues at sea, but as will be seen he was also to suffer his fair share of mishaps.

Smith had only a short time to settle into his new duties under Captain Irving before the *Republic* was chartered briefly to the Inman Line later that year. Smith stayed on the ship and it was during this period that he was involved in his first known maritime accident, albeit as a spectator. On 20 September 1885, the *Republic* was leaving New York Harbour under the compulsory control of one of the harbour pilots as too was the outward-bound Cunard liner, the SS *Aurania*. As the two ships neared one another in Gedney's Channel, what exactly happened is not clear, but certainly confusion arose in the minds of the harbour pilots concerned as to what course the opposing ship was taking, and suddenly the two vessels collided. The *Aurania*'s bow smashed into the side of the *Republic*'s nose breaking her stem off 2ft above the waterline, while the Cunard vessel received a heavy blow to the stern. Of the two, the *Republic* came off worst and had to be dry-docked for a fortnight for repairs before she could sail. The *Aurania*, though dented, was still intact and so sailed as normal.

The only matter of interest in 1886 was that Smith would have first seen the iconic landmark that today dominates New York Harbour, namely the Statue of Liberty. A gift from the people of France to the young United States of America, the statue was erected on the uninhabited Bedloe's Island in the upper bay and the passengers and crews of passing ships doubtless looked on with interest as the giant steel and copper form slowly took shape over a number of months before being officially unveiled on 28 October 1886. Smith, though, would not have seen the statue in all its glory until the *Republic* reached New York on 13 November that year. Doubtless he had read of its construction, though he would not have witnessed any of this as the *Republic* does not seem to have made any crossings to the States since May. As sailors, Smith and the other officers of the *Republic* had a far more important reason to take note of the statue than those of more casual spectators, as from 1886 to 1902, the Statue of Liberty also served as a lighthouse to incoming ships.

Marriage and Command

Ted's old school friend Spencer Till, by now a fairly successful solicitor in the Potteries, later recalled that it was in 1886 or early 1887 that he received an invitation from Smith to meet him in Liverpool. Upon their meeting, Smith treated his friend to a personal tour of the *Republic*. Presently they were joined here by a young woman and after the introductions Smith announced, perhaps not unexpectedly to his friend, that he and the lady were engaged to be married, and as the happy couple were off to see an exhibition then being held in Liverpool, they invited Till to join them.[13]

On Thursday 13 January 1887, at St Oswald's, the parish church of Winwick, near Warrington, Lieutenant Edward John Smith married Sarah Eleanor Pennington. Eleanor, as she preferred to be called, was twenty-six years old, ten years Smith's junior, a slim, pretty woman, brown-haired and fresh-faced, with a thin pointed nose. In the only extant photograph of her, taken in about 1900, which was widely reproduced in books and papers around the world after the *Titanic* disaster, Eleanor can be seen seated self-consciously with her infant daughter Helen Melville on her lap. In the picture she has that starched formality as do most figures in Victorian or Edwardian photos, or perhaps it is shyness we are seeing. Indeed, there is a veiled suggestion in a letter written a few years later that she was somewhat camera-shy, yet in those earlier years she would have perhaps cut a far more striking figure.

Winwick was Eleanor's home territory. As she noted on the marriage certificate she was the daughter of the late William Pennington, a local farmer, one of a number of farmers of that name in the surrounding area. In the 1881 census, William Pennington was still alive and the owner of 147 acres of land employing five labourers and three household servants at their family farm at Newton-in-Makerfield, modern-day Newton-le-Willows. It was there that Eleanor was born in 1861. She must have had fond memories of growing up there at Woodhead Farm, as she and her husband later named their family home in Southampton 'Woodhead' in its honour. Perhaps it was not only happy childhood memories, though, that prompted the name, as the Penningtons' substantial home was doubtless one of the places that the young couple did their courting.

With the wedding being virtually on their doorstep, the Penningtons and Eleanor's friends were doubtless at the church in some numbers, but so too were Smith's family and friends. His best man seems to have been Thomas Jones, a brewer from Runcorn, who is referred to in a couple more documents in Smith's later life. His mother and Thyrza and her family were no doubt present and Joseph Hancock was definitely there with his wife and children. By now Ted's half-brother had given up the sea for good. He is last mentioned as the captain of the 1,413-ton *Mohur* in 1882 and though there may have been other ships that we do not know of, the chances are good that Joseph's life at sea was now over and he had gone into partnership with William Edward Heath of Birkenhead to form a company, Hancock, Heath & Co., of Victoria Buildings, Liverpool. Certainly by 1891, Joseph was an established ships stores dealer and provision merchant, commuting from his home in Birkenhead over to Liverpool, while William Heath kept the firm's books.

But we shall return to the altar at St Oswald's, where Edward and Eleanor were joined in holy matrimony, after banns, before God and in the face of this congregation, by the curate, James Carson. On the marriage certificate, Smith and his new wife signed themselves as being residents of Tuebrook and among other details Smith put down that his father had been a potter rather than the more polite title of 'grocer' that Edward Smith had been buried under. The only other matter of interest is that they called a large number of witnesses for their marriage – five rather than the required two. These were: Thomas Jones, Joseph Hancock, John William Pennington, Maria Annie Pennington and one Mary Privett Rooker.

The Smiths initially set up home locally at Spar Well Cottage, which like Woodhead Farm still stands today. However, perhaps for convenience and because it would give Smith a little more time at home with his new wife, they soon moved to Liverpool and within a couple of years were living at 39 Cambridge Road in Seaforth, a district that fronted the Liverpool docks.

On an intimate level, Eleanor called her husband 'Ted', or 'Teddy', while he affectionately called her 'My only dear one'. After his years of nomadic bachelor's existence, Eleanor doubtless gave him a settled home life to return to. The two of them seem to have enjoyed a steady, happy marriage that prospered despite Smith's long periods at sea. His career prospects too were coming to fruition and in April 1887, almost as a wedding present from the White Star Line, Smith was given temporary command of the *Republic*, but this only lasted until August that year, when he was transferred back to the glamorous *Britannic* as her popular first officer.

It was in February 1888 that Smith put himself forward to be tested for the extra master mariner's certificate of competency. Entry for this examination was purely voluntary and was intended for those masters who wished to push their skills to the limit and gain certificates for the highest grade of training offered by the British Board of Trade. Though a master's ordinary certificate would suffice for any master in sailing ships, the increasingly technical nature of steamship travel was soon seen to require something more of a ship's commanding officer, though it was not yet compulsary. Bertram Hayes notes in his autobiography that it was not until 1897 that the White Star management sent a missive around suggesting that the extra master's certificate would ensure that its holders would be favourably considered for promotion and Hayes promptly rushed to gain one. Smith, though, was well ahead of the game, nine years ahead to be precise.

As might be expected, this exam was as tough as it could get. Because it was usually the case that the vessels that such highly qualified masters would command would often make trips to the East Indies or the Pacific, under the navigation section the candidates were required to work out a lunar observation by both sun and star; to determine the latitude by the moon; by polar star off the meridian; and also by double altitude of the sun and to verify their result by the navigational process known as Sumner's method. The candidate would also have to be able to calculate the altitudes of the sun or star they took a sighting off when they could not be clearly observed for the purposes of lunar fixes; to find the error of a watch by the method of equal latitudes and to correct the altitude observed with an artificial horizon. To earn the certificate for a foreign-going ship he also had to understand how to observe and apply the deviation of a compass and how to deduce the direction and speed of the current by dead reckoning and by observation. As his job would involve travelling across great expances he would also be required to explain the nature of great circle sailing and know how to practically apply that knowledge on a voyage. Great circle sailing required a master to solve complex problems using spherical trigonometry. An examination question would give the candidate a hypothetical route from one point on the globe to another, and he would be required to list all the turning points on the course and the courses to be steered between them. Such calculations alone could cover a couple of pages, but the candidate was not required to supply the calculations within the context of the examination. The candidate was also required to show his understanding of the law of storms, so far as to know how to best escape hurricanes and the tropical storms of the East and West Indies.

To the landsman all this seems like an arcane science and it was no easy matter for the most experienced seaman, little wonder that some who earned their master's certificate never made or attempted the higher grade. After all this brainwork the practicalities of the seamanship section probably came as a blessed relief to Smith and the other candidates. In this he was examined as to how he would heave a ship down should an accident befall the vessel abroad; to get lower masts in and out and to perform any other actions of a similar nature that the examiner saw fit to tax him with.

The fee was again £2, with half being returned if he failed the exam. This was just as well as on his first attempt on 14 February, for the first time in his career Ted

Smith failed an exam, losing out on the navigation section. Undaunted, he applied again three days later, well aware that the future success of his career depended on his passing these exams. On 20 February, he passed the tests and gained his blue paper signed by the examiners in lieu of the far more ornate certificate to come.

As an extra master mariner, Ted Smith had certainly earned the right to his own ship and he received his first permanent White Star command in April 1888. The ship he got was the SS *Baltic*, the 'little Baltic' as she eventually became known to distinguish her from her later, much larger namesake that Smith also went on to command.

Built in 1871, she was the twin sister to the *Republic*; White Star built most of its ships in pairs – the *Baltic* and *Republic*, the *Germanic* and *Britannic* etc., though occasionally there was a one-off such as the *Oceanic*, or a trio such as the *Olympic*, *Titanic* and the *Gigantic*, later renamed *Britannic*. The 'little *Baltic*' grossed 3,707 tons and had been quite a ship in her heyday, having once gained the Blue Riband for her crossing of the Atlantic in 1873, in seven days, twenty hours and nine minutes. But by 1888, the *Baltic* was getting on and Smith was her last White Star captain, as later that year the ship was sold to the Holland American Line for £35,000. Renamed the *Veendam*, she continued in the Atlantic service for a further ten years, until she sank without loss of life after hitting a mid-Atlantic derelict in 1898.

Though his time aboard the *Baltic* was very short-lived – just two transatlantic return voyages – Captain Smith gained a couple of early admirers from his time aboard her. Mr and Mrs John Thallon were an American couple who were thoroughly impressed by the new, young White Star skipper and their comments written after his death reveal something of the bond that grew up between Smith and many of his regular passengers:

> We sailed with Captain Smith on the little 'Baltic' of the White Star Line, the first transatlantic Steamer which he ever commanded; and since then, a period of nearly thirty years, we have followed him from ship to ship; and had we not sailed from Naples April 5, 1912, we should undoubtedly have been with him on the 'Titanic', instead of crossing at the same time on the 'Cincinatti'. We always felt so safe with him, for one knew how deeply he felt the responsibility of his ship and of all on board. He has been a deeply cherished friend on sea and land all these years, and we hold him in love and veneration, and are proud that we could count so noble a man among our closest friends.[14]

The ship's final voyage for the White Star Line began from Liverpool on 5 May 1888. The voyage started as normal and the next day the ship called at Queenstown in Ireland. However, a broken low-pressure valve spindle forced Smith to return to that port and for repairs and she did not leave Queenstown again until 3a.m., on 8 May.

After leaving the *Baltic* in May 1888, in June Smith briefly took command of the *Britannic*, though perhaps only as acting captain as he is noted in some records as having been a ship's mate at this time. The *Britannic* still seems to have been the apple of Smith's eye and in an act which seems to have shown his pride in having finally achieved this long-sought-after command, he sent a large framed photograph of the ship to his old school friend Spencer Till. He was not, however, aboard her for too long on this occasion, being discharged on 12 September due to his being sick.[15] On 8 December 1888, he was over his illness and back at work in charge of the new White Star cattle transporter *Cufic* for her maiden voyage from Liverpool to New York. She weighed 4,660 tons, was 444ft long, had four masts and a single funnel and was at that time the largest tramp cargo ship in the world and as such should be counted as a feather in Smith's cap, even if she was not a glamourous passenger steamer like the *Britannic*. The *Cufic* arrived at the Pierpont Stores in Brooklyn on 21 December, just in time for Christmas, attracting a small amount of attention from jobbing reporters who noted that Captain Smith had brought her over. Probably as a result of the good publicity this voyage generated, the jaunt with the *Cufic* also brought Smith to the attention of the White Star Line's senior management, in this case Thomas Ismay's son, J. Bruce Ismay. He would inherit his father's business and later play a controversial role in the voyage of the *Titanic* and in the subsequent inquiries he noted that he had known Smith for a good many years, first becoming aware of him when he took the *Cufic* out for her maiden voyage.[16]

In January 1889, Smith was back on the *Republic* as her full commander. There had been a few changes since he had last been on the ship – most notably a second-class section had been added. Second class drew a line between the opulence of first-class travel and the much more spartan accommodation offered by steerage. It was a sign of the times that it was mostly designed to cater for the professional classes and the wealthier working classes who increasingly took their business abroad, who wanted cheaper travel than first class afforded but with more style and comfort than steerage offered. Again, however, as with the *Baltic*, Smith seems to have been given command of the *Republic* merely to be one of those seeing her to the end of her White Star career. Later that year she, like the 'little *Baltic*', was sold to the Holland American Line for £35,000 and renamed the *Maasdam*, following the style of name change that her sister ship had undergone the year before. Before that came to pass, though, the *Republic* gave Smith his first test of the responsibility he had taken on as the commander of an ocean liner.

The incident happened on Smith's thirty-ninth birthday, 27 January 1889. The *Republic* arrived off Sandy Hook on the approach to New York Harbour and promptly ran aground. She was pretty firmly stuck and it took five hours of vigorous work on the part of the master and crew before the ship was finally refloated. After this delay, the *Republic* made speed to arrive at New York. When she finally moored up at the White Star pier and her passengers had all disembarked, the day seemed to have given Smith nothing more annoying than an upset journey, but as the officers and crew were closing the ship down prior to disembarking, down below in the bowels of the ship tragedy struck. In one of the boiler rooms, the furnace flue to a lower forward boiler fractured and a jet of superheated steam shot out into the room which was still crowded with firemen, stokers and engineers. Those in the path of the jet were blown across the room and lay scalded and screaming for help where they lay. At first, newspapers spoke of a large loss of life, some reporting upwards of fourteen fatalities, but this number more accurately reflected the number actually caught in the blast. These included Fireman James Borden, Oiler Samuel Ward, Stoker Patrick Hughes, Sixth Engineer James Dyer (or Dwyer), Fireman James Collins, Fourth Engineer Thomas McFarland, Fireman James Ward and Trimmer John Leonard. Second Engineer Yates and Fifth Engineer Ebbs were also badly burned in the accident.

Captain Smith would have been called immediately and after viewing the carnage it was probably on his or the ship's surgeon's orders that a team of surgeons were called for from the local authorities. While the remaining engineers and stokers dealt with the venting steam, parties of medical men arrived and went in to help the casualties. Most had suffered severe burning to their hands and faces and their moans and screams were heart-rending. The surgeons tended the most serious cases first, several being so badly injured that they were unable to stand. Help was therefore summoned from Smith and his crew and the casualties were placed on stretchers and then hoisted onto the wharf with tackle and the ship's cargo cranes. Doubts were expressed for the engineers Dyer and McFarland, Fireman Collins and Trimmer Leonard and indeed three of them subsequently died. Though sources do vary, the final toll seems to have been three dead and seven seriously injured.

It had been a terrible business and Smith was probably as shaken as anybody by the tragedy on this day of all days. As ship's captain it was his onerous task to account for the accident to the authorities and console with the relatives of the dead and injured. As well as this, he also had to have his ship checked over to see what damage had been sustained. Once the fires were out and the steam cleared from her boilers and pipes, engineers and marine inspectors came in to look over the boiler room. Despite the carnage it had caused, the boiler flue was found to be only slightly damaged and the inspectors confidently predicted that it could be fully repaired and the ship ready for sea in a few hours.[17]

Lieutenant Smith RNR

A few months earlier in August 1888, Smith had applied to and joined the ranks of the Royal Naval Reserve, the auxiliary force of merchant seamen who in times of war, or during any other form of national emergency, could be called upon to serve as naval officers. After applying to join the RNR, prospective officers needed to undergo an official interview at the Admiralty in Whitehall. This Smith did and was quickly accepted. Normally, new officers were entered into the service as sub-lieutenants, but because he held a master's certificate Smith was qualified as a full lieutenant and it is in the full dress uniform of a lieutenant in the RNR that he can be seen in the framed sepia photograph which hangs in Hanley Town Hall. Once he had joined, Smith had the right to have the letters 'RNR' after his name and providing a certain proportion of his crew were in the Reserve, his ship could henceforth fly the blue ensign of the RNR, rather than the red ensign of the merchant navy; officers were presented with an official warrant legitimising this and Smith had warrant No.690.

This and other details including his leaving the *Britannic* due to illness are recorded in Smith's RNR records held at the National Archives in Kew and these also tell us about the training he now underwent. All Reserve officers were required to undergo a period of drill aboard a RNR training ship and from 26 February to 1 March 1889, Smith did his stint aboard HMS *Eagle*, an old, dismasted wooden frigate moored at Liverpool. Here he underwent training on the use of big guns, rifles and the use of a cutlass, his ability and conduct being variously labelled as 'fair', 'good' and 'very good' from week to week.[18] One thing is for sure, Smith would have enjoyed himself, for as Bertram Hayes noted, the time spent aboard the *Eagle* was good fun, with officers getting up bands and organising parties when they were not training, but as far as practical experience for modern warfare went, it was laughable:

> I am not definitely certain that the guns we were drilled at were those with which she was supplied when she was originally commissioned as a man-of-war – in 1794 I think it was; but they might well have been, as they were old iron muzzle-loaders, and we had to train them with rope tackles – good exercise even if not of much use in teaching modern gunnery. The guiding principal with the Admiralty may have been that a sound training in the classics – the old muzzle-loaders taking the place of Greek or Latin – is the best foundation for a good education, but, if so, we were never informed of it by any of our instructors, so perhaps didn't take as much interest in the drill as we otherwise might have done.
>
> It was not very encouraging, either, to be told by the instructor at the end of a long lecture on fuses, sights and what not: 'You musn't remember any of that, gentlemen, when you go into the Navy to do your twelve months. It's all hopsolete and only used for the purpose of passing your test in this ship.'[19]

As the passage notes, there was the option of going for a further twelve months training with the Royal Navy, but many officers never bothered, opting to stay with their companies and the continuity of Smith's service records at this time indicates that he was one of these.

On the last day of his training, Smith received his RNR certificate of competancy, No.207. With his new honours tagged on after his name he then passed almost blithely from one command to another over the next few years. From April 1889 to July 1889, Captain Smith commanded the *Celtic*, the first White Star ship he had served on. He then went over to the Pacific station one more time when he took charge of another of his old ships, the *Coptic*, for a voyage out to Australia and New Zealand.

Smith had been given command of the *Coptic* following a rather unfortunate incident that had occurred under her former commander, Captain Burton. During the *Coptic's* last journey all had gone well until shortly after the ship left Rio de Janeiro on the homeward leg of her long journey in late 1889. On leaving Rio, the ship would then be steered on a course ESE between Pai and Mai Islands (modern-day Pai and Mãe) before turning up along the Atlantic coast. This was the standard route used by European outward bounders, but care was needed in negociating the passage between Pai and Mai, even on a moonlit night as that one was. It seems, however, that Captain Burton had forgotten this and perhaps confused by the high speed the ship was making, he altered course much too early and as a result at about 1a.m. on 12 October, the ship ran aground off the southern end of Mai Island, impaling herself on a rock which unbeknownst to her crew at the time left her with a substancial hole in her forehold. The ship had refloated at high tide and apparently convinced that there was little damage Captain Burton had then attempted to continue the journey, but by 10a.m. there was 24ft of water in the forehold, the crew were protesting at the danger and so he decided to return the ship to Rio, docking there later that evening. The passengers were promptly taken off and cargos removed or dumped overboard and over the next week or so repairs were carried out, the hole in the ship's hull being repaired with wood and the space behind it filled with bricks and cement. Thus shored up, on the 30th, the *Coptic* set off on her return to Britain, albeit minus her original passengers who had long since taken another ship. The *Coptic* arrived safely at Plymouth early on the morning of 20 November where, *The Times* noted matter-of-factly, she deposited her overdue mails before setting off an hour later for London.

Everyone was glad that the ship had made it home safely, but the shipping authorities were less than pleased with Captain Burton and his officers, who were quickly and quietly removed from duty pending an inquiry into the events at Rio. Hasty repairs were effected to the damaged *Coptic* and a new crew headed by Captain E.J. Smith were brought in, not perhaps so much as a replacement crew to keep the timetable up and running, as the proverbial new brooms brought in to sweep away Captain Burton's mess.

The *Coptic* thus set out from the port of London on 12 December 1889, calling at Plymouth on the 14th and the ship sailed south via Tenerife before making her way south to the Cape of Good Hope. The ship called at Cape Town on 6 January and by 26 January she had arrived at Hobart, Tasmania. A few days later she touched at Wellington, New Zealand, before moving onto other ports. It is known that she departed Lyttelton, New Zealand, on 20 February, but it was not until March that Smith sailed the *Coptic* into Rio de Janeiro. His departure from that port was without incident and after an uneventful journey the ship arrived back at Plymouth on 7 April 1890. That, though, was Smith's only journey in command of the *Coptic*, after which he returned to the Atlantic service.

By this time, the unfortunate Captain Burton had been thoroughly raked over the official coals. In February the inquest into his actions had not gone well and he had found himself stripped of his master's certificate for six months, forcing him to jog along on a first mate's competancy until the term was up. Ironically, though, for many years Captain Burton would have the last laugh as following the *Titanic* disaster (which made Captain Smith everybody's favourite 'ill-fated' skipper to tag a mishap onto) it would be Smith, not Captain Burton, who would be blamed for the Rio de Janeiro grounding. The story persisted until new research opportunities opened up in the early years of the twenty-first century, giving the lie to this fable.[20]

In late March, Smith was in command of another ship for a month, the steamer SS *Runic*. During his time aboard the *Runic* he had one famous passenger, but in this case of the equine variety. The celebrated Irish racehorse Clear-the-Way, winner of the 1888 Irish Grand National, had been purchased by Edward D. Morgan of Westbury, Long Island, and Captain Smith had the task of getting the horse and his human passengers there in one piece.

Smith was at sea transporting this famous horse when the 1891 census was taken, though Eleanor was resident at their new home at 4 Marine Crescent in Crosby, Liverpool. This distinctive house with its imposing gate posts, arched upper-floor windows and balcony looks very grand, though it may not have looked that way when the Smiths lived there.

The census is actually more valuable for providing us with an update as to what was happening with the Smith, Hancock and Harrington clans. For instance, Ted's mother Catherine was still going strong at eighty-four and had for a time at least returned to Hanley where she was living with her grandson James Harrington – the same J.W.S. Harrington who had gone to sea as ship's boy aboard the *Lizzie Fennell* fourteen years earlier. Catherine was now listed as a retired grocer, while twenty-nine-year-old James, having given up the sea and married, now worked as a painter and decorator. He, his wife Martha, their young daughter Daisy and the elderly Catherine lived at 34 Market Street, Hanley.

James's mother Thyrza, now fifty-four, and William, now fifty-five, their seventeen-year-old son Edward and a fourteen-year-old domestic servant Mary Ellen Lynn, all lived at 30 Greenway Road, Runcorn. William Harrington had followed the family trend and is listed on the census return as a 'sea going engineer', while his son Edward was evidently following in his father's footsteps working as an 'apprentice engine maker'.

In 1891, Joseph Hancock, his wife Susanna and a teenage domestic servant named Annie Harrison were residing at 70 Bridge Street, Birkenhead, having recently moved from nearby Neville Road. As already noted, Joseph had left the sea and by this time he listed his occupation as 'ship's stores dealer'.

May 1891 saw Smith's return as captain of the *Britannic* and barring one short break he was to retain command of his favourite White Star vessel for nearly four years. Later that year in August, Smith and the *Britannic* made the papers when they were involved in a rescue. On the morning of 6 August, the *Britannic*'s lookout spotted a small fishing yawl with a couple of occupants who were shouting and waving desperately for attention. Smith ordered the ship stopped and the men were taken aboard. They were two French fishermen, Adrian Leroy and Hyppolite Fresel, of the fishing smack *L'Active*. They had been out in the smaller boat tending to their nets when an incredibly thick fog had rolled in and losing all sense of direction they could not find their way back to their smack. Marooned in their small boat with no food and water, they drifted for some days and had experienced some rough weather before they finally saw the *Britannic*.

Their story touched the passengers who immediately organised a collection which raised the equivalent of $40 for the rescued fishermen. Leroy and Fresel stayed aboard the *Britannic* until the ship reached New York where they were turned over to the French Consul who would arrange their return home. It came to light here that exactly the same thing had happened to two other French fishermen who were rescued by the Dutch tank steamship *La Campine*.[21]

A few months later a similar pea-souper delayed the *Britannic's* departure from New York. The fog had rolled in on 6 November shortly before the ship set off and at first it may not have seemed too bad as Smith and a number of other captains took their ships out. Within a short distance, though, it became clear that this was no ordinary fog. A great blanket of mist had rolled over the lower bay and the pilots and skippers realising the danger brought proceedings to a halt. The *Britannic*, *Augusta Victoria* and the *Noorland* anchored near the Statue of Liberty, while several approaching steamers including the White Star SS *Majestic* lay anchored further along the bay near to a quarantine dock. At its worst visability was reduced to 10 yards and the ships had to regularly sound their whistles in warning. The New York newspapers later told stories of the confusion caused by the fog, of ferries going astray, trains delayed and a massive crush of people using the Brooklyn Bridge as there was no other way to cross. For nearly twenty-four hours virtually all sea and river traffic was brought to a halt. By the morning of 7 November, though, the situation had improved. From dawn the mist had begun to thin and by 9a.m. the crew of the *Britannic* and other steamers could see well enough to proceed and were soon on their way.[22]

When the *Britannic* returned to New York on 21 November, it was after experiencing the roughest crossing that the ship had suffered in seventeen years of Atlantic service. She had left Liverpool on the 11th when a terrific storm was sweeping around the British Isles and playing merry hell with the shipping. The *Britannic* immediately ran into a monstrous boiling sea that sent massive volumes of water crashing down over the decks. The passengers stayed below decks and the deck crew were compelled to cling to ropes to keep from being swept overboard. One sea crashed into the vessel, swept over the decks and carried with it Quartermaster Thomas McKenzie, who as he went over the railing let out a shriek of despair before he vanished into the angry waves. The cry for man overboard went up and Smith and the bridge crew were immediately informed, but in such conditions nothing could be done for him. The *Britannic* sailed on and continued to meet rough weather for the remainder of the voyage, arriving in New York over a day late.[23]

Yet more rough weather awaited the *Britannic* right at the end of the year. After leaving Liverpool on 9 December, the ship experienced a series of misadventures. On the seventh day out the *Britannic* ran into a storm which she weathered well enough, but as the storm was abating it was found necessary to stop the ship's engines for repairs to a damaged steam pipe. This took several hours, but it was just the beginning of their problems. At 1a.m., on the Thursday a monster wave crashed over the ship. This smashed a portion of the ship's bridge into splinters and carried away a large portion of the remainder. Chief Officer Thomas was on duty at the time and narrowly escaped being dragged overboard, escaping with a badly cut head and an injured arm which effectively put him out of action for the remainder of the voyage. The report carried in the newspapers told of the anxiety of the passengers at this time, but there was no panic and all breathed a sigh of relief when the storm finally blew itself out on the Friday.[24]

At the beginning of 1892, a new facility opened its doors in New York Harbour, namely the Ellis Island Station. The station was designed to process immigrants and to act as a form of quarantine, in which capacity it dealt mainly with the poorer steerage passengers who were deemed more likely to be a public health risk. Before this opened, New York State had received the newcomers at the Castle Garden on the Battery. By the 1890s, though, the numbers arriving due to political and economic instability, wars and oppressions in Europe and elsewhere, had swelled enormously and the small Castle Garden establishment was being swamped. As a result, the US government had stepped in and constructed a new federally operated immigration facility on Ellis Island. Initially an enormous wooden structure built of Georgia pine, the Ellis Island Station opened its doors on 1 January 1892, receiving its first immigrants the next day.

The immigrant ships did not actually stop at Ellis Island, proceeding instead to their company piers further up the bay. First- and second-class passengers were not normally required to undergo the inspection process at Ellis Island, they usually underwent a very cursory examination aboard ship. The reasoning behind this was that anyone who could afford to pay for a first- or second-class ticket was less likely to be insolvent and have been in places where they would have been exposed to any dangerous diseases that would cause them to end up in institutions or hospitals, or otherwise be a burden upon the local medical facilities or the state. They did, however, have to go to Ellis Island if it was discovered on arrival that they were sick or had any legal problems. If there were no such problems, though, they simply passed through customs and into the country.

The steerage passengers, meantime, were transported over to the station and underwent a series of examinations at Ellis Island to check that they could not only afford to come to the United States, but that they were well enough to be allowed in. Those that failed to satisfy the inspectors were sent back to where they came from. To aid this quarantine process the shipping companies were expected to keep the steerage passengers segregated from those in first and second class. This apparently draconian measure, which later came in for such critcism after the *Titanic* disaster, was as much a condition laid down by the American authorities as a quirk of the British class system.

Ellis Island would become a very regular call for Smith and his ships over the years apart from a brief hiatus of three years after a fire gutted the facility in 1897. In the meantime Smith and the *Britannic* were latecomers to Ellis Island and the ship did not offload her first batch of passengers here until 22 January, a full three weeks after the facility had first opened its doors.

In June 1893, Smith left the ship for a month to captain the *Adriatic* for one journey to the States and back, but by 12 July, he was back with the *Britannic*. One journey followed another, again with little to report. It doubtless seemed that way too when Smith took the ship out on her sixth crossing, but little did he know that he would not see his mother again.

Since the census was taken two years previously, Catherine Smith had returned to Runcorn where she lived with her daughter Thyrza and her family at 30 Greenway Road. Her death certificate indicates that she had been suffering from senility, which had probably prompted her daughter to take her in and look after her at the end of her life. Certainly it was here where Catherine died on 1 November aged eighty-six. The cause of death was given as senile decay and hemiplegia or the paralysis of half of her body, probably as the result of a stroke. Catherine was buried on 4 November at Runcorn Cemetery.[25] Unlike that of her husband, Catherine's grave has a stone, in pink granite. This carries the inscription:

> In Loving Memory of
> CATHERINE SMITH
> Relict of EDWARD SMITH
> of Hanley Staffordshire
> Died 1st November 1893
> Aged 86 years

The *Britannic* left Liverpool for New York on the day she died and the crew list for the voyage shows that Smith was aboard, so her death was probably sudden and unexpected as Smith may have been granted leave had he known she was dying. In the days before wireless, ship to shore messages could only be relayed by word of mouth from other vessels, so the chances are that Smith did not hear of his mother's death and funeral until he reached New York on 10 November, or even after he returned home. Doubtless on arriving back he visited the grave and consoled with his relatives, but he did not take any time away from work and led the *Britannic* out on her next voyage on 29 November.

'The Perfect Sea Captain'

It seems that it was from Smith's captaincy of the *Britannic* that he began to establish the sterling reputation that would over the next few years propel him to the top of his profession. First and perhaps most importantly, he gained note as a captain that crews enjoyed sailing under. His first duty was of course to them, motivating them in a positive way so that the ship ran smoothly. Some never cut the mustard in this respect and the position of captain gave power to many pompous and exacting martinets, men who cared more about getting the job done than treating their fellow workers like human beings; the exigencies of liner travel, the opinions of passengers and fellow crewmen and doubtless the wary eyes of company officials made sure that few of these amounted to anything. Captain Smith, though, found the perfect line; he was disciplined, but as much as his exhalted position allowed he treated the members of his crew in a friendly manner. Steward Samuel Rule, who served under Smith on numerous ships starting back when the skipper had been a junior officer, later said of him, 'A better man never walked a deck. His crew knew him to be a good, kind-hearted man, and we looked upon him as a sort of father.' [26]

This kind of recommendation shows in a large way the secret of Captain Smith's growing success from this time onwards. A happy and efficient liner was after all far more pleasant to the passengers than a merely efficient ship and from the company's point of view this was no bad thing as it was also a liner captain's duty, albeit an unofficial one, to cultivate an image that would attract customers, especially the rich and famous, many of whom would become valued regular travellers. As the journeys took much longer than those of modern airline travel, so the captain received much more exposure to the passengers, unless the weather was bad enough to keep him constantly on the bridge. However, when the weather was fine and the journey smooth, the privilege of sitting at the captain's table was much sought after by first-class passengers.

In this capacity, Smith's obligations were a combination of those of the modern airline pilot, hotel manager and PR man; he always had to be pleasant, presentable and confident. For the company choosing a captain was, therefore, not only a matter of picking the best qualified sailor, but also the best qualified host, diplomat, friend and confidant, sometimes marriage counsellor, sounding-board and sympathetic ear. Captain Smith apparently ticked all these boxes and his intelligence and charm seem to have worked well on the majority of the passengers he met and gained him many admirers, a few of whom later recalled their times in his company. One of these regular travellers was Mr J.E. Hodder Williams of the publishers Hodder and Stoughton, who after the *Titanic* disaster provided an interesting pen portrait of the by then famous White Star skipper as he had held court on his ships:

We crossed with him on many ships and in many companies, through seas fair and foul, and to us he was and will ever be, the perfect sea captain... He was amazingly well informed on every phase of present-day affairs and that was hardly to be wondered at, for scarcely a well-known man or woman who crossed the Atlantic during the last twenty years but had at some time sat at his table. He read widely, but men more than books. He was a good listener, on the whole, although he liked to get in a yarn himself now and again, but he had scant patience with bores or people who 'gushed'. I have seen him quell both... He had an infinite respect – I think that is the right word – for the sea. Absolutely fearless, he had no illusions as to man's power in the face of the infinite. He would never prophesy an hour ahead. If you asked him about times of arrival, it was always 'if all goes well'. I am sure now that he must have had many terrible secrets of narrowly averted tragedies locked away behind those sailor eyes of his... An inspiring man to meet was our friend Captain Smith, an inspiring man to serve under, if need be, to die with.[27]

Another regular of his, who first met Captain Smith during his time aboard the *Britannic*, was Kate Douglas-Wiggin, the future author of *Rebecca of Sunnybrook Farm*. As she notes here she had travelled with Smith several times over the last few years and like many of her fellow travellers in first class she thereafter began to follow him from ship to ship and she later described – with perhaps some slight exaggeration in places – how their early shipboard acquaintance had broadened into friendship:

I knew Captain Smith from the time of the old 'Britannic' until the day of his death. The routine of life on the smaller, slower ships of earlier years made it possible to form real friendships, made it possible to know the man by whose side you sat three times a day for a voyage of considerably more than a week. This was my pleasure and privilege, season after season, for I crossed the ocean with Captain Smith twenty times or more.

There were no electric lights then, no 'Georgian' or 'Louis XIV' suites, no gymnasiums or Turkish baths, no gorgeous dining saloons with meals at all hours, but there were, perhaps, a few minor compensations, and I can remember certain voyages when great inventors and scientists, earls and countesses, authors and musicians and statesmen, made a 'Captain's table' as notable and distinguished as that of any London or New York dinner.

At such times Captain Smith was an admirable host; modest, dignified, appreciative; his own contributions to the conversation showing not only the quantity of his information, but the high quality of his mind.

My knowledge of him was furthered from time to time by informal meetings at my own house in America, or at his home in England, where I saw him in his happy and delightful family life.

One did not need so many opportunities as these to divine the character of the man. His face, his manner, his voice, the grasp of his hand, showed simplicity, directness and strength. There was never any variableness about him 'neither shadow of turning'. He never flattered or curried favour with any one, or indulged in any

small talk of policy, but his blunt, straightforward, seamanlike speech, his keen sense
of humour, his essential kindness, his sunny smile – all these seemed to be just so
many visible expressions of a character intrinsically upright and trustworthy. A kind
of steady loyalty, to his profession, his duty, his friends, and his own ideal, always
seemed to me the compass by which his life was set. [28]

In her autobiography Kate tells a delightful little tale of Captain Smith playing
cupid at the captain's table by introducing her to her future husband. It started on a
sunny morning in May 1894, when Kate again turned up at White Star's New York
terminus at the foot of West 10th Street, to take the *Britannic* over to Europe. By this
time she had become something of a favourite of Captain Smith's and she noted
that, when he came down for his meals in the first-class saloon, Smith (who from her
description of the scene appears to have sat at the head of one of the *Britannic's* long
tables), usually placed her at his right hand at table and here they enjoyed a very easy-
going familiarity, which would pay dividends for Kate on this voyage.

As she walked up the gangplank, Kate spotted Smith and waved in reply to his
greeting and though the captain never appeared in the first-class saloon on a sailing
day, Kate managed to collar him for a brief interview before luncheon.

'Captain, dear,' she said, 'I was never so tired in my life and I must rest on this
voyage. I don't want to meet anyone except those at our end of the table.'

'All right,' Smith replied with a quizzical glance. 'You'll agree that I never was
much of an "introducer". There's an awfully nice chap on my left, who has made
twelve or fifteen voyages with me; the Earl and Countess of R. are seated next to
you, and across the table Mr William Shakespeare, the London musician, and his wife.'

'That sounds delightful!' she answered. 'No one could "seat" a dinner-party with
more discretion.'

Kate went down to luncheon very late that day and the people at table had nearly
finished the meal. They all made a few brief remarks to one another, with a view to
deciding what sort of companionship might be had during a nine-day voyage. She
thought both the Earl and Countess of R. had most delightful and democratic manners,
and the 'nice chap' Smith had mentioned as sitting opposite her and named on the
list as George C. Riggs, New York City, did indeed look interesting. Captain Smith
had told her that Mr Riggs was an American, though to her eyes he looked British;
however, she liked that. What really caught her attention, though, was his crop of curly
hair, which she found very attractive. That superficial impression recorded, though,
Kate dismissed him, and all the others, from her mind. When she learned that the
captain would not be going down to dinner, Kate, not wishing to brave the scrutiny of
strangers without Smith as their genial host, dined on deck and went early to her cabin.

The next day at breakfast, though, Captain Smith arrived, all smiles, and formally
introduced his table companions to each other and they had a very merry meal
together. Kate soon warmed to George Riggs and during the morning she walked
the deck with her new acquaintance and later went to tea in the captain's cabin,

where Mr Riggs and one or two others were present. For Kate, the hitherto confirmed spinster, it was the beginning of a whirlwind romance which blossomed further when she and George Riggs landed in the United States.[29]

Smith's command of the *Britannic* would end in April 1895, but before he departed her bridge he had had the pleasure of welcoming aboard the newly married George and Kate Riggs – the former Kate Douglas-Wiggin – taking the boat out for their honeymoon; they chose to travel on the *Britannic* and under Smith out of a sense of loyalty and probably by way of a thank you to the captain for having introduced them.[30]

Someone else who could also have said a great deal about Smith at this time was Bertram Fox Hayes, the future White Star captain and commodore of the line, who during 1893 and 1894 served as first officer under Captain Smith and his Chief Officer Cornelius Lancaster, or occasionally as acting chief officer himself when Lancaster was away. Hayes later wrote his autobiography, but though of interest being written by a contemporary of Smith's, his book *Hull Down* contains no mention of his former skipper whatsoever, nor of the *Titanic* disaster. By this time Hayes had retired, the *Titanic* and any of the major figures related to it were anathema to the White Star management and perhaps fearing for his pension Hayes produced a very tame account of his time with the company. He does relate one story, though, that took place aboard the *Britannic*, probably during his time under Smith.

On one voyage the *Britannic* had amongst its passengers a number of prize fighters, one of them being the famous black Australian boxer Peter Jackson. Jackson was a decent, quiet, self-respecting man who did not mix much with the other fighters and went to bed at a reasonable time. The others were a different matter, however; they were noisy and unruly and caused a great deal of anxiety to the crew especially towards closing time in the smoking room.

Things came to a head one evening when the banter between the boxers started to get very ugly and two of the men seemed ready to settle their differences by fighting, which would have caused a great deal of annoyance to the other passengers and no end of trouble for the crew. The ordinary methods of keeping the peace were of no use and understandably no one wished to tackle a couple of experienced prize-fighters when they were liquored-up. All this was reaching its climax when somebody thought of Peter Jackson. He had already turned in, but very kindly turned out again and soon had the two troublemakers under control. Catching them both in his powerful hands, he banged them together then frog-marched the stunned men down to their respective cabins and told them to stay there. They did as they were told.[31]

Two Family Funerals

It was during his last few voyages aboard the *Britannic* that Ted Smith's brother-in-law, William Harrington, died at the age of fifty-seven. Judging by the tally of his voyages, Smith seems to have been ashore in Britain when William died on 1 March 1895. Pat Lacey, a descendant of the Harringtons, noted that both William and Thyrza Harrington were regarded with great affection by their grandchildren, but also with some trepidation. In those days children were expected to be seen and not heard and such was the case in the Harrington household, especially as William had not liked noise. Both Ted and Joseph were well known to the Harrington's children, and Ted especially was regarded more as a big brother to them than an uncle, a role he seems to have fulfilled with a number of his nephews and nieces on both sides of the family, many of whom were close contemporaries of his age-wise and he was doubtless on hand now with the rest of the family to comfort them and his sister Thyrza on their loss. He probably attended the funeral which took place at Hanley Municipal Cemetery a few days later. The grave is marked by an ornate gravestone, perhaps the most flamboyant of any of Smith's relations. Here, William's remains were later joined by those of his wife Thyrza when she died over twenty years later.

After two more voyages aboard the *Britannic*, Captain Smith was notified that he was to be transferred to the *Britannic*'s sister ship SS *Germanic* and was to remain ashore on leave until his time came to take over. Perhaps the news came as a disappointment, the *Britannic* had after all been the ship that first attracted him to join the White Star Line. However, there were new ships on the horizon and the break had other compensations, for Smith had led a very busy life over the last few years, so was probably glad to at last spend a little quality time with his wife and visit his family and friends. This was probably just as well in one case as on 1 May 1895, exactly two months after William Harrington's death, Ted's half-brother Joseph died in Liverpool. His death came as a complete surprise to everyone, as apart from a few weeks of illness just after Christmas, Joseph had been in apparent good health. On that May morning, Joseph was in Liverpool and at about 11a.m. he was coming through the arcade from the Fish Market into Lime Street when he was seen to stagger and fall. People nearby rushed over and called for an ambulance which soon arrived from the Southern Hospital. It was, however, too late; Joseph had suffered a massive heart attack and he died where he fell. Taken initially to the hospital, his body was subsequently removed to the Prince's Dock Mortuary.

As one newspaper report noted, at first the police had only a vague notion as to whom this respectable-looking man was. They had the name Hancock in their possession and an inventory of the items found on his body. These included: a purse containing money, a silver keyless watch (No.1845), a steel Albert chain, a pair of spectacles in a case, eyeglasses, a pocket knife and three railway tickets. Presently, however, a positive identification was made and a second local newspaper carried a brief, but much more studied account of Joseph's life, noting that he had commanded Andrew Gibson's ships for nearly forty years prior to giving up the sea and going into business.[32]

Joseph was buried three days later at 2p.m. on Saturday 4 May at St Hilary's, the parish church of Wallasey, near Birkenhead, the same churchyard in which another of

Smith's old captains Benjamin Gleadell had been buried in 1888.[33] This picturesque and singular churchyard with its nineteenth-century church and an older surviving tower situated some little distance away surrounded by graves, was a favourite subject of the photographer Francis Frith, whose lens captured its Gothic splendour on a number of occasions during his career. Standing as it does at the peak of the hill dominating Wallasey, it commands a distant view of the Mersey estuary where Joseph had captained his own ships so many years before. His family and many friends and collegues from Andrew Gibson & Co., William Heath and James Carr from his present company and many others attended the ceremony. His gravestone still stands there, greeny brown and mottled with age, but the simple inscription gives no hint of his origins, nor of the adventurous life that this potter's son from Penkhull had led. It reads simply: 'In Loving Memory of Joseph Hancock, who entered into rest 1st May 1895, aged sixty-two years. In life beloved, in death lamented.'

Nor does the laconic headstone give any indication that Joseph was a wealthy man. Some time previously he had made a will and his entry in the probate index for that year reads:

HANCOCK, Joseph of 2-Victoria Place Seacombe, Cheshire, died 1 May 1895 at Lime Street, Liverpool. Probate Chester 20 June to William Heath bookkeeper and James Carr ships stores dealer. Effects £5191 12s. 2d.

How much went to his family is not made clear.

4

THE *MAJESTIC* YEARS

Following his brother's funeral Ted Smith took command of the *Germanic* for two transatlantic voyages; on 5 June the ship arrived in Queenstown in seven days, two hours and twenty-one minutes, the fastest east-bound time the twenty-year-old ship had ever achieved. However, his tenure aboard the *Germanic* was short-lived and in early July Smith was moved on once again, this time being appointed to command the SS *Majestic*, taking over from Captain Henry Parsell who had been transferred to shore duty to superintend the construction of the *Georgic* in Belfast. In doing so, Parsell was succeeded as the line's senior captain by J.G. Cameron of the *Teutonic*, and with Smith taking the *Majestic*, command of the *Germanic* was given to Captain E.R. McKinstry. Smith, meanwhile, would find himself treading the *Majestic's* bridge for most of the next nine years, making her his longest-held command.

Like all of the White Star ships of the Ismay era, the *Majestic* was a Northern Irish lass, born in the great shipyard of Harland & Wolff in Belfast in the late 1880s and delivered to White Star in March 1890. Both she and her sister ship the *Teutonic* were partly funded by the British Government under the proviso that they would have use of the ships for transport duties in wartime and the White Star management agreed to this.

The ship measured 582ft from stem to stern with a 57.7ft beam and weighed in at 9,965 tons and had accommodation for 1,490 passengers. As far as speed was concerned at her launch it was impressive enough, the *Majestic* having been built at a time when White Star still jousted for the coveted Blue Riband. Her two triple-expansion steam engines could push her to a very respectable 20 knots and although her maiden voyage had disappointed, on a west-bound voyage in August 1891, the ship snatched the title from the previous holder the *City of Paris*, with an average speed of 20.1 knots. The *Majestic* only held onto her laurels for a fortnight, however, her record being beaten by her sister ship *Teutonic*, which in turn lost the honour a year later when the *City of Paris* won it back. Since then faster ships had come into the competition and the *Majestic* had relaxed back into the role of a dependable albeit luxurious workhorse.

The *Majestic's* first voyage with Smith at the helm coincided with the formal opening of the Riverside Station for Atlantic travellers that made access to the

Liverpool docks much easier. Many of the White Star Line's directors came down on a special train for the ceremony and the first ship to benefit from the station was the *Majestic*. Mrs Ismay who attended the gathering with her husband noted in her diary that Captain Smith was in charge for the first time.[1]

Joining Smith aboard the *Majestic* were his old chief officer, forty-two-year-old Liverpool-born Cornelius Lancaster who had served with Smith in that capacity aboard the *Britannic* since at least December 1892, and First Officer J.B. Rawson who had been with Smith probably since 1894. They were familiar faces on a new ship which would have been a comfort to him.

Smith, though, was destined to form at least one long friendship with a member of the *Majestic's* crew. The ship's surgeon Dr William Francis Norman O'Loughlin was the same age as Smith. Born in Tralee, Ireland, he was orphaned soon afterwards and had been raised and educated by his uncle, but this had in no way held him back and he went on to study at Trinity College Dublin and then the Royal College of Surgeons in Dublin. At the age of twenty-one, poor health had prompted him to pursue a career at sea and so he became a ship's surgeon, a profession he would follow for the next forty years.

Dr O'Loughlin had served on a number of ships since then and had been aboard the *Majestic* for several years before Smith took command. He had a reputation as a keen sportsman and when ashore he was a regular team member whenever the ship got up a crew to take on another ship or local team. On 17 June for instance, he was part of the team that took on the Summer eleven of the Staten Island Cricket Club. Though he and another crew member gave the best innings, the *Majestic's* team still suffered a drubbing of fifty-seven runs to the Summer eleven's 155 runs.[2]

Like Smith, O'Loughlin seems to have been blessed with a great deal of personal charm which worked equally well with the crew and passengers, male and female. Stewardess Violet Jessop who later knew the good doctor, recalled in her memoirs that she and other members of the crew often popped their heads around his door for a dose of his cheery banter. She also noted that though he remained a lifelong bachelor, O'Loughlin had cultivated the reputation for being something of a ladies' man and decorated his surgery with photographs of the many beautiful and famous women passengers who had been his patients. Over the years he also became firm friends with numerous notable men such as Thomas Andrews, the nephew of Lord Pirrie, owner of Harland & Wolff; financier J. Pierpont Morgan; the White Star Line's chairman J. Bruce Ismay; and now, most fatefully perhaps, with Captain Edward John Smith. Fatefully, because O'Loughlin would with a few exceptions follow Smith from ship to ship over the next two decades, serving as chief surgeon on all the big ships Smith would command including the *Titanic*. O'Loughlin, like his old friend, would not survive that disaster.

Passengers, Reunions and Races

The first trip back and forth across the Atlantic passed without incident but the second trip to the States was interrupted when at 1.10p.m. on 10 August, thirty-four-year-old Swedish steerage passenger John H. Johnsen committed suicide by throwing himself over the rail from the after main deck. Alerted to what had happened Captain Smith stopped the ship as quickly as he could and two lifeboats were manned and lowered into the water, but no trace could be found of the man. After searching for an hour the boats returned to the steamer and the *Majestic* continued with her voyage. Mr Johnsen, it was supposed, had gone temporarily insane.[3]

The *Majestic*'s third trip to the USA, which started from Liverpool on 4 September and finished in New York on the 11th, also caught the interest of newspapermen as it was a very fast crossing of the Atlantic, the trip taking six days and thirty minutes. This was achieved despite the ship encountering some very rough weather. The *Majestic* had met with moderate to strong westerly winds up to 8 September, but then the wind had shifted sharply to the north and *Majestic* was plunged into the heart of a fearsome gale with high seas. The wind shifted yet again on the 9th, first to the north-west then to the south-west, but there was no let up in the heavy going until late in the afternoon when the winds moderated. The weather was much calmer from then until the ship reached New York.

Among the passengers for this swift if rough crossing was the former reporter, explorer and recently elected MP, Henry Morton Stanley, the man who had 'presumed' so famously when he finally located Dr Livingstone in the heart of Africa many years before. Like most press snippets, we only get half the story, there being no indication as to why Stanley and his family were abroad, whether for business or pleasure.

Another passenger for this voyage who became a good friend of Smith's ashore was Colonel William Washington Gordon (1834–1912), one of Savannah's leading citizens. A former lawyer and Confederate army officer during the American Civil War, Gordon became by turns a cotton merchant, state legislator and would presently gain promotion to brigadier general during the Spanish-American War of 1898. Their acquaintance may have been an old one, for as Gordon had been a Savannah cotton merchant it may not be too far-fetched to suppose that Smith had got to know him during the days when he was transporting cotton aboard the *Lizzie Fennell*. Certainly the two were on good terms and many years later Smith was still sending General Gordon his best wishes.[4]

According to Smith's old school friend William Jones, it was at this time that he met Smith for the last time when the captain briefly returned to the Potteries. According to Mr Jones's account, Smith had just completed two or three journeys in command of the *Majestic* and had returned to Hanley to see his brother-in-law.[5] As already noted, William Harrington had in fact recently died and Mr Jones may have actually seen Smith earlier that year, perhaps if he had attended William's funeral at Hanley Cemetery. Alternatively, Smith could have been in town to meet with

William and Thyrza's son James Harrington, who had served under him on the *Lizzie Fennell*. Smith kept in contact with his nephew and perhaps kept his eye on him after his father's death; certainly James later delivered an emotional eulogy at Smith's memorial and a number of the captain's personal items were passed down to James Harrington after the *Titanic* disaster, including the decorated loving cup that Smith had acquired on passing his master's exam in 1875.

There was, though, another possible reason why Smith may have paid a visit to the Potteries at this time. In 1911, a newspaper article noted that sixteen years previously in 1895, Captain Smith had been invited to attend an Etruria British School reunion planned by some of the old boys and timed so that it would coincide with Smith's shore leave. Though no exact date is given and efforts to trace the reunion in the local newspapers has proven fruitless, according to reports it was well attended, many coming to pay their respects to their old teacher, Alfred Smith, who had long since retired from the school. Smith's old friend Spencer Till attended the get-together as did Edmund Jones, Jesse Shirley, Mr H.B. Shirley, Mr Hall of the Potteries Electric Traction Company and Major Cecil Wedgwood of the famous potting family, who would later go on to be the first Mayor of the newly federated Stoke-on-Trent in 1910. In a separate report three other individuals are also mentioned; there was a Mr D. Hughes and a Mr Smallwood as well as a gentleman from Hull whose initials were W.T., but whose surname is unreadable in the old paper. There were many more there, however, for as Spencer Till noted, a group photograph was taken by a Mr Govern; some years later in 1913, Till wrote sadly to Smith's widow that seventeen of those in the photograph, including Alfred and Ted Smith, were dead.[6]

Whatever the reason for his visit to the Potteries, Smith was soon back at work and a couple of voyages later found him making the news once more, pulling off quite a coup in the race to win the Atlantic mail contract to the States. This was highly coveted and in late 1895 the honour was up for grabs. Though she may have long since lost the Blue Riband, *Majestic* was put forward as a candidate to run against the new American liner *St Louis*.

The race started from New York on 17 October 1895. The *St Louis* had a head start, leaving the North River at 11a.m., four hours before its rival. Despite the fact that the *St Louis* would have to sail 275 miles further than the *Majestic*, the New York postal authority had complete faith in her. The ship carried a post office with postal workers to sort the mail prior to arrival; the *Majestic* did not. As a result, the American ship was given twice the amount of mail that the *Majestic* was to carry. Then there was the rail advantage once she reached Britain, the *St Louis* was heading for Southampton, whereas the *Majestic* was as usual bound for Liverpool via Queenstown. As the aim of the race was to get the New York mails to London first, Southampton's proximity to the capital could be telling. To the American press the ten-year mail contract that depended on this competition was as good as in the bag.

Predictably, there was no fanfare for the departure of the British ship when Smith took her out at 3p.m. the same day. Once away from the coast of America for the next few days there was silence until on 24 October the news came back that the *St Louis* had lost the race, but more through sheer bad luck than anything else. Some 800 miles from Southampton, the *St Louis* had been caught in a moderate gale. A high sea broke her rudder and for the rest of the journey her skipper Captain Randle had steered the ship with her propellors.

The *St Louis* was seen signalling off Prawle Point on the morning of the 24th and two tugs were sent out to meet her at the Needles to ease her passage into Southampton. Everyone aboard was well, but the ungainly progression over the last few days had given Smith and the *Majestic* time to land the mails at Queenstown well ahead of the *St Louis*. By default White Star got the contract to carry the US mails for the next ten years. For White Star it was no mean victory; the mail contract, as well as carrying the caché afforded to mail boats, was also a nice little earner, netting the company an estimated $644,800 a year. For the newly appointed skipper of the *Majestic*, his victory over the *St Louis* was a good start to his prestigious new command and even if chance had played a good part in it, it was still a feather in his cap with the White Star management.[7]

The Storm King

Some months passed before Smith and the *Majestic* were back in the news again. The new year was as usual one of rough weather and storms. On 18 February 1896, whilst en route to Liverpool, the *Majestic* arrived off Queenstown in such a heavy sea that the tenders that were to take off the mails and passengers could not come alongside. With no other option, the *Majestic*, therefore, continued on her way, the passengers and mail still aboard. Then a few weeks later, having left New York on 8 April 1896, the ship experienced two days of rough gales, with waves crashing over the ship and passengers confined to their cabins. That the latter was necessary was shown when a sailor was lost overboard in the storm. Then another four months pass and we catch a glimpse of the ship in fine weather and smooth seas making the fastest west-bound voyage of her career thus far, a time of five days, seventeen hours and fifty-six minutes, twelve minutes better than her previous best four years before, but it was now too slow to secure the Blue Riband. Then in November, newspapers reported that a steward named Creal committed suicide from the *Majestic* by throwing himself overboard.[8]

At some point in his career, though when exactly is unclear, Captain Smith began to be referred to in some quarters as 'the Storm King' in setting out or bringing his ships home through the worst weather. One newspaper report from 1896 sheds some light on how this reputation came about.

On 15 December that year, a major storm set in over New York during the afternoon. By evening this had developed into a severe snow storm and Sandy Hook was reporting winds of 40mph, adding that the snow was thick offshore. Telegraph lines were down and off the coast a schooner had been abandoned by her crew and was drifting before the wind, presenting a serious hazard to shipping. The thick snow had cut down and delayed river traffic and severely disrupted travel across the board. By the next morning the weather was still appalling. Two snow-caked steamers had reached Ellis Island that morning, but nothing was leaving the port. The *St Louis*, *Noorland* and *Majestic* were docked and it was doubted that any of them would leave that day. Smith, though, was not daunted by the storm and readied his ship for sea.

The *Majestic* left port late on the 16th and sailed straight into the maelstrom. Newspaper reports of the voyage spoke of ferocious winds, snow and sleet blasting across the decks and of towering waves crashing over the rails, while the passengers locked their doors and otherwise kept below decks as the *Majestic* ploughed across the Atlantic. If the weather was bad at the start of the journey, on the third day a further hazard was thrown into the mix when an iceberg loomed into sight. Smith was on the bridge almost constantly during the voyage and he now doubtless gave the berg a very wide berth, reporting on it when the battered ship reached Queenstown. Despite the terrible conditions which slowed the journey, the ship made landfall at Queenstown at 11a.m. on 24 December and probably reached Liverpool later that day or early in the morning on Christmas Day.[9]

The year 1897 was an auspicious one in Britain, for that year Queen Victoria had been on the throne for sixty years. The diamond jubilee celebrations would see large numbers of officials and visitors flocking to Britain from around the world to join in the festivities. The *Majestic* played her part in transporting some of these over from North America, one of her most important passengers being the Hon. Whitelaw Reid, the special ambassador selected to represent the American government at the celebrations. He came bearing a letter of congratulations from President McKinley. Reid, his family and over 1,200 other passengers were landed at Liverpool on 10 June 1897. Most immediately clambered aboard the trains bound for London. Amongst those who came across with him were many expatriates, who had made the trip back to Britain for the jubilee and who were surprised at how Liverpool had grown since they had left the country many years before.[10]

Liverpool had indeed changed a great deal in the thirty years that Ted Smith had been living and working there. In 1871, shortly after he had first arrived, Liverpool was an impressively large collection of townships with a population of 493,405 people. It was granted city status in 1880 and by the time of the jubilee, had grown into one of the greatest ports in the Empire, with a population of about 650,000 people. In 1895, over 3,000 ships entered and cleared the docks that year, shifting 95 million tons of imports and 90 million tons of exports and each year had showed a marked increase on the last. During that time over half a dozen new docks had been opened on the river front to accommodate this increased trade.

Some of these docks can be seen in an early film of Liverpool made by the Lumiere brothers in 1896 and these reveal that despite the revolution in steam, the bulk of the world's cargo was still being transported by sailing ships. Dozens of sailing vessels crowd the wharfs and unloading sheds with an occasional glimpse of a compact steamer going about its business, clearing the dock or steaming along the Mersey.

The wealth generated by this trade was considerable and had allowed the city fathers to indulge in ostentatious displays of civic pride. The Lumieres' camera recorded the many high-fronted shops, tall porticoed civic structures and streets teeming with horse-drawn carts and omnibuses. Most notable though, are the crowds of people, from curious children, shop and dock workers, office workers, policemen and the occasional upper-class gent in topper and tails.

· The high-class building projects had barely touched the waterfront. Liverpool's Pier Head is today dominated by the 'Three Graces' – the Royal Liver Building, the Cunard Building and the Port of Liverpool Building, but these iconic structures would not be built until the early decades of the twentieth century. White Star, however, had taken the plunge. Up until 1895, the company headquarters had been located at 10 Water Street, but that year the company started construction on its new offices just around the corner at 30 James Street, situated just behind the docks. By 1897, the building was finished and open for business.

The new building, which still stands to this day to the rear of the 'Three Graces', is a stylish Gothic confection of dressed grey stone and red and cream bricks with high roofs, Dormer windows and round corner turrets, one of which held the office of J. Bruce Ismay, the son of Thomas Ismay, who as chief executive now held the reins in his father's firm. From here it was said that Ismay could keep an eye not only on his own ships, but also those of his rivals, most notably Cunard, and as a now valued senior skipper Smith doubtless had occasion to pass through its doors on more than one instance over the next few years.

Whilst ex-patriots were admiring the bigger, improved Liverpool prior to setting off for London, back in the United States, New York's Harbour lost one of its prominent structures when on 14 June the Ellis Island Station went up in flames. Though no lives were lost, the fire gutted the massive wooden structure and most of the Federal and State immigration records dating back to 1855 were destroyed in the blaze. The US government quickly ordered a replacement facility to be built with the proviso that the structure would be fireproof. This, though, would not be ready for some years and in the meantime, the processing of immigrants was moved to the company piers. This necessitated some delay and confusion for Smith and his fellow captains and crews at first, but within a matter of a few weeks the system was running smoothly.

'Mel'

We hear nothing more of note about Smith and his good ship for the rest of 1897, but in the latter half of the year he was given plenty to think about at home when Eleanor announced that she was pregnant. The couple had been married now for just over ten years and this appears to have been Eleanor's first and only pregnancy.

Doubtless the nomadic lifestyle led by her husband had stopped them starting a family earlier. The fact that both of them seem to have been doting parents perhaps indicates that they may have happily had more children had the circumstances been more conducive, but it was not to be. Nonetheless, it was doubtless a happy time for both of them.

Not that Ted Smith was there, though, to see Eleanor through much of her term. During the latter half of 1897, he undertook five more return trips to the States and three more in 1898. Being as busy as he was there was a good chance that Smith would not be there for the birth of his child and doubtless Eleanor had someone looking after her during her final weeks. Fortune, though, seems to have smiled on the sea captain and the indications are that he was in Liverpool when on 2 April 1898, Eleanor gave birth to a daughter at their family home 20 Alexandra Road, Waterloo.

Ted himself would later go to register the birth on 3 May. The baby girl would prosper. In a picture probably taken at the turn of the century which was reproduced in newspapers and books after the *Titanic* disaster, she is seen as a cherubic curly-haired infant seated on her mother's knee, though by that time she was actually a fourteen-year-old schoolgirl.

She was baptised Helen Melville Smith, but like her mother before her she preferred to be known by her middle name, Melville. This rather masculine-sounding Scottish name was an unusual one for a girl even by Victorian standards. Pat Lacey suggests that the baby girl's middle name came from Melville House in Fife, where she claims Ted and Eleanor had taken holidays in the past. John Pladdys in a well-known article on her, also ascribed the name to her parents' love for Scotland.[11] Despite her preference for her middle name, Melville softened its clunkiness in going by the shortened version of 'Mel'. Her father, though, gave her a few nicknames, one was alluded to by Eleanor after his death when she referred to Melville as 'his Gillie' – girly. But as J.E. Hodder Williams noted, he often also referred to her by another nickname, 'Babs', which was probably a pet form of baby.[12]

Though he was often away Smith would dote on his daughter, buying her presents and organising little parties for her when he was ashore. In John Pladdys' article there is a picture of Mel seated on the grass in the back garden of the Smith's future Southampton home, looking for all the world like a well-dressed Alice in Wonderland, a lapdog on her knees and a caged bird on the lawn nearby, presents perhaps from her father. He also wrote small notes to her, many of which she preserved. Such a one is dated 29 November 1906. Illustrated by Smith with a stylised bird carrying a letter addressed to Mel in its beak, he wrote underneath:

My dear Daughter,
I could not catch a little Bunny to send you on my letter so send you this card by this little bird. I hope mother & you and Gladys are well. I shall soon be home.
(D.V./Your loving)
Daddy

The note though brief gives a few more insights into the relative enigma that is E.J. Smith. John Pladdys notes that in his messages to Mel that Smith always alluded to future events with the initials 'D.V.' ('deo volente' – 'God willing', or 'if all goes well' as Hodder Williams had noted), though who 'Gladys' was remains a mystery. But above all it is a touching message showing a father missing his child.[13]

The Transport Captain

As already noted, during all this domestic excitement Ted Smith had still been at work. For the most part it was run-of-the-mill, though occasionally there was some press excitement when the *Majestic* docked. On 10 March 1898 for instance, the ship arrived in New York with a cargo of gold bullion worth £2,582,500.[14] Since February, the ship had also been sailing back and forth through potentially hostile waters. After years of tension over Cuba and as a result of the sinking of the US warship USS *Maine* in Havana Harbour, the United States had declared war on Spain. Most of the war would take place at sea being slugged out around Spain's colonies, which were being reinforced by Spanish battleships sailing from the homeland. As a result, the American and European press were eager for any news regarding the Spanish ships and pounced on the skippers, crews and passengers of the transatlantic steamers hoping for easy copy. As representatives of a neutral power, though, Smith and his crew had been advised by the White Star management to say nothing.

Smith was doubtless still rather sky-high from the birth of his daughter when he found himself sailing into this tricky situation on returning to duty in mid-April. *Majestic* arrived in New York on 14 April and by the 27th she was back at Queenstown. During the return crossing, at midnight on the previous Saturday, whilst some 1,700 miles west of the British Isles, the *Majestic* apparently passed a battleship and three torpedo boats heading west and it was presumed that they were Spanish vessels. The report was unconfirmed as Smith and his people kept a diplomatic silence on the matter and J. Bruce Ismay denied the rumour when the *Majestic* docked. Not so the passengers who quite freely related what they believed they had seen to waiting reporters.[15]

Smith may, anyhow, have had more pressing matters to deal with. A small report carried in the American newspapers described how on arriving at Liverpool later that same day, the *Majestic* collided heavily with the quay, damaging her stem and breaking several of her plates, causing her to leak. The damage, though, was not as serious as this sounds and the ship sailed for New York as scheduled on 5 May.[16]

The next time we hear about the *Majestic* is on 1 September 1898, when the ship sailed from Liverpool carrying amongst her more notable passengers Mr Joseph Chamberlain, the Secretary of State for the Colonies, and his wife. Chamberlain was on his way to the States to discuss an Anglo-American alliance. During the journey back to Britain a month later, again aboard Smith's ship, Mr Chamberlain and his wife presided at a concert given aboard the liner where he gave a speech intimating that to his mind the Anglo-American alliance was to be settled in a short time. He returned to Britain fully convinced of that fact.[17]

In late January 1899, Smith and his crew welcomed another famous man aboard the *Majestic*, arguably more influential than Joseph Chamberlain. Rudyard Kipling, one of the most famous writers of the Victorian era, and his American wife, took passage to the United States. On arrival in the States, they and the other passengers had to wait up to five hours for the customs inspectors to carry out the new stringent examinations of all the luggage. Kipling and his family planned to visit Mrs Kipling's family in Vermont, but whilst in New York he and two of his children developed pneumonia and though it was touch-and-go for a while – Kipling was described as 'hovering between life and death' – he would recover, though his six-year-old daughter Josephine was not so lucky, succumbing to her illness on 6 March. On 29 March, Kipling's father John also came over on the *Majestic* to see his ailing son.[18]

Apart from another bout of stormy weather that Smith reported in mid-February and the usual press notices concerning notable travellers and ship arrivals and departures, the rest of the year is something of a blank; Smith and the *Majestic* warranted little interest from the press. Later that year, though, Smith, like many other senior British merchant captains, found themselves very much in the limelight when they became involved, albeit in a small way, in one of their own nation's wars. The second Boer War had broken out between British Cape Colony and the small neighbouring Boer republics. Regarded at first as merely another little war of empire, it turned out to be one of the hardest-fought conflicts of the Victorian age. Though small in number compared to the forces brought against them, the better armed, motivated and much more mobile Boer commandos proved formidable foes and it took two years, nearly half a million imperial troops and several punishing British defeats before the Boers were finally overwhelmed.

As the conflict developed and sucked in more and more soldiers, there were criticisms from some quarters that the Admiralty seemed to have chartered the slowest merchant vessels they could find to send out reinforcements to the war zone. Stung into action as a result, they chartered several faster liners including three top White Star vessels, Smith's *Majestic*, Captain Lindsay's SS *Cymric* and the *Britannic* under Bertram Hayes. As all three were RNR officers they got to take their ships out to the war zone in person.

The *Majestic* was at sea and out of contact when the news reached New York on 14 November that the ship was to be taken up as a transport. Two days later on the morning of the 16th, the ship arrived at New York after a rough crossing that had obliged the passengers to remain indoors. It was here that an outward-bound British merchantman saluted the liner with a blast from her whistles which lasted five minutes. Puzzled by the display, Smith must have mentioned it to the pilot who then informed him that his vessel had been chartered as a troop transport. As a result, the merchantman received an equally long blast from the *Majestic's* whistles in reply. The news was greeted with delight by the *Majestic's* officers.

'Well, this is good news,' said Purser Brandt. 'Will we go? Well, of course we will. Every man on board will stay with the ship if he can.' Smith was a little more circumspect when reporters accosted him on the dock, eager for his opinion.

'Yes, I have received unofficial information that the vessel is to be sent to South Africa but I cannot say what my orders are until I hear from the office of the line. I cannot say anything until then.'

Only right and proper, but it was obvious to all that like his men he was delighted at the prospect of war service. [19]

When it came time for the *Majestic* to return home on 22 November, before departure, Smith's American friends presented him with a large floral horseshoe with the inscription 'Safe Return' on it. Later, as the ship left her berth and set off down New York Harbour, the *Majestic* received a 'noisy godsend' from many of the ships in the harbour, led by the White Star ships *Cymric* and *Georgic*. [20]

On arriving back at Liverpool on 29 November, Smith and the crew of the *Majestic* learnt of the death of Thomas Ismay on 23 November. Though he had retired in 1892, Thomas had retained the chairmanship of the line and still took an active interest in its fortunes even though the day-to-day running had passed to his son J. Bruce Ismay. The death would have been keenly felt by the senior commanders such as Smith, most of whom owed much of the success in their careers and indeed their advancement to the skill that Thomas Ismay had shown in building up his great shipping company. Bertram Hayes, who took a certain pride in being the last commander appointed by the old chairman, wrote of him, 'He was always just and considerate to us in all circumstances, and took a personal interest in our welfare.' [21] The younger Ismay now took up the mantle of chairmanship and while his ship was being prepared for its new duties, Smith doubtless went to pay his respects and condolences to the Ismay family.

The *Majestic*, meantime, was taken out of passenger service and dock crews moved in to prepare her for much more rough and ready duty. A photograph of Hayes's *Britannic* from this period shows that she had her hull painted white and 'No.62' stencilled on her side, but it is unclear how much of a transformation the *Majestic* underwent. A photograph held at the Southampton City Museum shows troops aboard the *Majestic*, but the portion of her hull that can be seen seems grey, or possibly black. Even if she were not repainted, the ship would have certainly been cleared of its most valuable fittings; expensive flooring was covered over with boarding to deal with thousands of hobnail boots. She was fitted for seventy officers and more than 2,000 men. The bulk of them were berthed aft, where room was made for 101 messes by removing the second-class cabins and the third-class married passengers' quarters. Another forty messes were accommodated forward. As might be expected, the officers had the first-class saloons and cabins for their accommodation, except for a portion reserved for a hospital. All this refitting was carried out in less than a fortnight, after which extensive stores were laid down for the longer journey and her bunkers were filled with as much coal as she could carry. As a result the ship lay deep in the water, drawing 29ft, and to avoid getting stranded by low tides she had rested at anchor in the river since the previous Sunday.

Smith's officers for the trip down to the Cape were Chief Officer James O. Carter, First Officer A.E. Rimmer; Second officer H.W. Seile-Dibb; Third Officer E.R. White; Chief Engineer J. Barber; and ship's surgeon A.W. McKenzie. Under them they had an experienced crew that would remain largely unchanged until the ship re-entered passenger service early the next year. With the officers and crew in place, troop transport No.68 as the *Majestic* was now designated, was ready to take on her passengers.

For this first voyage, Smith and the *Majestic* were to take to the Cape the 1st Battalion York and Lancaster Regiment, drafts of the 1st Battalion Somerset Light Infantry, 1st Battalion the Border Regiment, King's Royal Rifles, the Rifle Brigade, depot companies of the Royal Army Medical Corps Field Hospital and details. There was also a single passenger, the Spanish military attaché who would accompany the troops to the war zone. These were to arrive on the morning of 13 December 1899. The dock authorities and civil powers knew from experience that there would be crowds gathered to see the soldiers off and stringent arrangements were therefore made to afford a speedy trouble-free loading. A cordon was drawn around the docks and tickets were issued to those who needed to enter.

Reporters were there to describe the scene that morning. The *Majestic*, all ablaze with electric lights, had lain at the Prince's landing stage all night. As the morning came, cold and grey with a scattering of snow to be seen on the distant roofs, the police moved in, as too did the first crowds waiting for the troop trains that would unload at the quayside. The first train carrying the Border Regiment draft arrived from Shorncliffe Barracks a little before 8a.m. The soldiers had travelled all night, they were stiff and cold from the journey, but were soon piling out of the wagons and the dock front became a sea of pale khaki, intermingled with the darker clothes of the police, civilian officials and White Star personnel. In place of passengers' luggage, rifles and kit bags were piled before the ship ready for loading. The soldiers were very pleased with an arrangement made by the White Star Line with the British Workmen's Public-house Association to provide a canteen on the landing stage. On alighting every man had a cup of coffee and a meat pie. Things were decidedly chaotic at first but the need to get on and get the first contingent on board and out of the way as quickly as possible before more arrived soon motivated them.

More trains arrived and the same scenes presented themselves, while the crowd of well-wishers and onlookers increased outside the cordon, cheering and waving flags as the soldiers' trains arrived. The last of these pulled into the docks at 10.30a.m. and the next four or five hours were a busy time for Captain Smith and his crew. In total 2,068 officers and men had to be shown to their places around the ship, where they then probably received a lecture on the dos and don'ts of life aboard a ship at sea. Smith doubtless had to meet the senior officers of these various detachments and he and his own officers would have arranged rotas for meals and exercise for the different contingents.

Only when everything had been sorted out did the ship leave the Prince's landing stage at 3p.m. To those on the dock the *Majestic* seemed to be one living, moving forest of men from stem to stern. Despite the long night journey, the cold and the fatigue none of the soldiers went below until they had seen the last of their friends who crowded the shore to bid them farewell. Clad in their thick grey overcoats, they clustered along the upper deck, the rigging and every vantage point they could find, waving their caps and handkerchiefs. One of the regimental bands was playing military airs on deck, but the men began to sing 'God Save the Queen' so loudly that the band gave up the struggle and joined in. As the ship swung round and began to move away a chorus of whistles arose from the nearest steamers, some of them crowded with sightseers, who waved and cheered. It was a moving moment and the people of Liverpool had risen to the occasion.

The ship, though, did not finally leave the Mersey until 7p.m. that evening and the delayed departure may have been partly due to the fact that a dramatic rescue was taking place. One unfortunate aspect attendant on this popular departure was that many of the soldiers had turned up extremely drunk, drink having been thrust upon them by well meaning friends. This now nearly had fatal results when one Private W. Cooper of the Somerset Light Infantry, who had been hanging drunkenly onto the ratlines, loosened his grip and fell overboard into the ice cold Mersey. One of the *Majestic*'s crew, twenty-one-year-old Canadian Butcher's Mate Ilted John Morris, immediately sprang into the water after him through a porthole and at great personal risk, as both men were dangerously near to the ship's twin screws, he supported Private Cooper until they were both pulled from the water. A reporter who witnessed the scene saw Private Cooper taken away in a cab in a state of utter intoxication.[22]

The *Majestic* left the Mersey that night after lying at anchor off New Brighton for some hours. In the meantime the brave butcher's mate Ilted Morris (who later received the Royal Humane Society's Bronze Medal for his actions)[23], a chastened, hung-over Private Cooper and two or three other soldiers who had been left behind were put on board by the White Star tender *Magnetic*.

Then they were off. However, despite giving in to the popular clamour for faster transport ships, the Admiralty laid a leaden hand on its merchant greyhounds, restricting their cruising speed to a maximum of 17½ knots. This despite the fact that White Star would have been only too happy to let Smith and his fellow captains push their ships up to 19 knots. Nonetheless, *Majestic* made fairly good time. There was a day and a half stopover at St Vincent in the Cape Verde Islands off the west coast of Africa to take on more coal, the ship then crossed the equator and followed the long coast of the continent down to Cape Colony itself. The long sea journey gave the soldiers ample time to practice their shooting and as Bertram Hayes recalled, the sight of lines of soldiers drawn up on parade along the ship's decks became a very familiar scene. Doubtless Christmas was celebrated in style on the 25th, hearty meals being culled from the ship's stores.

During the voyage down there the crew list noted one tragedy when a trimmer, twenty-year-old Peter Doran, died as a result of asphyxiation, but otherwise the voyage was trouble-free. Then on 30 December, seventeen days after leaving Liverpool, the *Majestic* came in sight of Table Mountain and shortly afterwards she arrived at Cape Town, the capital of the British colony. Here some of the troops departed, but that evening the *Majestic* moved on to Durban in Natal province, where most of her troops disembarked. A few days after this, *Lloyd's List* once again placed the *Majestic* back at Cape Town, where she remained for a couple of weeks. It may have been during this long interlude that Smith, that proud son of the Empire, did a little imperial sightseeing, on one occasion visiting the estate of the late Cecil Rhodes, just outside Cape Town.[24]

For the return journey back to Britain, the *Majestic* took on a party of 183 wounded, many of them from the Battle of Belmont, an incompetently fought action that had taken place at the end of November 1899. Amongst the wounded from the battle were General Featherstonhaugh, Major Dalrymple Hamilton of the Scots Guards and Mr E.F. Knight, a reporter from the *Morning Post* newspaper, who had got a little too close to the action and lost an arm to a dum dum bullet. With these and others aboard, the ship finally sailed on 17 January 1900. She again stopped at St Vincent and arrived in Southampton Water early on 2 February.

It was a bitterly cold morning at Southampton and although snow had been falling for some hours there was a fairly good attendance of friends and relations awaiting the *Majestic's* arrival. The *Majestic* was early in dock, but the wounded were not landed immediately. This arose from the fact that the ship was initially placed at a berth where there was only a partially completed shed in which a special train was waiting for Netley. Colonel Stackpole, the man in charge of all transport arrangements at the port, did not consider it advisable to allow injured men to disembark in so bleak and cold a spot and so the vessel was ordered to another berth, which delayed the disembarkation for some time.[25]

There was no return to Liverpool at this point, the next batch of reinforcements joined the ship at Southampton. These were the 3rd (Militia) Battalion the Lancashire Regiment, 3rd (Militia) Battalion the Welsh Regiment and two contingents of reinforcements for the Guards Brigade and the Highland Light Infantry, a total of 1,864 men. A few of the ship's crew changed places with others and a new officer C.C. Boase replaced Third Officer White on Smith's bridge.

Once again cheered on its way by a large crowd, the *Majestic* sailed from Southampton's Pembroke Dock at 3.45p.m. on 12 February and a week later again touched at St Vincent, reaching Cape Town on 1 March. Twelve days later the ship had again moved to Durban where she stayed for a few days before returning to Cape Town. Here she took on 350 sick and wounded officers and men and on 22 March the ship set off back to Britain. By 6 April, *Majestic* had arrived back at Southampton and by the 11th she had reached Liverpool again where she was soon converted back to a passenger liner.[26]

Back in Business

His Boer War service over, for Captain Smith it was back to business as usual for the next year, but with a few changes, not the least of which was virtually an entirely new bridge crew. Of the team that took the *Majestic* to South Africa and back only H.W. Seile-Dibb remained with the ship. The new chief was thirty-eight-year-old W. Herbert Calvert; Charles Edwin Stark was first officer; Seile-Dibb returned as second officer; E.F. Crosby was third and the fourth officer was J.R. Jones. Even Seile-Dibb would be gone a voyage later and there would be numerous changes of officers during the rest of the year, all of which was probably quite troublesome for Smith. Once again, though, for the most part Smith's return to North Atlantic service remains a blank so far as his life is concerned. One incidental thing we do know about is that from late 1900, Smith's ships were again sending people through Ellis Island, the new fireproof facility having been officially opened for business on 17 December that year. It is not until March 1901, though, that we catch up with Smith again when it was reported that when the ship arrived in New York on the 14th one of her passengers was the Italian inventor and wireless pioneer Guglielmo Marconi. He had sailed to the States for a month-long trip to investigate possible sites for wireless radio stations in New England and other sites along the North American Atlantic coast. He told waiting reporters that the North German Lloyd steamship line would be the first to install his new wireless apparatus, but he could not say what other shipping lines would adopt it. As it turned out most of the major shipping lines would follow suit, the White Star Line taking the plunge five years later. Marconi's apparatus would soon prove its worth and for Smith at least the wireless system would play a significant part at the very end of his career.

In the meantime, shortly after Smith's arrival at New York, he was called upon to take part in a naval court to pass judgement on the crew of a British ship that had been wrecked off the American coast. The *Camperdown*, a British steamer carrying 20,000 bags of sugar, had become stranded on the Cape Lookout Shoals on 4 March and all attempts to help and communicate with the crew had been hampered by heavy seas and thick hazy weather. For nearly three days the ship had bumped about on the shoals until early on the 7th it floated free. The crew then went to the captain and asked him to put into Norfolk, Virginia, as the ship was surely damaged. However, having sounded his ship the skipper was sure they could still make it to New York, but the crew disagreed and refused to work and obey orders. It was a clear case of mutiny and the *Camperdown*'s captain immediately ordered the twelve ringleaders arrested and the ship was brought in by the rest of the crew. Here, the twelve men were given over to the New York Police, but as they were serving under the British flag they were then handed over to the British Consul.

Thus, on 11 March, the mutineeers were marshalled into Sir Percy Sanderson's office where they were charged with wilful disobedience to lawful orders and wilful neglect of duty. The Consul General had called upon the two most senior British skippers then in port, namely Smith and Captain Edward Taylor of the steamer *Sabine* to sit in with him. The hearing lasted for five days in which eight separate testimonies were heard. After listening to all the arguements Sanderson, Smith and Taylor concluded that it had been a mutiny and Sir Percy delivered his verdict on the 16th. After outlining the events he said:

> There has been throughout a manifest endeavor to dictate to the Captain, and a spirit of insubordination has been shown such as renders a seaman especially a danger to himself and to all who sail with him. This court will do all it can to mark its sense of the gravity of this offense.

The court stopped short of imposing a prison sentence, but ordered that each of the twelve men be fined fourteen days' pay plus expenses attributable to their arrest and the court's proceedings.[27]

His stint on the bench over, Smith returned to Britain in time to be included in the 1901 census. At the time, namely the night of 31 March 1901, the *Majestic* was in Liverpool, but the master 'Edward James Smith' (sic) was not aboard. The vessel held a handful of men under the command of Third Officer John Aitken. Nor was Smith at 17 Marine Crescent; his home was being looked after by his mother-in-law, Sarah Pennington, her daughter Maria and two servants the cook Kate Chambers and the teenage housemaid Annie Brett. Ted, Eleanor and Mel were instead visiting Smith's old friend Thomas Jones and his family at 32 Leinster Gardens in Runcorn. Mr Jones was no longer listed as a brewer, but as a much more upmarket-sounding 'spirit merchant'.

Smith and his friends were on the up as too were some of his relations; in the Potteries, his nephew and old shipmate James Harrington was prospering as a builder and decorator. But it was not a bed of roses for all of his relatives and since the death of her husband William, Ted's half-sister Thyrza, now sixty years old, had fallen on harder times. According to the census she now worked as a domestic servant for one William Edward Hand and his family at 22 Manning Road, Southport. Mr Hand was originally from Newcastle-under-Lyme in Staffordshire, so Thyrza may have gained employment through an old acquaintance.

A few days after the census, Smith was back aboard the *Majestic*, bound for New York once more. What would have otherwise been a normal, mundane journey, was made slightly more interesting when, on 7 April, a bolt fractured in the *Majestic*'s starboard engine and the ship limped along awkwardly on her port engine whilst repairs were effected, all of which delayed the ship's arrival in New York by a day.

Later that same year, the *Majestic* was again in the news when at 5a.m. on 7 August, a fire broke out in one of the ship's linen closets just before she arrived at New York. A hole was made in the deck above the closet and water was poured in. This appeared to extinguish the blaze, however five hours later clouds of billowing smoke was again seen coming from the closet, which forced breakfasting saloon passengers, including millionaire John D. Rockefeller, to flee the promenade deck until the fire was brought under control. This time, steam from the ship's boilers was injected into the recess and this finally did the trick. The fire, which appears to have been caused by sparks from electrical wires, caused no injuries to passengers or crew and there was no serious damage done to the ship.[28]

Early the next year, the crew of the *Majestic* saw a whole ship ablaze. On 3 January 1902, the *Majestic* was mid-Atlantic when smoke was sighted in the distance and presently the source of the blaze hove into view. This was the Canadian schooner *Clifton of Windsor*. Smith noted the name of the ship and that the vessel had been abandoned and reported the sighting when they made port. Other press reports told the rest of the story. Disabled and flooded in a storm, the schooner's crew had sent up distress signals that were soon answered by the steamer *Exeter City*. On close inspection the *Clifton of Windsor* was seen to be unsalvageable and the crew was evacuated. The ship now low in the water was deemed a hazard to navigation and set alight and she attracted the attention of many more passing ships as a result.

In early March 1902, the sea caused more damage to the *Majestic* than any fire did, when en route to New York the ship ran into a terrific storm. It was near midnight on the Saturday and the ship was battling her way through huge seas mid-ocean. Smith was on the bridge keeping an anxious eye on the situation which had all the potential of turning worse at any minute. Then suddenly it did, when a terrific wave crashed over the ship, and when it receded the forward lifeboat had gone as well as the davits that held it and not a rope or anything was left to show that a lifeboat had hung there. Smith had seen what happened and immediately had the crew fix extra ropes to the rest of the boats as a precaution.

There was again a fair turnover in officers aboard the *Majestic* in 1902. One man who arrived in mid-July was to play a role later on in Smith's career. On 14 July, the *Majestic* was set to start her latest voyage. Smith was in command, thirty-nine-year-old Alexander Hambleton was chief officer, A.E.S. Cooper was first, A.W. Barker was second and J. Mawdsley was initially down as third with G. Morgan as fourth. At the last minute, though, Mawdsley was transferred and his place was taken by a fresh-faced twenty-eight-year-old named Charles Herbert Lightoller.

Despite his youthful looks, Lightoller had crammed a lifetime's worth of adventure into his time at sea. Since the age of seventeen he had been shipwrecked on a desert island, survived a fire at sea, a cyclone and a serious bout of malaria. Giving up the sea at one point he had gone to the Yukon to join the gold rush but without success, worked as a cowboy and then journeyed across North America as a hobo, riding in railway wagons to make his way back to the east coast. Arriving back in Britain penniless, he decided to return to his old career and joined the White Star Line in 1900. Since then had seen service aboard the small steamers *Medic* and *Georgic*, having left the latter to join the *Majestic*.

His service with the line thus far had been a mix of the rough and the smooth. In 1900, he had nearly scuppered his career by a prank that he and some of his fellow officers had pulled on the citizens of Sydney, Australia. Finding the locals obsessed with news of the Boer War, early one morning Lightoller, accompanied by four midshipmen, quietly rowed to the town's fortress and climbed its tower. Here they fixed a makeshift Boer flag on the tower's lightning conductor before loading a cannon with 14lb of blasting powder, then lighting a 50ft fuse before they quickly made their escape back to the *Medic* to watch the spectacle – and the town's reaction – in comfort.

In the furore that erupted after this escapade, only Lightoller's honesty and upright attitude in not divulging the names of his co-conspirators saved his bacon and after paying for the damage the ship quietly sailed away from the controversy.

Adventurous, hot-headed and puckish the youthful Lightoller may have been, but there was a serious and dutiful side to him too, for on his journeys to the Pacific and back he also netted himself a wife, Sylvia, whom he had met aboard ship. Perhaps as a result of his marriage, by the time he joined the *Majestic*, this rough diamond had become perhaps a little smoother around the edges and showed all the makings of a fine officer, though his sense of adventure – and an unerring ability to be where the action was – stayed with him for the rest of his life. Ten years later he was to be the senior surviving officer of the *Titanic*; during the First World War he survived another shipwreck then commanded torpedo boats and destroyers and twice earned the Distinguished Service Cross for his actions; then in the dark days of 1940, at the age of sixty-six, he and the crew of his motor launch *Sundowner* were one of the many 'little ships' that helped to pluck the beleaguered men of the BEF off the beaches of Dunkirk. Lightoller died in London in 1952 from heart disease, his condition possibly exacerbated by the killer London smog that year.

On 14 July 1902, though, Lightoller, or 'Lights' as he was known to his peers, was the new boy on the bridge. It would have been interesting to see what his fellow officers made of him at this time. Certainly he was personable, loyal and had the ability to make fast friends, but, as would be seen later in his career, he could also be exacting and intolerant of anyone who did not follow orders to the letter, or of anyone he believed had shown poor judgement. What Captain Smith made of him is equally unknown, though he seems to have found Lightoller to be good at his job and was happy to have him aboard ship. We do, however, have Lightoller's opinion of Smith, which to put it mildly was glowing.

Lightoller had sailed with many captains and endured the odd tyrant or two, but he both liked and admired Smith who lived up to his expectations in a sea captain, governing not by force but by 'accepted discipline, tact, his own personality and good common sense'[29]. He described Captain Smith as having a quiet and friendly nature fronted by an invariably warm smile which perhaps sat incongruously with the bluff, hearty image that his appearance seemed to convey. Not that Smith could not seadog-it with the best of them when he needed to and occasionally Lightoller heard the skipper bark out an order that brought an errant crewman back to his duties with a bump. But usually it was not necessary; both officers and crew knew where they stood with him and as a result he ran a happy ship.

Lightoller recalled a number of things about Smith's confident, swashbuckling style of seamanship which he quite admired. He said, for instance, that it was an education to watch Smith con his ship through the intricate channels into New York Harbour, a manoeuvre he undertook at full speed. There was one particularly bad corner known as the South-West Spit that used to make his officers swell with pride and not a little awe as he swung the ship through, judging his distances to a nicety, the ship heeling over to the helm with just a few feet to spare between the banks and either end of the ship. Of course, as we know, he did not always get it right, occasionally Smith's bravura left his ship temporarily high and dry, but it was pretty impressive when he did. Smith was sometimes not too delicate when it came to mooring his ship and Lightoller recalled that the *Majestic* might occasionally strike a hard knuckle of the wharf a hefty blow, but beyond denting a few plates or scraping off some paint there was no harm done.

Lightoller served aboard the *Majestic* for several years before moving on to other vessels prior to reuniting with his old skipper aboard the *Titanic*. Despite what happened to the *Titanic,* Lightoller remembered Smith as one of the ablest sea captains he had ever sailed under: 'He was a great favourite and a man any officer would give his ears to sail under.'[30]

An Interlude and a Farewell

Throughout 1902, Smith and other White Star employees would have listened with interest to the news of the changes taking place at the top of the company structure. After a round of negotiations, in February that year, J. Bruce Ismay had agreed to sell the line for £10 million to the International Navigation Co. Ltd, a British subsidiary of what later that year would become the International Mercantile Marine, a shipping trust headed by the American financier J.P. Morgan. Many have since averred that this now made White Star an American company, though the issue is very fuzzy. The IMM was not 'owned' as such by J.P. Morgan or anybody else and though many of the IMM's major financiers were American, the trust's shares were freely traded on the New York stock exchange and so there were doubtless many British investors with a finger in the IMM pie. The best that can be said is that White Star was now owned by a British corporation that was owned by an American-based trust the majority of whose investors were American.

Certainly for White Star's employees very little changed. There was no Americanisation of the line, White Star ships were still British registered, flew the

British flag and carried largely British crews. Indeed, had an American officer come aboard and attempted to take command of a White Star vessel, it would technically have been an act of war. Furthermore, they still answered to the same boss, as despite J. Bruce Ismay's apparent lack of sentiment in selling off the family jewels, he had in fact negotiated a lucrative deal that saw him retained as the Line's managing director. The IMM had been purchasing shipping lines since the 1890s, with an eye on securing a monopoly on the North Atlantic trade and the White Star Line was now undoubtedly the jewel in the trust's crown. This put Ismay in an important position in the IMM hierarchy that would pay dividends in a couple of years, when he was elected its president with full control of its finances.

A boost in their finances may have been the main sweetener on the deal as White Star's stock improved immediately on its purchase, rising from £3 million to £24 million almost overnight. As a result, the deal was successfully ratified by the shareholders in May that year and the cash payment for the purchase was paid over in December.

It was as this deal was being finalised that the *Majestic* was being taken out of service for an extensive refit. This may or may not have been prompted by the favourable changes in the company's fortunes, though there is no doubt that an upgrade was long overdue for the now ageing liner and this may have been on the cards for a while. This upgrade was necessary if the *Majestic* was to compete with the newer, faster ships on the North Atlantic service.

Majestic made her final voyage of 1902 in November, arriving in New York on the 20th. When she returned home, though, she was taken out of service and while the *Majestic* underwent her refit, Smith was once again given command of the *Germanic*. The ship was still going strong with over 300 transatlantic crossings to her name, but now like her sister *Britannic*, she was getting on, a fact noted by the New York papers. This would be Smith's last stint as her commander, but it was a memorable farewell, though for all the wrong reasons.

Captain Smith took the ship out from Liverpool on 31 December 1902. There were only a few passengers making the crossing, forty-five in first class and 101 in steerage. After nearly nine days at sea, at 6.10p.m. on 9 January *Germanic*'s lights were sighted of Fire Island before New York and the ship crossed the bar two hours later. Like all the ship's crawling into the harbour that morning the *Germanic*'s bridge and all of her upper works were encrusted in snow, the vessel having sailed through a fearsome Atlantic storm. Her troubles, though, had not ended. Early the next morning having passed her quarantine, the *Germanic* was cruising along the North River past pier 46 en route to her own berth, when the ship struck and sank a garbage scow, one of a number being pulled by a tug. The two men aboard the scow, James Mullen and Daniel McCarthey, jumped overboard and grabbing hold of the tow line they managed to pull themselves over to another scow. The *Germanic* proceeded on and finally moored at the White Star pier.[31]

If that journey had been rough with one thing and another, it was nothing compared to the next trip from Liverpool to New York that began on 4 February.

This time *Germanic* carried forty-five cabin passengers and 181 steerage, all of whom were in for the roughest ride imaginable. Once again just over nine days later the ship sailed into New York Harbour, looking this time little the worse for her voyage, but the passengers had a hair-raising tale to tell the waiting reporters. The journey had been hellish and the *Germanic* had encountered gales and seas which at their worst even daunted 'Storm King' Smith at the helm.

Of the nine stormy days they endured probably the worst was the previous Monday when the ship logged only 333 nautical miles.[32] That day, two port side portholes were blown in by large waves and the ship was shaken so violently that any pleasure or relief to be gained from eating and sleeping was out of the question. But there was more to come. From 2a.m. on the Thursday until 7a.m. the following day, the *Germanic* ran into a succession of the fiercest gales. At times during those grim hours the ship made virtually no headway, making only a little over 5 knots an hour. Then the seas became so confused and the waves so intimidating that Smith had the crew pour oil onto the waters in an effort to calm matters down. Some of the passengers described how the waves looked like great mountains towering before them, recalling how some appeared to come to a dead stop and seemed almost to wait for the liner to butt into them, much to the alarm of all on board. It was a great relief, therefore, when the American coast was sighted and they knew that their terrifying ordeal was over.[33]

After this second rough voyage, Captain Smith's trips with the *Germanic* were more run-of-the-mill. There were two more journeys to New York and back again, the last of which started from Liverpool on 8 April 1903. On his return to Britain at the beginning of May, Smith managed to get some precious time with his family. Indeed, it was concern for what provisions he should make for his family that dominated his thinking at this time. Perhaps the storms he had experienced aboard the *Germanic* had worried him more than usual and now that he had the chance he decided to contact his solicitor J.W. Thompson of Liverpool and have his last will and testament drawn up in full legal fashion. This was signed and witnessed at the family home, 17 Marine Crescent, Waterloo, on 11 May 1903. Smith left everything to his wife, with the condition that should she die or remarry then the entire property would pass to Mel. The executors of the will were two of his friends, David Cooke of 6 Adelaide Terrace, Waterloo, and his old friend Thomas Jones of the Nook, Runcorn in Cheshire. The will was then witnessed by Eleanor's sister Maria and Mr Thompson the solicitor.[34]

In late May the *Majestic* re-entered service after her overhaul. Smith would have been keen to look over his old ship and see what exactly the boys at Harland & Wolff had done for her. Superficially, the most notable change to the *Majestic* was that the ship had lost one of her three masts. The mizzenmast had been removed from her stern and the mainmast moved further back to give the ship a more symmetrical appearance. The forecastle had also been extended, but the real changes had been in passenger accommodation. In first class, the deck house on the upper deck had been extended and at the front of it a new house had been built containing ten additional staterooms, some of them en suite. The sun deck had been extended further forward to shelter passengers in wet weather. The first-class library had been remodelled, the covering over the saloon dome having been removed adding considerably to the size of the room. Another dramatic change was the fitting of a new ornamental glass dome over the first-class dining saloon.

In second class, the saloon which was formerly housed in a deck house was now situated on the main deck and enlarged, while the space it had occupied had also been turned into ten new staterooms for second-class passengers and a further twelve had been provided in other spaces.

Third class too had seen some major changes. New, comfortably furnished dining rooms had been provided along with a number of separate two- and four-berth rooms in place of the open berths which had previously been the only accommodation for steerage passengers. With these improvements, accommodation-wise the *Majestic* was for the time being ranked amongst the most modern ships afloat.

Yet these upgrades had not only been confined to passenger accommodation. Smith discovered that the captain's cabin was now placed on the boat deck and a new chartroom and wheelhouse had been erected on the bridge. To the captain so used to this sturdy ship it must have seemed like a brand new command.

In May, Smith moved back smoothly to the *Majestic* and voyage then followed voyage, through weather foul and fair over the next few months. In November, there was a pause filled with some pleasure and pride when the voyages undertaken by the transport ships during the Boer War were rewarded. Three White Star captains, including Smith, were awarded the Transport Medal with the 'South Africa' clasp on its red and blue ribbon. Though some recipients were lucky enough to receive their awards from the King himself, not everyone was so fortunate and Captain Smith was presented with his medal by the Director of Transports on 26 November 1903 and from then on he wore the medal proudly on his uniform. Seven other members of his old crew also received the medal including Chief Officer J.O. Carter and Surgeon A.W. McKenzie. First Officer A.E. Rimmer had died in the interim and his medal was presented to his widow. [35]

The *Majestic* and her newly decorated skipper returned to duty in January 1904. There was one uneventful voyage and the journey after that was equally run-of-the-mill, at least until the ship docked at Liverpool on 12 February. Here, customs officials searching through the baggage of a Hungarian passenger, Ivan Sjubanovic, made an alarming find. Packed beneath a false bottom in his luggage they discovered 18lb of dynamite and 3,360 detonators. This was immediately confiscated and the man was arrested, being remanded into custody until 20 February.

Under interrogation the man actually turned out to be thirty-year-old Ivan Lymbanovic, who with a companion had bought a ticket in Pittsburg. His eventual destination was given as Karlstadt in Croatia, then part of the Austro-Hungarian Empire and a hotbed of terrorist activity. Terrorist threats were taken as seriously in the early twentieth century as they are today and Lymbanovic's actions were thoroughly investigated, though as things stood the future did not look too rosy for the man. However, just a month after his arrest, Lymbanovic was released. The police had made enquiries in Pittsburg and had found the man to be of good character. Though his reasons for being in possession of the explosives and detonators was never explained, the charge of unlawful possession of explosives was dropped. He did not get off scot-free, though, being then promptly slapped with a £10 fine for smuggling.[36]

Captain Smith took the *Majestic* out for five more transatlantic round trips, but his time as her skipper was now almost over. It would be no overstatement to say that his nine years aboard her had been the making of him. When he took over the *Majestic* he had been an up and coming star so far as ship's captains went, well respected but still something of a junior player. Now, though, with several of the older captains having retired, Smith and some of his near contemporaries such as Herbert Haddock and Bertram Hayes were becoming the captains of choice on the transatlantic run not only for the passengers but also for the harder heads in the White Star management. To these men would go the coveted commands of the new breeds of bigger steamships that were now coming onto the scene. These had begun to appear at the turn of the century and Smith being weighed in the balance was perhaps still found wanting, but by 1904, White Star had evidently decided that it was time for the popular Lieutenant Smith of the *Majestic* to take on one of the big boats.

5

BALTIC AND ADRIATIC

In 1901, the first in what would be a quartet of larger White Star vessels, popularly known as 'the Big Four', burst upon the shipping scene. This was the *Celtic*, which at 20, 880 tons and 700ft in length was the biggest ship in the world at that time. Under the command of Captain H. St John Lindsay, the *Celtic* set out on her maiden voyage in July 1901. In February 1903, the second of the four, the 21, 000-ton *Cedric*, another world-beater in size, set out for New York under the command of Captain Herbert James Haddock. A year later the third liner, named *Baltic*, was delivered to White Star and the command of this latest liner was given to the popular commander of the *Majestic*, Lieutenant Edward John Smith.

For Smith, the command of the *Baltic* was a major moment in his career and perhaps a rather daunting one at first. The *Baltic* at 23,876 tons (again the biggest ship afloat) was nearly 14,000 tons heavier than the *Majestic*, indeed, over twice the weight of his old command. The *Baltic* was 726ft long, 18ft longer than the *Kaiser Wilhelm II* of the North German Lloyd Line which had formerly held the record. Her width was 75ft and the ship had eight decks, four of them above the main deck. She carried a crew of 350, had accommodation for 3,000 passengers and a cargo capacity of 28,000 tons.

When it came to speed, White Star had given up on questing for the Blue Riband. Her engines, the four-cylinder, triple-expansion variety, were good workhorses but nothing special and at best averaged a speed of 17 knots. Instead, White Star now concentrated on its strong suit, creating more luxurious interiors than any of their older ships or other shipping lines provided. There was a sumptuous first-class smoking room and library on the upper promenade and as contemporary photographs show the main first-class dining saloon was a very ornate confection with pillars and stucco and upholstered chairs ranged around the dining tables. The facilities and accommodation in second and third class, though much more utilitarian, were still much better than could be found on other ships.

One thing that had suffered as a result of the increase in ship size, though, was lifeboat provision. By this time, ship design and tonnage had effectively outstripped the British Board of Trade regulations governing lifeboat provision. These were now hopelessly outdated and held that vessels exceeding 10,000 tons were only legally required to carry sixteen lifeboats, irrespective of how many people they carried. These deficiencies would be starkly highlighted by the *Titanic* disaster and White Star officials found themselves being quizzed intensely over the matter. In fact, White Star ships tended to be much better provided for than many of their rivals. Cunard's *Mauretania* and *Lusitania*, for instance, only had space in their lifeboats for 32 per cent of the total company aboard and some ships carried even fewer boats. The *Baltic* carried twenty lifeboats, four more than was legally required, but even so, these could accommodate only 43 per cent of the total number of passengers and crew that the ship could carry. This rather alarming statistic rarely if ever made its way into the newspaper reports about these shiny new ships, though some such as the journalist W.T. Stead, were fully aware of the matter and campaigned albeit ineffectually to get things altered. Ironically, Stead would lose his life aboard the *Titanic* as a direct result of this lack of boats.

Smith finished his last stint on the *Majestic* in May 1904. He must have had mixed feelings about leaving the vessel that had been his home from home for the past nine years, but the ship was now well past her prime and six years later she was downgraded to a reserve vessel. She did, however, come back into front line service one last time when she filled the gap left in the services by the loss of the *Titanic*. In the meantime, the ship was given into the capable hands of one of Smith's old officers, Captain Bertram Hayes, while Smith went to Belfast to bring out the *Baltic*. Here he oversaw her sea trials before making the short crossing to Liverpool where, leaving the ship with a skeleton shipkeeping crew, he took a few days with his family.

On 29 June, Smith went back aboard the *Baltic* and plunged immediately into the task of getting his new vessel ready for sea, meeting with his Chief Officer Thomas Kidwell, formerly of the *Celtic*, whose experience of these big ships would doubtless be useful to his skipper. Their meeting was also a reunion as Kidwell had served under Smith before as a much more junior officer aboard the *Britannic* and *Majestic*. Included in the morning's meetings were the ship's surgeon W.E. Graham, Chief Purser Hugh McElroy (who would later serve under Smith on the *Titanic*), Chief Steward H. Wovenden and Chief Engineer H. Crawford Boyle, who, like Chief Officer Kidwell, had come in from the *Celtic*.

Also there for the maiden voyage was another man who would come to figure large in the story of the *Titanic*, consulting engineer Thomas Andrews, heading the Harland & Wolff Guarantee Group that would check the *Baltic* over on her first trip to see if anything needed changing or improving upon. Andrews was a fine marine engineer and the nephew to Lord William Pirrie, Harland & Wolff's owner. He and Smith may have already been acquainted, but if not they would certainly see enough of one another over the next few years as Smith led out one after another of White Star's new vessels.

For this maiden voyage the ship took on well below her total capacity of passengers, setting off with 209 in first class, 142 in second class and 555 in steerage, 906 in total. Among the first-class passengers was J.P. Morgan, the founder of the IMM, the conglomerate that controlled the White Star Line. After the usual stops, the voyage across the Atlantic was uneventful but pleasant and everyone declared themselves to be delighted with the new ship. As they reached the approaches to New York Harbour, Smith showed that he was by no means fazed by the size of the new vessel. The channel being clear he took her around the Southwest Spit at full speed as he had with the *Majestic*. 'She behaved admirably,' Smith later noted to reporters as the *Baltic* swung through the channel. Then, though, the speed was reduced and Pilot Johnson, who guided all the big ships into New York, took the *Baltic* into the harbour.

As the ship entered the bay on the breast of the tide on 8 July, thousands of eyes followed her progress. As soon as she appeared in the upper bay steamboats, ferries, tugs and all manner of small sailing craft went out of their way to give all of those on board a better view of the big ship as it passed, while others moving in the opposite direction moved aside as she approached. One of the smaller vessels that tagged on was J.P. Morgan's personal steam yacht *Corsair*, which ran for a time alongside the *Baltic*, the small black yacht looking like a child's toy alongside the big liner. Then as the *Baltic* approached the docking piers hundreds of whistles and hooters started sounding and flags were dipped as the vessel finally reached her destination.[1]

Reporters swarmed to meet the wealthy passengers, eager for their comments as they disembarked and the White Star officers and officials came forward to give their pennyworth. All of them from Smith down were pleased with the ship. The following Monday, the New York public were allowed to tour the vessel to see for themselves what this latest White Star behemoth had to offer. There was an admission charge of 25 cents, the proceeds going to seaman's charities.

Messages: By Wireless, Letter and Bell

The voyages undertaken over the next few months excited no great press interest, but after February 1905 (though the exact date is not yet known), six White Star vessels gained a new apparatus that would prove in many cases to be a real life saver. It was not extra boats, though, but the new wireless system recently perfected by Guglielmo Marconi, who had travelled to America aboard the *Majestic* some years earlier.[2]

The wireless was operated from a small cabin, probably situated near to the bridge, with cables reaching up to the antenna which comprised a set of wires suspended between the ship's masts. The advent of the wireless brought two new crew members aboard; the wireless operators were essentially employed and trained by the Marconi company, but soon became accepted as an integral part of a ship's company providing not only a ship to shore message service for passengers, but also sending and receiving valuable information relating to navigation and distress signals. In a matter of years the ether was alive with the crackle of the electrical pulses of Morse code.

From the outset big vessels such as the *Baltic* and its successors carried two wirelessmen who between them could keep a twenty-four-hour watch. This was not the case with smaller vessels whose lone operators needed to sleep. This still left a narrow gap in which things could go disastrously wrong. This, like the lack of lifeboats on bigger vessels, was something that would become blindingly clear as a direct result of the *Titanic* disaster.

Smith, therefore, was one of the first captains in the Atlantic trade to have this new tool at his disposal and by the time of the *Titanic* disaster he had been familiar with its presence for seven years and would have seen how useful it was. This obvious fact gives the lie to the notion that Smith blatantly ignored the wireless messages he received on that fateful voyage. However, as with any new form of communication – the internet is the best recent example – the pros also had their cons. Ready access to information could lead to information overload, the few nuggets of useful data were buried in a mass of inconsequential details; anyone who has tried to write the life of an early twentieth-century merchant captain using information available on the net knows the truth of this. Equally, it might have promoted complacency. Sorting through all this and dealing with what was relevant would become a regular chore for skippers to add to their many other duties.

The Marconi system was especially useful in getting news from ship to shore. This too could have its up and downside; on one hand it could cause a great deal of concern when its piecemeal messages came through declaring for instance that a ship was in difficulties, but on the other it was a quick way of allaying fears if vessels were overdue. Such a case was the *Baltic*'s journey to the States that began on 10 May 1905. This was a memorable one for more than one reason and was reported at some length in the American papers. For a start there was a huge and distinguished passenger list. Both second and third class were full and first class had 389 passengers, which though not full was certainly the largest number she had ever carried. The most notable of these were the Duke of Sutherland, who with a couple of friends was hoping to make a tour of the Pacific Coast, a Brazilian Ambassador to the United States, railway magnate Charles M. Schwab returning home after a trip to Russia and the American composer and conductor John Philip Sousa who with his band was also returning home after a very successful tour of Britain. Sousa did not come back empty-handed for as well as numerous other gifts and purchases he brought back a Gordon setter, an English setter and a black retriever who were housed in special kennels aboard ship. Like many Americans, Sousa had been astonished at just how well his works had been received in Britain, most notably 'The Stars and Stripes Forever' which had become a much requested hit during his tour. By way of a fond farewell to the country, Sousa and his band assembled on the *Baltic*'s deck shortly after going aboard and played the ship away from the Liverpool landing stage. The crowds gathered to see the ship off, cheering loudly to their renditions of 'Auld Lang Syne' and 'The Star Spangled Banner'.

The *Baltic* and her passengers enjoyed three days of fine weather but on Sunday 14th the *Baltic* encountered a bad mid-Atlantic storm. Winds blew with terrific fury creating a heavy swell and head sea which slowed the *Baltic*'s progress for twenty-four hours. Huge green waves came crashing over the bow and readers in the library three decks above later recalled how they had watched with some surprise and trepidation as the waves crashed against the windows. As each successive wave passed them by, *Baltic*'s propellors were lifted out of the sea which caused them to race unhealthily.

At 12.30p.m. on the Sunday, the situation became a little more desperate when whilst in the act of reversing the engines to curb the racing of the propellors, the clutch broke down and Smith had no option but to stop the ship while his engineers effected the necessary repairs. Two black balls signifying 'Not under control, but no need of assistance' were raised on the forward rigging and passengers said that oil was poured onto the sea to calm the waves down, though officers when interviewed claimed that the ship was stable enough on its own. Smith then had a notice posted on the bulletin boards in the various saloons announcing that the ship would be stopped for four hours whilst repairs were carried out on the damaged machinery and he assured the passengers that there was no danger. Nor did there seem to be, for despite the storm and sea growling around them the *Baltic* hardly rolled and when passengers sat down for luncheon there were only a few absentees. During the meal some of the crockery slid about, but most agreed that it was nothing serious and decided anyhow that the storm made for an interesting spectacle.

The ship got under way again later that afternoon, though at a greatly reduced speed while the engineers continued with their repairs. The effects of the storm and the stopping of the ship had reduced the *Baltic*'s daily run from over 400 to 237 nautical miles. The storm rapidly blew itself out overnight and once the repairs were fully effected the ship was pushed up to speed once more. The next day she travelled 388 miles, on Tuesday she covered 415, though the day after that she managed only 407 miles having run into a thick bank of fog.

The storm had made the journey memorable and reportable, but the rest of the journey was not lacking in incidents of note. On Tuesday night, Sousa and his band gave a concert in the first-class saloon at which $325 was collected for the Seamen's Hospitals in New York and Liverpool. Then up got the Duke of Sutherland, who in keeping with his rather eccentric nature had come to the concert wearing tan shoes with his dinner suit, much to the amusement of some and consternation of others, and gave possibly the shortest speech on record for a chairman of such an entertainment. Estimates varied as to how many words he actually used; some claimed a laconic seventeen, while others bumped it up to an erudite twenty-five, yet everyone agreed he had said all that needed to be said.

News of the *Baltic*'s adventures had by now reached London via the steamer *Oceanic* which had been in wireless contact with the *Baltic* whilst she was stopped. The news of her delay was then telegraphed to New York via the transatlantic cable. Here it caused a great deal of concern amongst those waiting for friends and relatives, much more so than aboard the *Baltic* where a light-hearted game of cricket was being played out between the married couples and the single passengers when the ship's Marconi office started receiving the first urgent enquiries. The ship reached

New York on 19 May, the journey having taken just fifteen minutes' short of eight days.[3]

After the usual stopover, the ship set off back to Britain. The weather had eased now, but this voyage also had its share of drama. On 29 May, an American steerage passenger named B.F. Seeson committed suicide by throwing himself into the sea. Other passengers witnessed him jumping and alerted the crew. Smith stopped the ship and a boat was lowered, but no trace of Mr Seeson could be found.[4]

After the next voyage to the States and back, Captain Smith managed to have a week off, a welcome respite from his work. The *Baltic* was proving to be popular (indeed, she would remain the most popular of the 'Big Four') and White Star was making the most of it. This meant that Smith had little time at home during the turn around, but now he spent a week with his family getting to know his young daughter better and enjoying time with his dogs. It seems that he also used the time to make a decision over one of his commitments. Smith had been an officer in the Royal Naval Reserve for nearly seventeen years and had done his bit during the Boer War, but now at the age of fifty-five, with his career technically beginning the wind-down towards retirement, he decided to quit the RNR. At his request he was placed on the retired list, notice of which appeared in *The Times*. The small notice mentioned that Lieutenant Smith had been retired 'with permission to assume the rank of Commander', which rank he henceforth used aboard his ships. By the time the notice appeared, though, Smith was back at sea again.[5]

On arrival at New York, Smith penned a letter to his nephew Frank Hancock. Frank had emigrated to the States some years previously and settled in one of Smith's old stamping grounds, Savannah, Georgia. In the letter, the first in a short series of five held today at the Blunt White Library at Mystic Seaport, Conneticut, USA, we get to see Edward John Smith the family man enquiring after relatives and friends, a very different figure from the tragic skipper of the *Titanic*.

The letter opens with Smith regretting that Frank had not been able to take a trip north as he had been looking forward to meeting him for a chat. Evidently work had prevented Frank from travelling, so Smith did not hold it against him, being in the same situation himself. Smith had, it seems, been hoping to hear family news of how Frank's mother Anna and the rest of the family were faring, but he concluded that no news was good news. He then mentioned his recent break at home and the *Baltic*'s popularity and how he would be busy aboard her for the foreseeable future. He had hopes of meeting up with Frank if he was ever up that way on business. The letter concludes in an interesting fashion by alluding to a number of mutual aquaintances in Savannah. Smith sends his best wishes to General Gordon, Churchill and Myers. Mr Myers was mentioned earlier in the letter for having secured a good position, though his identity remains a mystery. The other two, though, can be tentatively identified. 'General Gordon' was most likely the same William Washington Gordon who we first met during the stormy crossing to America in September 1895. The identification of Mr Churchill is less clear cut, though Pat Lacey in her well-researched, fact-based novel, claims that he was in fact one Winston Churchill, a gradute of the United States Naval Academy, who had given up the sea to write novels. In closing his letter, Smith also noted that if Frank happened to see one George Walker who had been very kind to the young Captain Smith of the *Lizzie Fennell*, he must send him his regards, though he conceded that he may have forgotten him after so many years.[6]

In early January 1906, the *Baltic's* Marconi system came in for a little mis-use when it seemed to start getting the Edwardian equivalent of spam emails. The American press reported on 13 January that the *Baltic* had just arrived from Liverpool and that when she was two days out from Queenstown three spoof news bulletins, supposedly from the liner *Columbia*, were posted on the ship's bulletin board.

The bulletins were written on genuine Marconi blanks and two were to the effect that Thomas W. Lawson of Boston had committed suicide in a Boston hotel and that Japan had presented an ultimatum to Germany demanding that the latter country withdraw all of her troops immediately from Chinese territory. Neither, of course, was true.

Captain Smith was dining in the first-class saloon when he heard about the messages and immediately ordered them to be taken down. He then started an investigation and found out that no messages had been received from the *Columbia*. The perpetrator of the gag, described charmingly by one officer as, 'one of those deucedly funny chaps', was never discovered.[7]

In late May and early June, Smith appeared in the American newspapers reporting on a great transatlantic race between two other famous steamers. He described how a couple of days earlier the *Baltic* had been passed by the French Line steamer *Provence* and the Hamburg-American Line vessel, *Deutschland*, both heading for Europe. As they passed the *Baltic* the two ships were at best only 5 miles apart making full steam in a great ocean race. Smith described the scene:

> We passed the two ocean racers at about six o'clock on Thursday night. The Provence loomed up first, reeling off the knots at the rate of 22¾ an hour, 1¾ faster than she had ever travelled before. She was 129 miles east of Sandy Hook.
>
> Five minutes later the big funnels of the Deutschland hove into sight. She was making 23½ an hour, and had picked up five miles of the lead which the Provence had on sailing from New York.
>
> I have never seen two ships cut through the water at the rate the two liners were going, except the little torpedo boat destroyers, and bigger ships would have made even them hustle. It appeared to me that if the German boat can keep up the pace she was making when I passed her she should win out in the race.[8]

The papers could not get enough of Smith that day as he also reported how on approaching New York, the *Baltic* had detected the submarine bell of the Scotland Lightship. This device takes a little explaining. Essentially, it was an underwater warning bell carried by lightships, which served as an extra warning and navigational beacon in thick weather when even the lightship's lamps could be obscured. Operated by a chamber of compressed air, the bell would toll and microphones set up in small chambers on either side of a ship's bow were set to detect the sound. From both chambers wires ran up to a small device known as the indicator box. This could be operated by throwing a handle to one side to activate the starboard microphone and connect it to the telephone on the bridge and the other one to do the same for the port microphone. When the bell was detected the captain merely had to turn his vessel so that the sound of the bell could be detected with equal intensity from each side to know that his ship was pointing in the direction from which the sound was coming. From this he could then take a navigational bearing from the nearest lightship that was fitted with a submarine bell, the positions of which were marked on his standard charts.

The US government had recently installed submarine bells on a number of lightships from Maine to Florida and ship's captains had been asked to report any data regarding them. As the *Baltic* had pushed forward cautiously through a dense fog on the approaches to New York, the Scotland Lightship bell was detected. This gave Smith an instant bearing, which was useful as it was impossible to see the lightship. Once ashore, Smith reported the successful contact and he discovered that he was the first navigator to make such a report, which was then promptly reported in the morning newspapers.[9]

The next time that Smith and the *Baltic* appeared in the news was as the result of a far more tragic event. On 30 June, the *New York Times* carried the story of how on the morning of the 25th whilst at sea, steerage passenger thirty-four-year-old Mrs Julia Agnes 'Nellie' Frawley of New Britain, Conneticut, gave birth to triplets, all of whom died a few hours after birth, the mother herself dying in childbirth.

News of the tragedy in steerage travelled through the ship and cast a gloom over the voyage. On Tuesday night, the body of Mrs Frawley and her three babies were lowered over the side, the burial service being read by the ship's purser. The *Baltic* arrived in New York on the 29th and among those waiting on the pier for their loved ones was Mrs Frawley's husband, who had no inkling of the tragedy that had occurred. None of the passengers could gather up the courage to go and break the news to the poor man, neither it seems could Captain Smith, who delegated the purser to go and tell Mr Frawley that his wife and babies were all dead. In a terrible scene, Mr Frawley broke down utterly on hearing the news. Eventually, he went aboard the ship to collect his wife's luggage and belongings and then still weeping profusely, he left the pier.[10]

Smith's time with the *Baltic* was now almost over. The last instance that he seems to have been mentioned in connection with the ship was on 16 November that year when on arrival at New York he reported their having passed the abandoned and waterlogged barque *Marion C.*, now a dangerous derelict lying in the track of the ocean liners. After that, there were three more transatlantic journeys before he had a new command on his hands.

The *Adriatic* and Southampton

In January 1907, White Star suddenly announced that it would be moving some of its transatlantic services from Liverpool to Southampton, principally its Wednesday mail service to the States. This would be served primarily by the line's new ship, the last of the 'Big Four', the RMS *Adriatic*, which was due to enter service in May 1907.

There were several reasons for this change, which brought rapid and vehement protests from both the Liverpool and Queenstown authorities. For one thing, Southampton's deep water harbour provided excellent moorage which would come into its own as the vessels increased in size further. The most pressing reasons, though, were economic. White Star was losing valuable trade by staying bound to Liverpool as many transatlantic travellers were finding the Channel ports a much more convenient and comfortable route by which they could reach London or the continent. This business was being picked up by French or, increasingly, by German steamship companies. White Star's decision to base not only the *Adriatic*, but also the *Oceanic*, *Teutonic* and *Majestic* in Southampton immediately led to the suspicion in Liverpool that Cunard would also be shifting its services to Southampton, though this would not happen until 1914. White Star was not abandoning its home port, indeed, the other three 'Big Four' – *Celtic*, *Cedric*, *Baltic* plus the *Arabic* would continue to run mail services from Liverpool, though these would now depart on Thursdays rather than Wednesdays. By way of proof that the new Southampton service was a separate entity, it was christened the United States and Royal Mail Service. This, though, did little to diminish the significance of the move, for as events would show the new prestige liners would all sail from Southampton and some, such as the *Titanic*, never visited their home port.

By the time this news broke, Smith probably knew that he too would be sailing from Southampton from now onwards, as he had been chosen to skipper the *Adriatic*, the *Baltic* now being handed over to Captain J.B. Ransom. Giving the new command to Smith had seemed the natural choice, as with the retirement of John G. Cameron of the *Oceanic* at the beginning of the year Smith had become the White Star Line's senior skipper.

The RMS *Adriatic* was the only one of the 'Big Four' not to emerge as the largest ship in the world when she entered service; that title lay temporarily at least with the German liner *Kaiserin Auguste Victoria*. Nevertheless, at 24,541 tons, *Adriatic* was the biggest of the four sisters, though her dimensions were essentially those of the *Baltic*.

As the new big White Star ship, *Adriatic* had the pick of the crews. Smith was in charge and doubtless under him was a bevy of experienced officers. There were some familiar faces, his old friend Dr O'Loughlin had joined the ship as ship's surgeon and another notable figure so far as our story is concerned was First Officer William McMaster Murdoch, Captain Cameron's former first officer on the *Oceanic*. There is no indication that the two of them had served together before, but Smith and Murdoch would work together fairly solidly for the next five years.

Born in Dalbeattie in Dumfries and Galloway, Scotland, in 1871, Murdoch's father and grandfather had been ship's captains and at the earliest opportunity he too had gone to sea. In many ways his early career echoes that of Smith. Like him, Murdoch started in sailing ships and within a matter of a few years was progressing rapidly through the ranks, though unlike Smith he never got to command a sailing vessel. Joining the White Star Line in 1900, Murdoch had seen service in a number of vessels, gaining a good deal of practical experience and a reputation as a quick thinker. In 1903, he joined the White Star liner *Arabic* as second officer on the North Atlantic run. Here his cool head and rapid judgement of a situation prevented a disaster when one night a ship was spotted bearing down on the *Arabic* out of the darkness. First Officer Fox on watch immediately ordered the quartermaster to steer hard-to-port. Murdoch, though, realised that this would actually cause a collision and rushing into the wheelhouse he brushed the quartermaster aside and held the course steady. Had the ship turned as instructed the *Arabic* would have been struck amidships or in the stern, but thanks to his quick thinking the two brushed by within a couple of inches of each other.

Since then, Murdoch had progressed steadily up the chain of command, impressing numerous people as he did so and by the time he joined the *Adriatic* he was widely regarded as an upcoming star of the line with a good future ahead of him. As it was, he already had plans for his own future well in hand. During one of his earlier voyages he had become friends with a young woman, Ada Banks. The two had corresponded ever since and Ada had recently agreed to marry him. They would be married in September 1907.

The next few years, though, would be something of a mixed bag for this ambitious sailor as aside from the highpoints of his marriage and his transfer to the new big ships as they came online, his career would seem to stutter albeit briefly to a halt. The position of chief officer beckoned, but for one reason or another Murdoch never quite achieved that sought for position en route to his own captaincy. He would briefly be designated as chief officer aboard the *Titanic*, but would again be superseded by another for the ship's maiden voyage. Was it just bad luck, or was his career being blocked by a glut of commanders who would not move into retirement, or perhaps even actively scuppered his advancement? Conspiracy theories abound around Murdoch as much as they do around Smith who some tout as his promotional nemesis. Exasperated he may have been, but it is unlikely that a man like Murdoch would have suffered to stay aboard Smith's ships if this was the case. And in any case, Murdoch would have become chief officer of the *Titanic* under Smith immediately after that ship's maiden voyage. This, though, was not to be as he perished in the disaster, for First Officer William Murdoch would be the officer on watch that fateful night in 1912 when the iceberg was spotted and another life-or-death snap judgement was called for.

The *Adriatic*'s maiden voyage would at least start from Liverpool on 8 May 1907. After stopping at Queenstown to pick up the last of her passengers, the *Adriatic* carried 2,502 passengers across the Atlantic, a larger number than the much more famous *Titanic* later carried for hers. The lifeboat provision being as poor as it was, had disaster struck, the loss of life could have also been worse than that of the *Titanic*.

The crossing was smooth, though the weather varied over the seven days. She arrived in New York on 16 May in heavy weather. As the ship was being warped into the dock, one of the first-class passengers suffered an accident. The son of Republican National Committee man R.C. Kerens was waving to his brother on the dock when he slipped and fell against an iron stanchion, striking his jaw and dislocating it. The boy was in agony, but help was soon at hand in the form of ship's surgeon Dr O'Loughlin and Dr Ingram of Roosevelt Hospital, who had been waiting on the pier, both of whom gave immediate assistance, setting the boy's jaw in fifteen minutes, with every hope that he would do well.

The press were there to record this misfortune and to greet the ship and her other passengers. They noted that all hands were full of praise for the way Captain Smith and his officers had handled the vessel and the passengers too were pleased with the journey. There had been no jars and one passenger commented that had he not caught the occasional glimpse of the ocean he could have easily forgotten that he was on a ship at sea.[11]

During the stopover, Captain Smith also gave an interview to reporters in New York. Smith never seems to have found it easy discussing his experiences but this interview is notable for the fact that he does actually give us a brief glimpse beneath the gold leaf and starched jacket of command. Here it seems there was still something of the romantic youth who forty years earlier had gone to sea for an adventure and never quite got over it. However, we also get to see what Smith had become, namely a somewhat predictable company man touting his firm's wares and displaying an attitude towards his job that arguably bordered on overconfidence.

The reporters started by quizzing him about any difficulties he had handling such a large ship. Smith replied that he had grown up in the service, and it meant little to him that he had been transferred from a small vessel to a big ship and then to a bigger ship and finally to the biggest of them all.

'One might think that a captain taken from a small ship and put on a big one might feel the transition,' he said. 'Not at all. The skippers of the big vessels have grown up to them, year after year, through all these years. First there was the sailing vessel and then what we would now call small ships – they were big in the days gone by – and finally the giants to-day.'

Though ships were bigger and much more comfortable, this steady progression had by no means sanitised sailing nor robbed Smith of his love of the sea and his appreciation of its power:

The love of the ocean that took me to sea as a boy has never quite left me. In a way, a certain amount of wonder never leaves me, especially as I observe from the bridge a vessel plunging up and down in the trough of the seas, fighting her way through and over great waves, tumbling and yet keeping on her keel, and going on and on – I wonder how she does it, how she can keep afloat in such seas, and how she can go on and on safely to port. There is wild grandeur, too, that appeals to me in the sea. A man never outgrows that.

Yet, for all of that, Smith added that he was not in awe of the sea and he confessed that he found a crowded London street much more awe-inspiring. The ocean, after all, was his very familiar workplace, '... a great domain of well-defined paths, with degrees of latitude and longitude slipping by like telegraph poles.'

When quizzed on the matter of ship safety, though, he would not go so far as to claim that the *Adriatic* was unsinkable. Captain Smith had confidence in her design and maintained that shipbuilding was such a perfect art nowadays:

> ... that absolute disaster, involving the passengers is inconceivable. Whatever happens, there will be time enough before the vessel sinks to save the life of every person on board. I will go a bit further. I will say that I cannot imagine any condition that would cause the vessel to founder. Modern shipbuilding has gone beyond that. There will be bigger boats. The depth of harbours seems to be the great drawback at present. I cannot say, of course, just what the limit will be, but the larger boat will surely come.

Damning lines had just been bestowed on history had the listening reporters but known it, but at the time they were more interested in getting Smith's views on the sudden vogue for faster ships. This was an obvious reference to Cunard's latest vessels that now easily outpaced White Star's liners and it gave Smith the opportunity to put forward his own company's policy.

'Speed will not develop with size, so far as merchantmen are concerned.' Smith replied:

> The travelling public prefers the large comfortable boat of average speed, and anyway that is the boat that pays. High speed eats up money mile by mile, and extreme high speed is suicidal. There will be high speed boats for use as transports and a wise government will assist steamship companies in paying for them, as the English Government is now doing in the cases of the *Lusitania* and *Mauretania*, twenty-five knot boats; but no steamship company will put them out merely as a commercial venture.

Smith rounded off the interview by noting:

> When any one asks me how I can best describe my experiences of nearly forty years at sea I merely say uneventful. Of course, there have been winter gales and

storms and fog and the like, but in all my experience I have never been in an accident of any sort worth speaking about. I have seen but one vessel in distress in all my years at sea, a brig, the crew of which was taken off in a small boat in charge of my third officer. I never saw a wreck and have never been wrecked, nor was I ever in any predicament that threatened to end in disaster of any sort. You see, I am not very good material for a story.

But an officer standing nearby cut in with his own remark. 'Don't forget when you write of the captain's uneventful life to put in that it is the great captain who doesn't let things happen.'[12]

There were a few days in port, time for interested New Yorkers to tour the berthed vessel for a small fee, but the ship was restocked, fresh passengers came aboard and the *Adriatic* sailed for home once more. This time, though, home was not Liverpool; the ship was now making for Southampton.

On the return leg of her maiden voyage the *Adriatic* made White Star's first call at Plymouth which became a regular port of call for east-bound ships until the beginning of the First World War. The ship then proceeded on to Southampton. In his autobiography, George Bowyer later recalled the arrival of RMS *Adriatic* at Southampton. He had good reason to; 'Uncle' George as he was affectionately known to a generation of skippers was the Trinity House pilot tasked with guiding the world's prestige liners in and out of Southampton Water. The *Adriatic* was one of the new generation of large ships, but Bowyer had some experience with her class of vessel. In April and early May, he had piloted the *Adriatic*'s older sister *Celtic*, when she had taken up the sailings of an American line steamer which was laid up at the time. He did not seem overly daunted by the bulk of the new ships and was waiting when the *Adriatic* was reported in the offing.

The arrival of the White Star ship was a cause for civic celebration in Southampton. As Smith, under Pilot Bowyer's direction, conned his ship up Southampton Water, a large crowd gathered at the quay to greet them. As the ship came into dock, the main street was illuminated and town bells were rung. At the quay an official delegation from the council and the harbour board waited to greet the vessel, for as a local newspaper reporter noted, 'the vast importance of the move south of the White Star cannot yet be estimated at its true importance.'[13] The local officials could certainly see that it was a major boon, however, and laid on all its civic finery to proclaim as much.

On 3 June, the *Adriatic* was opened up to the public and the good round number of 8,888 people visited the ship, excellent publicity for the line and beneficial to the local community as the proceeds went to the local hospitals. Two days later, George Bowyer recorded that the ship sailed from its new home port for the first time. The Isle of Wight steamer *Prince of Wales*, full of well-wishers, followed the ship down as far as Osborne, 'when they wished the *Adriatic* Bon Voyage and returned to Southampton.'[14]

At Home with the Smiths

The move of services to Southampton meant that the Smiths too had to leave Liverpool where they had lived for the last fifteen years and make a new home in a strange new port. It would be a serious wrench for both of them, leaving behind both of their families and their friends, but in quitting Liverpool Smith also had to give up many obligations ashore. For instance, for some time he had been an executive member of the Liverpool branch of the Mercantile Marine Service Association. This body represented the interests of ship's masters and was in effect a sort of union. It ensured a high level of training for prospective officers and was in charge of running the training ships for cadets such as HMS *Conway*. There is no indication as to when Smith joined the Association, or what function he served in it, though his membership was noted in a number of small pieces following the *Titanic* disaster. These indicated that his membership lapsed on his removal to Southampton in 1907.[15]

But for the sake of Smith's career they had little choice but to move south to a new city and a new home. They settled on a large red brick, twin-gabled house in Winn Road, situated in the select Westwood Park district of Southampton. This they named 'Woodhead' in honour of the Pennington family farm where Eleanor had grown up. There is no way of knowing if the house was purchased before the opening of the new service or immediately after, though given Captain Smith's busy schedule the former seems the most likely. When their Liverpool home was sold their belongings were sent down followed by the Smiths themselves and by their maid Annie Brett, who is noted in the 1911 census and when she contributed to Smith's memorial gave her address as Southampton. Then, ensconced in their new home they would have set about turning it into a comfortable living space. By 1912, they certainly had the maid and a cook by the name of Mabel Inkpen and their new home boasted one of the still relatively new telephones; the Smiths' number was Southampton 1,400.

Here, Smith could just relax and be the family man, and time with his family was indeed precious to him. Some of his passengers, such as the Bishop of Willesden, noted that while Smith came across as a forward thinker, he was only too happy to put aside weightier matters and to chat amiably about his life at home. Kate Douglas-Wiggin actually witnessed some of this at first hand. On trips to Britain, she and her husband occasionally visited with the Smiths where, 'I saw him in his happy and delightful family life.' Another regular passenger of his, the publisher J.E. Hodder Williams, recalled how:

> In the little tea parties in his private state-room we learned to know the genial, warm-hearted family man; his face would light as he recounted the little intimacies of his life ashore, as he told of his wife and the trouble she had with the dogs he loved, of his little girl and her delight with the presents he brought her and the parties he had planned for her.[16]

One gets the impression from the letters that Smith wrote to his nephew Frank that he would have liked a little more shore leave. Whilst in command of the *Baltic* in 1905, he noted that the ship had been kept very busy and he was thankful for an extra week at home to get better acquainted with his daughter. She, he admitted in a letter in 1910, was a great comfort to her mother in her lonely life ashore. He also bemoaned the fact that in the last three months he had only had two days at home, 'not very satisfactory!'[17] he commented tersely. Home life was a rare commodity, Smith tended to feel that he had very little contact with either his family or their new home.

Eleanor too was perhaps less than enamoured with her new life in Southampton. The move, as her husband's comment notes, had meant that her life had become a relatively lonely one away from their family and friends in the north. Certainly following the *Titanic* disaster she commented in a letter to Frank that she would soon quit the house and so she did, moving back to Cheshire and Lancashire, though the move may have also been prompted by the now painful associations the place held for her. Added to this was the general ill-feeling with which Captain Smith's memory was regarded by the grieving citizens of Southampton. Though the town abounds with *Titanic* memorials, there were none erected there to Captain Smith.

Mel too, in spite of the presents and the parties, had little lasting contact with her new family home as she was soon enrolled at a boarding school. Ted, though, had his calm harbour and when not spending time with his family or entertaining the occasional visitors, he unwound in his study either reading or smoking. In later life, Mel recalled how her father would sit quietly smoking and he would only allow her in the room if she kept still and did not disturb the cloud of blue smoke that hung around his head.

When this paled, as he again noted to some of his friends, Smith enjoyed nothing better than spending time with the dogs that gave him such pleasure and his wife so many pains. In one famous photograph Captain Smith is pictured on the deck of one of his ships (possibly the *Baltic* or *Adriatic*) with his cigar in its holder in one hand, while the other held on to a short leash around the neck of a large, pale, shaggy Borzoi, or Russian Wolfhound. Hodder Williams' account indicates that Smith owned more than one animal and newspapers noted that Smith was fond of walking his dogs in the nearby New Forest.

The Millionaires' Captain

Ted Smith's command of the *Adriatic* had got off to a good start with the switch to Southampton and for the rest of 1907, his journeys to and from the States appear to have been trouble-free and he was the toast of ocean-going society. In July, living up to his nickname of the Storm King, Smith pushed his ship through an electrical storm and a snowstorm, but then quelled a third much more human tempest with a little well-honed diplomacy. After an evening's concert given by the vaudeville entertainers Clarice Vance and Pearl Jones, the $50 raised was handed to the ship's orchestra to divide amongst themselves. However, in stepped Mr Appleyard the ship's purser, who attempted to appropriate the money for the Seaman's Fund, much to the fury of the two women and their audience. Things looked black for a while until Smith suavely stepped into the fray. 'It shall be as the ladies wish.' He ruled and with cheers all around the money went to the orchestra.[18]

The accounts agree that it was in such ways, more by fair dealing and friendliness rather than flattery that Smith endeared himself to his first-class passengers. By all accounts it was this straightforward personal charm that attracted the right kind of customers earning him another nickname in the process, that of 'the millionaires' captain'. It is unclear as to when and if he did become said darling of the millionaire and smart set, though as the story above shows and the accounts of the Thallons and Kate Douglas-Wiggin indicate, his fan-base had been steadily growing with each successive command. His promotion to the *Adriatic* seemed further proof of this reputation.

Yet, for all that, it is easy to generalise and to get caught up in the mania that still to this day seems to touch all things *Titanic*. To read or watch some modern versions of the story, one might think that the *Titanic* was the be-all-and-end-all of Edwardian shipbuilding and as will be seen she was nothing of the sort. So too seems to be the case with Ted Smith. He is held up in many accounts as a shining example, the alpha and omega of ship's captains of the period. In fact, he was just one of a number of skippers whose pictures and stories graced the New York society pages and there is no indication prior to the *Titanic* disaster that he was regarded as the first among equals. *The Fort Wayne Journal-Gazette* of 18 September 1908 carried an article entitled 'The Steamship Captain as he Appears To-day'. Though Smith gets a passing mention, the article concentrates on Captains Kaempff and Knuth, two German commanders whose moustachioed and bearded faces smile benignly out of the old paper and whose deeds and awards are listed almost with a touch of awe.

Later that year, a Sunday supplement of the *New York Times* carried a picture spread of fourteen well-known liner captains. To modern eyes this in itself seems rather strange. To see photographs of fourteen grizzled seamen as opposed to the silicon, botox, steroid and computer-enhanced models, sports and film stars whose pictures would today grace such supplements, is in itself an interesting sign of the times and perhaps a rather sad comment on our own much more trivialised era. Smith is there in this rogue's gallery, as too are Captains Stenger, Froelich, Mills, Nierich, Van der Zee, Dempwolf, Charles, Schweke, Warr, Knuth, Doxrud, Barr and Passow.[19]

Yet, if Smith was not perhaps the paragon among sea captains that popular legend would have us believe, he was still very highly regarded by many very famous and influential people who both at sea and ashore actively sought out his company if not his approbation. And with such a wide set of acquaintances made aboard ship, Smith's social life in between voyages was anything but dull. Kate Douglas-Wiggin noted that Smith occasionally visited her and her family whilst ashore, but she was just one of an intellectual and artistic social set – not just millionaires – who mixed with White Star's paramount skipper.

Following the *Titanic* disaster, the *Oakland Tribune* ran a small article about Captain Smith, noting that he 'was a very popular man in New York clubdom'.[20] One of his club-going friends, the actor William Faversham, had apparently been telling stories of Captain Smith to a select group of fellow Bohemians a couple night before news of the *Titanic's* fate shocked everyone. One of the stories dealt with a dinner given at the Lambs Club, of which Faversham was a member. Though the story is not dated, Lambs Club records show that Faversham joined in 1897, so it may have been at the turn of the century. The Lambs Club was the actors' club of New York and the meal was given in honour of the British actor Sir Johnston Forbes-Robertson. Captain Smith had been invited, probably by Faversham, who was also there and another of Smith's actor friends, and Lambs Club member, John Drew, one of the ancestors of the Barrymore acting dynasty, was on hand to deliver one of the after dinner speeches.

It had been a hilarious affair and John Drew was full of the party atmosphere and not a little drunk when he got up to deliver his speech. Instead of doing this, however, Drew launched himself into a fulsome address to his friend Faversham, or 'Favvy' as he called him. Drew, thoroughly in his cups, went on so long and in such a fashion that the whole company including William Faversham became very uneasy and wondered when he would finish. Finally, Drew took his eyes off Faversham and caught the amused glance of Captain Smith seated nearby.

'Well, well,' exclaimed Drew, who suddenly realised that he was making a fool of himself, 'there's my dear old friend Ted Smith. Captain Smith transports people – and so does "Favvy".' With that, Drew finally shut up and sat down.[21]

Another club that Smith may have attended was the Metropolitan Club, sometimes referred to as 'the Millionaire's Club.' This had been established by financier J.P. Morgan and the Vanderbilts in 1891 to rival the older New York gentlemen's clubs that had snubbed the 'new money' millionaires such as Morgan. As will be seen, a party was held there in Smith's honour a few years later, and another reason why he may have been a regular guest at the club was because he was a very good friend of J.P. Morgan himself. Morgan was a terror in the business world and many people thought him a difficult person to get to know, but appearances could be deceptive. One White Star officer later wrote, 'Most of us were a little frightened of him, unnecessarily, for though apparently austere he had a very kind heart. I always think of him at Church Service on board, attended regularly, joining us lustily in his favourite hymns, with a deep basso voice.'[22]

Morgan and Smith seem to have hit it off early in the captain's career, the former, occasionally with his wife and children, had been travelling on Smith's ships for many years and they had become so well acquainted that Captain Smith and the Morgans often spent their leisure time together, along with other wealthy families during Smith's stopovers in the States. In one newspaper report from 1907, shortly after taking over the *Adriatic*, we see these two giants of the shipping world involved in a very informal and for the time rather hair-raising incident.

After arriving in New York on 5 September, Captain Smith, J.P. Morgan and Colonel Oswald Latrube of New York, spent a few days at Allen Winden, the Lenox, Massachusetts, estate of millionaire Charles Lanier. On the afternoon of 8 September, the party drove to nearby Pittsfield so that Mr Morgan could catch 'the millionaires express' on the New York, New Haven and Hartford railroad for New York. The four men made the journey in Mr Lanier's $15,000 car.

They had, however, left their journey a little late and arrived at the station just as the last carriage of the train disappeared around a curve in the road. Mr Morgan was alarmed as he needed to be in New York by the next day, so after a quick interview, the station master agreed to telegraph ahead and have the train held for a few minutes at Lee, 12 miles to the south of Pittsfield.

They only had a short time to get there but luckily for all concerned between Pittsfield and Lee there stretched a fine state highway. Mr Lanier got his car onto this and the driver put his foot down. The car roared down fashionable South Street at the then alarming speed of 40mph. Once out of the city, the car was pushed up to 60mph. En route the road passed through Lenox, where the police had set up a speed trap to deter would-be road hogs. Not that it had any effect in this instance and the car swept past the police so quickly that the surprised officers could not get a good look at the licence plate.

Out of Lenox, the car tore down the long bank into Lee. In the vehicle an anxious Mr Morgan sat, watch in hand, hoping they would not lose too much time. Coming into Lee's main street, the speeding car made a spectacular sight for the locals, who came out to see what the fuss was about. Pulling up outside the station, Mr Morgan, Captain Smith and Colonel Latrube jumped out to find the train waiting for them. They had made the trip from Pittsfield almost as quickly as the train and the conductor assured the passengers that the journey had been delayed by only two minutes. Morgan clambered aboard and was last seen waving goodbye to his friends as the train pulled away.[23]

Southampton to New York

On arriving back in New York after his car escapade, Captain Smith discovered that for his return journey back to Britain he would be taking personal responsibility for a passenger. Late on 10 September, a beautiful young woman, said to be the daughter of a millionaire London banker, was secretly brought aboard the *Adriatic* by six stewards, strapped securely to a stretcher.

She was well dressed and seemed quite respectable, being named on the passenger list as twenty-eight-year-old Miss Jessie Hyman, though this appears to have been an alias. She had arrived in the United States on 31 May aboard the *Oceanic* and went to stay with her brother at 213 Christopher Street, Brooklyn. But Jessie, if that was her real name, was a troubled individual and rapidly became unhinged and tried to take her own life. She was taken to the sanatorium at Flushing, Long Island, where her violent behaviour came to the notice of officials, who, finding her quite insane and of a suicidal disposition, ordered her restrained and deported.

Smith and Dr O'Loughlin were there to meet the sanatorium officials, who told the two men that she would have to be watched carefully and Smith was informed that he would be held personally responsible if anything happened to her during the voyage. They promised to see that she was well guarded and she was taken to one of finest suites on the liner. Here it seems her bonds were loosened to see if she would behave, but she immediately became violent and the attendants only restrained her after a fierce struggle. It probably came as a relief to all concerned when a few days later the young woman was deposited safely in Southampton, where others took responsibility for her.[24]

The New Year found the *Adriatic* riding out another bout of bad Atlantic weather. On one journey in late January 1908, the weather was varied. Early on in the voyage, the ship passed through a balmy light rain storm, then the sun came out and the passengers and crew were treated to a magnificent rainbow. As the ship neared New York, though, the weather grew worse and Smith stayed rigidly on the bridge as the *Adriatic* ploughed through a hurricane. He reported winds of 90mph, reducing the ship's headway at times to 15 knots.

Most of the passengers were unconcerned. The *Adriatic* weathered the storm well and the Storm King at the helm knew what he was doing. In first class, some of the men found themselves being fleeced by an expert lady poker player whose deeds warranted a mention in the *New York Times*. The only people who may have been worried were those who had to make connections. One frequent voyager was John Sharman from Yorkshire, a retired merchant who travelled for his health. He had already pre-booked his return journey to Liverpool from New York aboard the *Mauretania* on the 25th, though because of the storm there was no guarantee that the *Adriatic* would be on time.

Sure enough, for the *Adriatic* and many other ships there was no access to New York Harbour on 24 January. The pilot would not come out on account of the dangers of trying to bring vessels through the intricate approach to Sandy Hook. Within sight of America, Smith had to order the anchors dropped and the passengers would spend another night at sea.

By the next morning, though, the storm and eased and the *Adriatic* was one of the first ships brought into quarantine. A short time later she landed her passengers. The inveterate traveller John Sharman learnt that the *Mauretania* was now in the river outward bound for Liverpool. For most people this would have been a disappointment, but undeterred Mr Sharman quickly loaded his baggage aboard a tug and set off in pursuit of the departing liner. The *New York Times* noted that this was fairly normal practice for him. Mr Sharman had made eighty-eight trips to New York, but never spent more than a few hours in the city before catching a tugboat to some liner returning back across the Atlantic. [25]

If Smith was not dealing with peripatetic travellers, then he was hearing about his crew robbing the passengers. This would have ranged from petty larceny that was probably dealt with under ship's discipline, to major acts that required the police. One such incident occurred on 10 October 1908, when four crewmen were charged with looting passengers' luggage whilst the vessel was at sea. Hordes of stolen property to the value of $15,000 were found hidden around the ship.

The thefts were discovered when the longshoreman went aboard to unload the luggage and discovered that a number of trunks had been broken into. The main victim was Captain H.B. Blagrave, who had come aboard with six hunting dogs, a case of guns and several large trunks, one of which had been emptied and others interfered with. The thefts were immediately reported and Detective Edward Mallen employed by White Star was summoned to investigate, and hardly had the passengers' luggage begun to be unloaded than he and other detectives came aboard.

It was soon discovered that the baggage hold had been broken into and that the crime was obviously the work of crew members. A search of the stewards' quarters was without result, so the detectives proceeded to the quarters of the firemen and other crew. There they began to find traces of the missing luggage, some hidden in dunnage bags, under bunks, or hidden in out of the way places. Suspicions soon centred on four men, William Chalk, William Henry, Harry Cavendish and James Kelly, who were arrested. They soon admitted to the crime, telling how four days after the *Adriatic* left Queenstown they had broken into the hold, two keeping watch while the other two quickly rifled what they could. This did not require much effort on their part, as each trunk proved to be a goldmine in expensive goods. The men told the detectives where other items were hidden away and these were returned to their rightful owners while the four men were taken off to jail. [26]

Just over a month later, the *Adriatic* was the scene of more drama. The first occurred on 19 November, the day after leaving Southampton and prior to reaching Queenstown, when the body of first-class passenger John Krause was discovered in his cabin. The bedroom steward had grown concerned that he had seen nothing of this passenger since they had left Southampton. As a result that purser forced an entrance into the locked cabin and found Krause's body on the floor. He had cut his own throat and two bloodstained safety razors were found by his side and an empty whisky bottle was found nearby. Smith was informed and Dr O'Loughlin was summoned and concluded unsurprisingly that the man had bled to death. The body, he noted, was cold and he had been dead for quite some time. His body was handed over to the authorities when the ship reached Queenstown the next day, while the man's effects were carried on over to New York where they were handed over to his family.

The US papers gave some explanation as to Mr Krause's actions. He had been connected to the Pacific State and Sunset Telegraph Company of San Francisco and was apparently fleeing a subpoena that would have forced him to testify in the San Francisco graft scandal, where public money had been siphoned off by private companies. This had obviously played on his mind and the result was his suicide.[27]

These were just a few of the troubles that could beset an ocean voyage. Another danger awaiting the unwary travellers, notably any naive first-class passengers, were the professional gamblers who regularly took passage on the prestige liners in search of rich pickings. These had become something of a curse and the failure of the shipping lines to stop them reflected badly on their reputations. However, in time wary officers and stewards knew who to look out for and took steps to warn passengers of their presence aboard. On 27 February 1909, the *Syracuse Herald* reported that nine professional gamblers – described by the press as 'a jolly bunch' – who had made the westward passage on the *Adriatic* which had docked in New York the day before, had fared badly.

Several days earlier, soon after the *Adriatic* had cleared Cherbourg, Captain Smith was notified that the nine gamblers were on board. He immediately took a very proactive stance and issued orders that notices informing the passengers of the gamblers' presence aboard were to be posted in conspicuous places. The gamblers took the hint and made little effort to relieve the passengers of their money.

Three of the party did manage to get a small poker game going at one point, during which they spent about $50 on refreshments. Two passengers lost about $38 between them. It was estimated, however, that the gamblers had spent about $1,400 for their passage, which, contrasted with their $38 winnings, meant that for once they came off much worse than their potential victims.[28]

Half a dozen voyages later, though, found Smith and other ships officers on the receiving end where officialdom was concerned. By August 1909, New York had a new, energetic customs officer, Collector William Loeb, who was determined to stamp out the bringing ashore of numerous small articles from the steamships that arrived from overseas.

Almost every steamer and passenger vessel arriving at the port brought with it hundreds of small articles not listed on the manifest. Most of these were brought over by passengers as presents for friends, for their own use ashore, or perhaps to sell. Crew members too came ashore with dutiable goods that had previously escaped the lax watch formerly kept at the piers. This was not the case under Collector Loeb, who quickly stamped his mark on the service and whose vigilance rapidly netted hundreds of items worth thousands of dollars. Loeb and his men were good at their jobs, but it seemed after a little while that no one's dignity was to be spared, not even the ship's captain's. Matters came to a head in August, when men under the command of Collector Lutz took things a little too far. Captain Finch of the White Star vessel *Arabic* was left incandescent with rage at being unceremoniously frisked on his own gangplank and in front of his passengers and crew by two of Lutz's heavies. On 16 August, Captain Smith also came up against the same flinty attitude when he and Dr O'Loughlin reported to the Customs Office, prior to taking a trip up to

Marblehead to J.P. Morgan's residence on the Hudson River, where they had been invited to spend a few days.

Both men duly presented their valises for inspection. Each of them was carrying a box of cigars, the seals of which had been broken. In spite of their protests, these were confiscated, as too was a bottle of whisky in Dr O'Loughlin's valise. The two left the office thoroughly disgusted at their treatment and left for their trip. The customs men had managed to get away thus far with the treatment meted out to Captain Finch, but Captain Smith was a very different bird with at least one very influential friend. On reaching their destination Smith and O'Loughlin had obviously complained to Morgan about the indignity. Their mood could have hardly been helped if they happened to catch the papers the next day when their names and misdemeanor were reported under the headline 'Smugglers Plan to Outwit Loeb'. Incensed at the treatment his friends had suffered, Morgan immediately complained to no less a person than President Taft. The press soon caught wind of this and pursuing the story sought out Collector Loeb whose men had so embarrassed the country.[29]

All of which came as a surprise to Collector Loeb who, quite innocent, had been away on a fishing trip whilst his men pursued their draconian policy. He came back to New York to find his office besieged by the press looking for an explanation for his actions. It transpired that he had issued no orders to stop and search ship's captains. Acting on their own, his men had overstepped their authority and the treatment of men such as Captain Finch had been completely unwarranted. To say Loeb was cross would be an understatement and the comments he made to the press pulled no punches in regards to the stupidity of some of his staff. Lutz and his men had gone too far and he put their actions down to simmering discontent in his force over the abolition of the night inspectors and the formation of the marine police, though he in no way elaborated on this. He then added darkly that he knew who some of the other perpetrators were and that he wouldn't forget what they had done to injure the reputation of the service. He further noted that he had now issued strict instructions regarding the treatment in future to be accorded to the captains of ocean liners and their officers. They were not to be searched or interfered with in any way as they went about their duties.[30]

When reading through a tally of round-trip voyages, it is easy to forget that each voyage had its fair share of incidents both good and bad. Thus far 1909 sounds a rather grim year, but there were lighter moments for Smith and the crew of the *Adriatic*. On one occasion for instance, Captain Smith was able to entertain his passengers and indulge his interest in dogs. Two days out whilst en route to New York and on discovering that there were more than the usual number of pedigree dogs travelling with the passengers, first-class passenger Dr C.Y. Ford of Canada began to interest the dog owners in an exhibition. There was general approval for the idea and the owners met in the saloon of the vessel to organise the contest. Dr George Taylor of New York was to be the referee and Dr Ford was the judge. Thus on Tuesday 5 October with Smith's blessing and under his patronage the first-class passengers and crew organised the 'Adriatic Kennel Club', which was reported to be the first dog show ever held on the high seas.

The deck was specially decorated for the occasion and the dog owners and their pets turned out in the afternoon just as they would at any dog show ashore, though in less formal dress. There were sixteen entries in total and the winners were awarded small souvenir silver cups acquired from the ship's barber engraved '*Adriatic*'.

The prize for best in show was chosen by J.J. Manning of New York and went to a dog named Lilly, a griffon soyeau purchased in France by Miss Bertron, the daughter of S.R. Bertron of New York. Other prize winners were a dalmation and a so-called 'golden fox' dog belonging to David Elkins; a Blenhein spaniel owned by Mrs W. Ritter of Cleveland; an Austrian pomeranian and miniture pomeranian belonging to Mrs J.J. Vatable of New York; a black pomeranian owned by Mrs E.C. Jourgensen of Brooklyn; a miniture pomeranian belonging to Mrs M.H. Behr of New York; an Aberdeen terrier the property of Mrs Wain of Philadelphia; and a Scottish terrier owned by R.B. Van Cortlandt.

The competitors seem to have entered the contest in all seriousness, but were not above seeing the lighter side of things and there was a great deal of hilarity when some wag tried to enter the two ship's cats as 'nice hounds'. [31]

On the next journey, though, Smith's name was again in the newspapers for all the wrong reasons when on arriving in New York Harbour at 3.20a.m. on 4 November, the *Adriatic* ran aground on a sandbank at the entrance to the Ambrose Channel. This incident was not recorded in the ship's log book, though it was eagerly reported in the New York papers.

The ship was carrying 881 passengers including pioneer aviator Orville Wright and his sister Katherine, but they and the other passengers had to wait patiently as efforts were made to free the vessel. In a wireless message to the agents, Captain Smith asked for tugs to be sent out. The ship, though firmly stuck, was in no danger and he was sure that she would float free on the next tide. If that was not the case, he made arrangements for another steamer to come down to take off the passengers and their hand baggage.

This, however, was not necessary, for as predicted the ship moved on the next tide. Captain Smith had the ship's water tanks emptied and a line was passed from the wrecking tug *Merrick-Chapman*. At 8.10a.m., the tug pulled *Adriatic* free of the sand and towed her into deeper water. There was no damage and the ship proceeded up the bay to quarantine. [32]

There was more grim news reported in early 1910, when the ship suffered another suicide. On 12 March, as the *Adriatic* pulled away from her pier in New York, English acrobat Edward 'Beppo' Ettridge committed suicide by shooting himself through the head. He was discovered in the cabin of fellow vaudevillian Alfred Burgess and when Dr O'Loughlin was called he presumed that the dead man was Burgess and wrote out the certificate to the effect that the latter had been found '... with a bullet wound in his head.' However, when the body was returned to the pier on a tug the misidentification was corrected.

Once again in 1910, we get another letter from Captain Smith written to his nephew Frank Hancock. Of the three surviving letters by his own hand, this one dated 28 April 1910, and penned on the *Adriatic*'s fifth arrival in New York that year, is probably the most fascinating and yet the most frustrating from a biographer's point of view. There are references to a couple of people whom we would like to know better, but who stubbornly refuse to be identified. By way of compensation, though, we do catch a few more glimpses of E.J. Smith when he didn't have a reporter jotting down his every word. Smith in the raw is much more interesting.

Captain Smith wrote in reply to a 'nice chatty letter' he had received from Frank. He added that it was good to receive a cheerful note occasionally as most of the letters he received from his family tended to be rather depressing. He mentions a letter from someone named 'Lill', which gave him a poor account of John, though there is no indication as to who these two were exactly and what part of the family they belonged to, as they do not seem to relate to any of his relatives that we know of. He goes on to congratulate Frank on his success at work and over his growing family, referring briefly to Eleanor and Melville and their lonely life ashore while he was at sea. He also hoped at some point to take a trip to visit Frank in Savannah, or arrange to meet him should the latter ever be in New York on business.

The middle of the letter begins with Smith noting that Mrs Mallock would be aboard the *Adriatic* on the next crossing to Southampton. This was probably Mrs Christian Mallock, the thirty-nine-year-old wife of cotton exporter John Mallock, both of whom were listed in 1910 US census as residents of Chatham County, Savannah. A letter from one Christian Mallock was sent to Frank after the *Titanic* disaster, which seems to confirm this identification. Smith was glad to note that he would be having a friendly face aboard ship and then commented that while it took all sorts of people to make a world, ocean travel did seem to bring out the worst in people. This was hardly the kind of comment he would have made to a journalist, but it does show the real man who was rather weary of dealing with an irksome, demanding public. On top of these more general problems, he noted that he was suffering staff changes. White Star currently had two ships laid up and with the glut of available officers this provided, the company had decided to send all of its available RNR officers to undergo the required drill. As a result, on the past three voyages Captain Smith had seen several changes in his command staff including two chief officers he had never sailed with before. It was all very trying as was his lack of time with his family. Evidently John Mallock had offered to put his car at Smith's disposal should he come to Savannah. The thought of visiting Savannah and the other ports from his days aboard the *Lizzie Fennell* evidently appealed to him, though he did not doubt that things would have changed considerably in the interim. He was, though, a busy man and looked set to get even busier as the *Olympic*, the first of White Star's latest breed of super liner, was ready to enter service in July 1911. He then ended the letter by sending his regards to Frank's wife, who had met him some years earlier.

The crew lists from the period show that he did indeed suffer a few staff changes in early 1910, though he seems to have taken on only one new chief officer, Joseph Evans, who took over from Chief Officer E.J. English who had been with the *Adriatic* since late 1908. Along with Evans came a new second officer, C.C. Boase, who had served with Smith in a more junior capacity aboard the *Majestic*, both of them joining the ship on 26 January. Boase was promoted to first officer for the next voyage when William Murdoch left the ship, either on leave or to undergo his RNR drill, reverting back to second when Murdoch returned to the fold for the next journey.

Chief Officer Joseph Evans also stayed on and later followed Smith, for one journey at least, when he took over the *Olympic*. When he joined the *Adriatic*, Evans was fifty-one years old and would lead a blameless but unspectacular career, happily serving out his remaining years at sea as chief officer on several vessels but never rising to have a command of his own. He does, however, win the prize for the most misidentified officer of the White Star Line, being regularly cited in photographs as his successor, Chief Officer Henry Wilde of the *Olympic* and *Titanic*.

On 20 June 1910, Smith was in receipt of another medal to go with his rather lonely looking Transport Medal. In light of his long service with the Royal Naval Reserve, he along with a number of other officers, was awarded the Royal Naval Reserve Officer's Decoration.[33] The decoration was granted for fifteen years commissioned service (sub-lieutenant and above) in the RNR. This was a far more ostentatious award than the Transport Medal, a filigree of brass and silver bearing the royal cipher and hung on a green ribbon and its award allowed Smith the distinction of having the letters 'R.D.' (Reserve Decoration) after his name. Like the Transport Medal, Smith would wear this new gong displayed on the left breast of his dark uniform, this more exhaulted award taking precedence over the campaign medal. These are the two medals he is seen wearing on later famous photos of him aboard the *Olympic* and *Titanic*.

In August 1910, there occurred what some have called a 'mutiny' among the *Adriatic's* firemen, though what actually happened was more like a strike, the principal reason for the trouble being money.

The *Adriatic* was due to leave Southampton on 10 August, however, on 8 August as a result of a rather vague ongoing pay dispute, 100 union firemen walked off the ship. The union was seeking a 10s rise in the firemens' wages and had also taken umbrage at White Star, who they claimed were hiring men in New York via the Church of England Mission there, who were physically unable to work in a stokehold.

The union then threatened to walk out on other White Star vessels and Cunard's *Mauretania* unless their demands were met. The police threw a cordon around the White Star dock, but the firemen were confident that the ship could not leave. However, much to their surprise, on 10 April the ships sailed as planned, the stokeholds being manned temporarily by office workers and other shore employees. After leaving Southampton and passing down the Solent, Smith stopped his ship off the Isle of Wight, where White Star had gathered 100 firemen who were waiting on a tug. These replaced the office workers who were dismissed and they were joined by a further seventeen firemen when the ship reached Queenstown.

Due to the fact that the new stokers were unfamiliar with the big ship and could not make enough steam, the *Adriatic* was a few hours late arriving in New York on the night of 18 August. Once the ship docked, forty or fifty of the replacement stokers promptly deserted, much to the horror of the US authorities and to the chagrin of White Star. There, though, this curious tale ends, on both sides of the Atlantic. No further articles told of the deserters in the United States and by the time the *Adriatic* returned to Southampton, the dispute there had effectively fizzled out without spreading to any other vessels.[34]

6

THE WEDNESDAY SHIP

For the next six months, Captain Smith conned the *Adriatic* back and forth across the Atlantic without any more serious upsets to spoil his remaining time on board her. The 'Big Four' had made quite a splash since they first appeared in 1901, but the shipping world had moved on since then and even the relatively new *Adriatic* found herself easily matched or outmatched by ships operated by White Star's rivals. German and American vessels now vied for the prestige shipping lanes, but the company's biggest rival still by far was Cunard, which in 1907 had pulled off a remarkable coup with the launch in close succession of the *Lusitania* and *Mauretania*. Bankrolled by the British Government, no expense was spared to produce the two vessels. Powered by direct-drive turbine engines and engineered to a new radical design with powerful big propellers and rudders, these two 32,000-ton wonder ships had been designed by Cunard to top their rivals. With service speeds of 25 knots and top speeds in excess of 28 knots, the *Lusitania* and *Mauretania* easily outran anything else on the oceans. As a result, in 1907 the *Lusitania* did what she had been ostensibly designed for, she won the Blue Riband for the fastest west-bound crossing. The two Cunard ships then competed with one another for the next few years until the *Mauretania*'s record crossing in 1909 set a record that would stand for the next twenty years.

The appearance of these two transatlantic greyhounds on the shipping scene totally wrong-footed Cunard's rivals. The Germans had lost the Blue Riband and the IMM conglomerate, of which White Star was now a key component, lost its growing stranglehold on the North Atlantic trade. For travellers, businessmen and even emigrants who wanted to get across the Atlantic as quickly as possible, there was quite literally nothing to match the *Lusitania* and *Mauretania*, certainly not the smaller, slower, albeit more luxurious White Star ships.

There was, however, a flaw in Cunard's plans. Despite their size and impressive speed, the two ships were not enough to maintain a regular bus service back and forth between Europe and the United States, a third ship being required. As a result, until that problem was rectified with the launch some years later of the *Aquitania*, White Star with it slower but much more regular sailings kept a firm hold on the market. Nevertheless, it was clear to the IMM and White Star management that the new Cunarders were the shape of things to come and they would have to produce a new breed of vessel to compete. To this end in 1907, J. Bruce Ismay met with Lord William Pirrie of Harland & Wolff to discuss the matter. Between them they thrashed out a plan to construct a new class of White Star liner, bigger and finer than anything Cunard or their other rivals could offer. These would also replace some of their own now ageing transatlantic liners on the New York run. The vessels, to be over 40,000 tons each, were given the names *Olympic, Titanic* and *Gigantic* (though the latter was renamed *Britannic* after the *Titanic* disaster, as White Star did not wish to remind people of that disaster with such a similar name). There was little point in trying to compete with Cunard speed-wise, so following the tradition of the 'Big Four', the emphasis was to be placed on comfort, safety, reliability, luxury and size.

The design for the new vessels was soon finalised. This was by no means radical, being merely an upsizing and streamlining of the tried and tested designs that Harland & Wolff had been producing for White Star for the last few decades, but with a little more showmanship to equal Cunard's big ships. The *Olympic*-class ships were originally designed to have three funnels, but as Cunard's new ships had four funnels, a fourth – a ventilation dummy – was added to the White Star ships for effect. It seems that White Star's new vessels not only had to be bigger, but look the part as well.

Within two years of this meeting, the keels of the *Olympic* and the *Titanic* had been laid down in two specially constructed docks at Harland & Wolff. In 1910, the *Olympic* was launched and another year was given over to constructing her upper works and fitting her out.

Like her sister after her, the *Olympic* began her career as the largest ship in the world. In overall length she measured 882ft 9in, was 92ft 6in wide and 104ft from keel to bridge. Period newspapers made efforts to convey the size of the ship in more visible terms, placing a drawing of her amidst the buildings of central London in one, or putting the ship on end against the Eiffel Tower and the Egyptian pyramids in another. In gross tonnage the *Olympic* weighed 45,324 tons and she displaced an estimated 60,000 tons in the water. The ship had accommodation for over 3,500 people.

Eschewing the modern direct drive turbines used by Cunard, motive power, up to an estimated top speed of 24–25 knots, came from two triple-expansion steam engines powering the ship's wing propellers and a smaller turbine engine for the central propeller. These were fed by twenty-nine boilers, arranged in rows through six separate compartments amidships. The boilers also supplied the heating for the ship's massive plumbing system, not only to the cabins but also to the galleys, the ship's swimming bath and the elegant first-class saunas and Turkish baths.

There were sporting facilities: the squash court on G deck and a fully equipped gymnasium on A deck, both of which came with their own professional instructor. Reading rooms and smoking rooms were decorated to the latest taste and with great attention to detail, sporting specially commissioned works of art. The ship's restaurants were equally extensive, affording the last word in elegance. This, of course, was in first class, but the facilities for second- and third-class passengers, though less elegant, were considered the best on any ship afloat.

But the greatest luxury undoubtedly went into the cabins. For those in second or third class, these were essentially utilitarian, very similar to what we expect today, but in first class, especially for those in the most expensive state rooms, comfort, luxury and sheer unadulterated elegance were the watchwords. Rooms were decorated with panelling and stucco and fitted out in a number of different styles with fine furniture, crockery and linen. Some staterooms housed four-poster beds, tapestries hung across the walls and beautiful glassware decorated rooms, along with ornate mirrors and light fittings and well-made high-class furniture. The decoration was limited only, perhaps, by the creativity of the various craftsmen employed in producing such beautiful settings.

The *Olympic* incorporated the latest safety features. Inside her hull, she was subdivided by fifteen watertight transverse bulkheads, making sixteen separate compartments. These were interconnected by a series of emergency watertight doors that in the event of flooding could be closed either singly by the engineer on the spot, or all of them automatically from the bridge. The hull itself was double bottomed, with a secondary hull built inside the main one. If the main hull of 1in-thick steel plate was breached, the designers were confident that the secondary hull would hold. The space in between these two hulls was approximately 7ft, easily enough for a man to walk through.

Yet given all these features, did the designers say that the ship was unsinkable? Of all the great legends surrounding the story of these *Olympic*-class liners and most notably the *Titanic*, the story that the ship was said to be unsinkable has been the most enduring and the most ironic in the light of what was to happen to two of the three *Olympic*-class liners. Sir Philip Gibbs in his contemporary work *The Deathless Story of the Titanic*, quotes White Star publicity as having said that the ship was unsinkable. The company did say this, albeit in a qualified manner. In 1911, White Star issued a small four-page publicity leaflet showing the two sisters, the *Olympic* and the *Titanic*, on the stocks at Harland & Wolff, accompanied by an artist's impression of how they would look when they were finished. The leaflet went on to describe the dimensions, weight and luxurious appointments of the two liners. Then, in the final paragraph came the fatal phrase, '... and as far as it is possible to do so, these two wonderful vessels are designed to be unsinkable.'[1]

These leaflets seem to have been intended for shipping offices and travel agents, but the vast majority were quietly withdrawn and destroyed after the *Titanic* disaster made their existence highly embarrassing.

Another source of the unsinkable legend was a contemporary shipping journal that reviewed the *Titanic* and described her as 'practically unsinkable'[2], but this may have been echoing White Star's own generalisation. Certainly, by the time the *Titanic* set sail many of the passengers had the spurious notion in their heads that the ship could not sink; this caused many to delay when disaster struck and cost them their lives.

Then there were the lifeboats. The *Olympic*-class ships had originally been designed to carry thirty-two boats, with capacity for well over 2,000 people, but in the event, the company decided that it could do without the extra expense that sixteen more lifeboats would create, deeming the ship's safe enough with her inbuilt safety features. So, the *Olympic* and *Titanic* received only the necessary sixteen lifeboats required by the British Board of Trade regulations, the same number as had been carried by the *Baltic* and the *Adriatic*. These were arranged eight either side of the ship, slung from Welin davits. The company also provided the ship with the four Engelhardt collapsible lifeboats that had been supplied to the 'Big Four'. These were wooden-keeled, canvas-sided craft, which looked flimsy but were perfectly seaworthy in calm conditions. These were lashed in place on the roof of the officers' quarters.

As his letter to his nephew Frank indicates, Smith seems to have known since the previous year that he was to be given command of the *Olympic*[3]. In February 1911, he handed command of the *Adriatic* over to Captain Bertram Hayes before going to join the *Olympic* in Belfast. Prior to taking the ship on, Smith found time to make a trip back to the Potteries to visit his family and friends there. Whilst there he stayed with his nephew J.W.S. Harrington. Evidently Smith was pleased at having been given command of the *Olympic* and may have already been over to see the new vessel as she was being fitted out. He now talked confidently about the strengths of the giant ship and Mrs Harrington remembered him saying words to the effect that the *Olympic* 'was firm as a church'.[4]

The long stint ashore that thus saw him mulling the pros and cons of his new command also saw Smith recorded in one last census. The 1911 census for England and Wales was taken on the night of Sunday 2 April 1911 and gives an interesting view of his family life in Southampton. Smith and Eleanor were present, aged sixty (sic) and forty-seven respectively, as too was Mel, now a bouncy thirteen year old. Their maid who had come down with them, Ann Brett aged twenty-seven, from Cheshire and cook Mabel Lucy Inkpen, twenty-two, from Dorset, made up the normal household. There were also two visitors there that night, Thomas Martin, a twenty-two-year-old medical student from Walkden in Lancashire, and twelve-year-old Florence May Curry from Eltham, Kent. Who these two were is unknown, though from their similarity in age we can speculate that Florence was one of Mel's friends who was stopping over. There was plenty of room for all of them at Woodhead as the census return noted that the Smith's home had no less than thirteen rooms. That, though, is the last family snapshot we get of the Smiths together, not so very long after this, of course, that peaceful household would be shattered for good.

In Belfast, the *Olympic* was now complete, the final expensive items of her interior decor were in place, her propellers had been checked over and the final coats of paint were applied. Preliminary trials were carried out on 2 May 1911 to make sure that her engines were in order ready for her sea trials. The people of Belfast were then allowed on board for a day to look around; the price was 5s a head, the proceeds going to the local hospitals.

According to his records Smith took command of the *Olympic* in May 1911 and was thus at the helm to oversee this final critical stage before she was passed over to White Star. Under him perhaps for this and certainly for the ship's maiden voyage was an experienced team of officers. On deck with him were Chief Officer Joseph Evans, First Officer William Murdoch, Second Officer Robert Hulme, Third Officer Henry Osbourne Cater, Fourth Officer David William Alexander, Fifth Officer Alphonse Martin Tulloch and Sixth Officer Harold Holehouse. William O'Loughlin was the ship's chief surgeon and the engines were under the charge of Chief Engineer Joseph Bell and his men. Under these men, the *Olympic*'s sea trials took place on 29 May 1911. Having been guided down Belfast Lough, her compasses were adjusted and once enough steam had been raised the ship was put through her paces. On Smith's orders she was pushed through a series of tests, one testing her turning circle. Other tests were no doubt carried out, but a clear record of the *Olympic*'s sea trials is sadly lacking, though it is known that there was no speed trial as such, but the ship surpassed her required service speed. At the end of proceedings, the ship's wireless was tuned and tested by her two wireless operators and a message was sent to Liverpool declaring the tests a complete success.

The *Olympic*'s certificate of seaworthiness, valid for a year, was signed and the new ship was handed over to the White Star Line on 31 May 1911. The delay of a couple of days had been due to White Star wishing to make this a handover part of a double event as the launch of the *Olympic*'s younger sister *Titanic* had been scheduled for that day.

Sure enough, the prospect of the spectacle afforded by the two *Olympic*-class liners attracted a huge crowd to the Belfast waterfront. Numerous invited guests including J.P. Morgan and J. Bruce Ismay were there to accept the *Olympic* into the IMM/ White Star fold and to oversee the launch of the *Titanic*. In the crowd, held high by his father, was a young lad named William McQuitty, who in later life would go on to produce the famous film *A Night to Remember*, which documented the loss of the *Titanic*. For now, though, he and many others watched as without the naming ceremony shown in that film (White Star did not believe in the practice), the wedges holding the ship in place were removed and to the cheers and gasps of the crowd *Titanic* glided down into the water, helped on her way by tons of grease and soft soap and dragging monumental piles of chains to slow her release. The launch was as smooth as that of the *Olympic*, indeed, the hull was exactly the same dimensions as her sister ship now sitting at anchor a short distance away. The only difference was that at her launch the *Olympic* had been painted white to make her more conspicuous, while the *Titanic* was painted black.

While the *Titanic* was removed to the outfitting basin to begin her transformation from an empty shell to a luxury liner, the *Olympic*, now the property of the White Star Line, left Belfast for a brief visit to her port of registry. The *Olympic* arrived at

Liverpool at 4.30p.m. on the 31st. The next day, for several hours, the ship was again open to the public at half a crown each. That evening, though, the ship departed for Southampton to make ready for her maiden voyage.

Running down from Liverpool and past the Welsh coast, the *Olympic* made good time. The ship passed The Lizard at 2.45 on the afternoon of 2 June and by the early hours of 3 June she was in the approaches to Southampton. Smith and his officers were well pleased with the new vessel's performance thus far, it boded well for this new class of super liner.

Having sent a wireless message ahead, the *Olympic* paused outside Southampton Water to pick up the harbour pilot, George Bowyer, the same man who had brought in Smith's previous command, the *Adriatic*. That experience and those with the big foreign ships had not, however, prepared Bowyer for the sheer size of the vessel that now loomed, lights blazing, out of the darkness. He and the crew of the Nab Lightship, 'could hardly believe our eyes there was such a ship.' Taken up to the bridge he was obviously still agog at the bulk of the *Olympic*. He said as much to a cheery Captain Smith when they met.

'Yes,' Smith replied, 'but after you have been on board for some time her size will wear off.'[5]

Perhaps somewhat daunted, Bowyer decided to take his time getting the new ship in. Having negotiated the approaches, five tugs came forward to help the ship into the Ocean Dock. This was not quite finished, only the *Olympic*'s berth, number 44 was ready, at the entrance to which were two sizeable 'dolphins', or buffers, which had been place there to protect those working on the two pier heads. By this time it was 3a.m., and in the dark and with the added difficulties presented by the dock entrance, Bowyer decided to take the ship in bow first. This would necessitate a rather tricky exit stern first on sailing day, but that could not be helped. For all that, *Olympic*'s arrival at Southampton passed without incident and by 4a.m., the ship was securely warped into her berth.

Though she had arrived in the dead of night, the *Olympic* did not want for a welcome from the people and officials of Southampton; the town had been eagerly awaiting the arrival of White Star's new behemoth. One of the ship's medical officers, Dr J.C.H. Beaumont, recalled that the *Olympic*, '…caused a sensation when she first appeared in Southampton… she looked colossal and even "uncanny" as she towered above the waterline… dwarfing all other craft within sight… To prevent visitors getting lost or strayed, parties had to be formed and led around by guides who were by no means sure of the direct route.'[6]

Among the first to visit the *Olympic* on the morning of its arrival was a party of council officials. At 11a.m., the Mayor of Southampton, Colonel E. Bance, arrived, accompanied by several aldermen and the town clerk. Smith was there dressed in his finery ready to receive them when they came aboard and after being given a tour of the ship, the visitors having been charmed and delighted with all they saw, Smith, the mayor and his party joined a large assembly of company executives and local officials for a splendid luncheon that was served in the first-class dining saloon to the accompaniment of the ship's orchestra.

The citizens of Southampton got their chance to look around the *Olympic* on 10 June, on payment of a small fee that went to the local charities. In the meantime, Smith probably left the ship in the charge of one of his officers, perhaps Chief Officer Evans, while he took a taxi home to Woodhead for a few days with his family.

During her stopover, the *Olympic* was loaded with stores for her maiden transatlantic voyage: thousands of tons of meat, fish, butter, sugar, fruit and vegetables as well as equally impressive amounts of drink, from straight forward tea and coffee up to the harder stuff, were brought aboard. The White Star stores also supplied thousands of tons of fresh linen from bed sheets to table napkins as well as crockery, cutlery and glass. Many local businesses benefited from the arrival of the *Olympic*, for instance flower merchants F.G. Bealing and Son, who provided 400 plants to decorate the ship's interiors. These were distributed to the reading and writing rooms, the à la carte restaurant and veranda cafe, while smaller plants were scattered in baskets or small pots throughout the ship's numerous lounges and public spaces.

The ship also needed thousands of tons of coal for the trip across the Atlantic. This was supplied by R. and J.H. Rea, who transferred 4,000 tons of coal from their barges into the *Olympic* in fifteen minutes, a world record in 1911. Though there was a coal porters strike in progress, enough strike breakers were available to bunker the ship, though this had necessitated searches being made as far away as the north of England to find enough to get the job done.

The strikers had hoped to cripple the passenger trade and delay the *Olympic*'s departure and there were lingering doubts even on the morning of 14 June that the *Olympic* would be able to get away that day. Early that afternoon, though, she began her maiden voyage, though hardly in the most stately manner. Crowds of people watched as Pilot Bowyer, with five tugs at his command, carefully eased her out of her dock stern first, then on down to the entrance to the Itchin where the new ship's turning circle had recently been dredged. It took an hour to get the ship out into the channel and facing in the right direction with her bow pointing down Southampton Water, but finally she was on her way.

As she was flying the RNR ensign, the *Olympic* was saluted loudly by the British warships moored at Spithead in preparation for the coronation of George V. After a trouble-free crossing of the Channel, the ship arrived at Cherbourg at 7p.m., on a fine summer's evening. Here, the two new tenders, *Nomadic* and *Traffic*, that had left Belfast on the same day as the bigger ship, ferried out the first batch of travellers from the continent. There followed an overnight run back along the English south coast and across St George's Channel to Queenstown in Ireland. Here, the *Olympic* picked up her final batch of travellers, including many Irish emigrants off to the States. For a maiden voyage the *Olympic* was not excessively well booked, which may be a reflection of the uncertainty caused by the coal strike. The ship carried 489 first-class, 263 second and 564 steerage passengers, a total of 1,316 people. In addition, in her capacity as a Royal Mail Steamer, *Olympic* also carried 2,500 bags of mail as well as about 2,000 tons of cargo.

Among the passengers were J. Bruce Ismay and his wife. Another of note was Colonel Thomas Denny of the famous Dumbarton firm of shipbuilders, who was making the trip to see how well the ship's main engines and turbine worked. Also on board, as on the maiden voyage of the *Adriatic*, was the Harland & Wolff Guarantee Group, headed once again by Thomas Andrews. Both Ismay and Andrews would make recommendations that would later be incorporated into the design of the *Titanic*. For instance, during this voyage, Ismay noted that the open deck space on B deck was too large and that not many passengers were using it. He went on to suggest that the *Titanic's* plans be altered to add more cabins to the promenade deck. These would include the famous private verandas to some of the swankier cabins on the *Titanic*.

Andrews, meantime, would spend the voyage wandering the ship, making detailed notes on anything that came to his attention. Some of his notes covered minor details of design, such as sponge holders being fitted in the private bathrooms on B and C decks, the numbering on promenade deck steamer chairs was to be altered and extra cane furniture was to provided for the popular first-class reception room. Other recommendations dealt in a minor way with ship's operations. Andrews had noted the trouble that the ship had leaving her dock and suggested that in future the Southampton pilots take up their position on the docking bridge on the poop deck if they were leaving stern first, as was the habit in Liverpool. He also recommended that warning boards announcing to other vessels that the ship carried triple screws were to be fixed permanently to the stern rails.

Many of his recommendations, though, this time as on previous occasions, were designed to make the crew's life easier. Indeed, Andrews was very highly regarded by the ordinary crewmen and women, for the thought he gave not only to their working spaces, but also to their accommodation. Stewardess Violet Jessop recorded in her memoirs how during this voyage, the victualling department presented Andrews with a magnificent walking stick for his efforts to improve their lot, which, she noted, was usually of secondary importance to passenger accommodation.[7] The *Olympic* incorporated some of these improvements, for instance there were now bathrooms for all the stewards. Jessop also later noted that Andrews regularly consulted with the stewards and stewardesses and when they first boarded the *Titanic* a year later, each went off eagerly in search of their own pet innovation.

Captain Smith also consulted with Andrews at some point and a couple of his recommendations stand out in the engineer's notes. Smith suggested the installation of protective sliding screens with round bulls eye windows to be fitted over the square windows on the navigating bridge as had been done on the *Adriatic*. Though the weather for the *Olympic's* maiden voyage was largely fine, in dirtier conditions the big square windows might blow out in a gale or fierce sea. As pictures of the *Olympic's* bridge later show this suggestion was soon acted upon.

The second of Andrews's notes relating directly to Captain Smith was concerned more with the skipper's comfort. Andrews noted that linoleum tiles should not be fitted in the captain's sitting room in which a full carpet was provided.

These considerations aside, for Ted Smith the *Olympic*'s inaugural voyage was pretty easy going. As was the case with all new ships, Smith broke her in gently, gradually increasing the number of boilers in use and her speed as the days passed. A similar process was carried out with the *Titanic* the next year. The increase in speed during the *Titanic*'s voyage, which was touched on by so many of Smith's critics, was like so many other aspects of that fateful journey, perfectly normal practice. Though Smith was undoubtedly a forceful sailor so far as his ships were concerned, rarely letting the weather conditions daunt him, it does not follow that he was foolhardy into the bargain and the *Olympic*'s maiden voyage offers evidence that when the conditions became dangerous Smith slowed his ship. He alluded to rougher weather conditions on the morning of 19 June, when he sent a wireless message:

On Board Olympic, via Cape Race
9.30a.m., June 19, 1911.
Up to this hour the Olympic has exceeded the speed promised by her builders, her average from noon Saturday to noon Sunday being 21.89 knots. Since passing Daunt's Rock at 4.22p.m., Thursday she has done the following: to noon Friday, 458 knots (sic); to noon Saturday, 524 knots; to noon Sunday 542 knots. Weather fine. Present weather outlook less favourable. At this writing all going smoothly.

The Olympic will probably reach the Ambrose Channel late to-night and come to her pier Wednesday morning.

As Smith notes in this message the weather on Monday 19 June closed in and he slowed the ship on account of fog, reducing her run to noon on Monday to 525 nautical miles travelled. The argument would be during the *Titanic*'s maiden voyage that J. Bruce Ismay urged Smith to push the ship at high speed despite Smith's misgivings, his interference and Smith's meek compliance supposedly contributing to the disaster. Yet here on a much more high-profile maiden voyage than the *Titanic*'s would be, we see Captain Smith completely in charge, sensibly slowing his vessel despite the fact that his supposedly publicity hungry managing director was aboard. Nor does Ismay appear to have in any way quibbled over Smith's decision on this or any previous occasion.

For the passengers the brief delay caused by the fog was just one of those things and all were unanimous in their praise of the new liner and thus it was a happy, satisfied crowd who landed at New York on the morning of 21 June.

The marine observer at Sandy Hook spotted the *Olympic*'s lights at 12.17a.m., when the ship was east of Fire Island, coming in at a fair rate of knots and some hours before her projected arrival. Shortly after this, Smith sent a message ahead that he expected to reach quarantine at about 3a.m.

Having picked up the New York pilot Julius Adler, the ship proceeded to quarantine and following the inspection by the New York Revenue Cutter at 7.45a.m., the *Olympic* began a processional up past Staten Island into New York Harbour. Despite the early hour, her arrival had drawn quite a crowd, not only lining the shore but out on the water. The ship was saluted and trailed by numerous motor boats and ferries as she made her way towards her berth at pier 59.

One ship that did not acknowledge the *Olympic* was the Cunarder *Lusitania*, which swung out into the river at 9a.m., just after the White Star liner had passed her. Reporters speculated rather mischievously that her skipper, Captain Charles, had either been too preoccupied with his own preparations for departure, or he was feeling too full of himself on his elevation to Commander of the Bath, that he failed to notice the *Olympic* as she slipped by.

Twelve tugs stood ready to bring the ship into dock under the pilot's instructions and as with her exit from Southampton this would prove a tricky business, taking nearly an hour to complete. Nor was it without some drama as one of the tugs, the *O.L. Hallenbeck*, got itself caught in the backwash from the *Olympic*'s propellers and found itself driven under the ship's stern. For a while it seemed that there was a minor disaster in the making as the tug's flagstaff shattered against the overhanging counter and its stern was forced lower and lower. Somehow the tug managed to break free and limped over to the safety of the nearest jetty. Reporters on the scene made light of the incident describing it as 'a playful touch', but it showed just how difficult it was for even experienced sailors and pilots to handle these big new liners. The tug's owners afterwards put in a lawsuit and White Star countered with their own. The case, though, was later dropped due to lack of evidence.

All this was a minor distraction, though. Hardly were the gangplanks in place than the passengers were filing off into a mass of pressmen and well-wishers. Reporters then swarmed aboard to get the low-down on how the ship had performed. Smith and his officers, immaculate in their white summer uniforms, were ready for them, praising the ship and offering up the swift, clipped sound bites that journalists love. Captain Smith said that the ship had done all that was expected of her and had behaved splendidly, though he conceded that there had been no really bad weather to test her seaworthiness, but he had no doubt that she would be steady enough in rough weather. The reporters were also interested in how she fared speed wise. 'Will she ever dock on Tuesday?' one of them broached.

'No,' Smith replied emphatically, 'and there will be no attempt to bring her in on Tuesday. She was built for a Wednesday ship, and her run this first voyage has demonstrated that she will fulfil the expectations of the builders.'[8]

This again was good PR, reflecting White Star's new softly softly approach when it came to the question of speed. They were not after the Blue Riband afterall, but there was little to be gained in advertising the fact that White Star ships were slower than their Cunard counterparts, so Smith blithely skirted the issue. The *Olympic* was built as a Wednesday ship but she was quite capable of a Tuesday arrival and before long his words would be given the lie, but as will be seen, the reasons behind this would be out of Smith's hands.

Meantime, the PR exercise slid easily and happily into the type of good-hearted banter between old workmates that makes for even better publicity. Purser Hugh McElroy noted to the reporters quizzing them about the size of the ship, that their daily inspection tour of the new vessel was fully 9 miles long. Smith disagreed saying it was only a third of that, but Dr O'Loughlin chipped in, commenting that it certainly seemed like 9 miles![9]

Then there were photographs galore. Some have Smith standing arms folded, looking wistfully and nobly to some far horizon as a good sea captain should; others show him looking somewhat cornered and wishing he was elsewhere. At some point he was also filmed strolling very self-consciously on the *Olympic's* starboard bridge wing, stopping occasionally to peer over the forward rail, or through the cabin window. It is good to see the Hanley lad moving and when he does it is with the rolling gait of a seaman, but he does look rather nonplussed.

All in all, though, everyone came away from the encounter thoroughly pleased. The passengers had tales of a pleasant journey on the new ship, the reporters had their scoop, while White Star and Captain Smith had the satisfaction of knowing they had a PR splash well done.

The next day the *Olympic* was the venue for a grand meal that was given to 600 White Star agents from across the United States. There must be some doubt, however, as to whether Smith attended this function, as he appears to have been otherwise engaged. Following the death of Edward VII in 1910, plans had long been in place for the coronation of George V, which was to take place on 22 June 1911 during the *Olympic's* first stopover in New York. For the British people at home and abroad and the loyal members of the colonies, it was to be a time of celebration and meals and festivals were being organised around the world to mark the event.

Had Smith been at sea, the chances are that some celebrations would have been held aboard the *Olympic* to mark the event. He was, though, in New York at the time. Here, despite the inevitable republican grumbling from some quarters, various dinners were being organised to cater for the numerous British and Canadian visitors to the city. The grandest of these was undoubtedly the coronation dinner to be laid on by the management in the summer garden and terrace of the Plaza Hotel, a massive new structure built overlooking New York's Central Park. This dinner was principally for those visitors and bigwigs who were to attend the coronation service at Trinity Church that afternoon. These included Courtenay W. Bennett, the British Consul General; William Gardener, the Vice Consul, as well as any other individuals who wished to book tables for the service and the soiree. By the eve of the coronation, several other notable Britons and Canadians had put their names down. There was Lady Drummond and a party from Montreal, Sir Daniel Mann, Lady Hickson and along with these Honourables and Ladies was Commander E.J. Smith. There were also a few pro-British Americans who would sit in for the feast, most notably the Presidents of the Pilgrims St Andrew's and St George's Societies.

The next day, the guests attended the church service to celebrate the coronation of their new King before retiring to the Plaza. Here, dressed in their best, the guests settled down for a fine dinner after which 'coronation favours' were distributed to the diners, the evening being accompanied and enlivened with a patriotic musical programme.[10]

On 23 June, the American public had the opportunity to have a look around the new ship. The gangways had been opened at 10a.m., and from then until 5p.m., the visitors filed around the ship in an endless chain, passing quickly along each deck, though it still took an hour of fast walking from any one visitor to take a complete tour of the vessel. More than 4,000 people toured the *Olympic* that day, which at 50 cents a head raised over $2,000 for seamen's charities. It was hoped that a similar number would take the tour on the 24th and sure enough they did.[11]

Clearly the RMS *Olympic* was a big hit with the travelling public on both sides of the Atlantic and so over the years she would continue to be, justly earning the nickname 'Old Reliable' from the passengers and crews that sailed on her. The ship continued in service through war and peace until hard economic times saw her laid off and scrapped in 1935, the first and – as it transpired – the last of the *Olympic*-class liners.

The ship took on more passengers for her return journey on 28 June: 731 in first, 495 in second and 1,075 in third class, a total of 2,301. The *Olympic* was also given a grand send off from New York. When the ship cast off at 3p.m., her departure was watched by a crowd of 10,000 people along the pier front, who cheered and waved handkerchiefs until the ship straightened up and set off down the bay, though many stood watching until the *Olympic* was out of sight.

There was some added excitement to the departure, as a lone aeroplane piloted by aviation pioneer Tommy Sopwith, flew overhead and dropped a package containing a letter of congratulation to Captain Smith and a pair of replacement spectacles for a passenger who had lost his. 'I was particularly glad to accomplish the flight,' Sopwith said after his jaunt, 'For I had been prevented from greeting the *Olympic* on her arrival and I did not want her first trip to America to be completed without extending my congratulations to her captain. There was a special letter for him in my bundle. I only hope he got it.'[12]

Unfortunately, for both Smith and his visually impaired passenger, it turned out to be a wasted sentiment as the package had missed the ship completely and sunk without trace.

The weather was again set fair and the *Olympic* made good time back to Southampton, maintaining an average speed of 21¾ knots. The ship arrived back home on 5 July, with the expectation of a far larger passenger list than had crossed for her maiden voyage, with over 700 first-class passengers alone.

In dock, White Star's new ship was given first-class treatment, cleaned out, reprovisioned and checked over. Thomas Andrews and the Guarantee Group went their ways, the former with his recommendations that would occasion some future work on the *Olympic*. The ship was also inspected underneath, a diver being sent down to check on the propellors. The inspections came back favourably, everything was in order.

Following the first voyage the *Olympic's* fifty-three-year-old Chief Officer Joseph Evans, who had followed Smith from the *Adriatic*, was transferred and a replacement arrived in the shape of thirty-eight-year-old Henry Tingle Wilde. A tall, broad set, handsome man teetering on the edge of permanent captaincy, Wilde had endured his fair share of woes during the last year and his transfer to the prestigious *Olympic* may have had a cheering effect. In December 1910, his wife had died, leaving Wilde with four young motherless children to provide for. His prospects seemed well set to provide for his family, though to do so meant that he was apart from his children more than he would have perhaps wished.

Smith seems to have taken to Wilde fairly quickly and from what little evidence survives the two of them developed a healthy rapport. It appears that Wilde was later transferred to the *Titanic* at Smith's behest and long after the two of them were dead, Smith's widow took a matronly interest in the welfare of Wilde's orphaned children, which may indicate that the two families were well acquainted ashore. But Wilde's appointment may not have been universally welcome. For instance, it doubtless came as another disappointment to the *Olympic's* ambitious First Officer William Murdoch, who had probably been hoping to take up the position of chief officer under Smith since his days on the *Adriatic*. As will be seen, Murdoch would be pipped at the post by Wilde yet again when they switched to the *Titanic*.

Fast Crossings and a Royal Visit

During her first year the *Olympic* was essentially being 'run in', she made some quick crossings. Her second transatlantic run took only five days, thirteen hours and six minutes, arriving at 10.30p.m. on the Tuesday evening, invalidating Smith's previous insistence that the *Olympic* was 'a Wednesday ship'. This early arrival, though, seems to have been prompted more by disagreements amongst the White Star management than through any design or recklessness on Smith's part. For the *Olympic's* second voyage, P.A.S. Franklin and other IMM Directors had recommended that the ship should dock on the Tuesday, so as to speed up the loading of the ship and her turnaround time, all of which would please the passengers and might just give the company an edge when it came to facing down the speed of the Cunarders. J. Bruce Ismay was not so keen on the idea at first, but demurred, saying that if it was discussed with Lord Pirrie, Captain Smith and Chief Engineer Joseph Bell and they were agreeable, then he would have no major objections. Smith and the others were duly consulted and on 11 August 1911, Ismay, under the corporate identity, wrote to Smith confirming, '… the verbal instructions given to you at Southampton last week that it will be right for you to go full speed when on the short track, subject to your considering it prudent and in the interests of safe navigation to do so. This instruction applies to both east-bound and west-bound voyages when on the short track.'

Writing from New York, Frederick Toppin, the vice-president of the IMM, wrote to Ismay on 18 August, enthusing that the decision would ensure that the ship would arrive in New York on Tuesday afternoons adding 'materially to her attractiveness and popularity on this side.' From the practical standpoint it also seemed beneficial in regard to coaling and reprovisioning. However, this idealised castle – or perhaps seaport – in the air took no account of the port authorities, who were largely inconvenienced by these early arrivals; berths and mooring gangs would be unavailable until their allotted time and anyhow ships could not practically depart any earlier as this would seriously upset the timetable. All in all, it was a bad plan, a management conceit that seemed good to them but to nobody else, and by the time Smith's successor Herbert Haddock took command of the *Olympic*, the management's view had shifted and on several occasions Captain Haddock was advised against arriving too early, unless the ship was on the short northern track used during the summer months and conditions had allowed it. There would be no concerted push to get to New York before time.

Yet, no opportunity was missed to show the ship off in all her glory and a few days after the *Olympic* arrived back in Britain and while she was still so spick and span and the pride of the British merchant fleet, the ship received some notable visitors. King Alphonso XIII of Spain and Queen Victoria Eugenie, the granddaughter of Queen Victoria, were in Britain on a royal visit and a tour of the new *Olympic* was on their itinerary. On 6 August 1911, they attended mass at St Michael's Church, East Cowes. Joining other royals they took luncheon with the Duke and Duchess of Connaught on the yacht *Alexandra*. The King and Queen of Spain afterwards went to Southampton aboard Princess Henry of Battenberg's personal yacht for their visit to the *Olympic*. No details exist of what they saw or did on their visit, but they came away thoroughly impressed with the ship and, it seems, with its genial skipper. The next year when the news broke that Smith had perished on the *Titanic*, King Alphonso sent a message to Eleanor via White Star, offering his condolences and sympathy at the death of her husband, whom he remembered meeting the year before on his visit to the *Olympic*.[13]

After this high point the *Olympic's* third voyage was run-of-the-mill, the ship carried a good number of passengers including an observer from the White Star Line's rival Cunard, who wrote a detailed description of the ship which was generally very favourable.

With the *Olympic's* fourth voyage there came a change in the schedule, albeit a temporary one, when the usual four-week sailing plan was changed to a three week one. This meant less time ashore for the crew, which must have been a sore point with Smith especially, who, as already noted, was rather displeased with the limited amount of time he already had with his family. Perhaps the discontent was widespread, or the change was simply to deal with a temporary situation, as by the New Year the schedule had reverted back to four weekly. But, as it happened, Smith and the crew of the *Olympic* were about to get a completely unscheduled break courtesy of the Royal Navy.

The *Olympic–Hawke* Collision

On 20 September 1911, the *Olympic*, again under the compulsory guidance of 'Uncle' George Bowyer, set off from Southampton on her fifth transatlantic voyage, departing the White Star dock at 11.20a.m. The weather was breezy, but set fair, fine sailing weather, though it was not the conditions that would give Smith problems on this voyage. First of all there were some minor staff problems to contend with. Shortly before the *Olympic* was set to sail some of the crew belonging to the British Seaman's and Fireman's Union had refused to serve aboard as there were two non-union workers aboard. To placate the crew and to get on with the voyage, the two men were dismissed from the ship and the *Olympic* was able to sail on time.

The ship duly set off down Southampton Water, reaching Calshot Castle at 12.29p.m., and the Black Jack Buoy a minute later. The ship reached Calshot Spit at 12.34 and moved along a southerly course of 65° West. *Olympic* then proceeded on towards Bramble Bank, the large shoal that dominates the entrance to Southampton Water. Once past that there are two routes out into the Channel, south-west down the Solent, or south-east past Spithead and past the Isle of Wight before setting off for Cherbourg. The Spithead route was Smith's preferred course.

The ship was making 17½ knots as she passed the North Thorn Buoy at about 12.37p.m. Three minutes later she cleared the Thorn Knoll Buoy at which point the port engine was put 'slow ahead' and the turbine engine was stopped. The ship's speed fell off, dropping to about 11 or 12 knots on approach to the turn around the West Bramble Buoy at about 12.42. The ship then let out two short blasts on her whistles to indicate to any other vessels nearby that she was executing a port turn. A minute later, the ship having turned the corner, she was straightened up and the telegraph rang down 'full speed ahead' to the engine room. The ship began slowly accelerating up to 20 knots, a slightly reduced 'full speed' for coastal waters.

As the *Olympic* was powering up, from his position on the poop deck, First Officer William Murdoch noticed a ship coming up a couple of miles astern. This was the 7,600-ton Royal Navy cruiser HMS *Hawke*. The ship had just completed her engine power trials and was making her way back to Portsmouth along the Spithead route. As the cruiser slowly gained on the *Olympic*, *Hawke*'s captain, Commander William Blunt, gave the liner a little more room in the Channel, but the ship's were on a convergent course. *Hawke* was travelling at about 15¼ knots and thus moving marginally faster than the *Olympic* at this point and soon drew alongside. As she drew level with the liner's bridge, though, the *Olympic* started to pull ahead as her speed increased.

On the *Olympic*, both Smith and Bowyer noted the *Hawke*'s movements. Smith later stated that he did not think there was any danger from the smaller vessel, but as the *Hawke* dropped back she began swinging towards the *Olympic*. Smith, watching from the bridge wing, was alarmed.

'I don't believe he will get under our stern, Bowyer,' he said, clearly under the impression that the *Hawke*'s commander was attempting to pass under the liner's stern.

'If she is going to strike, sir, let me know in time so I can put the helm hard over to port.' Said Bowyer. 'Is she going to strike, sir?'

'Yes, she is going to strike us in the stern!' Smith replied, alarmed by what he was seeing. 'He is starboarding and he is going to hit us.'

The scene aboard the *Hawke* was equally frantic. Commander Blunt had ordered the quartermaster at the wheel to turn away from the *Olympic*. The quartermaster accidentally turned the wheel the wrong way, but immediately corrected, but the *Hawke* took a sudden turn to port that was none of his doing.

'What are you doing?' Blunt yelled to the quartermaster. 'Port! Port, hard to port!'

'Helm jammed!' Yelled the quartermaster in reply as Blunt reversed first the port then the starboard engines to compensate. The three other men on the bridge including the captain joined the quartermaster and they all strained to turn the wheel, managing to force a 15° turn to starboard before the helm jammed again. In the grip of unseen forces the *Hawke* was now on a collision course with the *Olympic*.

Like most warships of her era, the *Hawke*, though well supplied with big guns and smaller ordnance, also carried an underwater ram designed to pierce and sink enemy ships should the situation, in extremis, demand it. With a sound like one of her big guns going off, this now pierced the *Olympic* in the starboard quarter and in the collision that followed the *Hawke* punched a ship-sized triangular hole in the liner's side. The noise of the collision was clearly heard by observers on the shore nearly a mile away.

With the *Olympic* still moving forward, the *Hawke* slipped back, scraping along the bigger ship and striking first the propellor shaft then the propellor itself, causing considerable damage along 40ft of the *Olympic*'s hull. Of the two, though, the *Hawke* undoubtedly fared the worse, her ram had broken off and her bow had been crushed back. As she was cast aside from the *Olympic*, the naval vessel listed heavily to port, nearly capsizing before she righted herself. On the other end of the collision, water poured into the ruptured *Olympic*, as on the bridge Smith and Bowyer reacted by sounding the alarm bell and closing the watertight doors, sealing her bulkheads. Pilot Bowyer then ordered the engines stopped.[14]

The watertight doors did their job and though shocking, the initial inrush was quickly contained. Two compartments were flooded and water had spilled through into a third before the steel doors banged down into place. The damage extended from below the waterline up to D deck, 40ft above. Some passenger areas had been damaged, but as most of the passengers were at lunch when the collision occurred no one was killed or injured. The incident was noted pithily in the ship's log: '12.46 Struck on starboard quarter by His Majesty's Ship.'

The voyage could not go on, but neither could the *Olympic* return to Southampton until the next high tide. Though the damage was serious, there was no danger of her sinking following the collision and when the ship was checked she was found to be drawing 35ft 6in of water aft, only a foot more than when she was fully loaded.

Smith and Pilot Bowyer took the ship over to Osbourne Bay, off Cowes on the Isle of Wight. There the 1,313 passengers, among them twenty millionaires worth $500 million between them, were taken off by tender and returned to Southampton where they had to make other travel arrangements. The *Olympic*, meantime, anchored for the night.

The next morning at 8.50a.m., the *Olympic*, assisted by a number of tugs from the Isle of Wight, slowly made her way from Osbourne Bay powered by her port engine. At 11a.m., she finally berthed at Southampton, where her cargos were offloaded and a party of divers and White Star officials took a look at the damage incurred. It was decided that this was too extensive to be dealt with there and she would have to be dry-docked and the only facilities large enough to take the *Olympic* were in the Belfast yard where she had been built.

Before anyone could contemplate sending the *Olympic* on the 600-mile trip back to Belfast, she had to be given a temporary patch. Steel plates were fixed in place to hold the damage below the waterline and the large hole in the ship's side was patched with wood. If this seemed bad, the other protagonist, HMS *Hawke*, did not get off so lightly. She was down at the nose and was now only staying afloat with vigorous pumping. The ship limped back to Portsmouth for extensive repairs that would take ten months to complete.

It would take over ten days for the temporary repairs to the *Olympic* to be completed. The disgruntled crew, short-changed as a result of the curtailed journey, left the ship at 5p.m. on 22 September. That same day Smith appeared in front of Leonard J. Paris, a public clerk of notary of Southampton, to whom he outlined in the insurance protest, his version of events. Mr Paris noted down that the *Olympic*, '...at 12.46p.m. while proceeding to Spithead was run into by HMS *Hawke* causing serious damage which compelled him [Smith] to anchor, and subsequently, namely at 8a.m. on the twenty-first day of September, returned to Southampton docks, where the vessel arrived at 10.30a.m. the same day.'[15]

Pursuant of Smith's insurance protest, White Star immediately sued the Admiralty and the *Hawke*'s captain, but this was soon countered by an Admiralty action for the damage done to HMS *Hawke*, which was then in the process of having 20ft of its bow removed. The White Star directors headed by J. Bruce Ismay held a private court of inquiry on the collision and here Smith and his officers were exonerated. However, the official inquiry into the events of 20 September 1911, which began on 16 November that year, was much less cut and dried. The commanders, officers and selected crewmen from both ships involved, as well as Pilot Bowyer, were brought in to testify, each in turn presenting his evidence. Captain Smith was the first witness. For the benefit of the court he described the *Olympic*'s course, speed and the ship's movements immediately before the collision. When he was asked whether he had any anxieties when he saw the *Hawke* running along abreast of the *Olympic*, he replied, 'No, not at all... She continued to overhaul until she got with her stem almost abreast of our bridge. I could see the stem through the aperture on the bridge shelter.'

He further recalled that the two vessels were virtually on a parallel course, then, 'We gathered speed, drew ahead a little, or she dropped astern.'

As for the *Hawke*'s sudden and unexpected turn to port: 'It seemed inconceivable,' he said, 'a manoeuvre I could not understand.'

'Did it occur to you at all, Captain Smith, that the ship had got out of control, the *Hawke* I mean?' He was asked.

'No.'

'Or that her steering gear had got out of control?'

'No, that did not occur to me.'[16]

Smith believed that the *Olympic* had fallen victim to a badly judged manoeuvre on the part of the *Hawke*'s skipper. All the White Star witnesses who were called gave the same impression, namely that the *Hawke* was at fault and that the Admiralty would be footing the *Olympic*'s repair bill.

However, things did not quite pan out that way. There was indecision in some of the answers given by Smith and his crew, which was in stark contrast to the assured accounts of the accident evinced by Commander Blunt and his men. Blunt made it clear that he believed that the manoeuvre he had made at 600ft distance from the *Olympic* had been prudent and presented no danger to the overtaking *Olympic*. Blunt was, of course, speaking before a sympathetic naval audience and no mention was made of the fact that the quartermaster at the wheel had initially turned the *Hawke* the wrong way, which may have had a bearing on how the *Hawke* reacted; that evidence, however, would not surface until a later appeal. White Star claimed that the navy had been careless, while the navy argued that the *Olympic* had gone too close to the *Hawke*. Each side stuck rigidly to their story, but there was another explanation given to the court, which with hindsight was the more likely cause of the accident.

George Baker, an official from the National Physical Laboratory, testified that the two vessels had in fact been victims of the suction set up between them. The science was then novel and as a result occasioned much lively debate in the newspapers at the time, but today it is a well accepted fact in the science of physics that all vessels whether cruising in air or water, produce a fluctuating series of fields of pressure around them as they move. The greater the vessel's bulk the more pronounced these fields of pressure become as too is the effect they can have on nearby craft. Increased pressure from the bow or stern of a vessel and decreased pressure from the middle cause forces of repulsion and attraction powerful enough to throw lesser craft around as if they were rag dolls. Mr Baker put it succinctly for the court: 'When one vessel overtakes another and is so placed that the bows feel the power of the reduced pressure and the stern is in the field of the increased pressure, the bow will turn in and the stern will move out.'

This was exactly what the *Hawke* experienced as the *Olympic* started to pull ahead of her and forced her into her unexpected turn. The forces that caused the accident had always existed, but it was only in the early years of the twentieth century, with the advent of these new, bigger, faster ships, that these formerly little-noticed hydrodynamics became a serious menace to shipping.

Baker's cogent explanation, though, made no impression on the old heads of the Admiralty Court. On 19 December 1911, Sir Samuel Adams for the Admiralty decided that the *Olympic* alone was to blame, the cause being negligent navigation on the part of Pilot Bowyer. The verdict saved White Star pride, the accident having occurred under compulsory pilotage, but it was not the outcome the company had looked for. They seem to have felt that the Admiralty's decision was self-serving in regards to one of their ships and as a result White Star lodged an appeal.

Smith was not pleased with the court's verdict any more than his bosses and in a letter to his nephew Frank, dated February 1912, he commented that though there was little chance of them overturning the verdict, their appeal showed at least that they were 'not taking it lying down'. A letter written to Frank by Eleanor following the *Titanic* disaster went a little further than this and accused the Admiralty of telling lies to make their case. As is the nature of these things, the appeal dragged on and did not in fact reach its conclusion until long after Smith himself was dead. On 5 April 1913, the Admiralty verdict was upheld and the White Star appeal was dismissed with costs. The company lodged a second appeal, this time taking it to the House of Lords and though new evidence was presented, not the least of which was the fact that the *Hawke's* quartermaster had initially turned his ship towards the *Olympic*, the verdict delivered on 9 November 1914 still fell against White Star.

Not that the court's verdict had any immediate effect on the careers of those involved. Commander Blunt was soon promoted to captain; 'Uncle' George Bowyer would continue to work as the paramount Southampton pilot for many years to come; and Smith's standing in the eyes of his employers remained unchanged. Though he was never officially elevated to the position of Commodore of the Fleet (for whatever reason, the position had become defunct some years before and would remain so until Bertram Hayes was given the title some years hence), as White Star's current senior skipper, he certainly occupied that lofty position. He was by now the highest paid man at sea, earning £1,250 a year, plus an extra £200 if he returned his ships in good order. From White Star's point of view the collision with the *Hawke*, though unfortunate, was not Smith's fault and they obviously felt that his were still the safest hands in whom they could entrust their new liners.

Meanwhile, the *Olympic*, back in Belfast, underwent repairs in dry dock, the reconstruction work costing about £103,000. Like that of her master, the ship's reputation remained untarnished. In some ways the accident had reinforced the 'unsinkable' image of the *Olympic* class liners, for the damage she had taken had been considerable but the ship remained afloat. The repairs to the *Olympic* also played a part in the events surrounding her younger sister, as one of the propellors intended for the *Titanic* was purloined to replace the one damaged by the *Hawke*. This bumped the *Titanic*'s maiden voyage back from 20 March 1912 to 10 April.

The voyage cancelled after the *Hawke* incident took place on 30 November 1911 and despite a delayed start due to fog, passed quietly and without incident. The return journey was remarkably quick, the *Olympic* completed the fastest passage she had yet made, her average speed being 22½ knots.

Nights to Remember

The latter half of 1911 is notable for the number of meals and celebrations that Smith attended or was invited to during his stopovers in the United States. These are interesting to relate as they not only reveal his popularity with the transatlantic smart set who, as will be seen, often organised parties in his honour, but also the breadth of his acquaintance over there, which was considerable and influential.

Just over a month before the *Olympic*'s collision with the *Hawke*, the *New York Times* noted that the evening before, on 16 August, General Charles Miller and his wife, who had returned on the *Olympic* that day, gave a small dinner party at the Waldorf Astoria for Captain Smith. This seems to have been a planned event rather than a casual invitation, as the report noted that there were large and small ships in the decorations and the ices were served from a miniature of the *Olympic*.[17]

On 7 December, another old soldier-cum-tycoon, Colonel William Hester, president of the *Brooklyn Daily Eagle* company, gave a birthday party at the Plaza Hotel, where Smith and others had celebrated King George's coronation in June. To this Mr Hester invited a number of his family and friends one of whom again was Captain Smith.[18]

The swankiest of these dinner parties, though, and certainly the most memorable for Smith, was that held in his honour at the Metropolitan Club – the so-called 'Millionaires' Club' – in New York on 28 December 1911. Rumours had abounded for some time that Smith was going to retire, but he was sailing still and should the rumours be true the party, to be attended by many of his wealthy clientele, would count by way of a thank you for the many years of service he had given. It may perhaps also be seen as a vote of confidence from his passengers after the rough ride he had endured following the *Olympic*'s collision with the *Hawke*.

It was a busy journey for the *Olympic*, Christmas being celebrated at sea, the last as it would turn out for Smith and many of those aboard the *Olympic*. The ship docked at New York on the 27th and the next evening Smith went to 'the Dinner' as he subsequently called it, though by the sparse accounts that survive it was more of a banquet than a simple meal.

The venue did justice to the occasion. The Metropolitan Club still stands to this day, occupying a prime corner spot at 1 East 60th Street. Standing four storeys high, though today dwarfed by the surrounding high-rises and sky scrapers, it still shouts wealth and exuberance. A great solid block of masonry with an elaborate pillared gateway, the interior of the club is decorated now as then in the Italian Renaissance style, with sweeping staircases, high ceilings and grand marbled doorways. Stucco and gilding decorate the grand rooms illuminated by high windows, large mirrors and elaborate period light fittings. Though ostensibly a gentlemen's club, there were rooms for guests and Smith may have perhaps been accorded one of these. If not, then he may have arrived in grand style and been escorted up to the main dining hall where the numerous invited guests were waiting. As he strolled up the stairs through this marble and gilt grandeur, Ted Smith could have been forgiven for thinking to himself that he had come a long way from that little brick house in Well Street.

The crowd that greeted him was select and telling. The American newspapers noted that among the guests were General Stewart, Mr A. Woodward, retired senator Chauncey M. Depew, William H. Truesdale, the vice-president and general manager of the Chicago Rock Island Railway, and W.A. Nash, a Justice of the Peace and deputy coroner. There were many more. Smith's old school friend Spencer Till later referred to a large framed photograph of 'the Dinner' that he saw on a visit to Eleanor, in which he noted the faces of many great and eminent men. In a letter to Frank Hancock, Eleanor also referred to the picture as a souvenir to hand down to Melville and her children. It was probably the same photo that was reproduced in a number of American papers after the *Titanic* disaster. The picture reveals that 'the Dinner' was a white tie and tails affair, held in a room that was draped with British and American flags. The numerous invited guests sat ranged on either side of two long tables, while Smith as the guest of honour can be seen standing between two close friends at a smaller table at the far end of the room. This off-duty picture answers one question about the good captain, namely what he had under his hat. Though he is some distance from the camera Smith appears to be bald or at least very thin on top.

Eleanor sent Frank a copy of the menu and noted further that Smith's own presentation menu from the meal was bound in white morocco leather and edged with silver bands. As accolades went, 'the Dinner' could not have been bettered as a source of great pleasure and pride for Captain Smith and his family, the crowning moment of his rise from the back streets of Hanley. Certainly, apart from his forthcoming command of the new *Titanic*, there would be no higher honours for him. If we believe the blurb that comes with the photo' it was profitable too as the gathering had raised $5,000 as a testimonial to Captain Smith.[19]

The Dinner seems to have passed unnoticed by the American papers at the time, accounts of it are merely given in retrospect; had the papers got wind of it, then our guest list here would be longer and the description of 'the Dinner' more detailed. Unfortunately for posterity, the privacy of the clubmen seems instead to have kept the affair very exclusive. Certainly one guest who was doubtless there was Smith's old friend J.P. Morgan, though whether he is among the many white-haired mustachioed faces staring up at the camera is unknown; for he may have avoided the big group shot as he tended to be touchy about being photographed due to his rosacea.

Morgan was certainly in town as two days after 'the Dinner', he turned up at the White Star pier fifteen minutes before the *Olympic* was due to sail. Though not mentioned on the passenger list he was spotted by reporters bidding farewell to his business partners before going aboard. He went straight to his suite, C57, where he looked over a few telegrams before telling the waiting reporters who had followed him that he was off to Egypt for the winter. That was all they were getting, though. They quizzed other notable passengers in the vain hope of perhaps eliciting some information as to the tycoon's doings, but all were unaware that he was aboard.

Smith doubtless knew that Morgan was aboard and had perhaps been told about his passage during 'the Dinner' and had kept it quiet. The whistles blew and the reporters and relatives were hustled ashore, then, waved off by hundreds of well-wishers and spectators, the *Olympic* set off back to Southampton.[20]

The End of Voyages

The first journey of the New Year was again a very rough ride. On 14 January, the *Olympic* ran into a storm of snow and towering seas that surprised Smith with their ferocity. Great waves dashed against and over the *Olympic*. One large wave lifted the ship's bow clean out of the water and as the ship sank down into the trough on the opposite side, another wave crashed down over the bow, ripping off a hatch cover, a strip of railing and damaging some of the deck machinery.

The journey was of some personal interest to Smith as a number of his family friends or acquaintances were crossing with him, though the bad weather limited his time in their company. In another of his letters to his nephew Frank, Smith notes that two mutual acquaintances of theirs, John Mallock and his wife Christian, had crossed with him on the previous trip as had a Mrs Brookfield about whom Frank had sent Smith a letter of introduction. Because the weather had been bad for some of the journey, he had only managed to catch a couple of conversations with the Mallocks at dinner. Of Mrs Brookfield, though, he had seen nothing. Though he had made arrangements to have her seated at his table, Smith discovered that she was actually in second class so he could do nothing in that respect. Smith did say, though, that Mrs Brookfield was well looked after and despite the bad weather would have been made comfortable on the trip.

Smith's letter to Frank was actually more of a brief reply to one of his, most of the time Smith is answering Frank's inquiries. His opinions on the verdict over the *Hawke* collision are voiced; he sends greetings to the Gordons and Churchills once again and muses on the fact that he and his family had not had any pictures taken for years and promised Frank one of the first when they had them done. Brief but friendly, to the point but covering several matters, it is the last of the letters in his hand to his American relative and it may be that the next time Frank heard about Ted Smith was under far more tragic circumstances. A whisper of that comes right at the end of the note, when Smith says that after one more voyage on the *Olympic* he would be leaving the ship to bring out the *Titanic* on 10 April.[21]

His prediction was completely accurate, but Smith's last days on the *Olympic* were not as smooth as he might have hoped. On the return journey to Britain following his letter to Frank, the ship gave him a little more trouble. On 24 February 1912, when the *Olympic* was some 750 miles off Newfoundland, the port side propellor shed a blade. To compensate, Smith ordered the two other engines to be run at full speed and as a result the ship arrived in Southampton more or less on time on 28 February. Unfortunately the loss of the propellor blade meant another trip to the dry dock in Belfast.

The *Olympic* arrived in Belfast once again in early March, where she was taken into dock by five tugs. Fitting a new propellor blade did not occasion as much attention as the damage she had suffered in the *Hawke* collision, but it did briefly bring her back into contact with her younger sister once more. The *Titanic* was undergoing her final fittings and getting ready for her sea trials at the end of the month. Soon the *Olympic* was in her graving dock and the repairs were effected promptly and on 7 March, the *Olympic* left the yard and sailed back to Southampton.

Smith's final voyage aboard RMS *Olympic* began on Thursday 14 March. The ship arrived in New York on the 20th after an unremarkable journey and Smith once again became the toast of his friends in America while the ship lay in dock. Whilst he was ashore his old friends Colonel William Hester and John J. Sinclair made arrangements for Smith to dine with them when he brought the *Titanic* over, an invitation he naturally accepted. Then, on the evening of the 22nd, the day before the return trip according to a report in the *New York Times* of 18 April, Smith dined with Mr and Mrs W.P. Willis at 138 Bowne Avenue in Flushing. Just as he had described the *Olympic* as 'firm as a church' to his relatives shortly before taking command, Smith now showed that he was just as confident about the *Titanic*. When Mr and Mrs Willis quizzed him about his forthcoming command he was enthusiastic as to its prospects, announcing to his hosts that he shared the confidence of her builders that it was impossible for her to sink. According to the report the Willis' gave, Smith looked forward to the most successful days of his seagoing career and forecast that the *Titanic* would set a new benchmark when it came to safety and comfort in ocean travel. He had no doubts that even if the ship received serious damage she could still make it to port.[22]

The next morning, Smith was back aboard his ship and when the *Olympic* departed she came away laden with as much coal as she could carry to add to the bunkers in Southampton, even carrying bags in vacant first- and second-class cabins. Britain was in the grip of a crippling coal strike that was affecting all walks of life. In Smith's home town in the Potteries as elsewhere in the country, working-class families were out scouring the slag heaps, coal picking to eke out what dwindling coal supplies they had for their daily needs. Unable to run their machines, factories were shutting down, railways were running reduced services and in the big ports the large coal-fired steamers were dropping by the wayside as the coal supply slowly ran out. The *Olympic*'s efforts were to help counteract this and to ensure that there was enough coal for her younger sister to make her projected maiden voyage on 10 April. White Star put as good a gloss on the situation as it could, saying – with a completely straight face, one assumes – that due to the unforeseen circumstances created by the coal strike, the *Olympic*'s passengers would be allowed a little more time to enjoy their luxurious cabins. The reason being that in order to conserve fuel the ship would be running at 20 rather than her normal service speed of 23 knots. As it turned out, however, the coal strike ended on 6 April and the coal situation was returning to normal when the *Titanic* sailed.

The *Olympic* docked at Southampton on 30 March 1912. That same day Smith would have cleared out his cabin as would a good number of his regular crew who would be following him to the *Titanic*. Indeed, Smith seems to have made a point of trying to keep the *Olympic* crew together. This is evidenced by the account of the *Olympic*'s junior Marconi wirelessman Alec Bagot. He and senior operator Ernie Moore had joined the *Olympic* when she returned to service after her collision with HMS *Hawke*. In the months since then they had seen little of Captain Smith, but as the ship had been approaching Southampton on this final voyage the skipper came in casually and unannounced. As he entered the wireless room the two operators sprang to their feet, but Smith immediately asked them to sit back down. He then added that as he was about to leave to take command of the *Titanic* he had come in to say goodbye.

The two operators were honoured by the unexpected visit and Moore said as much. Smith rested himself against a small desk just inside the cabin and asked if they had been happy aboard. Moore replied that they had and Smith noted that it was indeed a happy ship and that he would be very sorry to leave her.

Bagot gave an excellent pen portrait of Smith at that point, describing him as looking like a slimmer version of the late King Edward VII, a resemblance that they believed he tried to foster. All the while during this brief interview, Smith played with a toothpick, a curious habit of the captain's that Bagot had noted before, like holding a pencil or unlighted cigar between his lips. A passenger aboard the *Titanic* would make a similar observation a few weeks later, though under very different circumstances.

Bagot meantime was starting to wonder what the captain's visit was leading up to when Smith sprang another surprise on them. After saying that he was very satisfied with their work, he added that should they wish it he would recommend that both of them transfer over to the *Titanic* with him.

When Smith left, the two wirelessmen were delighted with the accolade. But on reflection, despite Smith's generous offer, they agreed that there would be little to gain by following the captain. There would be no extra pay and all their efforts to get the *Olympic's* wireless in tip-top condition would have been wasted. Then there was the fact that even though Smith would be leading the new ship out, when his retirement occurred some time in the near future, the *Titanic* would be the junior vessel, so what caché she carried would be brief. Finally and perhaps most telling, he and Moore were exhausted, Moore from a severe cold and Bagot from standing double-duty in his friend's stead. So neither of them fancied the idea of being plunged into all the hard work a new ship would entail.

So, to decide what to do, they flipped a coin; heads to go, tails to stay. It came down tails. Moore and Bagot stayed on the *Olympic* and it would be two other wirelessmen who sailed aboard the *Titanic.* In such small ways is history made, but as Bagot noted a good proportion of the ship's officers and crew transferred over to the *Titanic.*[23]

Some had already transferred over, First Officer Murdoch, slated as the *Titanic's* chief officer, had already gone to join the ship as too had Chief Engineer Joseph Bell. Smith's personal steward Arthur Paintin would follow Smith as too would numerous other *Olympic* crewmen and women when the vessel finally arrived in Southampton. Not everyone was originally meant to change over, Chief Officer Wilde was supposed to remain on the *Olympic*, but as will be seen fate had other things planned for him. Another of Smith's coterie who would also join the *Titanic* was his old friend Dr O'Loughlin, though it seems that he would have been content to stay where he was, not being too keen to up-sticks and move onto a new vessel when he had just got himself comfortable. Smith chided him for being lazy and told him to pack up his stuff and come with him.[24]

A Possible Retirement..?

Here, before both we and Smith get to the *Titanic*, we should touch on the rumours that Smith was on the verge of retirement. A legend has grown up that the *Titanic's* maiden voyage was to be Smith's last trip before retirement, a story which, like so many others attached to the coming disaster, would add a certain dramatic pathos to the skipper's actions. However, it has to be said that despite the rumours there was no concrete evidence that Smith was about to retire after the *Titanic's* maiden voyage; indeed, quite the contrary.

As noted earlier, stories of Smith's impending retirement had been doing the rounds since early 1911 and these may have helped to prompt the banquet given in his honour at the Metropolitan Club. On 6 June 1911, before the *Olympic's* maiden voyage, the *New York Times* reported that 'it is understood' that Captain Smith was going to retire by the end of the year, 'as he will have reached the age limit' of sixty.[25] It went on to say that he would then be replaced as captain of the *Olympic* and commodore (which as we have seen was a rank Smith never actually held) by Captain Herbert Haddock. The *Titanic*, it was said, was to be given to Bertram

Hayes. Some months earlier in November 1910, though he did not say anything about Smith retiring, J. Bruce Ismay had indicated that while Smith would have the *Olympic*, Captain Haddock would have the *Titanic* and the subsequent statement seemed to confirm this in part. Another statement carried in the *New York Times* on 19 November 1911 noted that Smith would indeed go to the *Titanic*, but when he retired in the summer of 1912, having reached the age limit, he would be succeeded by Captain Haddock. However, on 11 April 1912, just after the *Titanic* had set off on her maiden voyage, the *New York Times* carried yet another article in which it mentioned that a month earlier the rumour had spread that the *Titanic's* maiden voyage was to be Smith's final journey. This, though, had been countered on 10 April, when the New York office of the White Star Line had issued a denial and said that Smith would stay in command of the *Titanic* until the line commissioned 'a larger and finer vessel'. This appears to refer to the RMS *Gigantic*, the ship later hurriedly renamed *Britannic* after the *Titanic* disaster, which was then under construction at Harland & Wolff. As it turned out the First World War ensured that the new ship never saw service as a passenger liner, being employed as a hospital ship until it was sunk by a mine in the Mediterranean, but in the bright days of 1911 and 1912, no one was to know the horrors to come.

Of all the statements and rumours, the White Star denial is arguably the most believable as it was issued just before the sinking of the *Titanic* made the matter of Smith's retirement another touch of irony to place alongside the *Titanic's* 'unsinkable' label. But why did the rumours spring up in the first place? The simplest explanation is that Smith may indeed have been planning to retire, he was now sixty-two years old after all, but such was his reputation and popularity that he appears to have been asked to stay on as a further come-on to the seagoing public. The image of White Star's new ships with their well-liked premier captain at the helm seemed to be an unbeatable combination, White Star's publicity men may have even fanned the rumours of Smith's retirement as an added incentive. People who might otherwise have taken another ship might change their plans and switch over to the *Olympic* or the *Titanic* if they believed that they might have been a passenger on one of the last voyages commanded by the great Captain Edward John Smith. This may sound cynical, but one only has to look at the crowds attracted to the last games of famous sports stars, or final performances by notable singers or actors to see the truth in the matter.

So, had fate been kind, had ships not sunk and wars not started, Smith may have finally retired from the sea a year or two later after successfully captaining the RMS *Gigantic* to the States and back. His retirement may have engendered more awards, perhaps a knighthood as was later granted to Bertram Hayes and other senior captains. Smith's career may well have come to a shining end and barring the few mishaps he had acquired thus far, he would have doubtless left the scene quietly and without undue controversy and with a reputation second to none. Had fate been kind.

But fate was not kind and *Titanic* was waiting.

Hanley Market Square, seen here in 1904, had remained largely unchanged since Ted Smith's boyhood.

Crown Bank, Hanley, again little changed since the 1850s.

'Fresh Air From The Potteries'. The grim atmosphere and humour of the district is evident in this famous view.

Pottery pressers at work. This was the kind of work Ted Smith's father Edward was engaged in.

Well Street, Hanley, today.

St Mary's Church, Shelton, where Ted's parents were married in 1841.

Etruria in 1865. The British School stood behind the Etruria Chapel, the roof, white wall and windows of which can be seen on the far right of the picture. (University of Keele/Warrillow Collection)

The Etruria Wesleyan Chapel.

Smith's cousin Elizabeth Smith (standing) and her sister Sarah. Elizabeth married Mark Spode Mason, linking the Smiths to the Mason and Spode pottery dynasties. (Marjorie Burrett)

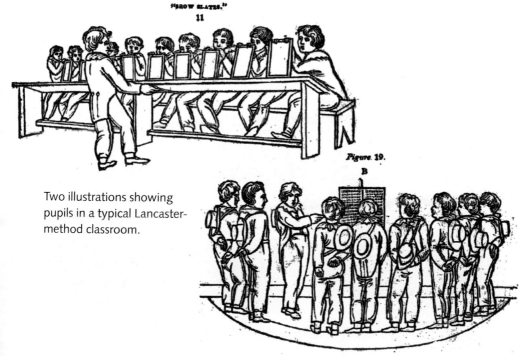

Two illustrations showing pupils in a typical Lancaster-method classroom.

A Nasmyth steam hammer, similar to the type Smith would have operated at the Etruria Forge.

Hong Kong harbour in the late nineteenth century.

Callao, Peru, in the 1860s.

Ships waiting for their supplies of guano at the Chincha Isles.

Western square riggers and Japanese vessels in Yokohama Bay in the late nineteenth century.

The Sailor's Home, Liverpool, where Smith occasionally lodged early in his career.

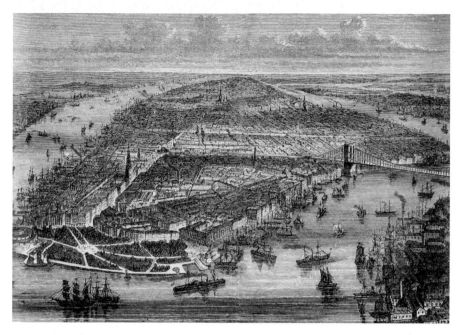

A stylised map of nineteenth-century New York. (W.T. Stead/*From the Old World to the New*)

Savannah, Georgia, one of Smith's ports of call aboard the *Lizzie Fennell*. Seen here are some of the timber yards and unloading sheds the trade ships frequented.

A ship of his own: Captain Smith appears in the New York papers.

Captain Benjamin Gleadell, SS *Celtic*.

Captain William Kidley, SS *Coptic*.

Captain Hamilton Perry, SS *Britannic*.

Captain Peter Irving, SS *Republic*.

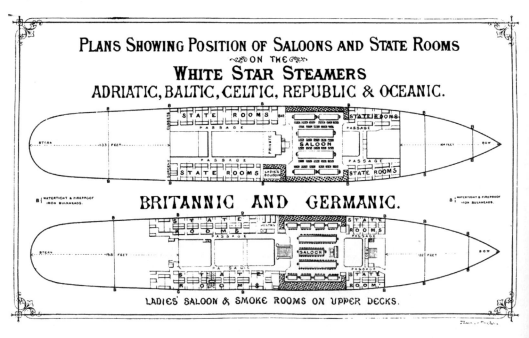

PLANS SHOWING POSITION OF SALOONS AND STATE ROOMS
ON THE
WHITE STAR STEAMERS
ADRIATIC, BALTIC, CELTIC, REPUBLIC & OCEANIC.

BRITANNIC AND GERMANIC.

LADIES' SALOON & SMOKE ROOMS ON UPPER DECKS.

Plans showing the passenger accommodation on some of the first White Star ships Smith served aboard.

One of Smith's early commands, the White Star steamer *Runic*.

The apple of Smith's eye, the *Britannic* serving as a troop ship during the Boer War. (Bertram Hayes/Hull Down)

Eleanor and Melville.

Catherine Smith's grave in Runcorn. (Steve Jones)

Joseph Hancock's grave, Wallasey.

An early photograph of Ted Smith when he took command of the *Majestic* in 1895.

The former White Star offices in Liverpool, opened in 1897.

The SS *Majestic* beside the Liverpool landing stage.

Another shot of the landing stage, where passengers embarked for the United States.

The first-class dining saloon on the *Majestic* with characters drawn from W.T. Stead's story *From the Old World to the New*. (W.T. Stead/*From the Old World to the New*)

The *St Louis*, the American ship that Smith's *Majestic* beat to secure the lucrative transatlantic mails in October 1895.

WHITE STAR LINE.

TWIN-SCREW R.M.S. "BALTIC."
23,884 TONS.

Smith's first big ship, RMS *Baltic*.

The *Baltic* taking on passengers at Liverpool.

The last of the 'Big Four', RMS *Adriatic*.

Southampton High Street.

Southampton docks.

The White Star docks, Southampton.

Queenstown Harbour, Ireland, the last stop before crossing the Atlantic.

Captain Smith leading his officers on one of his morning inspections aboard the *Adriatic*.

The *Adriatic*'s luxurious reading and writing room.

Allen Winden, the hill-top home of Smith's friend millionaire banker Charles Lanier, from where they and J.P. Morgan began their high-speed car ride in September 1907.

Smith's friend and founder of the IMM, financier J.P. Morgan.

One man and his dog. Smith and his pet Borzoi or Russian wolfhound, probably photographed aboard the *Baltic* or *Adriatic*. Note the cigar in its holder in his left hand.

Smith's medals, shown here in the order he wore them: left the RNR Long Service Medal on its green ribbon; and right the Transport Medal on its red and blue ribbon. (Ernie Luck)

RMS *Olympic*.

An excellent view
of the *Olympic*'s
upper decks.

A four-funneller, possibly the *Olympic*, entering New York harbour at night.

Smith in his summer whites. (University of Keele/
Warrillow Collection)

HMS *Hawke*.

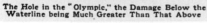
The Hole in the "Olympic," the Damage Below the Waterline being Much Greater Than That Above

The Bow of the "Hawke," the Damage being so Great That the Ram Has Been Mashed Flat

The damage sustained by the *Olympic* and HMS *Hawke* during their collision in 1911.

RMS *Titanic* departing Southampton.

The sepia photo of Smith in his RNR uniform in Hanley
Town Hall.

A close-up of the memorial plaque, Hanley Town Hall.

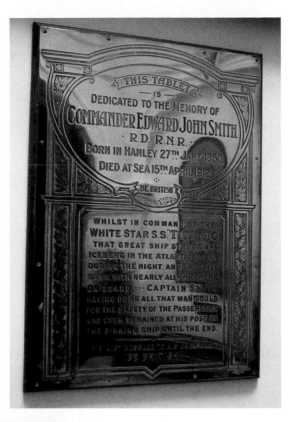

Smith's statue is unveiled in the Museum Grounds, Lichfield, by his daughter Melville.

Smith's statue today.

The original plaque which failed to mention the *Titanic*. The words 'Capt. of RMS Titanic' were added later.

William and Thyrza Harrington's grave, Hanley Cemetery.

Eleanor's grave at Brookwood.

Mel's grave, Brookwood.

TITANIC

Most of the officers who would serve aboard this soon to be infamous ship joined her in Belfast and were present during her final fittings and her forthcoming sea trials. First Officer William Murdoch had been promoted to chief officer of the *Titanic* and accompanied by another of Smith's old officers Charles Lightoller and David Blair as first and second officers respectively, he boarded the new vessel on 27 March 1912. Here they were joined by the ship's four junior officers and a couple of days later Commander Herbert Haddock came aboard and signed on as her first captain, probably as a formality as Smith was a latecomer, making his way independently from Southampton, and he took over on 1 April. Captain Haddock then left for Southampton in order to take command of the *Olympic*. A hand-written note attached to the first page of the crew agreement states that Smith had failed to sign the agreement and he had sent word that he would do so on the ship's return.[1] As a result, on paper at least, Captain Haddock retained command of the *Titanic* until it reached Southampton, but on 3 April he was sailing the *Olympic* to New York and it was actually Smith who commanded the *Titanic* for her sea trials and the subsequent delivery trip to Southampton.[2]

The engineering staff were putting the *Titanic*'s systems through their paces long before the sea trials proper. Chief Engineer Joseph Bell, having long since left the *Olympic* in the capable hands of Chief Engineer Robert Fleming, had been aboard the *Titanic* for several months, making sure that everything was as it should be in his department. His people also tested the deck machinery and on 25 March the engineers had test lowered the lifeboats as per regulations and everything was found to be in good working order.

The sea trials were initially scheduled for 1 April 1912, but were postponed to the next day due to high winds that made conditions potentially hazardous for an untried ship. On 2 April, the weather was fine and the *Titanic* was eased out into Belfast Lough by several tugs. The crew then worked their way through a series of equipment tests supervised by a gaggle of experts from Harland & Wolff and officials from the Board of Trade. One piece of equipment put through its paces at this juncture was the Marconi wireless which was located in a small cabin a little to the rear of the bridge. That this test was performed indicates that the two wireless men assigned to the

Titanic, twenty-four-year-old John 'Jack' Phillips and twenty-two-year-old Harold Bride, had already come aboard. Though technically ship's equipment, the wireless and its operators actually belonged to the Marconi Company and only its operators were qualified to test it.

A variety of speed and handling tests followed the equipment checks. These were designed to satisfy the Board of Trade inspectors as to the ship's seaworthiness. The *Titanic* had already been inspected on more than 2,000 occasions during her construction, but the start of her career as a passenger liner hinged on these final tests, though they were much less exhaustive than those carried out on the *Olympic*. One particular manoeuvre the ship executed was one that she would later repeat, though with much less satisfactory results than now. Whilst she was cruising along at 20 knots, the helm was put hard over to starboard and the engines were reversed. This was to test the ship's reaction to the wheel, her turning circle and her stopping distance. The *Titanic* came to a dead stop in 850 yards in three minutes and fifteen seconds.

The high point of the trials, though, was a running test during which the *Titanic* was run at 20 knots for two hours, taking her 44 miles out to sea then back again at the same speed. The Board of Trade officials were satisfied by what they saw and when the *Titanic* returned to Belfast Lough at 6p.m., her trials complete, she was awarded her certificate of seaworthiness. At 8p.m. that same evening the ship departed Belfast bound for Southampton. As well as the seventy-nine-strong skeleton crew aboard was the nine-man Harland & Wolff Guarantee Group, most of them shipyard workers, headed by Lord Pirrie's nephew Thomas Andrews. As with the *Olympic* and the *Adriatic* before her, Andrews and his men would use the *Titanic*'s maiden voyage to make sure the ship was running smoothly and to check her over on behalf of Harland & Wolff, noting down anything worthy of consideration, or in need of alteration.

The journey to Southampton was quick. Though the ship ran into a patchy fog between 2a.m. and 6a.m., she averaged a respectable 20 knots for the 570-mile voyage. Some sources believe that the ship was even pushed up to 23½ knots at one point, though this is by no means certain. If she did, then this was the highest speed the *Titanic* reached in her brief, inglorious career and had been achieved without even having all of her twenty-four boilers lit.

The journey gave Smith the chance to get to know the deck crew he would be working with. He knew Murdoch and Lightoller well enough, having served with them on numerous occasions over the years, but the four juniors he found aboard the ship were new men on his bridge.

Easily recognised on account of his moustache, thirty-four-year-old Third Officer Herbert John Pitman had been at sea for sixteen years and had joined the White Star Line in 1907. His previous ship had been the *Oceanic* and he had joined the *Titanic* for her sea trials in Belfast. He was noted as a talented administrator and for his friendly manner when dealing with the passengers, a talent he would use to the full later in his career when he transferred to the purser's department due to failing eyesight. Of all the officers on the *Titanic*, Pitman was the only one not to be a member of the Royal Naval Reserve, though he would end his long career by being awarded the MBE for his many years' service 'in dangerous waters'.

The *Titanic*'s fourth officer, twenty-eight-year-old Joseph Groves Boxhall, had like Pitman joined White Star in 1907 and served aboard the *Oceanic* and *Arabic* before joining the *Titanic* at Belfast. During his time aboard the *Oceanic*, Boxhall had come to know Charles Lightoller, who was the only officer he knew aboard this new big ship. Also like Pitman he would survive the *Titanic* disaster and continue his career at sea, eventually rising to the rank of chief officer, though like all the surviving officers he never commanded his own liner. Now, though, because of the shake-up, he found himself designated as navigator, a role usually assumed by the second officer. Smith seems to have been satisfied by his performance, though his projected position of the *Titanic* wreck has since been shown to be completely wrong.

Fifth Officer Harold Godfrey Lowe, aged twenty-nine, was about to make his first transatlantic voyage despite having been at sea since he had run away from home at the age of fourteen. Having first served off the African coast, he had joined the White Star Line in early 1911, seeing service on the *Belgic* and *Tropic* before receiving orders to join the *Titanic* at Belfast. A teetotaller, he could be glib and hot-headed when roused, as would be seen on several occasions during the disaster and the subsequent inquiries, which would give some the impression that he had been drinking. However, many would owe their lives to Lowe's impetuous nature in the events that would shortly unfold.

At twenty-four years old, Sixth Officer James Paul Moody was the youngest and most junior of the *Titanic*'s deck officers and the only one of these newcomers to lose his life in the forthcoming disaster. Having gone to sea in 1904, he had then attended King Edward VII Nautical School in London and passed his Masters Examination there in April 1911. After seeing service aboard the *Oceanic*, he too found himself transferred to the *Titanic*, which he thought of as quite a coup and he wrote home commenting gleefully that he had spent the past week 'trying to find my way around the big omnibus'. He was perhaps a little daunted too at the idea of serving under the famous Captain Smith, telling his sister that; 'Though I believe he's an awful stickler for discipline, he's popular with everybody.'[3]

He was indeed, and Smith would have found plenty of familiar faces in the other departments of the ship who were happy enough to be there with him. Tall, broad and genial, thirty-seven-year-old Chief Purser Hugh McElroy was an old hand who had served with Smith on the *Majestic*, *Adriatic* and most recently on the *Olympic*, while fifty-five-year-old Chief Steward Andrew Latimer had been with Smith since the *Adriatic*. As already noted, Chief Engineer Joseph Bell and Dr William O'Loughlin were also well known to Captain Smith. For the most part these senior staff had little control over who they served under, but other members of the crew did and when they came aboard many would have been familiar faces to Smith. It may be stretching a point to say that they followed Smith from ship to ship for the same reasons as the passengers, each probably had their own reasons, the main one undoubtedly being to keep serving with their immediate friends, but the old hard core of the *Adriatic* family had all but moved ship with Smith, first to the *Olympic* then onto the *Titanic*. There were many new faces to be sure, but at its centre the *Titanic* had an experienced crew, who had worked with one another on and off for many years. Unfortunately for most of them, this loyalty and camaraderie would prove fatal.

Smith also got to know another character in the drama, the *Titanic* itself, and get a feel for his new command, for though she was an *Olympic*-class vessel and as such very similar to her elder sister, there were new features that he would need to get to know. Most of these were cosmetic, but even that was something worth going to see. There were the new much more lavish suites on B deck, a larger à la carte restaurant and a brand new 'café parisien'. Other notable additions, situated just aft of the forward grand staircase, were the two 'millionaire's suites', each with their collection of rooms and exclusive enclosed promenades. In addition, the forward third of the promenade deck was enclosed with glass windows, a feature that clearly identifies pictures of the *Titanic* from those of the *Olympic*.

All of these alterations had upped the *Titanic*'s weight to 46,328 tons gross, just over 1,000 tons heavier than the *Olympic*, enough to make her (temporarily at least) the largest ship in the world. So the *Titanic* was bigger and plusher than her sister and her nearest rivals on the shipping scene, but apart from these differences there was nothing particularly magical about the ship, certainly nothing to warrant the somewhat contrived 'ship of dreams' tag that has sometimes been accorded her. Indeed, had the forthcoming disaster never occurred, it would be a fairly safe bet to say that the average man on the street would have never heard of the RMS *Titanic*. The ship, like so many great and famous vessels that plied the seas at that time, would have become just a footnote in maritime history, her travels and stories known to a select band of enthusiasts and historians. Only through her spectacular early death would *Titanic* achieve immortality.

The *Titanic* was in the English Channel by late evening on 3 April and the ship docked at White Star's berth 44 at shortly after midnight on 4 April. Apart from the meagre provisions of food and coal she had set out with the ship was empty and the next few days would be spent filling her up and getting her ready for the journey ahead.

The next day, Good Friday, the *Titanic* was decked out in her best with all of her flags fluttering from her masts and rigging, the only time she would get to dress in all her finery. The rest of the time in port was spent being loaded with the tons of silver, crockery, cutlery, linen, food, drink, coal, mail and cargo for her inaugural crossing. Several days before sailing hundreds of prospective crewmen and women turned up to sign on, before returning home to await the muster early on 10 April. During this period Smith went home for a couple of days and the ship was left under the charge of a small ship-keeping crew. There was also a shake-up in the senior officers at this time. Henry Wilde, Smith's chief officer on the *Olympic*, had been under the impression that he was to remain aboard that vessel under Captain Haddock, but at the last minute he had been told to remain ashore. Wilde was apparently tipped as the next captain of the *Oceanic*, but the coal strike had seen her and a number of other ships laid up for the duration. Though the strike was now over, it would be some time before normal service was resumed for White Star's lesser vessels and with Wilde at a loose end, it seems that it may have been at Smith's request that he was now transferred to the *Titanic* as chief for one voyage, coming aboard when the ship arrived in Southampton. But what to the company or to Smith may have seemed a straightforward act of sense, bringing his skilled chief officer with him for the new ship's maiden voyage, probably didn't go down too well with the other ship's officers. Murdoch, doubtless pleased to have made chief officer, was bumped back to first officer and Lightoller became second and their chagrin at being so unceremoniously demoted is easy to imagine, though they doubtless took it in as professional a manner as they could. Not that Wilde was overly pleased himself; he did not like his cabin and wrote almost prophetically to his sister that he had 'a queer feeling' about the *Titanic*. As the ship had a full compliment of junior officers the biggest loser – though as it turned out the biggest winner – was Second Officer David Blair, who had to leave the ship, taking with him the knowledge that the lookouts' binoculars were stored in his cabin.

Sailing Day

Shortly after 5a.m., on Wednesday 10 April 1912, dawn broke over Southampton with the promise of calm weather. At the docks, the *Titanic*, securely warped into White Star's berth number 44, showed a little more activity aboard her than there had been over the last six days. The ship-keeping crew, headed by Chief Officer Henry Wilde, were up early getting the vessel ready for the busy day ahead.

At 'Woodhead', their home in Winn Road, Ted and Eleanor Smith were also up early that morning perhaps taking breakfast together before he set off for work. The chances are that the couple were alone in the house apart from the cook and the maid, Melville may have been away at boarding school and so perhaps missed seeing her father before he set off aboard the *Titanic*.

Breakfast over, Smith then spent a little time in his study that morning, packing his bag and sorting whatever documents he needed for the voyage and it was here in 'the sacred room of his'[4], as Eleanor herself recalled, that the couple said their farewells. Then, at a little before 7a.m., Smith donned his overcoat and bowler hat before setting off as usual.

It was spring and outside, as a reporter later noted, the early flowers were coming into bloom in the captain's garden. As he made his way down the path, Smith spotted the paper lad, eleven-year-old Albert 'Ben' Benham, coming out of next door's garden, so he paused at the gate.

'All right son,' said Smith when the boy noticed him standing there, 'I'll take my paper.'

Ben handed the paper over then moved on to finish his round. It had hardly been the most dramatic moment in history, but young Benham would remember that brief meeting for the rest of his life.[5]

Smith had probably ordered a taxi to take him down to the docks as Winn Road was some distance from the noisy bustling harbour front and his route would have taken him through the centre of Southampton before turning down the hill towards the sea. From here there was a clear view down to the waterfront and the *Titanic*'s four funnels would have been easily visible, towering over the neighbouring ships and buildings.

Alighting at the docks, Captain Smith boarded the *Titanic* at 7.30a.m., and made his way to the bridge where he received the day's sailing report from Chief Officer Wilde, then made his way to his quarters. As on the *Olympic*, these were situated just behind the bridge on the starboard side of the boat deck and could be reached by cutting through the wheelhouse and chart room, thus providing him with quick and easy access to the bridge should any problems occur. His quarters consisted of a sitting room, bedroom and a private lavatory complete with a bath. The latter was an elaborate affair fitted with four taps, two for hot or cold fresh water, two for hot or cold salt water, a luxury only usually afforded to first-class passengers.

These rooms were Smith's home away from home and having signed back onto the ship's crew list on 6 April he had probably already added a few personal touches. Being an avid reader, Smith usually kept a small library of books in his quarters and although it was strictly against regulations, if one account is to be believed the captain kept a bottle or two here, most likely for entertaining as there is no evidence that he was a secret toper whilst on duty. He was attended here by his own private steward Arthur Paintin, who would bring Smith his meals and messages should he be obliged to remain on or near to the bridge.

In his cabin Smith changed into his uniform. This consisted of a pair of dark blue trousers, white shirt and blue neck tie, a dark blue waistcoat and over the top of this he had the choice of wearing a short dark blue double-breasted 'undress' jacket, or the longer double-breasted silk-lined Edwardian frock coat decorated by two rows of five gold buttons on the front: pictures of Smith on the *Titanic* show him wearing the latter style of coat. On the cuff of each sleeve were four gold rings, the topmost looped, denoting the rank of commander. As usual, pinned high on his left breast he wore the green-ribboned RNR long-service decoration and the Transport Medal on its red and blue ribbon. The final touch was his small dark blue peaked cap, bearing the gold laurels, crown and red pennant badge of the White Star Line. To distinguish his position as the ship's commander, the brim of the hat was decorated with a row of gold oak leaves.

As already noted, there was a summer uniform, a single-breasted affair made in white cotton, and he is seen wearing this in the famous portrait taken aboard the

Olympic and in the newsreel of him strolling on the ship's bridge. It was, however, only April, a time of wind and rain squalls, so Smith and his men stuck to the more saturnine colours. Other pictures from Smith's time aboard the *Olympic* show that he occasionally made a jaunty nod towards the paler uniform by sporting the white peaked cap with the darker dress.

Smith's uniforms were tailored at Savile Row, London, evidence for this came to light in 2004 with the auction of six Savile Row tailor's customer address books, though the name of the firm was never mentioned. Clients gave their name, the name of their home town and perhaps a little more information was recorded such as the date. On one page, at the bottom, was the name 'Edward Smith'. He gave his home town as 'Hanley' and additional information, if any were needed to prove that this was our man, were the words 'White Star' pencilled in the same space.[6]

Once Captain Smith had changed into his expensive, made-to-measure uniform, he was joined by Wilde and together the two officers went through the sailing report.

While the ship's two most senior officers talked, outside a wave of noise grew as over 900 men and women of varying ages and seagoing experience poured through the dock gates. Anyone hoping to crew on the *Titanic* need to arrive on time for the Board of Trade muster at 8a.m., as there was little chance of sailing without being present for registration.

Just over a third of the places aboard the ship were for the trimmers, boilermen, stokers and firemen who worked down in the bowels of the ship shovelling coal and feeding the furnaces that powered the ship's engines and fed her massive hot water system. Their transatlantic journey took place in what were often cramped, hot, airless and noisy environments, far removed from the luxuries enjoyed by the passengers. Another 290 crew members, on the other hand, would become familiar faces to many of the passengers, namely the stewards and stewardesses who attended their needs. The remaining crew held down a variety of different jobs. There were pantrymen, lift attendants, sports and PT instructors, librarians, bar staff, barbers, postal staff, cooks, bakers, waiters and even a masseur. Also aboard, albeit as second-class passengers rather than crew, was a small professional ship's band, whose members were the pick of White Star's musicians, or had been poached from other shipping companies.

While the crew gathered on the quay, a long, black Daimler Benz limousine pulled up beside the ship. A chauffeur dressed in a green uniform climbed out and opened the doors to let the passengers out. These were J. Bruce Ismay the chairman of the White Star Line and his wife Florence and their children, who now stood looking up at the huge vessel before them and chatting in an animated fashion. Mrs Ismay and the children would not be travelling aboard the *Titanic* and were about to set off on a motor car tour through Wales, but Bruce Ismay would be making the crossing to New York, accompanied by his butler, secretary and steward.

At 8a.m., the Blue Ensign was hoisted up at the stern and the crew muster began. As the crew began to assemble on deck or in the corridors, the ship's articles, or crew list for each department, were distributed to each of the department heads. The inspectors, Captain Smith, Captain Benjamin Steele, Dr O'Loughlin and his assistant Dr Edward Simpson stood to one side. Smith's task was basically monitorial; he would meet and assist the officials, who would check the vessel and crew before allowing it to go to sea. Captain Steele was White Star's Marine Superintendent, who oversaw the muster while the crew members were checked over by the two doctors.

As the muster was going on, Captain Maurice Clarke, the Board of Trade official who had inspected the *Titanic* the previous day, came back aboard for a final inspection. During his time aboard he supervised the test lowering of lifeboat 15, helped by Fifth Officer Lowe and Sixth Officer Moody, who had assisted him the last time. The davit crew performed well and Clarke came away satisfied with the test.

Whether Smith was there to watch the test lowering is not clear, though doubtless he had an interview with Captain Clarke. He chose, however, not to inform Captain Clarke of one problem that had been discovered with the ship. A bunker fire had broken out in boiler room 6. This had probably been caused by the coal being damp when loaded and as it dried and slipped and settled, iron elements in the blocks had rubbed together striking a spark and combustion had occurred. Chief Engineer Bell was of the opinion that the fire had been smouldering deep in the coal for some time, possibly since the ship's sea trials nearly a fortnight earlier. His men were even now beginning to move the coal from the affected area, trying to locate the seat of the fire, but he assured Smith that everything was under control and that any damage the fire might cause would be minimal and confined to one small part of the transverse bulkhead. The integrity of the ship's hull would not be compromised.

While Smith was engaged in his duties, the junior officers gathered on the bridge where each in turn submitted their section reports to Chief Officer Wilde. Wilde read them through and deeming the ship ready for sea he informed the captain. On the basis of this, Smith wrote out his Master's Report for the company: 'I hereby report this ship loaded and ready for sea. The engines and boilers are in good order for the voyage, and all charts and sailing directions are up to date. Your obedient servant, Edward J. Smith.'

This report Smith handed to Captain Steele, the White Star superintendent, before he left the ship, while the muster rolls were given to Captain Clarke.

The muster finished at 9a.m., and the crew filed off to their various departments and duties. By this time the passenger lists for both first and second class were ready and Smith would have examined them with interest, noting the names of not a few old acquaintances of his, who would be travelling on the *Titanic's* first transatlantic crossing.

The first-class passengers began arriving at 9.30, many on the boat train that had left London's Waterloo Station earlier that morning. Hardly had they arrived and busy stewards had begun to whisk the rich and famous off to their cabins than the second-class passengers began coming aboard. Between 9.30 and 11a.m., the last passengers, those from third class, boarded the *Titanic*.

Smith may have been on hand to greet a few, but he was a busy man and although there are no records as to how he spent his time, there are a couple of witnesses who remember encountering the captain that morning. Marine artist Norman Wilkinson, whose paintings graced the smoking rooms on both the *Olympic* and the *Titanic*, was en route to Devon with a friend, but stopped off in Southampton to see the *Titanic* before she sailed. On reaching the jetty at the top of Southampton Water, Wilkinson took a look for the *Titanic* and seeing her still in dock he turned to his friend and said, 'What a bit of luck. I know the Captain. We will go aboard and look around the ship.'

A quartermaster at the head of the gangplank told them that Captain Smith was aboard and took Wilkinson and his friend along to Smith's cabin. Sure enough Captain Smith was there and he gave his visitors a warm welcome, but added that he was very busy and that he would get Purser McElroy to show them around the liner.[7]

Two other visitors to the ship that morning also encountered Smith. Captain Diaper, formerly of the Royal Mail Steam Packet Company, had taken his young son Roy to see the *Titanic* before she left. Captain Diaper knew Captain Smith of old and went aboard in search of him. Young Roy was amazed by what he saw and later recalled standing in front of a grand staircase whilst his father chatted with a tall bearded man in a frock coat and a small peaked cap. Smith did not speak to Roy, but he did bend down at one point and shake him by the hand. All the while this was going on Roy recalled that there was a tremendous amount of activity around them and Captain Smith was surrounded by people.[8]

Departure

By 11 o'clock, 'Uncle' George Bowyer, the Trinity House harbour pilot, had arrived aboard the *Titanic* and he spent some time discussing draught and displacement and turning circles with Captain Smith. Both of them were still only too aware that it was only eight months since the embarrassing encounter with HMS *Hawke* and neither of them wanted a repeat of that accident with White Star's new flagship.

As the midday departure time approached, the ship's whistles were sounded urging all non-passengers ashore and Captain Clarke departed at about this time too. When all the visitors and officials were gone, the covered gangplanks were drawn in and the gangways closed. Down in the bowels of the ship, meantime, Chief Engineer Bell had the ship's massive engines ticking over and now only waited for the order from Smith that would set them in motion.

Captain Smith was now on the bridge with Chief Officer Wilde and Pilot Bowyer. Here they were joined briefly by J. Bruce Ismay and Thomas Andrews, who exchanged greetings and proffered best wishes for a successful voyage with Smith and Wilde before they left the bridge. Now, with everything ready, documents signed and the crew at their duties, cargo stored, passengers accommodated and the engines making steam, Smith ordered the quartermaster to sound the whistles for departure. Three triple-tone hoots rang out load and clear over Southampton docks, alerting other traffic that the *Titanic* was under weigh. This was followed by a further trio once the Blue Peter was run up the mast. Pilot Bowyer then ordered tugs in to make fast forward and aft and as they took the strain under the immense bulk of the liner, the quayside mooring lines were cast off, the hawsers splashing into the water to be hauled aboard the ship by her crew. Slowly and carefully the five tugs then eased *Titanic* away from the wharf and into the River Test towards the newly dredged turning circle. Here, at Bowyer's command, the tugs manoeuvred the ship into the correct position for her departure. Only then did the tug lines slacken and fall and *Titanic* float free.

As the *Titanic* moved clear of the dock, shouted farewells and final messages from the crowds from friends and relatives who had followed the ship along the quayside echoed over the water. Apart from this, none of the other ships sounded their whistles or put on any other display as might have been expected for the maiden voyage of such a fine new liner. The *Titanic* was a working ship, the second in her class and from the start she would be treated as such.

On the bridge and then down in the engine room the ship's telegraphs jangled to 'Ahead Slow' and beneath the water the *Titanic*'s two main propellers slowly began to spin. Followed by final goodbyes shouted across the intervening ships, the *Titanic* slowly gained in speed, cruising gently forward past the numerous quays and the various ships warped in there, most casualties of the coal strike. Two of these vessels tied up at pier 38 were the *Oceanic* and the *New York* and as the *Titanic* eased past them they began to shift on their moorings. The hydrodynamics caused by the big ship's passage nearly had damaging results as several of the *New York*'s stern hawsers suddenly pulled taut, then snapped with several loud reports and she began to be drawn towards the cruising liner like metal to a magnet.

Smith and Bowyer, perhaps half expecting something like this after the *Hawke* incident, were quick to react. The order was rung down for 'Full Astern' and the starboard anchor was lowered down to the waterline ready to be deployed quickly if the situation demanded it. It was never used, though, as prompt action by Captain Gale on the tug *Vulcan*, which managed to get a line onto the *New York*, averted any danger. The tug took the strain just in time and there were gasps from the passengers crowding the rails as the *New York* was brought to a halt just 8ft from the *Titanic*.

There were fears that the *Oceanic* too would snap her moorings, but extra ropes were quickly laid on preventing a repeat of the *New York*'s escape. The *Vulcan* had by this time been joined by the tug *Hercules* and together they brought the *New York* under control and the *Titanic* was again able to proceed after a delay of almost an hour. It had been a close call and for those of a superstitious turn of mind it did not auger well for the forthcoming voyage.

Having negotiated Southampton Water, the *Titanic* steamed out towards the English Channel. The ship passed Spithead and the Isle of Wight, swapping pleasantries with a White Star tug as it did so. Seated in a boat off the Isle of Wight, his camera at the ready, was a local pharmacist and amateur ship photographer, who snapped the *Titanic* as she swept by. Smith, seeing this familiar figure, saluted him with four short blasts on the ship's whistle.

His duties done, Pilot Bowyer was dropped off at the Nab Light Vessel. The *Titanic* then turned south and passed out over a beautiful shimmering sea. It seemed as if she were alone apart from a knot of sleek, grey warships resting at anchor a short distance away. As the ship finally left the shores of Britain, a French Tricolour was run up the foremast ready for her Channel crossing to Cherbourg.

Cherbourg and Queenstown

The Channel crossing was uneventful and the *Titanic* dropped anchor in Cherbourg Harbour at 6.30p.m. She remained there for only an hour and a half, taking aboard more passengers and mail that were ferried over by the White Star tenders *Nomadic* and *Traffic*. In the evening twilight hundreds of people filed through the liner's gangways while those disembarking cross-Channel passengers were carried back to Cherbourg on the tenders when they had finished loading passengers and mail. By 8p.m. the tenders had steamed back to port, the gangways had been closed and the new passengers were being installed in their cabins. Smith ordered a triple blast of the ship's horns to signal that the *Titanic* was about to depart. Minutes later the anchors were raised and the *Titanic*, now a blaze of lights, slowly cruised out of the harbour. On reaching the sea her speed increased as she steamed west through the night towards Ireland.

During her first night at sea Smith had the *Titanic* put through her paces so that he and her crew would get a surer feel for the new vessel. On his orders the ship executed a series of long lazy 'S' turns to shake her down ready for the long voyage ahead. By dawn on the 11th, *Titanic* was steaming past Land's End before turning north-west up into St George's Channel. She was making good time and the engines pushing her along at a steady 21 knots were working well. Also, early that morning that other piece of vital ship's equipment, the compasses, were adjusted.

As the morning passed, the coast of Ireland loomed in the distance. Standing sentinel before that was the Daunt Light Vessel, where the ship paused to pick up John Cotter the Queenstown harbour pilot. As the ship made her way towards the harbour, a full emergency drill was held. Alarm bells were rung, red lights flashed and the watertight doors clanged shut along the length of the ship. Everything worked well and by 11.30a.m. *Titanic* had come to rest and lay at anchor a couple of miles off Roche Point near Queenstown, for here as at Cherbourg an exchange of mail and passengers would take place. Soon after the liner's arrival, two tenders, the aptly named *Ireland* and *America*, were glimpsed ferrying over the ship's compliment of passengers.

As the tenders moved up alongside, Smith ordered lifeboat number 2 to be swung out ready, just in case there were any accidents as the new arrivals came aboard, but the embarkation was trouble free. Captain Smith, however, was called upon to sport his PR hat one more time, as along with the new passengers, officials, well-wishers and harbour-front vendors, a gaggle of Irish pressmen also came aboard to get a look at White Star's newest addition to the fleet. They were allowed onto the officers' promenade deck where one of the photographers found Captain Smith chatting with Purser Hugh McElroy. Asking them to pose for him, the two officers obliged.

Some passengers too were disembarking here. One of these was a Jesuit priest, Father Francis Browne, who had boarded the *Titanic* at Southampton. A keen amateur photographer, Father Browne had made the most of his time aboard the *Titanic* and had been roaming the ship, snapping photos. Father Browne also took a few parting shots as he left the *Titanic*. One of these was taken from the tender looking up at the starboard wing of the *Titanic*'s bridge just in time to capture Captain Smith gazing down at them. It was the last surviving picture ever taken of him.

At 1.30p.m., Smith gave the order for the anchors to be raised and three loud but dreary hoots from the whistles echoed across Queenstown bay, signalling the *Titanic*'s departure. More orders followed and the engines kicked in, the propellers churning up clouds of mud in the water as the *Titanic*, turning a quarter circle, slowly eased away from its mooring, followed by hundreds of swooping, screaming seagulls that danced over the ship's wake until nightfall. Pausing briefly once again at the Daunt Light Vessel to drop off the Queenstown pilot, the ship then set off around the Irish coast towards the Atlantic and so began the final leg of her maiden voyage.

Transatlantic

The long haul across the Atlantic was to take five days with the *Titanic* due to arrive in New York early on 17 April. For the first two days life aboard the new liner was spent in much the same manner as on any long voyage with all the attendant pleasures and petty tribulations. Like the rest of the crew, most of the ship's officers worked through their shifts, standing watch or attending to duties of navigation, crew and passenger issues and the routine of running the ship. Smith, though, had little time to himself. Like everyone else he had to sleep and eat, but as the captain of the *Titanic* as much as when he took command of the *Lizzie Fennell*, he was never off duty, there were merely variations in how busy he was.

For instance, every morning, except on Sundays, he and his officers had to undertake the routine stem to stern top to bottom inspection of the vessel. Thus, at a little after 10a.m., Smith would receive in his quarters the chief engineer, purser, assistant purser, surgeon and chief steward, each of whom would then report on the state of their respective departments and of any developments since the last meeting. After this, at about 10.30, the captain and his officers would set off on their tour of the ship, taking in passenger accommodation, public rooms, dining saloons, bars and corridors, galleys, storerooms, the ship's hospital, engine rooms and holds. While

Smith led the way the officers trailing behind him took note of his comments on cleanliness and order as they went, ready to ensure that any problems were rectified before the next day's inspection. These inspections were also one of the few occasions when passengers in second and third class got to see the man at the helm. For instance, third-class passenger Gunnar Isidor Tenglin caught a glimpse of the sterner side of Smith's nature when on Saturday 13 April the captain dropped in on the third-class cabin quarters. Finding some of the crew lounging there he told them to keep out and according to Tenglin threatened to impose a £5 fine on any crew member found hanging around the passengers.[9]

After these inspections, Smith and his officers returned to the bridge where they discussed the main points raised on their inspection before the department heads returned to their duties, leaving Smith alone with his deck officers whom he took through the day's course for navigation.

At noon each day the available ship's officers would gather out on one of the wings of the bridge with their sextants to take bearings and so calculate the ship's position. This general reading was to provide as accurate an average as possible and hopefully rule out any individual error. Smith would have noted the results, perhaps rechecked it himself and then, as was his want, he would personally mark the ship's position on the main chart. Then for the rest of the day while his officers went about their own duties, Smith could often be found on the bridge, or working in the chart room. As things were obviously running well, the weather being fine and the sea calm, he would have also been able to relax a little in his sea cabin, reading, catching a few hours sleep, or taking a scrub in his private bathroom. He also spent some time socialising with the passengers, however he was always contacted should any messages arrive, or situations arise that required his immediate presence on the bridge.

Because of the routine of the first few days, he had not put in an appearance in the first-class à la carte restaurant. Once they had left the Irish coast, though, the weather being fine if a little chilly, Smith took regular meals with the first class passengers. He first appeared on Friday 12 April, when he was present during the evening meal where, contrary to popular belief, he did not sit at the head of a large table surrounded by the finest people, choosing instead a table for six in the centre section of the restaurant.

The stewards who knew Smith did not trouble to notice if he was there for meals, being too busy with their own duties. The passengers, though, paid more attention. First-class passenger Hugh Woolner had not sailed with Smith before and being keen to know what the captain looked like, early in the voyage he asked someone who did to point him out to him. He subsequently noted him at breakfast in the mornings and at dinner one evening.

Another first-class passenger, Elizabeth Lines, also asked a steward to point out Captain Smith. Mrs Lines later stated in a deposition to the US Limitation of Liability Hearings that she had seen Captain Smith talking to J. Bruce Ismay in the first-class reception room just after lunch on both the Friday and Saturday. On the first occasion she saw them as she passed by and they were still there chatting some time later. The next day, Saturday 13th, Mrs Lines had settled down in the reception room with a coffee when Ismay and Smith came in and took the same corner seat nearby where they ordered liqueurs and cigars and sat talking. For some time after noting their arrival she paid them scant attention until Ismay started talking in an animated fashion about their daily runs, comparing them favourably with the *Olympic*'s maiden voyage. Smith said nothing, merely nodding as Ismay rattled on, enthusing about the ship's performance and affirming confidently that at the rate they were going the ship would arrive on Tuesday. Mrs Lines said that the two of them sat there for two hours and that Mr Ismay carried the conversation, his attitude towards the captain striking her as being somewhat 'dictatorial'. [10]

Smith was in the restaurant that evening, where he dined in company with Ismay and Dr O'Loughlin. Despite his apparent annoyance at having been shifted so unceremoniously over to the *Titanic* at such short notice, O'Loughlin had cheered up and now raised a glass and proposed a toast. 'Let us drink to the mighty *Titanic*,' he said and with cries of approval everybody stood up and drank the toast. [11]

Smith like Ismay could afford to feel pleased about the way the ship was behaving. Admittedly, the *Titanic* had over the first few days developed a slight list to port. Several people noted this and Purser McElroy put it down to more coal being used from the starboard side. Here the smouldering coals in boiler room 6 were being hastily shovelled into the boilers in an effort to eradicate the bunker fire and this was the most likely cause for the *Titanic*'s imbalance.

Despite this, the *Titanic* was making good time and as Mr Ismay had noted earlier, the daily runs made for interesting reading. From noon on Thursday to noon Friday, *Titanic* had covered approximately 386 nautical miles; on Friday to Saturday the tally was 519 nautical miles; and from Saturday to Sunday she would cover 546 nautical miles. Despite numerous claims to the contrary, the *Titanic* was not attempting to win the Blue Riband, the *Olympic*-class liners being easily outmatched by the big Cunarders. An attempt on the *Olympic*'s personal best may have been on the cards as Ismay's one-sided conversation with Smith suggests, though this is by no means certain. What is clear is that despite later claims of excessive speed, the *Titanic* was never driven at full speed, though it seems likely that she may have attempted a high-speed run on the 15th or 16th. In the time leading up to the disaster, though, the *Titanic* moved at a rate of knots that would keep her on schedule for her projected arrival in New York on the 17th.

Since the beginning of the voyage, *Titanic*'s Marconi men, Jack Phillips and Harold Bride had been busy sending but also receiving messages from many other vessels. Sometimes these messages were simply nothing more than personal greetings and best wishes to Captain Smith and his new vessel. Others were intercepted messages to other ships, but as the ship moved away from Europe and towards America, many of these messages carried warnings of field ice and bergs off the Grand Banks. This was nothing unusual as each year between March and May, hundreds of icebergs, released from the icy grip of the northern seas by the spring thaw, made a migration south across the shipping lanes. These dragged with them a mass of icy debris like floe ice and the smallest type of bergs known as growlers, some no more than 15ft out of the water, that were by far the most numerous in any of these conglomerations. Add to this the wide crust of frozen sea water that formed around the hard core of the bergs and the ice fields that formed could be many miles in length and several miles thick, presenting a serious barrier to shipping.

Smith and the men under him had of course encountered ice fields many times in their long careers at sea and they treated icebergs with respect, giving them a very wide berth and with good reason; for the bulk of an iceberg being underwater meant that even a growler could do serious damage to a ship. Accepted wisdom, though, held that providing that the weather was good, that there were ample lookouts to spot any potential hazards, and that any intervening ice field was not continuous, then ships could navigate as normal, even at night. This was not a whim on the part of White Star, it was the practice of most Atlantic shipping companies at that time and when ships did slow down or stop, it was not because they had seen icebergs, but because they could not find a clear navigation. Otherwise they would continue on their way, the captains relying on their experience and the power of the steam engine that enabled them to cut away from the current that dictated the berg's movements. The messages, meantime, would alert approaching vessels to the danger spots. Among the vessels sending warnings were the *Avala*, *Californian*, *La Touraine*, *Montrose*, *President Lincoln*, *St Laurent*, *Corsican*, *East Point*, *Empress of Britain* and *Lackawanna*. Their reports were consistent, 'Field ice, some growlers, some bergs' along the latitude 41° 50' N.

One message received across the Atlantic on 11 April had been more dramatic and prophetic in the light of what was going to happen with the *Titanic* and shows the danger that even small ice presented. The French Line steamer *Niagra* had stopped due to ice. The crew discovered that she was damaged and immediately sent out a distress call. The *Carmania* was nearby and went to her aid and upon her arrival a message was sent out that further aid was unnecessary. The *Niagra* was lucky, the damage though serious was not fatal and the vessel managed to limp to New York.

Messages of one kind or another kept coming in up until about 11p.m., on the evening of Saturday 13 April, when all wireless communication with the *Titanic* ceased for a short time at least when the wireless broke down. The junior wireless operator Harold Bride was sent to inform Smith about the problem and after he had returned to the wireless room, he and Phillips broke with Marconi regulations. Main power having failed, they should have relied on battery power and waited until they got to New York where a Marconi engineer would have looked into the problem. Instead of waiting, though, the two young operators decided to try and find and fix the fault themselves, spurred on perhaps by the occasion and the knowledge that the wealthy clientele aboard would wish to make use of the system. As a result they would work throughout the night and it was not until 5a.m., the next morning that they discovered that part of the machinery known as the secretary was damaged and they hastened to repair the faulty part. That they did so was fortunate as in less than twenty-four hours that fragile transmitter would be the voice that would alert the world to the *Titanic*'s dramatic fate.

The Last Day

Sunday 14 April dawned, the first day shift rose and got to work, the passengers awoke and breakfasted in style and Captain Smith and his officers went about their duties. However, unlike the other six days of the week, on Sundays there was no stem to stern inspection of the *Titanic*. Instead, there should have been a lifeboat drill, but this never happened as Smith like many captains had forsaken the practice, relying instead on the test lowerings that had taken place under Captain Clarke's supervision at Southampton. When questioned at the British Inquiry, Clarke confirmed that the practice was a common one. He added that he had always regarded these test lowerings as inadequate but busy shipping lines such as White Star found it expedient as it saved time and in the end money.[12] Another major drawback was the fact that it was often the same crew members who carried out the tests and as a result most of the crew had very little experience in readying, lowering and loading the lifeboats.

With no major duties to attend to, Captain Smith seems to have spent most of the earlier part of the morning either on the bridge or nearby in his quarters. He was certainly on the bridge at 9a.m., when he was handed the first of many ice warnings that the Marconi men received that day. The message was from Captain Barr of the SS *Caronia*, reporting a mixed bag of icebergs, growlers and field ice in latitude 42° North to longitude 49° to 51° West. Smith acknowledged the message and showed it to Fourth Officer Boxhall who marked it down on the main chart. Smith would later show the message to Second Officer Lightoller at about 12.45p.m., whilst Murdoch was eating his lunch. When Murdoch reappeared Lightoller reported the message to him. The *Caronia*'s message showed that there was ice near to the *Titanic*'s projected course, albeit 300 miles away and somewhat to the south.

Just before 10.30a.m. Smith, dressed in his finery, walked to the first-class dining saloon where divine service was to be held. Many first-class passengers turned up for the service and Smith led the prayers and hymns which were drawn from the White Star Line's own prayer and hymn books. Similar services in second class and third class were held by Purser Reginald Barker and in third class by a passenger, Father Thomas Byles.

The service in first class ended at about 11.15 and shortly after this Captain Smith was back on the bridge. He was there when at 11.40 another ice warning was received, this time from the Dutch steamer *Noordam*, noting ice in roughly the same position that the *Caronia* had reported. Though Smith acknowledged the message, none of the surviving officers recalled seeing it. This is odd given that at noon most of them would have gathered on the bridge with their sextants to 'shoot the sun' and log their midday position. Then in accordance with White Star regulations Smith ordered the ship's whistles and engine room telegraphs to be tested and they were found to be in full working order.

While the passengers enjoyed their dinners, sat talking, reading, or strolled around the decks, more ice reports reached the *Titanic*. At 1.42p.m., Jack Phillips took a message from Smith's old command, RMS *Baltic*.

> Captain Smith, 'Titanic' – have had moderate, variable winds and clear, fine weather since leaving. Greek steamer 'Athenai' reports passing icebergs and large quantities of field ice today in lat. 41° 51'N, long. 49° 52'W. Last night we spoke German oiltank steamer 'Deutschland', Stettin to Philadelphia, not under control, short of coal lat. 40°, 42'N, long. 55°, 11'W. Wishes to be reported to New York and other steamers. Wish you and 'Titanic' all success – Commander.

Smith received and acknowledged this message. He had punctiliously shown Second Officer Lightoller the *Caronia's* message from earlier that morning, but instead of handing the new message over to the officers on watch, Smith carried it with him as he made his way to A deck. Here, as he walked aft, Smith encountered J. Bruce Ismay chatting with George and Eleanor Widener. The captain joined them for a short while and Ismay later testified that Captain Smith handed him the *Baltic's* message without comment. Ismay pocketed the message, but did not read it until later that afternoon when he showed it to some of the passengers. Lord Mersey, who headed the British disaster inquiry, later commented that it was highly irregular for Smith to have handed this message over to Ismay and improper of Ismay to have held onto it, though he concluded that it in no way affected how the ship would be navigated. We shall never know why Smith did hand the note over to Ismay, though many a conspiracy theory has been built around this and other small incidents. Whatever the reason, Smith did eventually recall his duty and would retrieve the errant message long before the ship entered the ice region.

At 1.45p.m., another message was intercepted by the *Titanic*, it was a private communication from the German steamer *Amerika* to the United States Hydrographic Office:

> 'Amerika' passed two large icebergs in 41° 27'N, 50° 8'W on the 14th April.

Probably due to the fact that this message was not directly addressed to the captain, Phillips did not seem to have thought of sending it to the bridge. Phillips had delivered several ice warnings to the bridge, but messages that required a reply from a ship's captain were headed with the code letters MSG for Masters' Service Gram. If the *Amerika's* message lacked the all important code letters then Phillips would have deemed it much less critical. Certainly none of the surviving officers recalled seeing it, Fourth Officer Boxhall stated that he was sure Captain Smith had not seen it, otherwise, 'the word would have been passed around right away – everybody would have known it.' That said, the *Baltic* message that Smith alone had seen was still in J. Bruce Ismay's pocket.

With the Grand Banks being menaced by ice, the *Titanic* was taking the southern track that was used during the winter months in an effort to avoid the worst of it, sailing much further south and south-west than during the summer, until she reached latitude 42° North and 47° West, a spot known to sailors as 'the corner'. Here the navigation was to change to a heading of nearly due west on a course for the Nantucket Lightship and the approaches to New York.

Third Officer Pitman recalled that the *Titanic* changed course at 5.50p.m. on Sunday 14 April. However, at the British Inquiry, he claimed that the ship should have turned earlier, at 5.00p.m. Pitman believed that the late course change meant that the *Titanic* travelled an extra 10 miles south than would have normally been the case, the implication being that this may have been done to avoid the ice that reports now showed was littering the southern track ahead of them. This notion, however, may be wrong and possibly came about from a growing need amongst the surviving officers to reconcile Boxhall's erroneous position of the wreck – which they all believed to be correct – with the ship's speed and the actual distances travelled. White Star's lawyers, eager to save face, may have later seized on this to prove that Captain Smith had shown extra caution in view of the ice reports he had been receiving. However, as Lord Mersey's inquiry suspected and as the position of the wreck seems to show, there is an equal amount of circumstantial evidence that Captain Smith turned the corner precisely where he should have done.[13]

Chief Officer Wilde and Sixth Officer Moody held the bridge at the time, but the turn would have been executed under Smith's supervision and at his say so. On the captain's word of command the quartermaster turned the wheel several points to starboard then held steady on the new heading. The ship answered slowly to the wheel, executing a graceful arc before straightening up again. With that the *Titanic* started on the home stretch for New York.

At 6p.m., as throughout the ship the passengers sat down for what for most would be their last meal, Second Officer Lightoller took over from Chief Officer Wilde on the bridge watch. Since Captain Smith had shown him the *Caronia* message earlier that day, Lightoller had totted up the distance in his head and concluded that they would be up in the ice at about 9.30p.m. Some time after coming on duty he asked Sixth Officer Moody his opinion on the matter and Moody suggested that 11p.m. would be the approximate time. Lightoller was puzzled by the difference, but supposed that Moody had seen a message that he had missed. Nonetheless, it was clear by anyone's calculations that they would be entering an ice region some time before midnight.

Lightoller was not unduly concerned; he like all the other senior officers aboard had sailed through ice many times before and besides, on such a calm, clear night he was sure that he would be able to spot even a growler with 'sufficient distinctness' at a distance of up to 2 miles away.

It was 7.10p.m. when Captain Smith located J. Bruce Ismay in the first-class smoking room. He had obviously realised by this point that he had been remiss in his duties in leaving the *Baltic*'s message with his boss and had come to collect it. Walking over to Ismay he asked, 'By the way, sir, have you got that telegram which I gave you this afternoon?' Ismay reached into his pocket.

'Yes,' he said, 'here it is.'

The captain took the paper, explaining, 'I want to put it up in the officer's chart room.'[14]

Smith had doubtless wanted to square that problem away before he left the bridge in charge of the watch officer, for if he had not already done so, after posting the note in the chart room he probably went to his quarters to wash and dress as he had been invited to a party to be held that evening by George and Eleanor Widener in the first-class restaurant.

By the time Smith left, the bridge would have been in darkness. The sun had set and the blinds in the wheelhouse had been drawn, the only illumination for the quartermaster at the wheel came from the compass binnacle and a small light on the courseboard. At 7.15, Lamp Trimmer Samuel Hemming came onto the bridge to report that all of the navigation lights had been lit. Lightoller had by this time gone for dinner and First Officer Murdoch standing in as temporary officer of the watch received Hemming's report. Having said his piece, Hemming was walking away when Murdoch called him back and told him to go and secure the forescuttle hatch on the fo'c'sle. A glow was coming from it and as they were entering an ice region Murdoch wanted everything dark before the bridge as any light would blind them to any objects ahead. Hemming did as he was instructed.

In the wireless room, having given their machine a short rest after a hard day's work, at 7.30p.m. the *Titanic*'s wireless operators turned their equipment back on and intercepted a message from the Leyland Line steamer *Californian* to the *Antillian*. The *Californian*, ahead of the *Titanic* on a more northerly track, was to play a controversial part in the night ahead. The message, meantime, was as follows:

To Captain, 'Antillian', 6.30p.m. apparent ship's time; lat. 42°3'N, long. 49° 9'W. Three large bergs five miles to southward of us. Regards. – Lord.

The message was delivered to the bridge by the junior Marconi operator, Harold Bride, but he did not remember to which officer. Lightoller did not recall receiving the message, so it may have been delivered to Murdoch before Lightoller returned to the bridge at 7. 35p.m.

The British Inquiry found that at the time of the collision, the *Titanic* had long since passed the danger posed by these bergs, as she was 50 miles to the westward of the reported sighting. The inquiry also felt that the small ice reported earlier by the *Caronia* would most likely have drifted well to the eastward and the large bergs still in the powerful tow of the Labrador Current would have been taken further south. That said, none of the officers on the *Titanic* were foolish enough to believe that they were out of danger and by now, despite the missed messages, everyone who needed to know had been cautioned to keep their eyes open.

8

NEMESIS

Smith does not seem to have been told about the message from the *Californian*. By that time he was no longer on the bridge, having made his way to the first-class restaurant, where he joined those passengers who had been invited to the Widener's party. The invited guests included John and Marian Thayer and their son Jack, Major Archibald Butt, the theatrical director Mr Henry B. Harris and his wife Irene. Mrs Harris attended the soirée despite having an injured arm and the captain, seeing her in difficulties, went over to her and congratulated her on her spirit. He then seated himself nearby at his usual table, where he was joined by the Thayers. He spent an enjoyable evening in their company and allowed himself the luxury of relaxing a little. He smoked a couple of his favourite cigars, but drank nothing alcoholic. Following the disaster, one passenger who had been seated at another table claimed that she had seen the captain drinking, but this was refuted by depositions from both Mrs Thayer and Mrs Widener, both of whom stated that not once had they seen Smith drinking that evening.[1]

The meal finished earlier than expected and at about 8.55p.m., well before the earliest estimate for entering the ice region, Captain Smith excused himself and made his way back to the bridge. There he met Lightoller, and after saying 'Good evening', he remarked on how cold it was.

'Yes, it is very cold, sir,' said Lightoller. 'In fact, it is only one degree above freezing. I have sent word down to the carpenter and rung up the engine room and told them that it is freezing or will be during the night.'

'There's not much wind,' said Smith.

'No, it is a flat calm as a matter of fact,' Lightoller replied.

'A flat calm,' Smith said thoughtfully.

'Yes, quite flat, there is no wind. It is a pity there is not a breeze.'

Smith would have understood what Lightoller meant, namely that the effect of the wind would raise waves around any icebergs making them more visible. By now his eyes were becoming accustomed to the dark and he could see the weather conditions for himself. 'It seems quite clear,' he said.

'Yes, it is perfectly clear,' said Lightoller.

It was indeed a beautiful night, there was not a cloud in the sky. The sea was smooth, and both of them could clearly see the stars rising and setting on the horizon. As they watched nature's floorshow the two men talked about the possibility of encountering ice in such conditions and how they would recognise it if they should see it – reminding themselves as to the indications that ice gives of its proximity. Despite the lack of a revealing wind, Lightoller was not worried. 'In any case,' he continued, 'there will be certain amount of reflected light from the bergs.'

'Oh yes, there will be a certain amount of reflected light,' said the captain.

Lightoller commented further that even if a berg was showing its blue side, the starlight would again help by giving it a white outline, which he felt would give him ample warning. Captain Smith agreed. Lightoller did not, however, discuss with the captain the difference between his and Moody's calculations as to when they would enter the ice region. Nor was there any mention yet of reducing the ship's speed. Smith did comment, though, that if it became in the slightest degree hazy there would be no option but to slow down. Sea fog or haze was a serious possibility in the ice region where the warm Gulf Stream and the cold Labrador Current merged.

Captain Smith remained on the bridge for about twenty-five minutes until around 9.20p.m., when he decided to go to his quarters. As he turned to go he said to Lightoller, 'If it becomes at all doubtful, let me know at once. I shall be just inside.'

'All right, sir,' said Lightoller. The second officer understood this order to refer to the weather and visibility and to inform Smith if there was any change.[2]

Lightoller then got Sixth Officer Moody to telephone the men in the crow's nest and tell them to keep a lookout for small ice and growlers and to pass the word on when the watch changed over. Moody spoke to lookout George Symons and passed on the order about small ice, but failed to mention growlers. Noting the oversight, Lightoller had Moody phone the lookouts again and added the order about growlers.

A little earlier that evening, senior Marconi operator Jack Phillips had established wireless communication with the Cape Race receiving station in Newfoundland, a sure indication that they were now on the last leg of their journey. For Phillips, though, the wireless link with North America meant working his way through a mass of passenger messages to friends, families and businesses. These ranged from simple greetings to detailed instructions. Phillips worked on alone, while in the adjacent sleeping quarters, Harold Bride snatched a few hours sleep. Because of the long hours the two of them had put in fixing the wireless the night before, they had altered their working watches and Bride was going to relieve Phillips at midnight rather than the usual 2a.m.

In between his own transmissions, Phillips was still taking ice warnings from ships in the region. At 9.30p.m., there was a message from the steamship *Mesaba* addressed to the *Titanic* and all east-bound ships:

'Ice report. In latitude 42° N to 41°, 25' N longitude 49° W to 50°, 3'W. Saw much heavy pack ice and great number large icebergs, also field ice. Weather good, clear.'

Phillips replied 'Received, thanks.' The *Mesaba*'s operator, knowing that the message pertained to navigation, waited for Phillips to reply that the message had gone to the captain and after waiting a time sent, 'Stand by' to prompt an answer from the *Titanic*, but Phillips had returned to sending passenger messages. This latest message lacked the all important code letters MSG, being sent as an 'ice report' and as a result yet another message never got sent to the bridge. It was a slight oversight but a telling one, especially as the bearings given in the message placed a large ice field in the *Titanic*'s immediate vicinity. Lightoller later claimed in a radio interview that had Smith received the *Mesaba*'s message he had no doubts that the captain would have stopped the ship until morning. But would he? It is easy to be wise with hindsight mingled with forgivable loyalty to a dead comrade, but with no disrespect to Lightoller it has to be said that had the message reached Smith, under the procedures of the period it would probably not have prompted him to slow or stop his ship unless he found the navigation blocked; it was after all a clear night over a calm sea, Lightoller himself had said as much, but the message may have caused Smith to have extra lookouts posted, just to be on the safe side.

10p.m.–11.45p.m.

Lightoller's watch ended at 10p.m., when First Officer Murdoch arrived to take over. Before he left the bridge, Lightoller drew Murdoch's attention to the night order book with its footnote about possible ice hazards and the book was initialled by each officer in turn to show that both had seen it. Lightoller further noted that they would be up around the ice any time now.

Murdoch was not left alone on the bridge, besides him there was Fourth Officer Boxhall and Sixth Officer Moody as well as two quartermasters, one piloting the ship, the other on standby; there too occasionally was Captain Smith.

Over the years a story has built up that following his talk with Lightoller, Captain Smith had gone for a sleep in his quarters only to be rudely awoken a couple of hours later when the ship struck the iceberg. This, however, was far from the case and at both the American and British inquiries into the *Titanic* disaster Fourth Officer Boxhall testified quite specifically that he saw the captain on numerous occasions that evening from when he first arrived on the bridge during Lightoller's watch, up until the time of the accident. Boxhall spent much of his watch working out stellar observations and reporting the calculations to Smith, which explains how he came into contact with him so much. Sometimes Captain Smith was on the outer bridge or in his or the officers' chart rooms and occasionally he popped into the wheelhouse. Boxhall remembered talking with Smith at his chart room door and clearly recalled that at 10p.m. Captain Smith, as was his want, personally marked down their 7.30p.m. star position. Boxhall said that so far as he could tell, Smith never left the bridge during the watch, though he added that by the bridge he meant the square comprising the wheelhouse, chart rooms and the open bridge itself.[3]

If Smith had stood talking with Boxhall so freely and so often, then it makes sense to suppose that he also had a few conversations with First Officer Murdoch just as he had earlier with Lightoller, for the two of them had worked together for many years and because Smith was nearby during the bulk of Murdoch's watch. They doubtless mulled over the ice reports, but as both men were to perish in the disaster that would soon overtake the ship, the nature of any such conversations are now lost to history.

So, Smith was not asleep in his cabin, he was in fact at work, either plotting their progress thus far, puzzling a route around the reported ice, planning out the next day's navigation, or perhaps even taking time to complete the mass of official documents and requisitions he would have to present on reaching New York. The latter would have been an especially pressing task if, as has been suggested, the *Titanic* was to attempt a fast run and arrive a day earlier than scheduled.

Yet, if Smith was not asleep, being occupied as he was he could not be on the bridge all the time. He was certainly not there precisely an hour and forty minutes after Murdoch had arrived, when in the distance the crow's nest bell was heard being struck hard three times and then somewhere closer by a telephone began ringing.

At 10p.m., lookouts Frederick Fleet and Reginald Lee had come on duty. Climbing up the ladder inside the hollow foremast they emerged in the crow's nest, where they took over from the earlier shift that passed on the order to watch out for ice. The men were well wrapped up against the eye-watering, icy blast of air that greeted them as they stepped onto the exposed platform, the temperature by this time having dropped to freezing. Despite the chill, they had a cloudless starlit sky above them and their field of vision ahead was as clear as could be expected in the dark. They should have been issued with binoculars, but due to the shake up amongst the senior officers following Chief Officer Wilde's arrival, these had been mislaid before the voyage began. A lot of mileage has been made from this lack of binoculars and Fred Fleet, obviously feeling somewhat put-upon at the subsequent inquiries, maintained that had the lookouts been issued with their binoculars then the coming disaster could have been avoided. In truth, though, the binoculars would have been used more to examine in closer detail anything that the men made out with the naked eye rather than for any general scanning for danger. As it was, there seemed no real need for them because as well as being a clear night the sea before them was perfectly calm; had it not been so cold and windless they could not have wanted for better conditions. As Lightoller had noted earlier, in such conditions it might be reasonably supposed that they should be able to spot any of the icebergs they had been warned to watch out for long before they posed any serious danger to the ship.

As with the lookouts and deck crew on the bridge, the shifts switched over throughout the ship. In the galleys the bakers put the next day's loaves in the ovens, the 'boots' did his rounds collecting boots and shoes for an overnight polish, and the stewards cleared away in the public and dining rooms. Down in the bowels of the ship, the stokers, firemen and engineers of the 8 to 12 shift toiled away in temperatures in the 80° to 90°s F. In the wireless room, the senior Marconi operator Jack Phillips was still hard at work transmitting large numbers of passengers' messages to Cape Race. It was tiring work and by this stage Phillips was not in the mood for interruptions.

The Leyland Line steamer, *Californian*, had by then stopped in field ice. She was still ahead of the *Titanic* and about 10 to 19 miles to the north; her captain, Stanley Lord, had ordered extra ice warnings to ships in the area. The *Californian*'s wireless operator, Cyril Evans, dutifully called up the *Titanic*, but the ships were so close to each other that the boosted signal when it came through his headphones nearly deafened Jack Phillips, who in turn cut in with a terse transmission of his own: 'Keep out! Shut up! You're jamming my signal. I'm working Cape Race.'

Snubbed, the *Californian*'s operator had no option but to shut up, though out of interest he listened in to the new liner's wireless traffic for about another half an hour. He had been up early that morning and had stayed on duty longer than usual and when he finally gave up listening to the *Titanic* it was 11.30p.m. he switched off his set and went to bed. The *Californian* was only a small steamer and carried but one wireless operator, who was soon fast asleep. Over the next few hours the *Californian*'s officers would report to Captain Lord – who was taking a broken sleep in his chart room – that a ship several miles to the south was firing rockets. Presuming that they were company signals between ships with no wireless, Lord told his men to try and make contact with the Morse lamp, but to no avail; neither he nor his officers deemed it necessary to wake the sleeping wireless operator to find out what was happening.

The two lookouts in the crow's nest had now been on watch for an hour or so and Reg Lee thought that a slight haze had begun to form in the air. If a haze had been forming it may go some way to explaining why neither man reported seeing the telltale 'ice blink', which occurs when ice on the horizon reflects the starlight and which, with an ice field, gives the effect of a shimmering white line in the distance. Fred Fleet later agreed that a slight haze had risen, though others have disputed both his and Lee's testimony. It was more likely that they were seeing things; the rush of cold air caused by the *Titanic*'s forward motion was probably making their job difficult. Watery eyes made tired by facing into the unremitting cold blast for the last hour and a half could have easily become disorientated, seeing things that were not there, or not seeing things until too late as might have been the case a short time later.

Seven bells struck at 11.30 and the minutes slowly ticked by. It had been a quiet watch thus far and the two of them were probably looking forward to getting back to their warm bunks when the watch changed over at midnight, but at 11.40p.m., as Fred Fleet was staring into the darkness before them, something caught his eye. There was a darker patch ahead blocking out some of the stars. In a matter of seconds the dark patch resolved itself into an indistinct black mass and Fleet realised what he was looking at. Some 60ft out of the water and 500 yards dead ahead lay an iceberg. Eyewitnesses later described it as being dark blue in colour and triple-peaked with one great promontory that rose just slightly higher than the boat deck. Newspapers lacking sufficient information went wild with speculation, describing it in monstrous terms, though by iceberg standards it was unremarkable. Fourth Officer Boxhall for one was singularly unimpressed with the *Titanic's* nemesis when he caught sight of it, describing the berg as little more than a large growler. But everyone knew that they were seeing only a fraction of its mass, literally just the tip of the iceberg, and it was those parts they could not see that were the real danger.

'There is ice ahead,' said Fleet, though by then Reg Lee had also seen the berg. Fleet turned and rang the crow's nest bell hard, three times, the signal code for 'Object ahead'. He then reached across Lee and grabbed the telephone to the bridge. In the wheelhouse, alerted by the bell, Sixth Officer Moody answered immediately.

'Are you there?' asked Fleet.

'Yes. What do you see?'

'Iceberg right ahead.'

'Thank you.'

Moody went for the door to tell Murdoch, but from his position on the starboard wing of the bridge the first officer had heard the bell and seen the iceberg for himself. He had been in a situation like this before aboard the *Arabic* nine years earlier; then he knew that evasive action would end in disaster, now there was no option. Dashing onto the main bridge Murdoch shouted 'Hard a starboard!' to Quartermaster Hichens at the wheel, which under the helm orders then in use would actually turn the ship to port. Moody repeated the order and Hichens began to turn the wheel as quickly as he could. Murdoch meanwhile ran over to the engine room telegraphs and rang down the orders 'Stop Engines', then 'Full Astern', in the hope of avoiding the collision. Expert thinking has it that though done with the best intentions, this was a mistake on Murdoch's part. Robbing the ship of its speed, in effect making it turn more slowly, may have made the difference between a near miss and the now infamous collision.

In the wheelhouse, the wheel banged to a stop. 'The helm is hard over, sir,' said Moody. Slowly the bow of the ship began to turn, but as Hichens later reported, the *Titanic* had only turned twenty-two degrees to the south when he and everyone else on the bridge felt a shudder pass through the ship and heard an ominous grinding noise along the bottom of the vessel.

Just behind the bridge in the corridor outside the officers' quarters, Fourth Officer Boxhall had been walking towards the bridge when he felt the vessel tremble, but he did not break his stride. Standby Quartermaster Olliver had been aft to check on the compass and was also approaching the bridge when he too felt the ship shake for a few seconds; then he spotted the dark blue peak of an iceberg sailing past to starboard.

Only a matter of seconds had passed, the noise and shaking were over and the damage was done. Olliver arrived at the bridge and heard Murdoch call out 'Hard a port'. Hichens denied that the order was given, but at least two other witnesses stated that after her sharp turn to port the ship then turned to starboard. What Hichens did recall at this point was Captain Smith dashing out of the chart room, through the wheelhouse and onto the bridge. Boxhall arrived on the bridge in time to see Murdoch in the act of closing the watertight doors and throwing the switch. Looking around he found that Captain Smith had arrived at virtually the same time that he had.

'What have we struck?' asked Smith.

'We have struck an iceberg,' Murdoch replied, obviously shaken by events. 'I put her hard a starboard and ran the engines full astern, but it was too close. She hit it. I intended to port around it but she hit it before I could do any more.'

'Close the watertight doors.'

'The doors are already closed, sir.'

Smith then asked Murdoch if he had rung the emergency bell to warn that the doors were closing, the First Officer replied, 'Yes, sir.'

Alarmed, Smith stalked over to the cab on the starboard wing of the bridge and stuck his head out of the window. Murdoch and Boxhall followed him. Boxhall thought that he could make out the shape of the 'long-lying growler' some distance back off the ship's starboard quarter.[4]

To the rear of the bridge, in the officer's quarters, Second Officer Lightoller had been woken by the collision and now went out onto the deck in his bare feet to investigate. Looking forward he caught sight of Smith and Murdoch on the bridge, but he could make out nothing more and there seemed to be no obvious damage to the ship.

11.45p.m.–12.05a.m.

For some minutes after the collision a puzzled calm existed on the bridge. For despite the shudder that had passed through the *Titanic* and the grinding noise that had accompanied the sensation, to the naked eye there appeared to be no serious damage to the ship. There was physical evidence that a collision had occurred; ice had broken off the berg, scattered chunks of which now littered the forward well deck and starboard promenade, but otherwise the ship seemed intact. Staring down into the gloom Smith probably hoped at this stage that the damage was indeed superficial and as with the *O.L. Hallenbeck* and HMS *Hawke* incidents that the collision would count as little more than a serious and embarrassing bump. But, unlike on those two occasions, they were situated in mid-ocean; Smith could not afford to be complacent and the ship would have to be thoroughly checked. Fourth Officer Boxhall evidently thought likewise and whilst Captain Smith stood in the wing cabin further quizzing

Murdoch about the collision, on his own initiative Boxhall left the bridge and went to check the forward area.

With the engines backed the *Titanic* had come almost to a full stop by now, so Captain Smith turned away from the window and walked back to the main bridge cabin and laid his hands on the engine room telegraph which he moved to 'Half Ahead'. His action here is something of a puzzler, but it could be that Smith kept the ship going for a little longer, albeit at a reduced speed, while the vessel was checked over for damage. Then, apparently unaware that Boxhall had gone to check the forward area, Smith ordered Quartermaster Olliver to go and find the ship's carpenter and have him sound for damage. Though sheet metal had replaced the wooden planking of the old sailing ships, the ship's carpenter John Maxwell (or possibly the joiner John Hutchinson – many writers seem confused as to which) was still the man whose job it was to keep a weather eye on the ship's integrity and once he had the carpenter's report Smith would better know where he stood. Smith then went to the ship's wheelhouse to take a look at the ship's commutator in front of the compass. This small instrument, which resembled a clock, told how a ship was listing and now to Smith's alarm it clearly showed a 5° list to starboard.[5]

A moment or two later Boxhall reappeared on the bridge after his quick survey forward and reported what he had seen.

'I've been down below, sir, right down as far as I can go without removing any hatches or the tarpaulin, right through the Third Class accommodation forward and I don't see any signs of damage, not even a glass port broken.'

Though Boxhall's report sounded hopeful, the evidence of the commutator was not and as of yet neither Olliver nor the carpenter had appeared with a more detailed appraisal from the bowels of the ship.

'Did you see the carpenter anywhere Mr Boxhall?'

'No, sir, I didn't.'

'I do wish you would go down and find him, and tell him to sound the ship round forward and let me know right away.'[6]

By this time Quartermaster Olliver had encountered the carpenter in the working alleyway on E deck, in the act of sounding the vessel. What the carpenter discovered there so shocked him that shortly after Olliver had seen him, he went rushing up to the bridge. On the way he met Boxhall as the latter was coming down the stairs to A deck in search of him. 'The captain wants you to sound the ship,' said Boxhall.

'The ship is making water.' The man gasped by way of a reply and continued on to the bridge, while Boxhall went below to investigate further. On the bridge the carpenter reported his findings to the captain. An indication of what he probably told Smith was related by Boxhall many years later. The carpenter reported that the forepeak hatch had blown off and that the number one tarpaulin was ballooning up under pressure. Crewman John Poingdestre who had also met the carpenter recalled that the man had said he had been sounding the wells down in the firemen's compartment and found 7ft of water in them, all of which pointed to the unavoidable fact that the ship was making water fast. For Smith, this report must have been the first in a series of stunning blows that followed one after another in the first half an hour after the collision. The next came only a few moments after the carpenter had appeared, when Jago Smith, one of the postal clerks from the post office down on G deck, came with news that the mail hold one deck below the post office was filling rapidly with water.

By now it was clear to Captain Smith that this was much more serious than he had first imagined and the damage would need thorough investigation before anything more could be done. So, when Quartermaster Olliver reappeared shortly after this, Smith packed him off with a folded note for Chief Engineer Bell, probably asking for a damage report. After the quartermaster's departure, Smith or one of his officers rang down a final order to the engine room and stopped the ship for good.[7] There was nothing else Smith could do; it was now clear that the ship had taken damage and he would have to stop and check how serious it was before moving on.

While he stood waiting for Bell's report, more people crowded onto the bridge. Chief Officer Wilde came in with news that crewmen were reporting air whistling out of the forepeak tank in the prow, forced out under pressure by the rising sea water. It was at about this time too that J. Bruce Ismay first appeared on the bridge, wearing his suit over his pyjamas. He asked the captain why the ship had stopped and Smith informed him that they had struck ice. Ismay then asked him whether he thought the damage was serious, and Smith replied that he thought it was.[8]

There was probably more to the conversation than this, but Ismay in his own guarded account left the bridge after this apparently pithy exchange to go and get his overcoat from his cabin. As he made his way there, he met Chief Engineer Bell on his way to the bridge. To Ismay's dismay, Bell confirmed that the *Titanic* was badly damaged, but he believed that the pumps would keep the ship afloat. Whether Bell displayed such insouciance when he met Smith a few minutes later is unknown, but he would certainly have been able to give his increasingly concerned skipper a much more considered report than the fragmentary news he had been receiving thus far.

Boxhall too returned with bad news at about this time, confirming Jago Smith's story. Having met the postal clerk shortly after encountering the carpenter, Boxhall had been to the post office, where he found the sea only 2ft from the top of the stairwell and heavy mail bags were floating on the surface. The remaining mail clerks were hard at work stuffing bundles of letters into bags in the hope of getting them up to the higher decks, but it was a hopeless task.

'All right,' said Smith, digesting and processing the news. Boxhall noted that the captain then walked off the bridge; perhaps he had gone to see the damage for himself.

Smith does indeed seem to have gone down to take a look at the damage at about this time, though accounts are sketchy. Before setting off, though, he took the time to make his first visit to the Marconi room that evening. Here the two young operators had just changed over. Phillips, after his long stint sending to Cape Race, was in their sleeping berth getting ready for bed, while Bride was settling down at the wireless when Captain Smith popped his head through the doorway and said, 'We've struck an iceberg and I'm having an inspection made to tell us what it has done for us. You'd better get ready to send out a call for assistance. But don't send it until I tell you.'

The captain's inspection was probably carried out via the crew's companionways rather than the usual corridors, so as to avoid alarming the passengers. He seems to have been accompanied at first by Jago Smith and Purser McElroy. Stewardess Annie Robinson saw the mail man go up to the bridge then saw the three of them come down a few minutes later going in the direction of the mail room. Her account then indicates that she saw Smith with Thomas Andrews the Harland & Wolff managing director.[9] It is unknown as to whether Andrews noticed the collision or not, though according to the popular version of events he had been busy in his cabin and had not noticed a thing. The story then goes that it was only when Smith summoned a puzzled Andrews to the bridge that he informed him about the collision and asked him to accompany him on an inspection of the fo'c'sle, though there seems to be no primary source for this tale. According to the account given by one passenger to a newspaper, Andrews did feel the impact and was down in the bowels of the ship investigating the damage shortly after the accident had occurred, the implication being that Smith met him down there as he was undertaking his own quick inspection of the damaged compartments. Alternatively, Smith may have asked Andrews to go and take a look then followed him down to see for himself. In support of this theory there is the testimony of Steward James Johnston, who was in one of the saloons wondering what the shudder he had felt boded when he saw Mr Andrews going down towards the engine rooms and three or four minutes later he saw Smith going in the same direction.[10]

Whatever the case, as Smith moved along from one compartment to another, the full extent of the damage soon became horribly apparent. Water was gushing into the first five of the ship's watertight compartments. Stokers and trimmers caught by the initial inrush of water stood around bedraggled, though by this time the engineers had called many of them back to draw the boiler fires, an important task if they were to avoid a boiler explosion. In the past it was thought that the iceberg had torn a 300ft-long gash along the *Titanic*, prompting the writer Joseph Conrad to comment rather dramatically that the *Titanic* had been ripped open like a Huntley and Palmer biscuit box. Had this indeed happened, as was the case with the *Empress of Ireland,* which sank almost immediately with appalling loss of life after having her side ripped open by another ship in 1914, there would have been a cataclysmic flooding of the compartments that would have doomed the ship in a matter of minutes.

However, the findings of the team under Dr Robert Ballard who finally located the wreck of the *Titanic* in 1985, confirmed what a few researchers had already guessed. Rather than tearing through the hull, a finger of the berg had scored a line along the side of the ship causing the plates to buckle and pull apart. Rivets popped, metal sheared and gaps opened between the sheets of iron forming the hull. Rather than a continuous gash, there were intermittent splits along the hull. The damage occurred beneath the waterline but above the double-bottomed keel and as soon as the skin ruptured, powerful jets of sea water had blasted into the ship. Within the first ten minutes of the impact, the water had risen to 14ft above the keel in the forepeak and it was rising at an alarming rate in the other ruptured compartments. Only in boiler room 6 in compartment 5 was there any good news. The damage here was minimal, the hull having taken only about 6ft of damage before the *Titanic* and the iceberg had rolled apart. Pumps were being brought into action apparently with some success. These, though, were merely staving off an inevitable defeat, for the brief encounter with the berg had done enough damage to reveal the weakness in the *Titanic's* series of watertight compartments and bulkheads. In the bow section, the bulkheads separating the first five compartments were of equal height reaching up to E deck. However, the bulkhead between compartments 5 and 6 was smaller than those before it. With two compartments flooded, the *Titanic* would have limped into New York; three flooded would have left her dead in the water but still afloat. This, though, was now academic, because five compartments had been breached. As the weight increased in the bow it would slowly drag the ship down by the head and once the water spilled over into compartment No. 5, they would have reached the point of no return. Each compartment would then fill in turn, like the segments in an ice cube tray, back and back until the ship finally sank. Nothing they could do would stop it. Chief Engineer Bell's faith in the pumps if genuine was ill-founded, as these would only buy them a little more time. Both Captain Smith and Thomas Andrews were horrified by what they saw during their inspection. By this time the two of them appear to have been together assessing the damage; the ship's head barber Gus Weikman met both Andrews and the captain, apparently during this tour. Having felt the collision, Weikman was going up onto the deck when he met Andrews. Weikman asked if there was any danger and Andrews replied, 'My God, it's serious.' He then saw Captain Smith on the stairs and asked about the damage, but Smith remained tight-lipped and made no reply.[11]

First-class passenger Charles Stengel also saw Captain Smith at this time. Having gone up on the boat deck to see what was happening, Mr Stengel and his wife were going down to A deck when they saw Smith coming up; they presumed that he had just been down to inspect the damage. 'He had a very serious and a very grave face,' Stengel noted and turning to his wife he said, 'This is a very serious matter, I believe.'[12]

After only ten minutes Smith had seen enough and he and Andrews probably stood conferring for a few minutes. Where the interview took place is unknown as there is no mention of it having occurred on the bridge, nor is there a verbatim account of what actually passed between them, but a variation on the popular cinematic image of Andrews doing or having done the sums, explaining the situation as stated above and then informing Captain Smith that the ship was going to sink certainly fits the bill. It is known, though, that Thomas Andrews gave Smith an all-important deadline to work to, declaring that by his estimate the ship had an hour to an hour and a half left.[13] As it turned out, Andrew's estimate was pessimistic and the ship would actually survive for closer to two and a half hours yet. Smith, though, was not to know this and events would show that even this extra hour would prove to be very little time in which to do so many things and it would be this frantic race against the clock that would now determine Smith's course of action.

When Smith returned to the bridge he found a small knot of officers waiting for orders. It is probable that the two watch officers Moody and Murdoch were there, with Quartermaster Hichens out of sight but not out of earshot in the wheelhouse; Chief Officer Wilde was certainly present as too was Fourth Officer Boxhall who had reappeared on the bridge a few minutes earlier having in the meantime gone to inform Lightoller and Pitman about what had happened. Boxhall noticed J. Bruce Ismay, now wrapped in his overcoat, hovering around just outside the bridge. It was the first time the fourth officer had seen the White Star managing director during the voyage.

During his tour of the damaged compartments, Smith must have been wondering what he would have to do if things were indeed as bad as they seemed. Now that his worst fears had been confirmed he did not hesitate. Ismay remembered Smith turning to Wilde ordering the boats uncovered, Boxhall recalled the order too, while in the wheelhouse Quartermaster Hichens heard the skipper say, 'Get all the boats out and serve out the belts.'[14]

The time was now approximately 12.05a.m., on Monday 15 April 1912. At that precise moment the maiden voyage of the RMS *Titanic* ended and her evacuation began.

12.05a.m.–12.15a.m.

Captain Smith now found himself in an extraordinary situation, one that nothing in his forty-five years at sea could have prepared him for. He now knew that his ship, the White Star Line's new flagship, was sinking and that the 2,227 people aboard were in mortal danger. The prospect before him was not inviting. In the light of what he knew, it was imperative that he get the passengers to the lifeboats, but this in itself was problematic. For a start, evacuating that number of people in the middle of the night in freezing temperatures would have been daunting enough had the *Titanic* been provisioned with enough boats for all aboard, but the captain and his officers were fully aware that there was only space in the boats for half that number. Their best hope was that another vessel could come to their rescue in which case the *Titanic* would be the best lifeboat in the interim, but barring that Smith would have to be prepared to try and save as many as he could with the resources available to him. If circumstances had been perfect then each boat would have been launched filled to capacity and more, but this would take time, a luxury Smith now knew he did not have, as by Thomas Andrews' estimate the ship would sink long before all the boats were away. The logic was unavoidable: unless another vessel arrived in time then the greatest number could only be saved if the boats were in the water before the ship sank and took them with it.

Smith, therefore, seems now to have taken a conscious decision that would add substantially to the legend of the *Titanic* disaster. In what was probably the hardest decision he had ever taken in his life, Smith decided that though they would try to get as many into the lifeboats as would go, his real priority was to get the lifeboats off the ship as quickly as he could. Those passengers who were savvy or obedient enough to get into the boats when told to would be safe in any event and once the boats were in the water they would act as a safety net; more passengers could be loaded into them from the gangways and lower decks, or picked up from the water after the ship went down. Those left aboard, though, would have to take their chances with the ship, which meant they would go down with her unless aid did come. It was a calculated risk, but in what was rapidly turning into a no-win situation, it was the only option open to him.[15]

The main problems in all of this were the passengers and how he would get them to climb obediently into the boats as quickly as possible without the evacuation developing into a free-for-all. To manage this successfully, strict order would have to be maintained and a little deception employed to avoid any mass panic and a rush for the boats that might doom them all. To this end, when he apprised his officers of their situation and what was expected of them, Smith pointedly did not give them what would seem to be the obvious order – to abandon ship – as this would instantly tip off the passengers and would probably result in the very panic he feared. The illusion he wanted to maintain was that the ship, though damaged, was in no danger of sinking and was floating on its famous watertight compartments pending a rescue. Smith gave instructions that the passengers were to be placed in the boats as 'a precaution' in the light of the collision, *Birkenhead*-style priority being given to the most vulnerable, the women and children; for as had been seen in other disasters in the past such as the *Tayleur* in 1854 and the *Atlantic* in 1873, when such order was not, or could not be maintained and panic set in, the last people to make it into the lifeboats were the women and children.

His difficult decisions made, Captain Smith gave the required instructions then assigned his officers their new duties. Wilde was given the job of mustering the deck crew and uncovering the boats, while Murdoch was told to rouse the passengers and Mr Moody was sent to hunt out the list for the lifeboat stations. The remaining officers were sent to help Wilde with the boats. Chief Engineer Bell reappeared on the bridge and Smith received assurances from Bell that he and his men would keep the power supply running to the pumps and the ship's lights for as long as they could. Quartermaster Walter Wynn recalled that at this point he and another quartermaster were ordered by Smith to ready the two emergency boats before going to help uncover the rest of the boats. According to a newspaper account of the disaster given by ship's barber Gus Weikman, Smith also gave orders to 'some of the officers to get all the steerage passengers on one of the upper decks'.[16] Overhearing this, Weikman went off to help the third-class stewards, and then returned to the boat deck where he was immediately pressed into service getting the boats ready to be launched. It has to be said, though, that no other accounts note this order and in a statement to the American Inquiry, Weikman puts almost the exact words into Thomas Andrews' mouth. Equally, though, Smith could have given the order to one or more of those officers who did not survive and Andrews was merely repeating it.

By 12:10a.m., Smith's orders had begun percolating down through the ranks. All of his officers were now awake and most were now out on deck mustering their crews. On leaving the bridge, Chief Officer Wilde had ordered 'all hands on deck' which soon brought a crowd of sailors staggering groggily out into the cold night air, where they were set to work uncovering the boats and making sure that the small craft were supplied with bread and blankets. Others fitted the cranks to the davits or busied themselves hauling tight the falls and coiling them down on the deck, clear and ready for when they came to swing the boats out.

As the crew got to work, a shocking roar went up as steam began venting from the ship's boilers via the eight boiler relief pipes on the funnels. The din was incredible, making it difficult for the officers to make themselves heard over the noise. Conversely, for other members of the crew, the roar now blasting from the boiler pipes made their task somewhat easier as it woke up most of the passengers. Before going on deck to join his fellow officers and get on with his own duties with the lifeboats, First Officer Murdoch had passed on the captain's orders to the various heads of the crew departments. Tasked with the job of waking the passengers, the chief steward then got his own people up. Within minutes, stewards and stewardesses were going from door to door, urging their tired, puzzled passengers to put on warm clothing before helping them into their bulky life preservers and directing them to the stairs that led to the boat decks, assuring them at the same time, just as Smith had requested, that there was no serious danger and that this was only a precautionary measure.

For a while this calming tactic worked. Few of the passengers had any real notion of the danger, most having been asleep when the collision occurred. But as the stories of those who had seen the iceberg and felt the impact began to circulate, the seriousness of the situation became much more apparent and in the light of this many had more immediate considerations other than going to the boat deck. Some of the wealthy passengers, rather than doing as they were told, proceeded instead to the purser's office to get their valuables back from Purser Hugh McElroy and his assistants. Other first-class passengers, meanwhile, trusting to the safe reputation of the ship and exasperated by the mixed messages they were getting from the crew and the rumour mill, decided there was no real danger and at first remained in their cabins.

12.15a.m.–12.30a.m.

While his crew went to get the boats ready and empty the cabins, and as the passengers struggled with their own dilemmas, Captain Smith may have briefly left the bridge. At about this time Steward Charles MacKay saw him passing down the working staircase going along, he presumed, to the chief engineer's room. About ten minutes after that MacKay saw him come back. Certainly Smith was back on the bridge at about 12.15, going first to the chart room then to the Marconi room. When he got there he found the two young operators were now wide awake and wondering what all the noise outside boded.

'Send the call for assistance,' said Smith.

'What call should I send?' asked Phillips.

'The regulation international call for help. Just that.' The captain replied.

Smith then jotted down their estimated position, 41°, 44´ N, 50°, 24´ W, taken from that evening's dead reckoning, and then he vanished again. Smith doubtless knew the position was wrong, they were several hours past that location, but it was imperative to get a distress call out as early as possible; he could always correct their position once he knew someone was coming.

Meantime, the two wireless men powered up the transmitter, Phillips donned the headphones and got to work and within a matter of minutes they had their first reply from the steamer *Frankfurt*, 153 miles away. Bride dashed off to the boat deck to inform Smith. The captain asked him where the *Frankfurt* was, but Bride did not know so returned to the wireless cabin. It was the first of many such trips back and forth for the Marconi men that night as more and more ships made contact and the growing terseness of their transmissions to the outside world amply reflected the growing desperation aboard the *Titanic*.

As Bride's account indicates, at first Captain Smith stood watching the activity around the boats; indeed, he would spend a lot of that night there, waiting and watching. For after ordering the evacuation and putting out the call for assistance, despite his exalted position, Smith actually had very little to do. He had no boat station unlike his officers and for the most part his duties now became supervisory. In that respect it made sense for Smith to stay put and out of his officers' way, especially this early on in proceedings, as it made it easier for his men to get on with the task at hand. Plus seeing the captain of a vessel going around urging the passengers into the boats would hardly be conducive to the good order he hoped to maintain. Another advantage in staying put was that it made it easier for his men to find him when they needed instructions and sure enough they soon began turning up. Following the order to clear the boats, Fourth Officer Boxhall had gone out on deck and moved along the lines of boats, unlacing the covers, first on the port side, but as more crew crowded up onto the deck he moved over to starboard. Walking forward, he noticed Captain Smith standing nearby on the bridge and went over to report on some matter. Doubtless shouting to make himself heard above the noise of the venting steam, Smith asked if the men were getting on with clearing the boats. Boxhall replied, 'Yes, they are carrying on alright.' Then, having still not quite taken in the enormity of the situation, Boxhall asked, 'Is it really serious, sir?'

'Mr Andrews tells me that he gives her from an hour to an hour and a half,' Smith replied.[17]

Boxhall then asked the captain if he should send a distress signal. When Smith replied that he had already sent one, Boxhall asked what position had been sent and the captain told him that it had been the evening's dead reckoning. Boxhall then offered to calculate their present position. Smith told him to do so and Boxhall vanished into the chart room.

Hardly had the fourth officer disappeared, than Second Officer Lightoller appeared before Captain Smith. Lightoller had been getting the boats ready on the port side. Chief Officer Wilde had ordered him to uncover the boats but not to swing them out. Lightoller had done as he was told, but seeing no point in wasting time, the second officer then sought the captain on the forward part of the bridge to ask permission to swing the boats out. Due to the noise Lightoller had to cup his hands next to Smith's ear and shout his request to which the captain replied, 'Yes. Swing out.'

A few moments more and Boxhall came out of the chart room with what he took to be their current position, 41°, 46' N, 50°, 14' W. As it turned out this position was also wrong as was shown when the wreck of the *Titanic* was discovered in 1985, the broken remains of the ship being discovered some 18 miles astray of where Boxhall claimed she should have been and it was more by luck than design that the ship that came looking for the survivors the next morning actually found them. In a perfect world, Smith could perhaps have checked Boxhall's calculations himself, but he didn't and when the fourth officer presented the new position to his skipper, Smith trusted his junior and simply said, 'Take it to the Marconi room.'[18]

Some time later after the boats had been swung out, Third Officer Pitman walked onto the bridge and told the captain that a rather anxious man whom he suspected was the Line's chairman, J. Bruce Ismay, had come over whilst he was readying lifeboat No.5 and quizzed Pitman as to why he had not begun to put passengers into the lifeboats. Should he do so? 'Go ahead. Carry on,' said Smith.

Many passengers also recalled seeing Captain Smith during this early part of the evacuation, either close at hand or in the distance. Just after midnight, first-class passenger Marian Thayer was on the boat deck from where she caught sight of the captain giving orders on the port side of the bridge. The passengers' accounts also reveal that the captain did not remain exclusively on the bridge and perhaps a little while after this, two other first-class passengers, Martha Stevenson and Elizabeth Eustis, came to the iron stairs that led up to the forward boat deck. Here they found Smith waiting anxiously at the top of the stairs, a worried look on his face. Despite this, the captain waited courteously until the two sisters had come up the stairs before he had gone down. At about 12.30, Smith and Murdoch were spotted passing through first class going up towards the bridge. On the way they encountered a crowd of some fifty to sixty passengers who were gathered there waiting anxiously to hear what was happening. A French passenger, Alfred Omont, remembered that the two officers came over to talk to them all. Smith was chewing a toothpick and said, 'You had better put your life preservers on as a precaution.' Realising perhaps that ship's captains did not say things like that without good reason, M. Omont went immediately to his cabin to find his life preserver, and then returned to the boat deck.[19]

It seems to have been about now that Smith was also seen conversing rather anxiously with some of the better-known first-class passengers. Charles Stengel recorded, 'The first inkling I had of danger was when I saw the serious face of Captain Smith as he talked to George Widener of Philadelphia. I wouldn't have thought anything of it if I hadn't seen Captain Smith's face. Then I knew we were in danger.'[20]

Another first-class passenger, Mrs H.W. Bishop, also saw Smith saying something to multimillionaire J.J. Astor in an undertone. After their conversation, Astor came over and told the six people who were standing with his wife that they should put their life preservers on. Mrs Bishop went to find her husband who had returned to their stateroom and she had gone down two flights of stairs when from above she heard the captain announce to the whole company that everyone should put on their life preservers. A few minutes later, first-class passenger Emily Ryerson was looking anxiously out of her cabin door when a fellow passenger dashed past and said that the captain had just ordered everyone to put their life belts on.[21]

12.30a.m.–12.40a.m.

Slowly at first, the boat decks outside began filling up with passengers all bundled up in warm clothes and cumbersome life preservers. As the passengers appeared, the officers, unable to make themselves heard above the noise of venting steam, greeted the first arrivals with a resigned smile, but as the boats were being swung out the roar from the relief pipes suddenly spluttered then stopped, allowing everyone to talk more easily and presently the officers began calling for the women and children to come forward and step into the boats. Here, though, the crew started to encounter some difficulty with the passengers, not the panic they had initially feared, but a certain bullheadedness in the face of danger which hampered the loading of the first lifeboats. Having been pulled rudely from their warm beds in the middle of the night and hustled on to the cold, noisy boat deck with little or no explanation, many of the passengers were already disgruntled and confused and now a dash of panic was added to the mix by what they were expected to do next. As a number of survivors' accounts testify, at first most of the women passengers when faced with the prospect of sitting in a small boat swaying some 60ft above the sea, understandably preferred to stay on the deck, especially as there was as yet very little indication that the *Titanic* was seriously damaged. Hearing the 'women and children only' instructions, many of the women were also unwilling to leave their husbands and refused to get into the boats despite the entreaties of the crew.

The noise from the discharge pipes was shortly afterwards replaced by the sound of music drifting along the boat deck. Bandmaster Wallace Hartley, formerly of the Cunard Line, had brought his musicians up onto the deck and the evacuation suddenly acquired a musical accompaniment. The ship's orchestra was actually formed of two groups of musicians, which may account for the varying reports about what they played that night. The orchestra had been performing on the first-class stairwell, their intention no doubt being to keep panic to a minimum. They had struck up a series of cheerful, popular ragtime tunes which they carried on playing after transferring to the promenade deck. Here they would play for the rest of the evening, without apparently giving any thought to their own escape and reputedly signed off with perhaps one of the most poignant swan songs in history. Like so many others who might have added to our understanding of what happened that night, none of these men would survive the sinking and it is unclear, therefore, who might have ordered them up on deck, though Captain Smith seems the most likely candidate, perhaps when he and Murdoch were addressing the crowd in first class and where the orchestra were then stationed. Yet equally they may have gone up on their own recognisance after the bulk of the first-class passengers had moved up onto the boat deck. But whatever the case, their impromptu concert during the evacuation was another of the many remarkable happenings that night that would make this otherwise appalling event so memorable and their deed earned this small group of musicians something approaching cult status after the disaster.

Captain Smith appeared back on the boat deck just as Second Officer Lightoller was getting ready to load the first passengers into boat No.4, the second boat back on the port side of the ship. Lamp Trimmer Samuel Hemming was helping Lightoller when Smith told him to see that the boats were properly provided with lights and Hemming immediately went off in search of these, placing most in the starboard boats and a few in those on the port side.

Quite a few of the passengers waiting by Boat 4 were women with small children and Smith seems to have been considering this when he said to Lightoller, 'I want all the passengers to go down on A deck, because I intend they shall go into the boats from A deck.'

Lightoller agreed and asked the passengers to go below. It seems, though, that Captain Smith had confused the *Titanic* with his old command, the *Olympic*, and had forgotten that the forward part of the promenade deck on this new vessel was fully glazed, whereas it was completely open on the older ship. First-class passenger Hugh Woolner realised the mistake. Going up to Smith and saluting smartly, Woolner said, 'Haven't you forgotten, sir, that all those glass windows are closed?'

'By God, you're right!' Smith exclaimed. 'Call those people back.'[22]

Those passengers who had gone down duly came trooping back up the stairs but found much to their annoyance that their boat had been lowered to the deck below as instructed. By this time Smith had moved on but Lightoller still thought Smith's idea to be a workable one as the windows could be cranked open. There was also a wire hawser running along this part of the ship which was used as a mooring when the ship was being coaled, and this could be used to tie the boat to. The passengers, much to their exasperation, were ordered below once more. The windows, though, would take a while to open and the crew also discovered that the boat's descent would be hampered by the ship's sounding spar and this would have to be removed. As a result it would be another hour before Boat 4 was finally lowered to the sea. Some of the passengers would remain here waiting patiently, while others wandered off. Lightoller, unable to do any more with Boat 4 until these problems were resolved, moved on to deal with the next boat in line.

12.40a.m.–1.15a.m.

Meanwhile, Smith toured the lines of lowered boats. What had originally been only a handful of passengers gathered on the boat deck had now grown into crowds which he helped to supervise. Seaman John Poingdestre came up on to the boat deck at about this time and heard Smith pass the remark to the crew nearby, 'Start putting the women and children in the boats.'[23] Leading Fireman Charles Hendrickson heard something similar then watched the captain walk along and give his orders to the officers, or whoever was there, and they walked up and down to check that the orders were being carried out.[24] He even lent a hand when some of the passengers were having difficulties. Handing Mrs Compton and her family their life preservers, Smith smiled at her and said cheerfully, 'They will keep you warm if you don't have to use them.'[25]

In the wireless cabin, meanwhile, Jack Phillips was in communication with the Cunard liner *Carpathia*. Having learnt not to go sending Bride to Smith with half a story, he had waited until he heard back from the *Carpathia*'s Marconi operator that they were turning around and heading their way before he sent his junior off to find the captain. This time Bride had to struggle through a mass of people, the decks now being full of men and women scrambling to the boats. Smith was not in his cabin, but Bride soon found him in the wheelhouse and delivered the message. The captain followed the young wireless operator back to the Marconi room. Phillips was busy but Smith interrupted and asked what other ships he was in communication with. Phillips had been establishing communication with the *Olympic* some 500 miles away, so he told Smith that the *Olympic* was there.

'What are you sending?' Smith asked him.

'CQD,' Phillips replied.

Bride was on form and cut in with a quip. 'Send SOS. It's the new call, and it may be your last chance to send it.'

Despite the increasingly dire situation, the black humour was irresistible and they all laughed, including Smith. Still laughing, Phillips turned back to his machine and changed the signal to SOS.[26]

Smith, meantime, worked out the difference between the *Carpathia*'s position and the *Titanic*. From even this rough estimation, it was clear that at 58 miles away and on their side of the ice field, the *Carpathia* was the closest of the several vessels that had by this time answered the *Titanic*'s distress call. Her skipper, Captain Arthur Rostron, was pushing her hard, but even at full speed the smaller Cunard ship was still four hours away, too far away to reach the *Titanic* before she sank.

Yet, even as Captain Smith was in the wireless room talking to the Marconi men, on the bridge Fourth Officer Boxhall was studying a light on the horizon that the lookouts had spotted. It was situated near ahead, a point or two off the starboard bow and with his binoculars Boxhall could make out two masthead lights of what he took to be a steamer just below the horizon about 5 to 10 miles away. This may have been the steamer *Californian*, though there are many who dispute this. As already noted, that ship's captain and wireless operator were now asleep and its officers would soon be puzzled by what they saw next.

After studying the distant light for a short time to make sure of what he was seeing Boxhall went to find the captain, who was just returning to the bridge. The fourth officer told him about the ship. 'Shall I send up some distress rockets, sir?' Boxhall asked him.

'Yes, carry on with it,' Smith replied.

There was a store of distress rockets on the bridge and Boxhall had one of the crewmen hunt them out for him. Mounted on the starboard and port wings of the bridge were sockets from which the rockets could be launched. These distress rockets, though, were not simple fireworks, they were sizeable things and Boxhall needed to shoo everyone away each time he got ready to launch one. By tugging on a firing lanyard from a safe distance, the rocket launched with a roar and shot into the sky. It soared hundreds of feet into the air throwing out a white trail behind it before bursting overhead with a loud bang and scattering a shower of white stars above the ship.

Smith had stood nearby watching as the fourth officer readied and launched the first rocket and he now told Boxhall to fire one every five or six minutes. Also, as the distant vessel appeared to be within signalling range, Smith ordered Boxhall to use the Morse lamp situated atop of the wing cabins.

'Tell him to come at once,' Smith told his junior, 'we are sinking.'

Boxhall got to work between firing the rockets. By now there was a crowd of stewards and passengers standing on the boat deck and on the bridge staring anxiously at the far-off lights. Some of these said that they saw a light winking in reply, but neither Boxhall, nor Smith when he was there, saw any.[27]

The blasé humour that had characterised the proceedings thus took on a far different aspect as the first rockets went up. Some of the spectators were delighted at the free firework show, but others were profoundly worried as the use of rockets obviously meant that the ship was injured so badly enough that she required assistance from any ship near enough to see her. Others took the hint and began to hurry their families and friends towards the boats, or hurried back to their cabins, some for their valuables, others more wisely for their life preservers.

In fact, the first of the *Titanic's* lifeboats had gone into the water a few minutes earlier. At about 12.40a.m.[28] Boat 7 on the starboard side became the first to be lowered. As of yet still not enough people were convinced that the *Titanic* was in any real danger despite the efforts of the crew and few came forward to get into the boat. The boat's capacity was for sixty-five people, but it was launched with only twenty-eight aboard.

The loading had been supervised by First Officer Murdoch, who would supervise the boats on the starboard boat deck over the next couple of hours. Having seen Boat 7 into the water, Murdoch then moved along to the next boat in line, No.5, now being loaded by Third Officer Pitman and Fifth Officer Lowe who were being helped or hindered to varying degrees by J. Bruce Ismay, who had suddenly appeared and begun urging the two officers to get the boat loaded and launched. As already seen, Pitman had gone to Smith for permission to do so while Lowe, feeling thoroughly pestered, told Ismay to get out of his way. This outburst seems to have chastened the White Star director, who until his own escape from the ship behaved in a much more creditable manner, helping to load the passengers into the lifeboats without any attendant fuss. When Murdoch arrived the boat was filling up and he ordered Pitman to take charge of it. The boat left at 12.45 with forty-one people aboard.

Having lowered Boat 5, Murdoch and another officer then made their way over to Boat 3. Ordering a seaman into the boat, Murdoch began passing in the women and children. The number of women and children on the starboard side was low so when there were no more in sight he allowed some of the male passengers to get in. The boat was lowered at 12.55. Boat 3 held forty-three passengers and crew.

Due mainly to a lack of nearby passengers, or reluctance on the part of those who were there, thus far the boats were being sent away seriously under-loaded, but none more so than the next boat Murdoch attended, Boat 1. This was smaller than the main lifeboats and the twelve passengers and crew he now loaded aboard was well below the craft's capacity of forty and Murdoch perhaps sent the boat away with so few passengers thinking that the craft would return to pick up survivors from the water. As it happened, though, after the *Titanic* had sunk none of the crew felt that they could take the responsibility to do this and none of the passengers saw fit to remind them of their duty.

By most accounts Captain Smith seems to have spent most of his time touring the port side boat deck, but Seaman Frank Evans saw him on the starboard side just as Boat 1 was being lowered. Evans remembered that Smith, '…passed some remark to a tall military gentleman there with white spats on, but what it was I could not say, as I was attending to the fall; it was a tall military-looking gentleman who was giving orders as to lowering away forward or aft or both together.'[29]

Smith was still there a few minutes later when dining steward William Burke appeared on the starboard deck. Burke should have gone away with Boat 1, but on reaching the deck and finding that it had just left, he thought the next best thing to do was to assist with some other boat and helped with two boats on that side of the deck. But then the captain appeared and gave an order to the sailors that were working there to go aft and help with the last boat on that side. The sailors ran to assist at this boat, but Burke did not go. Instead he crossed to the port side and assisted with Boat 8 and Smith seems to have followed him.[30]

Compared to the lack of passengers on the starboard boat deck, the port side was now a bustling mass of people, many now sensibly gathering at the lifeboat stations. There were some who still refused to believe even now that there was any serious danger, but the boats had at least started to fill. At about 1.00a.m., Boat 8 was in the process of being loaded. Alfred Crawford, a first-class steward sent to crew the boat noted that Captain Smith appeared just before the boat was lowered. The Countess of Rothes, one of Smith's regular passengers also saw the captain who stood beside her as she waited to get into the boat. The Countess' maid Roberta Maioni went into the boat with her mistress and in 1926 penned a rather dramatic version of events for a short story competition run by the *Daily Express*. She wrote, 'An elderly officer, with tears streaming down his cheeks, helped us into one of the lifeboats. He was Captain Smith – the master of that ill-fated vessel.'[31]

The other witnesses, though, made no mention of a teary-eyed Captain Smith, merely a practical one. The Countess of Rothes heard him tell Able Seaman Tom Jones who had been placed in charge of the boat to row, '...straight for those ship's lights over there, leave the passengers aboard and return as soon as possible.'

Alfred Crawford's version of events was very similar. He saw Captain Smith point to a couple lights off to the north and heard him say, 'Pull for that vessel, land your people and return to the ship.'

Tom Jones remembered that Smith asked him whether the plug was in the boat and Jones answered, 'Yes, sir.'

'All right,' said Smith, 'any more ladies?' And he shouted twice more, 'Any more ladies?'[32]

Boat 8 was loaded with all the women and children that he could see, though there were still about thirty empty places. Some of the women started begging Captain Smith to let some of their men in to row and Tillie Taussig related bitterly how Smith allowed four incompetent stewards to get into the boat but refused to allow in any useful male passengers, such as her husband who was an expert oarsman. Emma Bucknell recalled the captain handing her a basket full of bread and chiding some of the men nearby when they started growing fractious. 'Behave yourselves like men!' He barked at them. 'Look at all of these women. See how splendid they are. Can't you behave like men?'[33]

Unlike Murdoch on the starboard side of the ship, who had allowed men into the boats when no more women could be found, Second Officer Lightoller, faced with this mass of humanity, had been insisting firmly on allowing only women and children into the lifeboats and if Smith had been inclined to let some of the men into the boat, to have done so he would have seriously undermined the authority of his junior officer on the spot, something he could not afford to do at such a time. The fact that Smith did not quibble with Murdoch over the several male occupants of Boat 1 a few minutes earlier, seems to support this view.

As a result Smith did not argue with Lightoller's approach and no male passengers were allowed into the boat. The captain then ordered Alfred Crawford to get in, then Smith and one of the stewards began to operate the forward falls while others worked the stern and the boat slowly descended towards the sea, watched by a crowd of men who moved away as the boat passed out of sight. There were only twenty-eight people aboard Boat 8. As the lifeboat began to descend Roberta Maioni claimed that she heard Smith say, 'Goodbye remember you are British.' But this may have been dramatic licence echoing what had, by 1926, become a popular phrase attached to the captain of the *Titanic*.[34] Certainly no one else in the boat noted Smith saying anything of the sort.

After watching boat No.8 descend, at about, 1.10a.m., Smith followed Lightoller forward to boat No.6. Major Arthur Peuchen, the vice-president of the Royal Canadian Yacht Club, was standing with a group of men watching as Boat 6 was being winched into position on the port side. He noted the arrival of Smith and Lightoller, one of whom called to them, 'We must get these masts and sails out of these boats; you might give us a hand.'

The men stepped forward to help and were soon passing women and children over the short gap into the boat. Smith also lent a hand, Hugh Woolner remembered him helping people in, saying, 'Come along, madam,' to encourage them to come forward. The boat soon filled up and after a short while the crew were calling for one more woman to fill it. The only one nearby was Mrs Lucien Smith, but she was loathe to leave her husband. Seeing Captain Smith standing nearby with a megaphone she went over and asked him if her husband could join her in the boat. But as with the entreaties around Boat 8, he remained inflexible. Ignoring Mrs Smith's individual plea he put the megaphone to his mouth and called out 'Women and children first!'[35]

Mrs Smith's husband took her aside and convinced her to get into the boat and eventually she did so and was saved. Her husband, however, did not survive and though in her affidavit to the Senate Inquiry she spoke of her pity for the captain who knew he had to stay with the ship, if we believe some of the reported comments she made after the disaster, she, like Mrs Taussig and a number of others, never quite forgave the captain for the accident or her own personal loss.

One of the women already in the boat who remembered Smith in a kindly light was Mrs Margaret Brown. On the way down, using an oar Mrs Brown fended the boat away from the ship's side when water gushing from a D deck porthole threatened to swamp them. It was at this point that she looked up and caught sight of Captain Smith with whom she had crossed the Atlantic twice before, the last time being three months previously. She thought the captain looked calm but resigned as he stared down at them, directing the crew to keep the boats together and make for the light in the distance.

It was then, though, that those in the boat realised that there were only two crewmen aboard, strangely enough these were lookout Fred Fleet who had first seen the iceberg and Quartermaster Hichens who had been at the wheel when the collision occurred, but neither of them were experienced in handling a lifeboat. Mrs Candee heard one of them call out as the boat was being lowered, 'Captain, we have no seamen.'

Up on the boat deck, Captain Smith turned and grabbed a boy by the arm and said, 'Here's one,' and sent him down to the boat. He, though, was found to be injured and a moment or two later a woman's voice was heard calling up to them that they still did not have enough men to sail the boat.

Lightoller looked around him. Nearby stood the group of male passengers who had helped to clear the boat. 'Any seamen there?' he called out.

'If you like, I will go,' said Major Peuchen, stepping forward.

'Are you a seaman?'

'I'm a yachtsman.'

'If you're sailor enough to get out on that fall you can go down,' said Lightoller.

Captain Smith, standing off to one side, suggested an alternative way into the boat. 'You had better go down below and break a window and get in through the window into the boat.'

Major Peuchen did not think much of that idea and he dismissed the suggestion out of hand noting, 'The captain was not quite himself; his idea was impractical if not downright dangerous.' A rather barbed comment that perhaps lends some credence to the reportedly dim view that the major took of Captain Smith. Instead, Peuchen grabbed one of the falls hanging from the nearest davit and lowered himself hand over hand down into the boat.[36]

Thus far, the evacuation had been proceeding calmly. The crowds of passengers waited patiently beside the lifeboats and most were well behaved and obeyed instructions. The men escorted the women and children up to the boats where there were tearful partings and shouted goodbyes. If any of them still believed the crew's stories that this was only a precautionary measure on the captain's part, the increasingly pronounced angle of the ship's bow and the thud of the distress rockets overhead told the real story. It was probably with this in mind that Smith had asked after the ship's small supply of handguns. Lightoller who related the story, said that it was Chief Officer Wilde who asked him to break out the firearms, but the order would have come from Smith; no junior would have been allowed to take that extreme decision. Having made the request of the chief officer, Wilde had then gone to ask Murdoch the first officer, who would have normally been in charge of the ship's guns, but he had not been the first when they were delivered, Lightoller had, hence the enquiry now. Lightoller for one thought that it was a waste of valuable time but took Wilde, Murdoch and Captain Smith to the locker where he had put the guns and handed them out, one apiece. Though things were as yet calm, there was no guarantee as the night went on that matters would remain that way and the weapons might be needed if panic set in.

Smith tucked the gun into the pocket of his overcoat and strolled back onto the bridge to check on Boxhall and his efforts to contact the ship on the horizon. He found that the fourth officer had been joined by two quartermasters, George Rowe and Alfred Bright, who had brought up two more crates of distress rockets and joined the officer in firing them, possibly from the opposite wing of the bridge. Smith stood with them for a time talking to the quartermasters and watching the rockets then checking to see if there was any response from the light on the horizon.

1.15a.m.–2a.m.

At 1.15a.m., Boat 16 was lowered with fifty passengers and crew. The water was by now up to about C deck and many were shocked to see how low the *Titanic* was in the water. The sea lapped over the name 'TITANIC' on the bow and soon after the prow finally vanished under the sea and water began to inch its way up the forecastle. The *Titanic*'s band was still playing its airy ragtime tunes, the sound of which could be heard in some of the nearest lifeboats. From their viewpoint, the *Titanic*, lit up brilliantly, lay dying in a sea that hardly seemed able to muster a light wave. Deep inside the ship the engineers and their men worked dragging hoses the length of the still unflooded compartments. Chief Engineer Bell had ordered that all the watertight doors aft of compartment No.4 were to be opened to facilitate this; each door could be closed as the men retreated. In the wireless room, Phillips was still tapping away, while Bride was employed shuttling messages to the bridge.

Crew accounts clearly reveal that some time before 1.30a.m., deep in the ship, concerted efforts were still being made to get more third-class passengers to safety. A group of second-class and third-class stewards had organised a system, probably at the behest of a senior steward, to get the passengers from the bow accommodation and others from the family accommodation at the rear of the ship up to the boat decks. On getting them out of their cabins the crewmen directed the passengers through emergency doors and along the crew companionway nicknamed 'Scotland Road' which ran along a good length of the ship and eventually connected with the first-class saloon companionway that had easier access up to the boat deck. At the other end, one of the ship's interpreters and a couple of stewards were also seen hustling third-class families from the rear of the ship through another emergency door into Scotland Road, and trying albeit with little success to get them to leave their luggage behind. These got onto the upper decks, though many of them were later seen crowded in the aft well deck far away from the available boats. Other third-class passengers made their own way up to the boats. Some climbed the rigging or scrambled along the

ship's cranes like lines of ants before dropping onto the boat decks. Others forced
their way through locked barriers and past formerly helpful crewmen, who lacking
orders from above suddenly becoming irritating jobsworths intent on stopping them.
In such ways many did make it to the boat decks and when the got there they were
treated no differently than the first- or second-class passengers, though according
to one account many refused to get into the boats, choosing like many first- and
second-class passengers to take shelter in the warm public rooms.

According to one newspaper account at least one third-class passenger saw Smith
at this time. The captain may have been on his way to pay a quick visit to the engine
room and in doing he seems to have encountered some of the third-class passengers
making their way up to the boats. Five days after the sinking, twenty-four-year-old
steerage passenger Bertha Mulvihill told the readers of the *Boston Post* how a friendly
sailor was taking her up to the boat deck where she would later escape in Boat 15. En
route she claimed to have seen a memorable sight:

> Some of the Italian men from way down in the steerage were screaming and
> fighting to get into the lifeboats. Captain Smith stood at the head of the passageway.
> He had a gun in his hand.
>
> 'Boys,' he said, 'you've got to do your duty here. It's the women and children first,
> and I'll shoot the first man who jumps into a boat.'
>
> But this didn't seem to have much effect on them, for they still fought to get
> into the boats. But the captain – oh, he was a good captain and a brave man – stood
> guard and wouldn't let the men get in before the women.[37]

Though the dialogue certainly sounds similar to some of Smith's reported speech
that night, the action-man image of the captain as a gun-totting Horatius guarding
the crossing seems rather incongruous, so it is a moot point as to whether this was
indeed Captain Smith, another officer, or merely a reporter's fabrication, of which,
sadly, there were many instances after the *Titanic* disaster.

Back on deck the orderly calm around the remaining boats was now beginning to
break apart and one officer at least was prepared to use his gun, albeit as a warning.
Panic had begun to spread as it became clear to most that the *Titanic* was indeed
sinking and Fifth Officer Lowe, standing next to Boat 14, fired shots along the side of
Titanic as several passengers tried to jump into the boat, which brought some order
to the situation. But it was not so much crowd control as the sheer mechanics of
loading and launching the lifeboats from what was now a severely tilted, listing ship
that caused the biggest problems for the boat crews. At 1.20, starboard side Boat 9 was
filled with fifty-eight people, including several men who were allowed in when no
more women and children could be found. There was some trouble loading the boat
for as well as her forward slope the *Titanic* was listing to starboard, which opened a
large gap between the deck and the hanging boat and nearly resulted in one woman
falling into the sea.

Five minutes later on the port side, Lightoller loaded forty people into Boat 12 before sending it off. The boat began its descent, but this was interrupted as it passed B deck when a male passenger jumped in and hid himself out of sight. Back on the starboard side, Boat 11 was also being lowered. With seventy passengers aboard, mostly second and third class, the boat was slightly overloaded and nearly suffered as a result. When the boat reached the water it found itself perilously close to the ship's pump discharge, a thick jet of water which would have easily swamped the boat if it had passed under it, but the crewmen managed to keep the craft clear and manning the oars they quickly pulled away from the ship's side. Second-class passenger Mrs Amin Jerwan recalled how the sailors in the boat voiced their ire towards Smith at that moment.

> Everybody on the ship blamed the captain. The sailor who rowed our boat told me that he had followed the sea for forty-five years and had never been in any kind of accident before except on the *Olympic* when she rammed the *Hawke*. 'That was under the same captain,' he said, 'and now I am having my second experience under him.'[38]

More drama attended the launching of the next two boats to be sent away. Boat 13 was lowered at 1.30, carrying sixty-four passengers, mostly third-class women and children, but also a few male passengers. Their boat also came close to the pump discharge, but those in the boat called out so loudly that those above operating the davits stopped the boat before it was too late. Using the oars the crew managed to push the boat clear of the discharge and 13 landed safely in the water. Hardly had one peril passed, however, than another appeared. Exhausted momentarily by their hard work, the sailors let the boat drift on its ropes, but this brought them right underneath Boat 15 which was just now being lowered, endangering the passengers in both boats. All the passengers started shouting, but those on the deck could not hear them and things seemed set for a tragedy in miniature. Some of those in Boat 13 were actually touching the bottom of Boat 15 at one point, but fortunately someone produced a knife, the ropes were cut and after a few more tense moments, Boat 13 pulled out of the way as Boat 15 landed in the water.

At 1.30a.m., Smith visited the wireless cabin to tell the operators that the engine room was flooding and Phillips promptly broadcast the message. Leaving the wireless room, Smith again returned to the bridge. Here he cast still hopeful glances at the distant ship's lights, but otherwise he stood watching the remaining boats being filled. Fourth Officer Boxhall, still busy signalling with the Morse lamp when not firing rockets, encountered Captain Smith for the last time standing by the wheelhouse door opposite the port side emergency boat No.2. A crowd of passengers, among them Mrs Mahala Douglas, were waiting to get in and she witnessed some of the fourth officer's exchange with the captain. Smith told Boxhall to take charge of the boat and help Chief Officer Wilde to load it. Before going to do so, Boxhall again pointed out the distant lights, but so far all their efforts to contact it had met with no response. Mrs Douglas remembered Smith saying, 'I want a megaphone.' Smith found his megaphone, then, before anyone got into the boat, he called out, 'How many of the crew are in that boat? Get out of there every man of you.' Elisabeth Allan, also waiting nearby, put a sharper edge on the speech. 'An "officer" came along and shouted to them: "Get out, you damned cowards; I'd like to see every one of you overboard."' To her surprise, Mrs Douglas saw a row of men from bow to stern crawl sheepishly over the side of the boat and back onto the deck. Miss Allen the heard the 'officer' say: 'Women and children into this boat,' and the passengers began to climb in.[39]

Though he had ordered Boxhall into a lifeboat, Smith had not given up hope that the lights in the distance could still be contacted. Quartermaster Rowe was still there firing rockets and the captain now asked him if he knew Morse code. Rowe replied that he knew some so Smith told him to keep signalling the ship in the distance.

Rowe took over the Morse lamp and in the intervals between launching further rockets he tapped out the distress message time and again, but there was no visible reply. After a short time, Rowe thought that he could make out another set of ship's lights. When he told the captain, Smith studied the light through his binoculars. He told Rowe presently, though, that it was just a planet winking low on the horizon and handed the young quartermaster his binoculars so that he could see for himself, telling Rowe as he did so that the *Carpathia* was nearby.[40]

While this was going on, Boat 2 had been filled and was now being lowered down the side. Smith walked over to the rail and looking down caught sight of Boxhall counting his passengers. Shouting down to him, Smith ordered the fourth officer to take his boat around to the gangway hatch on the starboard side of the ship and take on more passengers there. Smith may have also tried to attract the attention of other nearby boats at about this time as some accounts note that around now an officer's whistle was blown and Captain Smith was heard shouting, 'Come alongside,' to the lifeboats drifting nearby. He did this several times, but if anyone in the boats heard him, his orders were ignored and none returned.

Boat 4 on the port side had been the first boat swung out, but Lightoller had discovered that the ship's sounding spar was blocking its descent and needed to be removed, a process which took some time. In the meantime, the boat's passengers had to wait. The boat was finally lowered at 1.50a.m., by which time the angle of the ship had so increased that what was usually a distance of 60ft from the boat deck to the water had then shrunk to about 15ft. When the small craft eventually touched down, the passengers discovered that there were not enough sailors aboard, so a quartermaster was sent down one of the falls to help.

It was around now that Collapsible C on the starboard side was put into its davits and made ready for loading. Wilde was on hand to supervise the loading of this boat, but before he commenced he called out, asking who was in charge of the craft. Nearby on the bridge, Smith heard him. At that moment, as it was obvious by now that their efforts to contact the ship on the horizon were fruitless, Quartermaster Rowe asked Smith if he should fire any more rockets. 'No,' said Smith, 'get into that boat.' Nearby, Steward John Hardy had heard Smith calling out to the quartermaster about the rockets, but when the Rowe was gone Hardy saw Smith walk on the deck to watch the filling of the last boats. Rowe meantime went as told and after helping Chief Officer Wilde to load a few more passengers the quartermaster hopped into the boat.

Sitting in the boat with the other passengers when Rowe arrived was J. Bruce Ismay. He had stood watching Collapsible C being filled, but when no one else came forward and the boat began to be lowered, he and another first-class male passenger had stepped into it and sat down. It was a move that was to haunt Ismay for the rest of his life. The boat was lowered at about 2a.m., with thirty-nine people aboard.

2a.m.–2.15a.m.

By 2a.m., the forward slope of the *Titanic* was now quite pronounced, the bow was submerged; the foremast and rigging were sticking up out of the sea and the water was only 10ft below the promenade deck. Inside the ship the cabins, corridors and public rooms so full of life only a few hours before were all but deserted. The lifts stood empty, the teenage lift boys had been dismissed and left to fend for themselves and join the throng making its way towards the stern.

Though they had been the first sent up to the boats, there were also still plenty of first-class passengers on the deck, among them Henry and Irene Harris, the same woman whom Smith had congratulated on her spirit for attending the Widener's party with an injured arm. Now, though, if her own somewhat fanciful account is to be believed, as she, her husband and a couple of other passengers were crossing to the port boat deck via the bridge, she met the captain in a far less complimentary mood.

'My God, woman, why aren't you in a lifeboat?' Smith asked. The captain was standing nearby with Dr O'Loughlin and another first-class passenger, Major Archibald Butt. Mrs Harris kept repeating that she would not leave her husband which prompted an admiring comment from Dr O'Loughlin, 'Isn't she a brick?'

But Smith was having none of it.

'She's a little fool – she's handicapping her husband's chances of saving himself.'

'Can he be saved,' asked Mrs Harris, 'if I go?'

'Yes,' Smith declared, 'there are plenty of rafts in the stern and the men can make for them if you women give them the chance.'

Chastened, Mr and Mrs Harris quickly went through to the port boat deck where even now Lightoller was preparing another collapsible.[41]

There were no rafts, but three of the collapsibles remaining and Collapsible D, on the port side situated next to Boat 2's davits, was the easiest to swing out and load. Lightoller hurried forward and worked feverishly. The sea was now high on the forecastle, churning up through C to B deck and the large, square forward ports were taking in water. The collapsible boat was rigged up and a crowd formed around it instinctively. To hold them back Lightoller had crew members link arms around Collapsible D, while he asked for the women and children to come forward. Mr and Mrs Harris were in the crowd and along with many others Irene Harris was handed over into the boat.

Millionaire Frederick M. Hoyt was one of those on the deck watching gloomily as these last boats were being filled and lowered. Seeing the way things were going, Mr Hoyt realised that there was only one chance, he would have to swim for it and hope to get picked up by a lifeboat. Like everyone else he had thrown on thick, warm clothes, but he realised that these would be a hindrance in the water. He therefore returned to his state room and stripped down to his underwear before making his way back to the upper deck. Hoyt made his way forward to the bridge where he found Captain Smith. Mr Hoyt had known Smith for over fifteen years, but his final conversation that night did not amount to much. He sympathised with Smith about the accident and exchanged views over the inevitable outcome. Hoyt did not want to bother Smith with too many questions; he was sure the captain and many things to think about. 'But,' said Mr Hoyt, 'I feel like taking a drink before I take the plunge, don't you captain?'

Smith agreed with him and according to Mr Hoyt's account they went to Smith's cabin and both took a large drink to fortify them against the cold and doubtless to steady their nerves.

On returning to the deck, Smith said, 'You will have to jump and you had better do it soon.'

'Yes, I know it,' Mr Hoyt replied, 'but I won't take the plunge from this deck, but will go to one of the lower decks.'

'That will be better,' said Captain Smith, adding that he ought to go down to A deck to see if there were any boats alongside. Hoyt did so and found Collapsible D hanging from its davits. He jumped into the sea and swam around until the boat had been lowered and had pulled away from the *Titanic*. He then swam over and calling out to the crew he was plucked cold but alive from the water.[42]

As Hoyt was being rescued, nineteen-year-old steerage passenger Edward Dorking, having watched what he thought was the last boat depart the ship, decided to go below and collect his life preserver from underneath his bunk. His route took him past the engine room and as he passed the door he saw Captain Smith standing there, giving orders to the engine room crew. 'The perspiration was pouring down his face in streams,' Dorking recalled, 'but he was calm and collected, and as I recollect him now, he appeared like a marble statue after a rain.'[43]

If this was indeed Smith, then these may have been the last orders that he was able to pass onto the brave body of men who out of sight of the boats and with little hope of escape had fought with such dedication to keep the ship alive. Perhaps he was releasing them from their duty, though we shall never know. Dorking, meantime, passed on, though he never reached his bunk, the forward steerage section was now totally flooded, so he retreated to the deck and jumped. Luckily for him, Collapsible B passed by a short time later.

Dorking had been mistaken, however, as there were still two boats left. On the boat deck, Lightoller, Murdoch and Wilde and the crew dashed forward and got to work on them. The *Titanic* was sinking faster now and having returned to the bridge Smith watched as the sea began to boil up over the rails onto the port side of A deck one deck below him. Trimmer Samuel Hemming, helping with Collapsible B, had just jumped down to the deck from the roof of the officers' quarters, when he saw Captain Smith and heard him call out, 'Everyone over to the starboard side to keep the ship up as long as possible.'[44] Hemming and the others, probably including Chief Officer Wilde, followed Smith's orders and dashed over to starboard where they promptly got to work unshipping Collapsible A. The shift in weight trimmed the ship a little, but the end was now only a matter of minutes away. As they struggled to get the boat ready, the men saw Captain Smith reappear with a megaphone in his hand and heard him give the order he had been trying to avoid for most of that night, the final order to abandon ship. 'You've done your duty boys,' he called out to the men working on the boats. 'Now it's every man for himself.' Trimmer James McGann heard something similar. 'Well boys, it's every man for himself.'[45] As he walked past them all, megaphone in hand, Steward Edward Brown heard Smith say, 'Well, boys, do your best for the women and children and look out for yourselves.' Brown then watched Smith walk back to the bridge.[46]

Captain Smith then seems to have made his way to the Marconi room where Phillips and Bride were still stoically working over their wireless. Though isolated for the most part in their small cabin, the two young operators had worked tirelessly since the collision and Smith appreciated their efforts. 'Men, you have done your full duty,' he said quietly as he came into the room. 'You can do no more. Abandon your cabin. Now it's every man for himself. You look after yourselves. I release you. That's the way of it at this kind of time. Every man for himself.'[47]

Smith then left and seems to have again returned to the bridge. By this time the bridge, though not yet submerged, was probably swilling with water that came gushing up through the forward stairwells. Soon it would spill over the forward rails and if events continued as they had so far the bridge would have probably been swallowed by the sea in the same pedestrian manner as the bow and lower decks. So, if Smith in his last moments chose to linger here, fulfilling his role as a Hollywood-style tragic hero, staring out the windows and dwelling on the appalling events that had so suddenly overtaken him, he now had a few minutes grace in which to do so before the end. Popular tradition has him alone in these last moments, but that may not have been the case as hundreds of people were still dashing around the boat decks near to the bridge.[48] Two accounts, albeit second-hand ones, show that there were others nearby at the end. John Smith, an employee of a Merchant Marine Club in New York, claimed in a letter to his brother that he heard one *Titanic* officer, probably Lightoller, later describe how Chief Officer Wilde was last seen on the bridge smoking a cigarette, though there is no clear indication when exactly this was, or if Captain Smith was there at the time.[49] Ship's steward Frederick Ray testified that Smith's personal steward Arthur Paintin was also last seen on the bridge standing next to the captain. Ray was relating what he had heard and there is again no indication when Paintin was seen there, but as with Wilde, the end was as good a time as any.[50]

By this time, all the major lifeboats had gone and only two collapsibles remained fixed on top of the officers' quarters either side of the forward funnel. As the sea was creeping up the forward deck, Lightoller and his small team of men fought to unload Collapsible B. Lightoller still had hopes of getting some passengers away in the boat, but even as they were working, most of the passengers moved aft, unaware that there was still a chance of escape, and from the lifeboats, hundreds of people could be seen gathered up on the rising stern section.

The *Titanic's* band finished the last of the ragtime tunes that they had played all night, but according to some accounts before they laid down their instruments they struck up one final piece. Some claimed it was a popular tune called 'Autumn' (probably Joyce's 'Songe d'Automne', No.114 in the band's repertoire), others that it was the old hymn 'Nearer My God To Thee', which is said to have been the tune that bandmaster Wallace Hartley favoured for his own funeral.

2.15a.m.–2.20a.m.

The accounts of survivors describe how the final act in the tragedy of the *Titanic* was heralded by a great surge which occurred as the bridge went under, a sudden speeding up of the sinking which caught all of them unawares and which probably claimed more than a few of the many lives lost that night. By now the stern of the *Titanic* had lifted clear out of the water, not perhaps as high as movie depictions would have it, but enough to exert an enormous strain on the ship's superstructure and recent research has suggested that this final plunge occurred due to the fact that the ship's hull had already begun to rupture. Any breaks would have vented great pockets of air that would have kept the ship afloat a little longer and it also allowed a mass of seawater to flood in, pulling the ship down sharply. In essence, the theory is that the *Titanic* did not begin to break apart because she sank so suddenly, but sank so suddenly because she began to break apart.

Whatever the case, the sudden drop in the bow caused a large body of water to come rolling over the rails of the bridge. This forced its way along the two boat decks as the ship slid forward and dozens of passengers and crew were caught in the rush. Marconi man Harold Bride was now on top of the officers' quarters helping Lightoller and his crew to free Collapsible B, when the final plunge began. Perhaps hearing the cries that went up as the sea came crashing over onto the forward deck, he looked around and as he did so he caught sight of Captain Smith. The skipper had come outside and now dived from the bridge into the sea as it rose up before him; that was the last Bride ever saw of him.[51] Second-class passenger William Mellors, standing nearby, had heard Smith's final commands to the men on the roof of the officers' quarters and now saw him come out onto the deck. 'The brave old seaman was crying,' Mellors recalled. He then saw Smith jump from the bridge as the waters rose up over the rails.[52]

Bride and Mellors did not have time to dwell on Smith's disappearance, for a moment later the rising waters reached the officers' quarters. There were many passengers and crew still trying to launch the two remaining boats when the water hit them, flinging the boats and men into the sea. Among the other officers who now seem to have been lost were Chief Officer Wilde, First Officer Murdoch and Sixth Officer Moody, most of whom appear to have been helping with Collapsible A. Though tangled in ropes and rigging, this boat went into the water right side up and while swamped she stayed afloat due to her cork lining and many scrambled aboard her. On the opposite side of the ship, Collapsible B landed upside down and most of her crew were scattered in the process. Harold Bride hung onto an oarlock and though initially trapped under the boat he eventually managed to climb up onto the hull. Second Officer Lightoller had remained on the ship, but after checking to make sure that all the boats were away and there was nothing more to do, he dived into the sea. Though twice sucked under, blasts of escaping air blew him back to the surface both times and he too scrambled over to Collapsible B.

As the passengers and crew plunged into the water struggled to survive, the *Titanic*'s superstructure began to break apart. The guy wires on the forward funnel, unable to take the strain caused by the angle that the funnel had then attained, snapped, and with an unearthly roar the funnel buckled, then ripped free of the deck and crashed down into the water, killing dozens of swimmers. Fortunately for those who now clutched at Collapsible B, the falling funnel caused a wave that washed the boat to one side, safely out of harm's way.

As the *Titanic* began barrelling forward through the water, to those on the ship it seemed as if the sea rose rapidly along the boat decks, rushing through and over the partially crushed bridge and officers' quarters and down into the cauldron ripped open by the crashing funnel. Inside the ship the water blasted its way through steerage accommodation, spilled over the watertight bulkheads and swept through engine room No.4 into No.3 and further back, killing dozens of stokers and engineers who had no time to escape as it rushed through the innards of the ship.

Almost to the end, every light on the ship was ablaze, from portholes and upper staterooms and as high as the lonely lights on the ship's masts. But as the water climbed and reached the second funnel, the generators were flooded. As many witnesses later testified, one moment the ship was lit up brilliantly, filling their vision, when suddenly all the lights went out, winked back on dull and red for a moment and then went out for good. The only one that remained was a rear mast light run off a separate battery. All that could now be seen of the *Titanic* was her dark silhouette against a navy blue night sky that was dotted with brilliant stars that leapt out more vividly with the light from the ship having gone.

Only a brief pause followed when a thunderous roar could be heard by those in the boats as inside the *Titanic* a mass of loose objects began tumbling forward. Then more explosive sounds joined in as the strain of the raised stern proved too great and the ship began to snap in two. The break began on or near the rear expansion joint, an engineered gap in the superstructure that was designed to allow the ship to flex slightly in rough seas. This was now the weak spot, rendered even more fragile at that point by the presence of a number of large open public spaces in the upper decks. Splitting from the top, the *Titanic* burst asunder, toppling the remaining funnels, flinging pieces of superstructure into the sea and scattering a mass of coal, furniture, pottery and other material from its interior, which would sink down to form a huge debris field on the seabed.

Modern accident investigation has concluded, however, that the bow section did not sink straight away, but instead remained attached to the stern by a large strip of the keel and there is some belief that if the break had been clean at this point that the stern may have remained afloat, but fate was not so charitable. The stern, where hundreds of terrified passengers and crew were gathered, first fell back into the sea and the air inside did keep the rear portion of the ship afloat for a few minutes longer, until the weight of the now flooded bow section began to drag this last part of the *Titanic* down after it. The stern continued to rise, until some claimed that it finally reached an angle of about 65°–70°. It then stood there like a monolith for what seemed like an age, but then it gently settled back a little and finally began to slide under the water, slowly at first, but with increasing speed as more water began to invade the ruptured framework, escaping air blowing out doors and portholes. What remained of the rear half of the *Titanic's* central superstructure had already disappeared, but now the aft well deck and the poop deck were swallowed, followed by the propellers, the rudder and finally the last peak of the stern and the flagpole. A wave of passengers and crew went floundering into the sea as the water rose about them. Then the ship was gone, vanishing for good under a mass of churning water and debris.

2.20a.m. Onwards

As the wreckage showered down to the seabed, exploding, imploding and finally breaking apart as it did so, it took many people down with it, but hundreds of others were left in the water. Of these a few lucky individuals managed to get aboard Boat 4 which had still been near the *Titanic* as she went down and her passengers and crew managed to rescue eight men from the water, though two of these later died. That though, was the limit of Smith's safety net for those left in the water, for most of the other lifeboats never returned to the scene, as self-preservation had now become the order of the day. In the boats there was a general fear that if they did go back it would result in them being swamped, which was a genuine possibility. In some boats it was the passengers who protested when the crew showed signs that they were going back, while in others the crew themselves feared to return, much to the anger of the passengers. Many of the survivors would be forever haunted by what they did or did not do that night and by the memory of the terrible screams, first so loud and numerous, that gradually subsided as one by one the swimmers slowly sank into unconsciousness and froze to death in their life preservers.

Only one boat purposefully sailed back to pick up survivors; this was boat No.14 under Fifth Officer Lowe. Lowe too was fearful of venturing into the mass of people in the water immediately after the ship had gone, so he waited for a time for the screaming to die down. He then unloaded his passengers onto several other boats and he and four volunteers rowed back to where the *Titanic* had sunk. They found, though, that they had left it a bit too long as virtually all of those who had gone into the water had already perished. One of the crewmen, Joseph Scarrott, recalled the appalling scene as they gently pushed their boat through a sea of frozen bodies and he recalled how they all wept like children as they finally had to give up their search and return to the other boats. For their efforts Lowe and his men only managed to rescue three people, one of whom later died.

The lifeboats then drifted, having finally given up trying to reach the light on the horizon; after what they had been through, none now had the spirit to try. Instead they pulled in their oars and waited to see what the morning would bring.

It was a ship. Three hours after the *Titanic* had sunk and shortly before dawn, the small Cunard steamer *Carpathia* came weaving carefully through the ice field, firing rockets to announce her arrival and attract attention. The small ship had amazed her captain and crew but as dawn broke over the North Atlantic they found that they had arrived too late. For first light revealed not a stricken ship, low in the water, waiting for help, but a near pristine sea dotted with icebergs and an expanse of field ice and amongst this were the lifeboats. One after another these came alongside the small ship, some of them still half empty while others were now packed to the gunwales having taken on survivors from collapsibles A and B.

The roll call taken after those in the last lifeboat came aboard the *Carpathia* revealed an enormous loss of life. Out of the estimated 2,227 people aboard the *Titanic* when she had departed Queenstown four days earlier, only 705 people had been saved; approximately 1,522 people were missing. There were hundreds of widows and fatherless children now crowding the *Carpathia*'s decks. A good number of male passengers had survived, but most had not. Several millionaires and other men of note were numbered among the missing and for better or worse these would grab the headlines of waiting journalists, but across the board the figures made for tragic reading. In first class 119 men and eleven women and children had been lost; in second class it was 142 men and twenty-four women and children; the greatest loss of life among the passengers, though, was in third class, with 417 male casualties and 119 women and children, a total of 536. Here in some cases whole families had been wiped out and the disparity between the numbers saved in first and second class and those in steerage would soon cause a storm of controversy.

Though a good many of them had escaped the sinking ship, by far the heaviest loss was incurred by the *Titanic*'s crew, 685 of whom died in the disaster. The *Titanic* had gone to sea with thirty-five engineers, of whom none had survived; only eight of the 305 firemen and stokers had got away; three stewardesses died in the disaster; none of the teenage lift boys had survived, nor had any of the purser's or surgeon's departments; the five postal clerks had gone; the ship's band had died to a man. One group that had not suffered quite as heavily was the ship's deck officer cadre, only half of whom had been lost in the disaster. Three of the ship's officers, Pitman, Boxhall and Lowe had got away in charge of their respective boats, and Lightoller had clambered onto Collapsible B, but Sixth Officer Moody was dead and so too were First Officer Murdoch and Chief Officer Wilde. But by far the most notable casualty amongst the officers and indeed the crew was the ship's famous old skipper, Commander Edward John Smith. Like so many others, the millionaire's captain was dead.

MOMENTO MORI

The demise of the *Titanic* was one of the great unfolding news events of the early years of the twentieth century and even before the heavily laden *Carpathia* docked and landed the survivors at New York, the sinking of the great ship was headline news around the world. Early optimistic reports of everybody having been saved soon gave way to the grim truth of the matter as throughout the remainder of the *Carpathia's* journey to the United States, despite a severe case of frostbite, Harold Bride, the *Titanic's* sole surviving Marconi operator, helped the *Carpathia's* wireless man to transmit the names of survivors to the shore station at Cape Race. When the *Carpathia* finally arrived in New York Harbour, she was met by a large crowd of onlookers, friends and relatives, police, officials, medical staff and a host of reporters, all wanting to catch sight of the survivors and to discover more about the terrible disaster that had befallen the *Titanic*.

With the survivors on hand and before some could escape back to Britain, the US government convened the first official inquiry into the disaster. Over a seventeen-day period numerous crew and passengers, experts and officials were questioned and sometimes re-examined as to what exactly had happened to the *Titanic*. Perhaps because of the speed with which it had been arranged the US Inquiry turned into more of a talking shop than an in-depth investigation into the causes of the disaster. This accrued many and varied first-hand accounts which have proven to be of great interest to historians and researchers over the years. However, the investigators' lack of seagoing knowledge often exasperated *Titanic's* officers and crew. Second Officer Lightoller, the senior surviving officer, for one left the American Inquiry convinced that the whole thing had been a farce.

For Lightoller and many others there were more gruelling rounds of questions when they returned to Britain. The government set up their own inquiry under the chairmanship of Lord Mersey. In contrast to the American investigation this was more concerned with the technicalities of the disaster and fewer survivors were called in to testify. So, in retrospect these two inquiries complemented each other. Yet, not everyone was pleased with Lord Mersey's report either, as it glossed over far too many faults in maritime procedure and smacked of being a cover-up.

Though different in tone and despite their faults, both inquiries agreed on new guidelines to improve future ship safety. Ship's wirelesses were henceforth to be manned twenty-four hours a day and all sea-going vessels were to carry enough lifeboats or life rafts for all aboard, irrespective of the ship's tonnage. The inquiries also called for the formation of a body to monitor the flow of the ice through the North Atlantic and to ensure that such a terrible accident could never occur again. This became the International Ice Patrol, which today operates as a part of the US Coast Guard.

Many of the survivors were mentally scarred by that terrible night and effectively became victims of the *Titanic* after the fact, plagued by feelings of guilt and nightmares for years afterwards. Also, by having survived the disaster that had claimed so many, several notable first-class male survivors such as J. Bruce Ismay fell victim to the self-righteous ire of the press and saw their once fine reputations left in tatters. So too unwittingly did Captain Stanley Lord of the SS *Californian*, whose ship was deemed to be the vessel whose lights could be seen from the *Titanic*. As his officers had reported that a ship to their south was firing rockets that night and because Lord had not investigated further, his was a hard case to answer and he was censured by both inquiries for not going to the rescue of the *Titanic*.

Fair or unfair, the *Titanic* disaster had its 'villains', but at the same time it also had its heroes: the engineers; the band; Captain Rostron of the *Carpathia*, who was subsequently awarded a Medal of Honour by the United States; Jack Phillips, sticking to his wireless until the end, and Captain Smith. As was the custom at that time, because he was not there to offer evidence in his defence, Smith – though open to criticism of his seamanship – was exonerated of blame by both inquiries and certainly the stories of the bravery he displayed after the collision played a great part in his freedom from guilt in the eyes of the inquirers. From the very onset of the news of the disaster, the fate of this formerly admired and trusted seaman was a subject to grab the journalists' attention. There were early reports that he had shot himself in despair, while others claimed that he had been seen in the water after the ship went down and that when spotted he had refused to be rescued, or that he had handed a child into a lifeboat. There were also later reports that Smith had somehow managed to survive the disaster and made his way undetected to the United States. Some time after the disaster a sea captain who claimed an old acquaintance with Smith said that he saw him alive and well in Baltimore. There was also the story of a tramp named 'Whispering' Smith, who claimed shortly before his death that he was the former captain of the *Titanic*.

Perhaps the most famous account of his actions, though, which gained almost instant popularity in the wake of the disaster, is the story that Smith is supposed to have exhorted his crew to 'Be British!' as the ship was finally going under:

When the first signal was given to lower the boats, some of the crew pressed forward. It was then that the rallying cry came through the megaphone from the bridge, 'Be British, my men.' It was Capt. Smith's voice. Every man obeyed the command and faced death calmly. They knew that there was no hope and as the big, strong English seamen assisted the women and children into the boats they gave no sign that they realised that Capt. Smith's words 'Be British,' had sealed their fate. They remained at their posts and died like men.[1]

All well and good, you might think, but there is, though, no clear identification of 'John Johnson' the crew member who supposedly gave this account. The closest we get is Steward James Johnston, but though at the American Inquiry James Johnston mentioned seeing Smith on a number of occasions after the collision, he nowhere stated that Smith had said anything of the sort. It should also be noted here that the newspaper report above does not describe Smith's death. In fact if this report is to be believed, Smith told his men to 'Be British' pretty early on in the evening, not as the ship was going under. Maybe it happened, maybe it didn't; 'Be British' seems to have been a tale that simply grew in the telling.

It is now generally accepted by historians of the *Titanic* that the most likely of these fates, the one documented in this book, was that Smith returned to the bridge and dived into the sea when the ship began her final plunge. If that was the case it was also possible that Smith could have swum around in the water for a time and may have refused to let himself be rescued as some statements claim. The story of Captain Smith rescuing a baby was a popular one at the time and it seems to have provided some consolation for Smith's widow when she heard it; Eleanor referred to the supposed incident in a letter to Frank Hancock, though there are no indications that Smith, or anyone else, handed a child over to one of the boats. The suicide story is equally unlikely. The *Reuters* report that first mentioned his suicide was soon identified as a mistake, a mix-up of two separate messages. The appearances of Smith in America can be attributed to a case of mistaken identity and the ramblings of a worn-out old man seeking a morsel of fame.

All said though, the only certain thing about Smith's fate was that he was dead – the captain had gone down with his ship. Considering the odium heaped upon the likes of Ismay and Captain Lord, it was probably just as well that Smith had died, as had he lived the scandal would probably have destroyed him.

A Dollar for Captain Smith's Soul

At the other end of Southampton, in the wealthy quarter near the New Forest, grief has fallen not less heavily than in the poorer neighbourhoods. At Captain Smith's house the garden is full of spring flowers, but the blinds are half drawn as if to show that the fate of the captain is still in doubt. When I called this morning I was told by the maid that Mrs Smith was prostrated with grief. No communication has been received from the captain since he sailed from Southampton.[2]

The effect of the tragedy on Smith's family and friends, as was the case for all of
those whose loved ones had died, was of course, terrible. As the passage above
indicates, Eleanor Smith was shattered by the news and despite the anonymous
reporter's comments, she was at least one of the first to know that her husband was
dead and was thus spared the days of agony waiting outside the White Star offices in
Southampton. Here, every morning, hundreds of people gathered to read the list of
survivors' names. Outside the White Star offices were posted dozens of notices, one
of which a few days later was a small, sad message from the captain's widow:

> To my fellow sufferers,
> My heart overflows with grief for you all and is laden with the sorrow that you are
> weighed down with this terrible burden that has been thrust upon us. May God be
> with us and comfort us all. Yours in deep sympathy
> ELEANOR SMITH.[3]

There followed a national round of mourning and in virtually every church
memorial services were held, prayers said for the dead and thanks given for the
living. One of the earliest memorial services was in Southampton, attended by
Eleanor. The greatest service took place on 19 April at St Paul's Cathedral, which was
packed to overflowing. Dozens of memorial postcards were published, some to raise
funds for the families of the dead, and there were many that needed such support.
In Southampton, from where the *Titanic* had drawn most of her crew, whole
streets saw their menfolk decimated and no money coming in for the foreseeable
future. The *Titanic's* band had its own special fund as there was no provision for the
families of the dead men because the band was not officially a part of the crew, but
travelled as second-class passengers. Concerts were held, collections made and scores
of pieces of bad poetry and reams of pompous or sentimental sheet music were
churned out in an effort to raise funds for the bereaved and to commemorate the
disaster.

However, when what had started as genuine grief and sorrow for the victims and
their families began to turn into something more rabid, somebody had to speak
up. One of the leading literary lights of the day, playwright George Bernard Shaw,
wrote a letter to the *Daily News and Leader* on 14 May 1912, in which he said that he
was being driven to distraction by the overly romantic image being painted around
the disaster. Smith came in for some special treatment in his arguments, Shaw being
contemptuous of the captain being presented as some sort of superhero towering
over a shipload of other 'British' heroes. Six days later, Sir Arthur Conan Doyle,
the creator of Sherlock Holmes, wrote a reply in which he virtually accused Shaw
of lying and of showing a complete lack of compassion. Shaw attacked again on
22 May, saying that if anyone was sentimental or foolish enough to remind him that
Smith had gone down with his ship, they should be reminded that so too had the
ship's cat!

Conan Doyle was fighting a losing battle, Shaw loved nothing better than a bruising argument and though many of the examples that he touched upon in his arguments have since been dismissed as unlikely or just plain wrong, he did have a number of good points to make. By this time Smith was the darling of the popular press and a lot of pretty awful patriotic nonsense was being attached to his name, some of it dangerous nonsense as it distorted facts and attempted to cover up mistakes. Though his attacks were blunt and spared no one's feelings, Shaw's intentions were at least honest in this respect. He was trying to shake sense into people and make them see that what had happened was not an exercise designed to prove the nobility of the British in adversity, but a disaster of unparalleled dimensions, the lessons of which had been learnt the hard way because of mistakes in law, in operational procedures and in command. Conan Doyle for the conservative view, however, did not like Shaw's radical tone. His thoughts were with the victims of the disaster and their families, one of which was the Smith family to whom Shaw's comments would have read as nothing short of boorish insensitivity at such a time.

Shaw's views were, however, the exception rather than the rule and during the inquiries into the disaster, few aspersions had been cast on the captain's character. Men such as Herbert Lightoller had put up a stout defence of Smith's actions and motives before the commissioners. To many, notably the rich passengers who had been cultivated by Smith as a group of friends and valued customers, such a defence seemed perfectly correct. The tales of Smith's last moments spurred them on, notably the stories then doing the rounds, of him rescuing a child and uttering his super-patriotic 'last order', 'Be British!', both of which appealed powerfully to their sensibilities. To them such nobility of spirit surely demanded a permanent memorial and the obvious place to put this would be in the town of his birth.

However, this idea did not receive a great deal of support in the Potteries, where the name Edward John Smith was hardly known beyond the circle of his old friends or those who remembered him in connection with the folks who used to run the grocer's in Well Street. The local newspaper, the *Staffordshire Sentinel*, had quickly latched onto his connection with the Potteries and naturally followed the stories of his fate with interest and, to the paper's credit, with little sensationalism. Despite this, few people wished to be associated with the greatest maritime disaster in history, for fear perhaps that the curse of the *Titanic* might be catching. The controversy was, therefore, felt very powerfully in what in 1910 had become the Federation of Stoke-on-Trent. For this group of towns aspiring towards city status, the news of Smith's connection with the area was not seen as a good advertisement. Nobody denied that Smith had died bravely, but he had embarrassed the Potteries. So far as most of the council could see, Smith had not done anything for the area other than forever associate it with the *Titanic* disaster. Because of this the council made no move to commemorate Smith officially.

Though there was to be no official recognition of Smith, many of his old friends did make an effort to memorialise him in his home town. William M. Hampton, an old friend, backed by many of the Etruria British School's old boys, immediately proposed to start a subscription list for a memorial tablet. Hardly two days had passed since the disaster when the local paper carried this appeal, under the title 'Proposed Hanley Memorial to Captain Smith':

> Sir – Might I suggest it would be a gracious act to place a memorial tablet in some public building in Hanley to the memory of the late Captain E.J. Smith of the Titanic?
>
> It is well known that he was a native of Hanley, and I have (amongst many others who are now with us) known him personally since his schooldays, and have watched his career and have been proud that Hanley has produced such an eminent seaman. There are no doubt many who would like to show respect to his memory by subscribing towards the memorial. I would like to name 2s. 6d. as the limit of the subscriptions.
>
> Would it be asking too much for your sympathy in the matter, and receive any subscriptions which may be sent.
>
> - Yours etc. W. M. Hampton. Eastwood and Mousecroft Fire Brick and Marl Works, Hanley, April 17 1912.[4]

Actually, it was asking too much it seems, for though subscriptions began to arrive, they didn't exactly flood in and a short time afterwards another letter appeared in the *Sentinel*, this time from Mr Hampton's son, Thomas, who tried to jolt the local lethargy with a dose of patriotism:

> …I am sure there are hundreds of people in the Potteries who would only be too pleased to subscribe to such a fund to show our appreciation of Captain Smith's gallant conduct in this terrible disaster.
>
> Not only are 'we Potters' proud that he was an Englishman, but that he was a Potteryman and a Briton to the backbone.[5]

Actually, there were not hundreds of people in the Potteries who were willing to subscribe. Most people in the region were poor, most had never heard of E.J. Smith and could probably not have cared less about him. As a result subscriptions still only trickled in.

Eventually, though, enough contributions were taken and a total of £21 0s, 6d was raised. Shortly before the ceremony, which took place a year and a day after the disaster, a list naming the ninety-odd contributors was printed in the *Staffordshire Sentinel*. It had been decided that the plaque to Captain Smith was to be placed in the entrance to Hanley Town Hall and so it was that at 3p.m. on Tuesday 16 April 1913, the mayor stood up before a large crowd of dignitaries and officially unveiled the Potteries' only memorial to the captain of the *Titanic*, an ornamental cast metal plaque which read:

THIS TABLET IS DEDICATED TO THE MEMORY OF COMMANDER EDWARD JOHN SMITH, R.D., R.N.R. BORN IN HANLEY, 27 JANY 1850, DIED AT SEA, 15 APRIL 1912.

BE BRITISH.

WHILST IN COMMAND OF THE WHITE STAR S.S. '*TITANIC*' THAT GREAT SHIP STRUCK AN ICEBERG IN THE ATLANTIC OCEAN DURING THE NIGHT AND SPEEDILY SANK WITH NEARLY ALL WHO WERE ON BOARD. CAPTAIN SMITH HAVING DONE ALL MAN COULD DO FOR THE SAFETY OF PASSENGERS AND CREW REMAINED AT HIS POST ON THE SINKING SHIP UNTIL THE END. HIS LAST MESSAGE TO HIS CREW WAS 'BE BRITISH'.

The memorial tablet remained there until 1961, when during alterations to the town hall it was decided that there was no more room for it and it was handed over to Smith's old school, or rather the school that had replaced it. Following that school's closure in 1978, though, the plaque was re-housed back in the town hall in a small apse where couples newly married in the nearby registrar's office now come to have their photos taken. The highly polished brass plate sits beneath a large framed photograph of Smith dressed in his RNR dress uniform and from there like some Ruritanian master of ceremonies, he stares down benignly on the newlyweds and their families and friends.

Back in 1913, on 22 April, a week after the ceremony in Hanley, a similar event took place at the board school – this time the unveiling of another portrait. It was a photograph of Smith dressed in his white uniform and was presented to the school by some of its old boys, with the proviso that the ornately framed photograph was to be fixed in a conspicuous place in the school. The portrait hung there for many years and was later joined by the plaque from Hanley Town Hall. Before the school closed, the photograph was copied by *Sentinel* photographer and local historian, E.J.D. Warrillow, and now forms a part of the extensive Warrillow collection of photographs held at Keele University.

Before the ceremony took place, some of the old boys who had known Smith in his youth were asked to write to Eleanor Smith. It was a good plan and their recollections form the basis of the first chapter of this book, but it must have been a duty tinged with sadness for all concerned. Spencer Till and Edmund Jones wrote from the Potteries, while Joe Turner, by then the manager of Nobel's explosives factory, wrote from Perranporth in Cornwall. Eleanor replied to their letters with some passion, telling them that her husband had often joyfully recalled his childhood. Eleanor did not attend the unveiling ceremony, but Spencer Till spoke in her stead, relating to those gathered at the board school that he had recently had occasion to meet Eleanor when she paid a visit to a lifelong friend in Runcorn. During the visit, Mrs Smith had shown Till a number of photographs of her husband, including the one of him attending the large banquet thrown in his honour at the Metropolitan Club in December.

Captain Smith was not forgotten by his numerous friends on the other side of the Atlantic and there were lots of good thoughts towards him; for instance a meeting was convened at the Union League Club in New York by some of Smith's old friends to arrange for a fitting testimonial to his memory and to create a fund for his wife and daughter. A committee comprising Charles Lanier, J. Pierpont Morgan Jr, William A. Nash, William D. Sloane, John J. Sinclair, William Hester and others was appointed to oversee the project. William Nash at the Corn Exchange Bank was the treasurer.[6] However, it is unclear what, if any, memorials came of it; the newspapers carried no further indication of what form this testimonial took. Maybe these men had a hand in dedicating the one tablet that we know was raised in Smith's memory in the city, at the now demolished old Seaman's Church Institute at 25 South Street, New York. This read:

He sailed the sea for forty years.
Faithful in duty.
Friendly in spirit.
Firm in command.
Fearless in disaster.
He saved women and children
And went down with his ship.[7]

Smith's name was also freely banded about in an effort to raise the required funds for other memorials in the US. For instance, by June 1912, plans were afoot for what was known as the Women's Titanic Memorial. This was not, as might be supposed, a memorial to the women who had perished aboard the *Titanic*, but to the men who had died with the ship 'for the sake of the women and children'. The committee in charge of the memorial fund began taking collections from individuals across the country almost immediately. The newspapers reported the fund's progress, quoting letters occasionally. Captain Smith seems to have elicited, or was used to elicit, a great deal of sympathy from the women of America, young and old. According to a report in the *New York Times*, a young Chinese girl in California named Ying Lo, sent her contribution with the message: 'Memorial Day I am twelve years I send this dollar for Capt. Smith's soul.'[8]

A month later came another note from another twelve-year-old Chinese girl named Ah Ying of San Francisco, who had seemingly been similarly moved by Captain Smith's actions:

Dear Women's Titanic Memorial:
    I thought this was women's work, so I send a dollar. I am a little Chinese girl – Ah Ying. Ying is Chinese for eagle. Twelve years old. I go to school during the day and serve tea in a garden in the evening. I earned and worked for that dollar as a memorial to Capt. Smith. He went down holding a little child. Thank you. Yours truly
Ah Ying.[9]

It seems very touching, but the letter seems to be simply an expanded version of the first note with a similar name attached to it. It quite obviously pushes all the right buttons to elicit an emotional response from the paper's readers, be it shame or sympathy, which lends to a suspicion that this may just be a manufactured note couched in the style of a twelve-year-old girl just learning her English and designed to generate more money. Yet it is easy to be cynical and equally the notes might be quite genuine, though whether they were or not we will perhaps never know. Whatever the case, the memorial fund did find enough real women and girls to contribute their dollars for the souls of Captain Smith and the other men who gave up their lives on the *Titanic*. Though it was a while in coming, the Women's Memorial, showing a statue of a partially draped male figure with its arms outstretched to the side, was unveiled in Washington in 1931. Originally sited where the present-day Kennedy Centre stands, the memorial is now situated next to the Washington Channel near Fort Lesley J. McNair.

Placed on a Pedestal

Smith did get his own statue and its story began in November 1913, when a number of Smith's old friends and passengers, most notably the Bishop of Willesden, Lady Astor and the Duchess of Sutherland, formed the Captain Smith Memorial Committee. Disappointed perhaps by what few memorials had been grudgingly raised thus far, the committee's brief was to provide what they deemed a more fitting memorial to the old sailor. They were determined to have a statue of the man, but there was also to be a stained-glass window for Liverpool Cathedral while any extra money was to be donated to the Seaman's Orphanage in Southampton. Subscriptions to the fund were plentiful from some of the well-heeled citizens of Britain and America and Smith's old friends, but the committee received only three contributions from the Potteries.

The sculptress chosen for the commission of Smith's statue was Lady Kathleen Scott, the widow of Captain Robert Falcon Scott, 'Scott of the Antarctic', whose expedition to the South Pole in 1912 had ended so tragically for him and his men. The coming together of these two figures, Smith and Scott, both of them ripe for deification, is interesting to compare and contrast.[10] Though her own memoirs give no indication as to when she started work on the statue, Lady Scott decided upon constructing a bronze statue 7ft 8in high, to be mounted on a 7ft-high pedestal of Cornish granite. With this in process the only thing left to do then was to find somewhere to put the statue. The Potteries was approached, but it considered that it had got enough memorials to the man. So the committee were stuck until they lighted upon a small piece of pleasant parkland, known nowadays as Beacon Park, next to the museum in the picturesque south Staffordshire city of Lichfield. The council there were approached and, given the county connection with Smith, were willing to think it over. So the park was provisionally cited as the spot for the statue and everyone seemed happy, but the committee and their pet project were in for a rough ride.

There was a great deal of local anger when the citizens of Lichfield heard about the plans for the statue and a number of them banded together and presented a petition in protest. Their argument was plain and simple: Smith not only had nothing to do with Lichfield, but was not a historically notable figure. The reasons put forward by the Memorial Committee did not appease them and if anything, only went to show the embarrassment that the committee were beginning to feel about what was becoming a very contentious issue. The most artificial excuse offered was that Lichfield lay midway between London and Liverpool and was, therefore, easily accessible to American visitors. However, Lichfield was the capital of the diocese that covered Hanley and also had the advantage of also being in Staffordshire, Smith's native county. They might have also added that Lichfield, with its cathedral and other old buildings, its parks and its pleasant river walks was also a much prettier place than the hard industrial landscape of the Potteries. The committee may have in part alluded to this when they meekly added that they had 'other reasons'. Few passing American millionaires, no matter how highly they esteemed Smith's memory, were likely to have braved the Potteries in full blast if they had better things to be doing. But undoubtedly the main dilemma facing the Memorial Committee was that nobody else wanted the statue. The petitioners of Lichfield were fully aware of this particular 'other reason' and they made the perfectly valid statement to the effect that if Hanley did not want this honour, why should Lichfield?

The argument finally came to a head in a well-attended meeting of the Lichfield council. The mayor, Councillor Bridgeman JP, received the petition of protest only a few weeks before the statue was due to be unveiled in the Museum Grounds. The mayor said that he wished the whole affair to be discussed before an entire council in committee. However, Councillor Longstaff opposed this move in deference to the petitioners, saying that as it was a public petition, the whole matter should be discussed in open council. Councillor Longstaff failed to see any reason for taking up the matter in committee. However, Bridgeman opposed the move to an open council, which would delay matters, the main reason being that despite the local resistance the date was now fixed for the unveiling. The council had already decided to accept the statue and this eleventh hour attempt to scupper its unveiling had come too late.

Events in the council chamber ebbed and flowed along these lines for a short time, but eventually the town clerk was called upon to read out the petition from the protesters, which ran thus:

June 1914.

To His Worship the Mayor of Lichfield –

With respect to the acceptance of a statue to the late Captain Smith of the 'Titanic', and the decision to place the same in the Museum Grounds, we, the undersigned, desire to place before you our reasons for regarding such an action as undesirable, at the same time emphasising the fact that we do not in the least suggest any sense of reproach upon the memory of an admittedly brave sailor :-

i) His birthplace being in North Staffordshire, there is no claim upon the City.

ii) We are anxious for the reputation of our City that only such monuments should be erected as are by general consensus of opinion, representative of distinctly eminent men.

iii) We do not consider that there is any particular historical reason warranting the perpetuation of Captain Smith's memory in so marked a way as the erection of a statue would signify.

We trust, therefore, that the acceptance of the statue for erection here is not too late for reconsideration, and we respectfully ask that you will bring the matter forward in the right quarter.

In conclusion, we would urge the need for most careful consideration of any claim which purposes so near an association with the one statue of which we are all so justly proud, that of one of our greatest statesmen, the late King Edward VII.[11]

There followed a list of the seventy-three petitioners, mostly good citizens of Lichfield and a few army officers, the name of each being read out loud by the town clerk. Reading between the lines it seems that more than anything else, the petitioners were rather put out by the feeling that they were having the statue dumped onto their city. However, Councillor Raby for the conservatives read out next the names of the contributors to the Memorial Committee. These included the late Duke of Sutherland, the dowager Duchess of Arran, a former ambassador to the United States, assorted generals, colonels and admirals, churchmen, academics, Members of Parliament, naval captains, merchant commanders and Smith's old friend the American writer Kate Riggs, better known as Kate Douglas-Wiggin, who had written 'a moving tribute' to be read out when the statue was unveiled.

Councillor Raby then said that he would have liked to have talked to all who had signed the petition in protest, whom he believed had signed it unthinkingly, and that to him, the petition constituted a 'particularly ungracious' statement. Warming to his task, Raby drew upon newspaper accounts of Smith's bravery; he mentioned amongst other things that Lady Scott had sculpted the statue and he perpetuated a myth by saying that 'Be British' were 'words that would live as long as the English language'[12]. Councillor Longstaff for the petitioners was, however, still rather doubtful and added that though he felt that the words of the petition were rather unfortunate, he did not see any reason for anyone to launch into a defence of Captain Smith.

Councillor Raby completed his argument by telling the council that Queen Alexandra had been informed of the unveiling ceremony due to take place. That seemed to end the last of the many arguments between the critics and supporters of Smith, with the upshot of it all being that the petition was ordered to lie on the table. Despite the debate there had been little point in arguing the matter as the statue was there to stay.

The statue was unveiled on the warm and sunny afternoon of Wednesday 29 July 1914, by Smith's daughter, Melville. War clouds were gathering over Europe, indeed, the start of the First World War was now only a matter of days away and the ceremony was attended by all the pomp that could be mustered at this anxious time. There were many notable absentees who sent their apologies no doubt because of this, but there was still a large crowd of onlookers gathered at the Museum Grounds. On one side of the statue, a large contingent of the Royal Naval Reserve from Liverpool, dressed in their blue jackets, was drawn up under the command of Lieutenant Trant, who was also the White Star Line representative. Also there was a group of army buglers from nearby Whittington Barracks, their scarlet tunics contrasting brilliantly with the blue of the RNR and the bright green lawn and surrounding trees. There were representatives of the merchant navy, the Royal Navy, the police and the army. There should also have been a detachment of the South Staffordshire Regiment, who were to have provided a guard of honour, but they were away on manoeuvres, pending mobilisation.

As the civic procession made its way to the platform, the 'General Salute' was sounded by the buglers. The procession was headed by the sword and mace bearers, dressed in traditional uniforms. Then came the mayor and the sheriff dressed in robes of scarlet and blue. Aldermen and councillors filed onto the platform behind them, followed by the Bishop of Willesden; the Duchess of Sutherland; the statue's sculptor, Lady Kathleen Scott; Eleanor and Melville Smith; Lord Charles Beresford MP, dressed in a naval uniform, and Mr F.S. Stevenson, the honorary secretary to the memorial committee. The Mayor of Lichfield presided over the ceremony.

The message from Queen Alexandra was obviously a good starting point and was read out to the crowd:

> Her Majesty, as you are well aware, feels the most sincere and sympathetic interest in this movement and thinks this tribute to the good and brave man who died in the performance of his duties a most appropriate one. [13]

This perhaps was read out by the Bishop of Willesden; certainly he took over when the Queen's message had passed and he described the three or four journeys he had made with Smith and recalled something of their friendship.

The next to take the platform was the statuesque, elegant and eloquent Duchess of Sutherland, a character well known to the manufacturers in the Potteries as 'Meddlesome Millie', because of her investigation and criticism of the dangerous working practices workers had to endure. Being acquainted with the people of

Hanley, she was perhaps the most sympathetic of all to Smith's memory, being able to appreciate the leap he had made since his childhood. She also had a personal connection, being the widow of the same Duke of Sutherland who some years earlier had made the incredibly short speech after Sousa's band had given a concert aboard the *Baltic* and surprised his fellow guests by wearing tan shoes with his dinner suit. He too was now gone, having died the year before, and the Duchess recalled his journeying with Smith.

Mel, dressed in a pale hat and dress, sat with her mother near to the statue, quietly listening to these speeches. Eventually, though, she was invited to take the stand and, tugging at the sheeting, she revealed Lady Scott's statue of the captain of the *Titanic*. To those in the audience who had persevered in the face of criticism and difficulty to get the statue raised, it was a triumph.

Lord Charles Beresford then took the stand and talked about Smith's career, his patriotism and self-sacrifice, as too in various ways did the many others who got up in turn to speak: the Marquess of Salisbury; publisher J.E. Hodder Williams; Lady Diana Manners and her sister the Marchioness of Anglesey.

This all went on for some time, but when the ceremony ended it was with a vote of thanks being extended to Lady Scott and to Melville Smith. Eleanor Smith ended the ceremony by placing at the foot of the statue a wreath of red and white roses in memory of her husband.

EPILOGUE

The statue of Captain Smith is still there in Lichfield, little changed in the decades since it was unveiled. Despite the attentions over the years from birds, passing drunks or graffiti, the statue and its pedestal still remain as good looking as when it was first erected, a tribute to the local parks department. Like all statues of its ilk, the pose is allegorical. Smith stands with his arms folded, one leg poised forward confidently and his head held high and if he does seem to be surveying the immaculately manicured park with some undue interest, then it is presumably in much the same manner as he had once looked out intently across the grey Atlantic. Over time the bronze became green with age and as well as the patina of verdigris, a few extra words, 'Capt. of RMS Titanic', were later added to the pedestal to serve to enlighten the uninitiated. On the grass verge before it a small modern plaque explains in more detail who he was and why he was commemorated here in this fashion,[1] for nowhere on the original plaque is the name *Titanic* mentioned. Doubtless his friends and family had wished to remember him for something other than the disaster that took his life, but in choosing the wording they must also have had a weather-eye on the uncomfortable fact – as events in Lichfield had shown – that once the jingoism and soul-searching had faded, that unlucky ship and its associations had become very contentious issues indeed.

For the next four decades, as the world moved on to be rocked by other great and terrible events, Captain Smith's statue stood largely forgotten and he and his tale might have simply dwindled into obscurity. But then in the 1950s something remarkable happened when the story of the *Titanic* was rediscovered. Like so many aspects of the *Titanic* story, the reasons as to why it suddenly became and remains so popular to this day are hard to define. Some have come to see it as a morality tale, a corrective for all of the optimistic thoughts of the late nineteenth and early twentieth centuries. Others are attracted by the controversies, the personalities or the social and moral aspects of the tale. But perhaps the main reason why the tale resurfaced and survives so well, a reason which I doubt anyone would dispute, is the sheer dramatic power of this remarkable tale of high hubris and the inevitable fall. Certainly none of the other great or infamous disasters at sea that have occurred since then have captured the public's imagination in quite the same way as the *Titanic*.

In the resurgence of interest in the *Titanic* that followed, scores of books and articles were written or rescued from obscurity and this fascination continues to the present day, having recently entered a new dimension, namely cyberspace. Today the printed word's modern poor relation, the worldwide web, hosts numerous sites, some good, many bad, that have sprung up as a result of the continuing fascination with this famous ship and its passengers and crew. The story of the *Titanic* has also been immortalised on celluloid; at least four major films and numerous television dramas have been based around the disaster, as have stage shows and even a musical, and for better or worse these fictionalised renderings are perhaps the most accessible versions of events for the general public. [2]

Undoubtedly the biggest boost to modern interest in the *Titanic*, though, came in September 1985, when a joint American and French expedition discovered the broken wreck of the ship 13,000ft down on the Atlantic seabed. This astonishing discovery made headlines across the world, rewriting the history books almost overnight by proving not only that the ship had indeed broken in two as some eyewitnesses had claimed, but that the theory of the 300ft-long gash along the hull was an exaggeration. The discovery of the wreck also proved that Boxhall's position for the *Titanic* had been wrong and in doing so it relit old controversies such as the culpability of Captain Stanley Lord of the *Californian*. Further expeditions to the wreck over the years since then have disappointed and satisfied in equal measure. Survivors of the disaster amongst others wanted the ship left untouched as a sea grave, but this was not to be and numerous items have been retrieved or simply looted from the wreck. Some of these have advanced our knowledge of the people and events of that famous voyage, justifying their salvage; others though, have simply been acquired for monetary gain.

Because he played such a central role in events, hand in hand with the evolution of the *Titanic* from a subject of grief and controversy to something approaching an icon of popular culture, Captain Smith's reputation has also to some extent been salvaged over time, a fact reflected in the recent addition of the telling words to his statue's pedestal. From a superhero just after the disaster, to a *persona non grata* in the following years, the pendulum now seems to have swung back the other way a little.

The image of Captain Smith that has come to the fore since the 1950s has largely been shaped by the classier *Titanic* books such as Walter Lord's *A Night to Remember*. Other major influences are the cinematic versions of the story, be it Brian Aherne's 'Smith' leading the rather curious rousing singsong at the end of the 1953 film *Titanic*; Lawrence Naismith retiring to the bridge with quiet dignity in the movie version of *A Night to Remember*; or most recently, Bernard Hill shutting himself in the wheelhouse in the 1997 film *Titanic*. The latter film also played up another image touted by some authors, that Smith had suffered a mental breakdown after the collision. This image, however, like that of the resigned tragic hero enduring his own immolation to expiate his perceived sins, depends very much on a selective reading of the evidence.

Despite its many inaccuracies, this sympathetic modern image of Captain Smith as the rather lonely King Lear-like figure on the bridge of his last command, filled with despair, perhaps driven mad with grief, deserted by fortune, watching the green water slowly creeping up the glass in front of him, has proven popular and is likely to endure. It is a change in status that has not gone unnoticed in the two cities that might claim to have first dibs on his legacy: Stoke-on-Trent where he was born and Lichfield where his statue stands. Indeed, during the wave of *Titanic*-mania that took place following the discovery of the wreck in 1985, his statue, so long unloved and unwanted by either city, became a bone of contention between Stoke-on-Trent and Lichfield. In the Potteries calls were made for a statue of Smith to be erected in Hanley, or at least for the one in Lichfield to be resited to the town. Waking up to the potential this might hold for the local tourist industry, this last option was considered by the local council and a request was made to the Lichfield authorities for the statue there to be taken to Hanley. Lichfield, however, equally aware of the value the statue now had for their own city, flatly turned down the request and refused to relinquish that which so many of its inhabitants had once opposed so bitterly. Instead, Lichfield smartened the statue up, told people who he was, posted more information about him and otherwise made him more accessible to passing Brits or Americans enthralled by the great sea story. In Stoke-on-Trent, the debate began all over again a decade later, when Smith once more became hot property following the success in 1997 of the multi-Oscar-winning blockbuster *Titanic*. Knowing this time that it stood no chance of getting Lichfield's statue, Stoke-on-Trent pondered the problem of what to do as regarded remembering its erstwhile son, but this time beyond prompting the obligatory newspaper articles, for and against, that appear at such times, no more strenuous efforts were made to acquire or raise a statue to him in his birthplace.[3]

Had they been able to see into the future, what would the people who gathered in the Museum Grounds in Lichfield in 1914 have made of this petty carping of modern councils, or the ephemeral nature of successful books and movies and their attendant manias? This chaff of modern society would probably have prompted a mixture of pride, anger, astonishment and embarrassment from them, but there would at least have been the pleasure of knowing that their efforts to preserve his memory had not been in vain, even if it had taken a while. To them the statue stood for this, but for so much more; to his friends it was in memory of a man who, rising from a very humble home, had done remarkable things with his life and impressed them all in the process. To his family it was in lieu of the funeral they could never have.

For despite the trouble and recriminations it did and would prompt, the unveiling of the statue in Lichfield had been a sad but proud day for all of Edward John Smith's relations who had lived to see that moment. With that, though, the family quickly faded from the limelight. The Hancock and Harrington families relaxed back into the relative obscurity that is the lot of most people. They had attended the ceremony in some numbers. Thyrza Harrington, at seventy-eight the matriarch of the Smith and Hancock clans since the death of Catherine Smith, was there with many of her children and grandchildren. She would linger on for some years after, passing away finally on 13 January 1921 aged eighty-five, being buried in her husband's grave in Hanley Cemetery a few days later. Another attendee to the unveiling was Smith's nephew James William Sidney Harrington, who had served under him aboard the *Lizzie Fennell*, and with him were his wife and children. To some extent he became Smith's heir in the Potteries, inheriting several items that had belonged to his late uncle. Today, there are numerous descendants of the Hancocks, Harringtons and some of the older branches of the Smith family, who can still take a certain pride in their famous but often much-maligned relative.

Eleanor Smith remained a widow and like her husband's blood relatives she gently faded out of sight. Not long after the *Titanic* disaster, she wrote a long heartfelt letter to Smith's nephew Frank in the United States in which she indicated her desire to leave Southampton. Rumours persist even today that Eleanor and Mel were driven from their home as a result of the anger felt towards the *Titanic*'s captain in Southampton. It is more likely, though, as she noted in her letter, that the place now held too many unhappy associations for her and as her reason for being in Southampton was now gone she hoped to return home to the security and peace of her family and friends. Sure enough, within a few years she and Melville had returned to Cheshire where they lodged with her husband's old friend Thomas Jones and his family at The Nook, Runcorn.

She and her daughter did at least have the consolation that unlike many other families whose loved ones had died on the *Titanic*, they were still fairly well off. In the probate index for 1912, we read that Smith's will was issued on 15 November in London, the beneficiary being Sarah Eleanor Smith. Captain Smith's effects came to £3,186, 4s, 6d, a seemingly small amount. Indeed compared to say Chief Engineer Joseph Bell and others who left substantially more, Smith seems almost poor by comparison. Running the amount through an online calculator, though, tells the real story. In modern money (2007) this amounts to over £226,000 and going by the average wages at that time, Smith's will pretty much made millionaires of his wife and child. Though they may have suffered opprobrium after Smith's death, at least Eleanor and her daughter did not suffer penury.

During the First World War, Eleanor did briefly resurface and on 4 June 1915 she went to Liverpool for an interview with Mr Allan, an official of the Public Trustees Office. Eleanor, as Captain Smith's widow, added her voice to the growing clamour that the allowance being paid to the four orphaned children of Chief Officer Wilde be reconsidered. The committee had already increased provision for them in regard to paying for their education and a report on this was posted off to Eleanor.[4]

After the war, she saw her daughter Melville married and she became a grandmother to twins. But the last time we catch sight of Eleanor herself is on the occasion of her own death, which also made the news in a small way and, ironically enough, was itself the result of an unlooked-for collision.

In 1931, Eleanor was living at 41 Queen's Gate Gardens, Kensington, London. She had probably moved to the capital to be close to her daughter's family, Melville's husband being a stockbroker there. Eleanor was now sixty-nine years old and still active and on Sunday 28 April she was out and about when she was knocked down by a taxi cab in Cromwell Road, dying a short while later at St Mary Abbot's Hospital from a fractured skull.

There was a witness to what happened. At the inquest into Eleanor's death, Mrs Ann Gildea of Stanhope Gardens, South Kensington, described how, 'Mrs Smith seemed to walk into the taxi, which was coming along the road at a slow pace.'

The taxi driver's name was Robert Smith from Fulham, who said that he had no chance to avoid the accident. Eleanor and her late husband especially might have felt some sympathy with their namesake at this statement. A verdict of accidental death was returned by the coroner.[5]

Sarah Eleanor Smith was buried a few days later in the grounds of the London Necropolis at Brookwood, some miles out of the capital. To this day her grave can still be found in the older, much more tumble-down part of the cemetery, beyond the road that today bisects the site. Compared to many of the showy monuments and mausoleums nearby, the gravestone is relatively plain and the inscription it bears betters even Joseph Hancock's in its pithiness:

SARAH ELEANOR SMITH

17.6.61 – 28.4.31

WIDOW OF

CAPTAIN EDWARD JOHN SMITH

S.S. TITANIC

Through all the trials and tribulations she had endured since that terrible April in 1912, Eleanor had not forgotten her husband and now in stone, as in death, they were reunited.

Their daughter Melville lived long enough to see the resurgence of interest in the *Titanic* in the 1950s, but her own life since the death of her father had not been without its own share of tragedies. Melville and her mother stayed at Woodhead for a couple of years, before moving to London. It was here that Mel met and later married stockbroker Sidney Russell-Cooke in 1922 at St Mark's Church, Mayfair, an exclusive and wealthy part of the capital. They spent a lot of time at 'Bellcroft', their magnificent residence near Newport on the Isle of Wight, where Mel gave birth to twins, Simon and Priscilla, on 18 June 1923. In 1930, though, after only eight years of marriage, Sidney died in a bizarre shooting accident, the circumstances of which were never fully resolved.

Following her husband's death and then her mother's the following year, though she kept a small flat in London, Mel forsook the capital and in 1934 moved with her children to the quiet country village of in Leafield near Witney Oxfordshire. Her house here, named 'Pratts', had a large, beautiful garden to which she was henceforth devoted. To the villagers she made no secret of her father's tragic history and though one or two of the locals had their own strong opinions on the disaster, notably a retired admiral who blamed Smith for the sinking, she became and remained a respected member of the local community.

At home, Mel embroidered for pleasure and though she enjoyed the solitude her new home provided, she also liked socialising and there were many parties at Pratts, often attended by well-known personalities. She became good friends with the artist David Rhode and he moved into Pratts for a time and whilst there painted portraits of Melville and her two children. Mel was also a keen collector of paintings and she once pressed a fellow collector who had purchased a painting she wanted, until he agreed to sell it to her.

For the most part, though, she lived alone and never locked her doors. But, then again, she was never quite alone for like her father before her she kept dogs and was known to chain them up to her expensive furniture. Mel was not daunted by danger and gained a pilot's licence and flew all over the world. She also liked fast cars, owning her own sports car, and she frequently boasted about how fast she could drive the 70-odd miles to her flat in London.

With the advent of the Second World War, life for Mel and her children became harder as it did for everyone. Mel herself had kept busy during the war, enlisting in the local police and ambulance service and during her time at Leafield was involved in all the village activities. But she was to be hit by two more tragedies in the 1940s.

Her son Simon Russell-Cooke had joined the RAF, flying torpedo bombers, and was described by the commander of 144 Squadron as a popular officer with all ranks. He flew in several raids but was killed in action on 23 March 1944 whilst taking part in a successful operation against enemy shipping off the Norwegian coast. Piloting his aircraft through heavy flak, he pressed home his attack, releasing his torpedo, but afterwards it was observed that one of his aeroplane's engines was on fire and moments later the plane crashed into the sea. Simon and his navigator Flight Sergeant J.E. Beaman died in the crash; their bodies were never recovered. Simon was twenty years old; he had never married and left no children and is commemorated on panel 205 of the Air Forces Memorial at Runnymede in Surrey.

Melville's daughter Priscilla did get married, to barrister John Constantine Phipps, but she was very ill with polio and she did not long outlive her brother. Like him she died childless, in Selkirk, on 7 October 1947, aged just twenty-four.

In the years following this double blow, Mel may have been comforted to some degree by the growing interest in the *Titanic* disaster and the part her father had played in it. In 1953, Hollywood had produced a film loosely based around the story of the *Titanic* and in 1957 Mel visited the set of the film *A Night to Remember*. Here she met the veteran character actor Laurence Naismith, resplendent in his White Star uniform, who was playing Captain Smith in the film and Mel commented to reporters that he bore a strong resemblance to her father.

Back at Pratts, her life continued to be active until she herself died suddenly in 1973. On 18 August that year a neighbour called at the house and found her collapsed on the bed, having been preparing for a bath. She was rushed to the Radcliffe Infirmary in Oxford, but this hardy woman who had suffered perhaps more than her fair share of high-profile tragedy in life, was declared dead on arrival. Helen Melville Russell-Cooke, *née* Smith, was cremated and her ashes were buried in her husband's grave next to her mother's in Brookwood Cemetery.[6]

With her death Ted Smith's line and story had finally come to an end.

ENDNOTES

I

Made in the Potteries

1 A translation by Thomas Roscoe from Johann Georg Kohl's book *Reisen in England und Wales* (Dresden/Leipzig 1844). A typescript copy of the chapter dealing with the Potteries is available at Hanley Archives, pp.37-38.

2 *Victoria County History of Staffordshire, Vol. VIII* (London, University of London, 1963), pp.148-149.

3 'The Staffordshire Potteries' chapter from *The Land We Live In* (London: Charles Knight, 1848) p.33.

4 The *Morning Chronicle* is quoted in Marguerite W. Dupree's *Family Structure in the Staffordshire Potteries, 1840–1880* (Oxford, Clarendon, 1995), p.81. See also 'Inquiries into the State of Large Towns and Populous Districts 1843', quoted in *Local History Source Book G.12, State of Large Towns in North Staffordshire*, p.11. Available at Hanley Archives.

5 *Staffordshire Sentinel*, 7 January 1854.

6 Edward Smith and Samuel Sneyd are listed within a few places of one another in the directory which has been reprinted as Local History Source Book L.43 *A Directory of the Staffordshire Potteries 1818*, p.29.

7 George Smith's baptismal record on 1 December 1822, at the Charles Street Wesleyan Chapel, Hanley, is particularly useful as it names his mother and father, telling us his mother's maiden name and a little of her ancestry. LDS records note that the mother's name is 'Toms', though a look at the actual church record show that this was simply mis-transcribed. The history of the Smith family was traced by Mrs Norma Williamson, a descendant of George and Thirza Smith, who was good enough to share her research with me and provide fair copies of the much more detailed church records.

8 *North Staffordshire Mercury*, 7 August 1841.

9 A prime example can be seen in the *Evening Sentinel*, 16 April 1982. There is a photograph of the present-day 51 Well Street, which is identified as the birthplace of Captain Smith.

10 cf. *Slater's Classified Directory for Birmingham, Worcester and the Potteries* 1851 pp.446
    and 458, for the addresses of William Sedgley and Samuel Sneyd who lived on
    either side of the Smiths. George Smith and Thirza Leigh were married on
    8 October 1853 at Hanley Chapel. My thanks to Ernie Luck, who first drew my
    attention to the mistake over the number 51 and for his fine piece of detective
    work in locating the Smith's real address at the time of E.J. Smith's birth. A 1912
    edition of the *Daily Sketch* newspaper carried a picture of what was said to be
    the house where Smith was born, but the evidence is that the house had already
    been demolished.

11 Quoted in Phillip McCann, *Popular education and socialization in the nineteenth
    century* (London, Methuen, 1977), p.103.

12 *Staffordshire Sentinel*, 24 April 1913.

13 *Captain E.J. Smith Memorial: A Souvenir of July 29th, 1914* (Riverside, 7's Press,
    n.d.) p.31.

14 *Daily Sketch*, 25 April 1912.

15 *Staffordshire Sentinel*, 16 April 1913.

16 *Staffordshire Sentinel*, 24 April 1913.

17 *Daily Sketch*, 25 April 1912.

18 James Boswell, *The Life of Samuel Johnson* (Harmondsworth, Penguin Books,
    1986) pp.202–203.

19 Copies of Joseph's certificates of competency (ticket numbers 14,721 and
    15,310) can be obtained for a small fee from the National Maritime Museum.
    Further details of his two certificates are also held under BT127, boxes 8 and
    9 in the National Archives, Kew, and give the name of the ship as the *Hymen*.
    Accounts of the loss of the *Hymen* and the freeing of the hostages were carried
    in *The Times* on 12 and 19 June 1856.

20 Commander (later Admiral) Frederick Augustus Maxse's involvement in the
    raid, though not noted in either of the articles in *The Times*, is mentioned in the
    National Archives index. The Maxse Papers are held (under restricted access)
    at the West Sussex Record Office. The documents dealing with the raid on the
    pirate camp are under reference MAXSE/172.

21 J.W. Gambier, *Links in my Life on Land and Sea* (Woking and London: T.F.
    Unwin, 1907), p.59.

22 Ibid, p.62.

23 Between 1846 and 1856, eight ships were attacked and seized by Riff pirates –
    six British, one French, and one Prussian: *Ruth*, 30 March 1846; *Three Sisters*, 2
    November 1848; *Violet*, 5–6 October 1851; the Prussian vessel *Flora*, December
    1852; *Cuthbert Young*, 21 June 1854; the French ship *Jeune Dieppois*, 8 April 1855;
    Lively, 2 May 1855; and finally *Hymen*, 14 May 1856. A large number of smaller
    Spanish vessels were also seized. See: 'The Limits of Naval Power: The Merchant
    Brig *Three Sisters*, Riff Pirates and British Battleships' by Andrew Lambert, in
    Piracy and Maritime Crime: Historical and Modern Case Studies, Newport Paper
    35, (Newport, Rhode Island: Center for Naval Warfare Studies, January 2010)

pp.173-190. URL: Http://www.virginia.edu/colp/pdf/Piracy-and-Maritime-Crime-NWC-2010.pdf

24   Ernest Luck (2003) 'Charles Spode Mason and his Descendants' – *Mason's Collectors Club Newsletter*, No.144, November 2003. (Issue restricted to Members only.) George Smith had married Thirza Leigh at Hanley Chapel, 8 October 1853. Doubtless following the work, they moved from Hanley first to Chell in the north of the Potteries, then to May Bank, Wolstanton. The couple had nine children, Elizabeth being the eldest. On 23 April 1877, Elizabeth married Mark Spode Mason in Newcastle-under-Lyme. Though settled locally at first, in 1881 they moved to Yorkshire and over the next ten years becoming increasingly impoverished, they moved several times ending up in Great Grimsby, Lincolnshire, where in February 1891, Mark threw himself in front of a train and was killed instantly. Elizabeth was left with five children on her hands, and remarried the next year to George Johnson a local fisherman by whom she had two more children. Elizabeth Johnson, formerly Mason, *née* Smith, died on 4 April 1942.

25   *Daily Sketch*, 25 April 1912.

26   *Staffordshire Sentinel*, 24 April 1913.

27   *Oakland Tribune*, 19 April 1912. Ann O'Donnell was her married name; there is no indication of her maiden name.

28   *Staffordshire Sentinel*, 24 April 1913.

29   Smith's certificates of competency (No.14102) can be purchased from the National Maritime Museum.

2

Before the Mast

1   The *Staffordshire Sentinel*, 16 April 1913.

2   The *Southern Times*, 28 March 1891.

3   Maritime History Archive (MHA), Memorial University of Newfoundland, Canada, Agreement and Account of Crew, *Senator Weber*, Feb. 1867, ref: 51,475 (1868).

4   Captain E.J. Smith Memorial: A Souvenir of July 29th, 1914, p.30.

5   MHA, Memorial University of Newfoundland, Canada, Official Log Book, 'Senator Weber', February 1867, ref: 51,475 (1868) p.8.

6   Ibid, p.9.

7   Ibid, pp.10–11.

8   Ibid, p.12.

9   Ibid, p.13.

10   Ibid, p.14.

11   MHA, Agreement and Account of Crew, *Senator Weber*, Feb. 1867. The notification of the desertions can be found in the attached notes to the British Consul in San Francisco.

12   Charles Darwin, *The Voyage of the Beagle* (Ware, Wordsworth Editions Ltd, 1997), p.350.

13 Ephriam George Squier, *Peru: Incidents of Travel and Exploration in the Land of the Incas* (New York, Henry Holt & Co., 1877) p.30.

14 *Oakland Tribune*, 19 April 1912.

15 MHA, Agreement for Foreign-Going Ship, *Senator Weber*, Dec. 1868, ref: 51,475 (1870).

16 Ibid. A Japanese friend informs me that though to English speakers 'Mossa' seems a given name and 'Keechi' a family name, to Japanese ears the whole of 'Mossa Keechi' sounds more like a given name that consists of two letters, when it is written in Chinese characters, possibly the male name Masakichi or some variant. Though modern Japanese still use Chinese or Japanese characters to form their names they are also taught how to use the Latin alphabet to spell out their names. 'Mossa Keechi' doubtless lacked this ability and on being asked his name what he said was written down in the ship's records for him.

17 *Oakland Tribune*, 19 April 1912.

18 35 Victoria Sessional Papers (No.2A.) A. 1872, proceedings of the quarantine station, St John.

19 Merseyside Maritime Museum (MMM), Liverpool, Customs Bills of Entry, 17 July 1871.

20 MMM, Customs Bills of Entry, 4 March 1873.

21 MHA, Official Log Book, *Arzilla* April 1873–May 1874, ref: 46,615 (1874), p.5.

22 MHA, Official Log Book, *Arzilla* July–November 1874, ref: 46,615 (1874), p.8.

23 MMM, Customs Bills of Entry, 4 May 1875.

24 *Staffordshire Sentinel*, 16 April 1912.

25 MHA, Agreement and Account of Crew, *Lizzie Fennell*, May 1876–March 1877, ref: 64,485 (1877).

26 MHA, Agreement and Account of Crew, *Lizzie Fennell*, May–September 1877, ref: 64,485 (1877); MMM, Custom Bills of Entry, 13 September 1877.

27 MHA, Agreement and Account of Crew, *Lizzie Fennell*, October 1877–February 1878, ref: 64,485 (1878); MMM, Customs Bills of Entry, 28 February 1878.

28 Blunt White Library (BWL), Mystic Seaport, Mystic Connecticut, letter from Smith to Frank Hancock, 20 July 1905.

29 MMM, Customs Bills of Entry, 1 January 1880.

30 *Staffordshire Sentinel*, 16 April 1912.

31 Bertram Hayes, *Hull Down: Reminiscences of Wind-jammers, Troops and Travellers* (London, Cassell & Co. Ltd, 1925), p.62.

3

White Star

1 'The Transatlantic Captains' by Charles Algernon Dougherty. 1886, *Harper's New Monthly Magazine*, Vol.LXXIII Nos 435–26.

2 Board of Trade Wreck Report for *Lizzie Fennell*, 1881 (No.1164). URL: http://www.plimsoll.org/resources/SCCLibraries/WreckReports/14671.asp

3 *Reno Evening Gazette*, 8 June 1882.

4 Hayes, *Hull Down*, p.66.

5 *Captain E.J. Smith Memorial: A Souvenir of July 29th, 1914*, p.28.

6 *Oakland Tribune*, 19 April 1912.

7 Ibid, 17 April 1912.

8 Dougherty, *Harper's New Monthly Magazine*, pp.375–391.

9 Ibid.

10 *The Waukesha Freeman*, 19 June 1884.

11 *New York Times*, 28 July 1884.

12 Dougherty, *Harper's New Monthly Magazine*, pp.375–391.

13 *Staffordshire Sentinel*, 24 April 1913.

14 *Captain E.J. Smith Memorial: A Souvenir of July 29th, 1914*, pp.10–11.

15 The National Archives (TNA), ADM 240/3.

16 *New York Times*, 14 & 22 December 1888; US. Inq., Day 11, testimony of Joseph B. Ismay.

17 *New York Times*, 28 January 1889.

18 TNA, ADM 240/3.

19 Hayes, *Hull Down*, pp.68–69.

20 Mark Baber (2010), 'E.J. Smith, Coptic, Aground and Rio – Two out of three ain't bad?' *Encyclopedia Titanica Research*. URL:http://www.encyclopedia-titanica.org/e-j-smith-coptic-aground-and-rio---two-out-of-three-aint-bad-11534.html. See also *The Evening Post* (Wellington, New Zealand) 19 December 1889 and 31 January 1890, detailing the accident and then the new crew headed by Smith. Details of Captain Burton's trial were carried in the *West Coast Times*, 20 February 1890.

21 *New York Times*, 10 August 1891.

22 Ibid, 8 November 1891.

23 *The Daily Northwestern*, 21 November 1891.

24 *The Belfast News-Letter*, 1 January 1892.

25 Catherine's grave, number 223, is located in section 7 of Runcorn Cemetery; my thanks to Steve and Gill Jones for this information.

26 *St Ives Times*, 3 May 1912.

27 *Captain E.J. Smith Memorial: A Souvenir of July 29th, 1914*, pp.30–31.

28 Ibid, pp.32–33.

29 Kate Douglas-Wiggin, *My Garden of Memory* (Massachusetts: Houghton Mifflin Co., n.d.) pp.263–265.

30 Ibid, p.275.

31 Hayes, *Hull Down*, pp.70–71. Hayes supplies no further details and as Jackson made a number of Atlantic crossings during this period, the actual date is impossible to pin down.

32 *Liverpool Mercury & Liverpool Daily Post*, 2 May 1895.

33 *Liverpool Daily Courier*, 3 May 1895.

4

The Majestic *Years*

1 Wilton J. Oldham, *The Ismay Line* (London and Liverpool, 1961), p.125.
2 *New York Times*, 18 June 1895.
3 *Brooklyn Eagle*, 14 August 1895.
4 Ibid, 11 September 1895.
5 *Daily Sketch*, 25 April 1912.
6 *Staffordshire Sentinel*, 21 September 1911; 24 April 1913.
7 *The Daily Northwestern*, 18 October 1895; *Marion Daily Star*, 18 October 1895; *Daily Gazette & Bulletin*, 25 October 1895; *Steubenville Daily Herald*, 26 October 1895.
8 *New York Times*, 19 February 1896; *Fort Wayne Sentinel*, 15 April 1896; *North Adams Transcript*, 20 August 1896; *Fort Wayne News*, 25 November 1896.
9 *Centralia Enterprise & Tribune*, 19 December 1896; *Newark Daily Advocate*, 24 December 1896.
10 *The Liverpool Courier*, 7 & 10 June 1897.
11 Pat Lacey, *Master of the Titanic* (Surrey, The Book Guild, 1998), p.281; John Pladdys (1993) 'The Captain's Daughter: Helen Melville Russell-Cooke "Mel", 1898–1973', *Titanic Historical Society Commutator* Vol.17, No.2 1993, pp.61–64.
12 BWL, letter from Eleanor Smith to Frank Hancock, 16 June 1912; *Captain E.J. Smith Memorial*, p.30.
13 Pladdys, pp.61–64.
14 *Oakland Tribune*, 10 March 1898.
15 *Steubenville Herald*, 27 April 1898; *The Morning Star*, 29 April 1898.
16 *Manitoba Morning Free Press*, 2 May 1898.
17 *The Fort Wayne News*, 19 October 1898.
18 *Arizona Republican*, 24 January 1899.
19 *Brooklyn Eagle*, 16 November 1899.
20 *New York Times*, 23 November 1899.
21 Hayes, *Hull Down*, p.73.
22 *The Times*, 14 December 1899.
23 *Royal Humane Society Bronze Medal Citations* taken from the annual report 1900, case 30488.
24 *The Times*, 1 & 3 January 1900; *Town and Country*, 19 April 1902.
25 *The Times*, 18 January 1900; 3 February 1900.
26 Ibid, 13 February; 2 March; 15 March; 7 April 1900.
27 *New York Times*, 17 March 1901.
28 Ibid, 8 August 1901.
29 Jack Winocour (Ed.), *The Story of the Titanic: as told by its survivors* (Mineola, Dover Publications, Inc., 1960) p. 277.
30 Ibid, p.275.
31 *New York Times*, 10 January 1903.

32 An old Imperial nautical mile (nm) at 6,080ft is longer than a land mile at 5,280.23ft. Therefore 333 nm = 383.454 mi.

33 Ibid, 15 February 1903.

34 A copy of Smith's will is held at the City Centre Library and Archives, Hanley, under reference SP 192.

35 TNA, ADM 171, Sea Transport Medal Roll 1899–1902.

36 *Daily Northwestern*, 12 February 1904; *Atlanta Constitution*, 13 February 1904; *Altoona Mirror*, 19 February 1904.

5

Baltic *and* Adriatic

1 *New York Times*, 9 July 1904.

2 Private information from Parks Stephenson.

3 *New York Times*, 20 May 1905.

4 *Lincoln Evening News*, 1 June 1905.

5 *The Times*, 15 July 1905.

6 BWL, letter from Smith to Frank Hancock, 20 July 1905.

7 *New York Times*, 13 January 1906.

8 *Newark Advocate,* 2 June 1906.

9 *Oakland Tribune*, 2 June 1906.

10 *New York Times*, 30 June 1906. Mrs Frawley's death is confirmed on the online ship's manifest at www.ellisisland.org.

11 Ibid, 17 May 1907.

12 This report here is largely reconstructed since as of yet the full original interview remains elusive. The interview was quoted in part in some contemporary newspapers such as New Zealand's *Poverty Bay Herald*, 27 July 1907, but the bulk of the text comes from books and articles published after the *Titanic* disaster. These include *New York Times*, 16 April 1912; *Washington Times*, 17 April 1912; Logan Marshall (Ed.), *Sinking of the Titanic and Great Sea Disasters,* Chapter XX, available online at *Project Gutenburg*.

13 *Titanic Voices*, p.19.

14 Ibid. p.20.

15 *Staffordshire Advertiser*, 20 April 1912; also mentioned in the biography of Smith in the *Institute of Engineers Magazine*, 1912.

16 *Captain E.J. Smith Memorial: A Souvenir of July 29th, 1914*, p.30 & 33.

17 BWL letter to Frank Hancock, 28 April 1910.

18 *The Salt Lake Herald*, 18 July 1907.

19 *New York Times Sunday Supplement*, 8 November 1908.

20 *Oakland Tribune*, 20 April 1912.

21 Ibid.

22 J.C.H. Beaumont quoted in *Titanic Voices*, pp.16–17.

23 *New York Times*, 9 September 1907.

24 Ibid, 12 September 1907.

25 Ibid, 26 January 1908.

26 Ibid, 30 October 1908.

27 *The Syracuse Herald*, 20 November 1908.

28 Ibid, 27 February 1909.

29 *New York Times*, 17 August 1909.

30 *The Washington Post*, 18 August 1909.

31 *New York Times*, 8 October 1909.

32 *The Evening Post* (New York), 4 November 1909; *New York Herald*, 5 November 1909.

33 *The Times*, 25 June 1910.

34 *New York Times*, 9, 10, 11, 19 and 23 August 1910.

6

The Wednesday Ship

1   See: http://www.encyclopedia-titanica.org/discus/messages/5921/27883.html?1053408940

2   *The Shipbuilder* (summer, 1911): *The Irish News/Belfast Morning News*, 1 June 1911.

3   BWL, letter to Frank Hancock, 28 April 1910.

4   *Staffordshire Sentinel*, 16 April 1912.

5   *Titanic Voices: Memories from the Fateful Voyage* (Sutton Publishing Ltd, Stroud, 1997), p.33.

6   *Titanic Voices*, p.35.

7   *Titanic Survivor*, p.113.

8   *New York Times*, 22 June 1911.

9   Ibid.

10 *New York Times*, 21 June 1911.

11 Ibid, 24 June 1911.

12 Ibid, 29 June 1911.

13 *The Times*, 7 August 1911, p.8; 22 April 1912, p.12.

14 TNA, ADM 116/1163.

15 Copy of insurance protest, courtesy of Paris, Smith LLP, formerly Paris, Smith and Randall, solicitors, Southampton.

16 Quoted in Chirnside, *The Olympic Class Ships: Olympic, Titanic and Britannic*, p.71.

17 *New York Times*, 17 August 1911.

18 Ibid, 8 December 1911.

19 *Manitoba Morning Free Press*, 17 April 1912; *Staffordshire Sentinel*, 24 April 1913; the picture can be seen on the front page of *The Hawaiian Gazette*, 23 April 1912. URL: http://chroniclingamerica.loc.gov/lccn/sn83025121/1912-04-23/ed-1/seq-1/

20 *New York Times*, 31 December 1911.

21 BWL, letter to Frank Hancock, 14 February 1912.

22 *Worcester Evening Gazette*, 18 April 1912.

23 Alec Bagot (2010) 'Roaming Around: Memoirs of a Marconi operator'
    Encyclopedia Titanica (ref: #4,523, accessed 14th December 2010 06:55:13 PM).
    URL : http://www.encyclopedia-titanica.org/roaming-around-memoirs-
    marconi-operator.html.
24 J.C.H. Beaumont quoted in *Titanic Voices*, p.90.
25 Smith was already sixty-one when this was written, but White Star fudged
    the issue and Smith complied, pretending to be a few years younger. When he
    signed onto the *Titanic*, Smith gave his age as fifty-nine, but at the US Inquiry
    after the disaster, J. Bruce Ismay tactfully gave Smith's correct age of sixty-two.

7

Titanic

1 *Agreement and Account of Crew*, TNA, BT100/259; *Particulars of Engagement*
    (Belfast), Ulster Folk and Transport Museum, TRANS 2A/45 381.
 2 Ellis Island records for the arrival of RMS *Olympic*, 10 April 1912.
 3 Geoffrey Marcus, *The Maiden Voyage* (New English Library, 1976), p.33.
 4 BWL, letter from Eleanor Smith to Frank Hancock, 16 June 1912. URL: http://
    journeysintime.wordpress.com/the-captain-smith-letters-at-mystic-ct/
 5 Lee Raymond Collection, quoted in *Titanic Voices*, p.92.
 6 Robert L. White Single-owner Estate Auction, 15 May 2004. The auction
    was handled by Hantman's auctioneers, Maryland USA. The tailor's books
    were Lot 143 and sold for $6,000. URL: http://www.hantmans.com/pages/
    newsroom/040515_16_both/040515-16HILITES/NRsalehilitesMay15-16.html
 7 From Norman Wilkinson, *A Brush With Life*, 1969, quoted in *Titanic Voices*, p.94.
 8 City Heritage Oral History (Southampton) quoted in *Titanic Voices*, p.94
 9 *Burlington Daily Gazette*, 25 April 1912.
10 US Limitation of Liability Hearings, Deposition of Elizabeth L. Lines,
    27 October 1913.
11 *North Berks Herald*, 20 April 1912.
12 British Board of Trade Inquiry, Day 25, testimony of Maurice H. Clarke,
    questions 24,151–24,174.
13 The debate is a tortuous one and perhaps best left to people with an in-depth
    understanding of navigation. See the following discussion: http://www.
    encyclopedia-titanica.org/discus/messages/5664/111656.html?1144771518.
14 US. Inq., Day 11, testimony of Joseph B. Ismay.

8

Nemesis

1 US. Inq., Day 18, affidavit of Mrs George D. Widener.
 2 US. Inq., Day 1, testimony of Charles H. Lightoller; Br. Inq., Day 11, testimony
    of Charles Lightoller, questions 13,607–13,641.

3 US. Inq., Day 3, testimony of Joseph G. Boxhall; Br. Inq., Day 14, testimony of Joseph G. Boxhall, questions 16,924–16,927.

4 Boxhall, US. Inq., Day 3.

5 US. Inq., Day 5, testimony of Robert Hichens; Br. Inq., Day 3, testimony of Robert Hichens, questions 1,037–1,043.

6 (1962) Joseph Groves Boxhall – Radio Interview *Encyclopedia Titanica* (ref: #5,007, accessed 16 November 2010, 09:15:30p.m. URL: http://www.encyclopedia-titanica.org/Boxhall.html.

7 US. Inq., Day 7, testimony of Alfred Olliver.

8 Br. Inq., Day 16, testimony of Joseph B. Ismay, questions 18,510–18,517.

9 Ibid, Day 11, testimony of Annie Robinson, questions 13,282–13,283.

10 Ibid, Day 4, testimony of James Johnson, questions 3,363–3,371.

11 *Camden Post-Telegram*, 15 May 1912.

12 *New York Times*, 1 May 1912.

13 Br. Inq., Day 13, testimony of Joseph G. Boxhall, question 15,610. It is unclear, though, how long after the collision Smith said this and it may have been his own revised estimate.

14 Ibid, Day 3, testimony of Robert Hichens, question 1,041.

15 If this was indeed the sum of Smith's reasoning on the matter, then his judgment in this respect would be proven sound. For although the ship survived for an hour longer than estimated, even with that extension and sending the boats away woefully under-loaded in some cases, the crew would still only have enough time to launch eighteen of the boats in the proscribed manner, the last two being washed off the deck as the ship went under. Though any plan to evacuate more into the boats via the gangways seems to have fallen into disarray, the fact that the crew managed to clear the bulk of the boats and evacuate as many as they did probably owes much to the discipline Smith now insisted upon.

16 *Camden Post-Telegram*, 15 May 1912.

17 Br. Inq., Day 13, testimony of Joseph G. Boxhall, question 15,610.

18 Boxhall, US. Inq., Day 3.

19 *The Times*, 20 April 1912.

20 *Newark Star*, 19 April 1912.

21 US. Inq., Day 11, testimony of Helen Bishop; Day 16, affidavit of Emily Ryerson.

22 Ibid, Day 10, testimony of Hugh Woolner.

23 Br. Inq., Day 4, testimony of John Poingdestre, question 2,874.

24 Ibid, Day 5, testimony of Charles Hendrickson, question 4,990.

25 *Newark Evening News*, 19 April 1912.

26 Winocour, *The Story of the Titanic: as told by its survivors*, p.315.

27 Boxhall, US. Inq., Day 3.

28 For an in-depth revised look at the lifeboat launch times and the sequence they were launched in see: Bill Wormstedt, Tad Fitch and George Behe (2009) *Titanic:*

The Lifeboat Launching Sequence Re-Examined. URL: http://home.comcast.
net/~bwormst/titanic/lifeboats/lifeboats.htm

29   US. Inq., Day 7, testimony of Frank O. Evans.

30   Ibid, Day 9, testimony of William Burke.

31   Roberta Maioni (1926) 'My Maiden Voyage' *Encyclopedia Titanica* (ref: #9,097,
     accessed 21 November 2010, 08:58:27p.m.) URL: http://www.encyclopedia-
     titanica.org/Roberta-maioni-titanic-account.html.

32   US. Inq., Day 1 & Day 9, testimony of Alfred Crawford; also Br. Inq., Day 16,
     question 17,966; US. Inq., Day 7, testimony of Thomas Jones.

33   Tillie Taussig, *New York Times*, 22 April 1912; Emma Bucknell, quoted in Judith B.
     Geller, *Titanic: Women and Children First* (Somerset, Patrick Stephens Ltd, 1998)
     p.41.

34   Roberta Maioni (1926) 'My Maiden Voyage'.

35   US. Inq., Day 10, testimony of Hugh Woolner; Day 18, affidavit of Mrs Lucian
     P. Smith.

36   According to several newspaper reports, Peuchen was no fan of Smith's,
     regarding his sailing of the *Titanic* as criminally incompetent. He is said to have
     had a low opinion of him before the disaster and supposedly commented on
     hearing that Smith was in command, 'Surely, we are not going to have that
     man?' (*Toronto World*, 20 April 1912.) However, in his closing statement to the
     US Inquiry into the *Titanic* disaster, Peuchen utterly denied having made any of
     the newspaper comments ascribed to him regarding Captain Smith (US. Inq.,
     Day 4, testimony of Arthur G. Peuchen).

37   *Boston Post*, 20 April 1912.

38   *New York Times*, 19 April 1912.

39   US. Inq., Day 15, affidavit of Mahala Douglas. Account of Elisabeth Allen quoted
     in *The Story of the Titanic: as told by its survivors,* Jack Winocour (Ed.), p.201.

40   NMM, LMQ/7/2/21.

41   *Liberty*, 23 April 1932, quoted in *Titanic: Women and Children First* pp.51–52. Mrs
     Harris's full account is riddled with inconsistencies that throws much doubt on
     its accuracy, but the image of a by-now exasperated Captain Smith alarmed to
     find her still on board does have a ring of truth to it.

42   *The Peterson Morning Call*, 23 April 1912.

43   *Bureau County Republican* (Princetown Illinois), 2 May 1912.

44   US. Inq., Day 7, testimony of Samuel Hemming.

45   Walter Lord, *A Night to Remember* (Harmondsworth, Penguin Books, 1976)
     p.109.

46   Brit. Inq., Day 9, testimony of Edward Brown, questions 10,585–10,587.

47   Winocour, *The Story of the Titanic: as told by its survivors*, p.317.

48   Samuel Hemming in his testimony to the US Inquiry said there were still 100 or
     200 people still crowding the boat decks at this point.

49   Senan Molony (2006) 'The Portrush Letter' *ET Research* (ref: #5,005, accessed
     28 November 2010, 09:53:30p.m.) URL: http://www.encyclopedia-titanica.
     org/portrush.html.

50 US. Inq., Day 9, testimony of Frederick D. Ray.
51 Ibid, Day 2, testimony of Harold S. Bride.
52 Mellors' account from a contemporary memorial booklet quoted in: Robert L. Bracken (2008) William J. Mellors *ET Research* (ref: #5,988, accessed 12 November 2010, 09:10:59p.m.) URL: http://www.encyclopedia-titanica. org/william-mellors.html.

9

Momento Mori

1 *Worcester Evening Gazette*, 20 April 1912.
2 *Daily Sketch*, 17 April 1912.
3 *Southampton Times and Hampshire Press*, 20 April 1912.
4 *Staffordshire Sentinel*, 17 April 1912.
5 Ibid, 26 April 1912.
6 *New York Times*, 29 April 1912.
7 John P. Eaton (2005) 'A Captain's Career' ET Research (ref: #4,696, accessed 20 January 2011, 09:16:01p.m.). URL: http://www.encyclopedia-titanica.org/ titanic-captain-smith-a-captains-career.html
8 Ibid, 6 June 1912.
9 Ibid, 8 July 1912.
10 Curiously enough, Lady Scott was aboard a ship, reading an account of the *Titanic* disaster, when she received news that her husband's remains had been found.
11 *Lichfield Mercury*, 19 June 1914.
12 Ibid.
13 Captain E.J. Smith Memorial, pp.9–10.

10

Epilogue

1 In 2010, as a part of the Lichfield Historic Parks Project, the statue was finally cleaned, revealing the bronze statue as it would have been when it was first unveiled in 1914.
2 At the last count (2010), Smith has been portrayed in film and on TV by eleven different actors. See: http://www.imdb.com/character/ch0002347/
3 A good overview of the ink spilt over Smith's statue can be found in Stephanie Barczewski, *Titanic: A Night Remembered* (London, Hambledon and London, 2004) pp.180–183.
4 (1915) Letter re Officer Wilde Encyclopedia Titanica (ref: #4,201, accessed 23 November 2010, 07:41:22p.m.) URL: http://www.encyclopedia-titanica. org/letter-re-officer-wilde.html.
5 *The Kensington News*, (?) May 1931, partially dated newspaper cutting held in Lichfield Library.
6 Pladdys, pp.61–64.

BIBLIOGRAPHY

Books

Ballard, Dr Robert D., *The Discovery of the Titanic* (London: Hodder & Stoughton Ltd, 1987)

Barczewski, Stephanie, *Titanic: A Night Remembered* (London: Hambledon & London, 2004)

Behe, George, *Titanic: Psychic Forewarnings of Disaster* (Wellingborough: Patrick Stephens Ltd, 1988)

Chirnside, Mark, *The Olympic-Class Ships: Olympic Titanic Britannic* (Stroud: Tempus Publishing Ltd, 2004)

Cooper, Gary, *The Man Who Sank the Titanic? The Life and Times of Captain Edward J. Smith* (Alsager: Witan Books, 1992, 1998)

Davie, Michael, *The Titanic: The Full Story of a Tragedy* (London: Grafton Books, 1987)

Douglas-Wiggin, Kate, *My Garden of Memory* (Massachusetts: Houghton Mifflin Co., n.d.)

Eaton, John P & Haas, Charles A., *Titanic – Triumph and Tragedy: A Chronicle on Words and Pictures* (Wellingborough: Patrick Stephens Ltd, 1986)

Eaton, John P & Haas, Charles A., *Falling Star: Misadventures of White Star Line Ships* (Wellingborough: Patrick Stephens Ltd, 1989)

Gambier, J.W., *Links in my Life on Land and Sea* (Woking and London: T.F. Unwin, 1907)

Hart, Eva & Denney, Ronald C., *Shadow of the Titanic: A Survivor's Story* (Dartford: Greenwich University Press, 1994)

Hayes, Sir Bertram, *Hull Down: Reminiscences of Wind-jammers, Troops and Travellers* (London: Cassell & Co. Ltd, 1925)

Hutchings, David F., *RMS Titanic: A Modern Legend* (Launceston: Waterfront Publications, 1995)

Hyslop, Donald, Forsyth, Alastair & Jemima, Sheila, (Eds.), *Titanic Voices: Memories from the Fateful Voyage* (Stroud: Sutton Publishing Ltd, 1997)

Jessop, Violet & Maxtone-Graham, John (Ed.), *Titanic Survivor: The Memoirs of Violet Jessop Stewardess* (Stroud: Sutton Publishing Ltd, 1998)

Lacey, Pat, *Master of the Titanic* (Lewes: The Book Guild Ltd, 1997)

Lightoller, C.H., *Titanic and Other Ships* (London: Withy Grove Press, 1939)

Lord, Walter, *A Night to Remember* (London: Penguin Books, 1981)

Lord, Walter, *The Night Lives On* (London: Penguin Books, 1998)

Lynch, Don & Marschall, Ken, *Titanic: An Illustrated History* (London: Hodder & Stoughton, 1998)

Oldham, Wilton J., *The Ismay Line* (London and Liverpool, 1961)

Tibballs, Geoff, (Ed.), *The Mammoth Book of How it Happened – Titanic* (London: Constable & Robinson Ltd, 2002)

Wade, Wyn Craig, *The Titanic: End of a Dream* (London: Futura Publications Ltd, 1980)

Warrilow, E.J.D., *A Sociological History of the City of Stoke-on-Trent* (Stoke-on-Trent: Etruscan Publications, 1960)

Warrilow, E.J.D., *History of Etruria* (Stoke-on-Trent: Etruscan Publications, 1953)

Winocour, Jack, (Ed.), *The Story of the Titanic as told by its Survivors* (Mineola: Dover Publications Inc., 1960)

Captain E.J. Smith Memorial. A Souvenir of July 29, 1914 (Riverside: 7 C's Press, Inc., n.d.)

Morton Allan Directory of European Passenger Steamship Arrivals (Baltimore: Genealogical Publishing Co., Inc., 2001)

Victoria History of the Counties of England: Staffordshire (London: University Press, Vol. VIII, 1963)

White Star Line Official Guide 1877 (Douglas: Kinglish Ltd, 1989)

Printed Articles

Dougherty, Charles A., 'The Transatlantic Captains'. *Harper's New Monthly Magazine*, 1886, Vol. LXXIII, No. 435-26, pp. 375-391

Pladdys, John, 'The Captain's Daughter: Helen Melville Russell-Cooke "Mel", 1898–1973'. *Titanic Historical Society Commutator* Vol. 17, No. 2 1993, pp. 61–64

INDEX

THE TITANIC COLLECTION

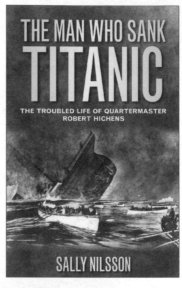
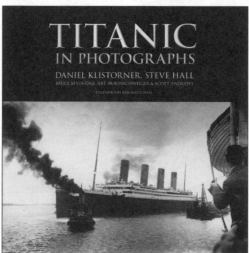